SAP PRESS e-books

Print or e-book, Kindle or iPad, workplace or airplane: Choose where and how to read your SAP PRESS books! You can now get all our titles as e-books, too:

- By download and online access
- For all popular devices
- And, of course, DRM-free

Convinced? Then go to www.sap-press.com and get your e-book today.

Sales and Operations Planning with SAP® IBP

 **PRESS**

SAP PRESS is a joint initiative of SAP and Rheinwerk Publishing. The know-how offered by SAP specialists combined with the expertise of Rheinwerk Publishing offers the reader expert books in the field. SAP PRESS features first-hand information and expert advice, and provides useful skills for professional decision-making.

SAP PRESS offers a variety of books on technical and business-related topics for the SAP user. For further information, please visit our website: *www.sap-press.com*.

Sandy Markin, Amit Sinha
SAP Integration Business Planning: Functionality and Implementation (2nd Edition)
2018, 504 pages, hardcover and e-book
www.sap-press.com/4615

Bhattacharjee, Monti, Perel, Vazquez
Logistics with SAP S/4HANA: An Introduction
2018, 400 pages, hardcover and e-book
www.sap-press.com/4485

Sandeep Pradhan
Demand and Supply Planning with SAP APO (2nd Edition)
2016, 831 pages, hardcover and e-book
www.sap-press.com/4011

Jochen Balla, Frank Layer
Production Planning with SAP APO (3rd Edition)
2016, 431 pages, hardcover and e-book
www.sap-press.com/3927

Raghav Jandhyala, Jeroen Kusters, Pramod Mane, Amit Sinha

Sales and Operations Planning with SAP® IBP

Rheinwerk
Publishing

Editor Meagan White
Acquisitions Editor Emily Nicholls
Copyeditor Melinda Rankin
Cover Design Graham Geary
Photo Credit Shutterstock.com/322483565/© hfzimages
Layout Design Vera Brauner
Production Kelly O'Callaghan
Typesetting III-Satz, Husby (Germany)
Printed and bound in the United States of America, on paper from sustainable sources

ISBN 978-1-4932-1674-1
© 2018 by Rheinwerk Publishing, Inc., Boston (MA)
1st edition 2018

Contents at a Glance

Dear Reader,

Wednesdays are a big deal.

Every week, our Editorial Board meets to discuss developments in the SAP world that impact demand in our market. We consider new book proposals, calculate projected sales, and forecast product costs. Consulting an updated production forecast, we balance the monthly publication schedule to optimize editors' skill sets, production schedules, and marketing resources. We compare sales and inventory reports and weigh reprints or new editions. Sometimes these meetings run long—but we always come away with a plan.

If this S&OP process sounds familiar to you, you're reading the right book. With SAP Integrated Business Planning, SAP has kicked its S&OP functionality up a notch. And between these pages, experts Raghav Jandhyala, Jeroen Kusters, Pramod Mane, and Amit Sinha offer a top-to-bottom look at this powerful application. With their guidance, you can set up and run your sales and operations planning—and be ready for next Wednesday.

So tell us what you think about *Sales and Operations Planning with SAP IBP*? Your comments and suggestions are the most useful tools to help us make our books the best they can be. Please feel free to contact me and share any praise or criticism you may have.

Thank you for purchasing a book from SAP PRESS!

Meagan White
Editor, SAP PRESS

meaganw@rheinwerk-publishing.com
www.sap-press.com
Rheinwerk Publishing · Boston, MA

Contents

4   Unconstrained Supply Planning   123

5   Constrained Supply Planning

6   Consolidation

7   Collaboration and Management by Exception

10   Configuring SAP IBP for Sales and Operations   309

11   Building Planning Views

12   Key Performance Indicators and Performance Monitoring

16   SAP IBP Case Studies

Foreword from Franz Hero

The pace of global supply chains has increased tremendously over the last few years. Global market trends—individualization of products and services, globalization, mobility, and connectivity—put even more pressure on existing structures. Modern technology offers a huge potential to further streamline and adapt the processes. Today, supply chain planners are pushed to operate in nearly real-time and produce more and more detailed plans to increase cost reduction and customer centricity. The sales and operations planning (S&OP) process is the centerpiece of this transformation. It needs strong and robust support to allow supply chains to cope with the changing demands of the world market.

The good news: IT technology adoption is moving ahead quickly to keep pace with changing market requirements. Big data cloud storage capabilities with powerful search and analytics functionality are the first step to a data-driven, responsive planning process. Modern IT platforms offer a comprehensive big data stack, but only the deep integration of the business data (collected from production sites, warehouses, suppliers, sales history, and customers) will unleash the full potential. The S&OP process brings these data points into a business context to create even more realistic supply chain plans. The next logical step is the collaboration between business partners in business networks in the cloud, already a reality with SAP Integrated Business Planning (SAP IBP).

SAP IBP is the best-of-breed solution for supply chain planning. It consists of five modules which can be operated as fully integrated or used as individual solutions. SAP IBP for sales and operations is at the center of these modules, which serves as a perfect starting point for customers. All modules are based on the same data model, nicely integrated with SAP IBP for demand, SAP IBP for inventory, SAP IBP for response and supply, and SAP Supply Chain Control Tower. The solution guides the user through all steps of the process, connecting all parties by a collaboration platform to ease data exchange and promote consensus building. Leveraging the built-in integration to all relevant business systems, SAP IBP gathers all data necessary to create a consistent and robust sales and operations plan. Best of all, SAP IBP offers a Microsoft Excel add-in that enables a gentle switch for planners to this solution. Built as a native cloud solution, SAP IBP is operated in the SAP data center, with new innovations delivered every quarter.

SAP IBP for sales and operations is at the center of a robust and reliable supply chain plan. Many organizations within and outside the enterprise need to collaborate to achieve this. This book combines all these different viewpoints regarding S&OP, both as an overview and in great detail. I congratulate the authors, Amit Sinha, Raghav Jandhyala, Pramod Mane, and Jeroen Kusters on their process, system, and business expertise. The book provides a gentle entry into S&OP and offers the detailed information needed for a successful process setup. Combined with business-proven tips from the authors' vast experience with the solution, this book is a must-read for everyone involved in supply chain planning.

Franz Hero
Head of Digital Supply Chain and Logistics Development
SAP SE

Foreword from Adam Mussomeli

Industries throughout the world today are moving at an increasingly frenzied pace, attempting to navigate dynamic market conditions, both address and capitalize on technological change, and restructure themselves to create competitive advantage as roles and expectations of workers, managers, customers, and consumers continue to change. This is turn is placing significant pressure on today's supply chains to be quicker and more agile, while still meeting or exceeding service, quality, and cost targets. Creating a synchronized, integrated orchestration of materials, services, and assets across supply chains and achieving these needs is made possible only through exceptional supply chain planning. *Sales and Operations Planning with SAP IBP* is the comprehensive authority on how to create a new-age management supply chain planning capability using the SAP IBP toolset.

Sales and Operations Planning with SAP IBP provides a detailed guide to designing and implementing SAB IBP to enable the sales and operations planning process required for tomorrow's supply chains. It provides a comprehensive overview of what sales and operations planning is and how to get the most out of it for your business, then cycles through all key parts of the process to include demand planning, supply planning (both unconstrained and constrained), and the executive management meeting, in which all decisions that result in operating margin and profit are made. Collaboration, analytics, management by exception, simulations, and other necessary capabilities are covered in great detail. Ultimately, this "thoughtware" is made real through the sharing of use cases that can be applied now and a multichapter treatment of how to build this planning cycle, matched to your business needs, into the SAP IBP toolset.

This excellent book, appropriate for everyone interested in creating or improving their sales and operations planning process, came to fruition through a collaboration between four very knowledgeable people: Amit Sinha and Jeroen Kusters from Deloitte, and Pramod Mane and Raghav Jandhyala from SAP. All four are practitioners well-experienced in creating sales and operations planning cycles across multiple industries and enabling them in SAP IBP. The wisdom they provide is worth considering because we know it works; it is wisdom earned through the hard labor of applied knowledge.

Adam Mussomeli
Principal and Global Cofounder, Digital Supply Networks
Deloitte Consulting LLP

Preface

We're excited to provide a comprehensive text on managing and optimizing sales and operations planning (S&OP) processes in SAP Integrated Business Planning (SAP IBP). S&OP is central to the supply chain planning process and is a crucial element joining demand and supply planning. It also integrates strategic plans with operations plans by leveraging information across teams and from external collaborative partners. S&OP is the most fundamental and essential capability of SAP IBP. The current end-to-end mature supply planning product has its roots in a solution aimed at optimizing S&OP processes. In this book, we aim to deliver end-to-end knowledge for the S&OP process and its implementation with SAP Integrated Business Planning for sales and operations.

This book will help you gain extensive knowledge of S&OP processes and their best usage through SAP IBP. S&OP processes are discussed in detail with coverage of their subprocesses, objectives, parties involved, value delivered, relevant analytics, and collaboration. This book also delves into the system application, configuration, and usage to manage S&OP processes in SAP IBP. In addition to S&OP, this book covers the details of supply chain analytics applications delivered through SAP Supply Chain Control Tower.

This book is your one-stop solution for understanding S&OP processes, system automation, digitization, and implementation of the processes through SAP IBP. In addition to the processes and system application, detailed configuration, tool building, data elements, integration objects, and collaboration applications are discussed in detail. This book doesn't require prior knowledge of supply chain management and SAP technology and aims to be a reference textbook for business users, system managers, and solution configurators and consultants.

Target Audience

The topics, coverage, and approach of this book make it relevant for a wide variety of readers, ranging from business managers to business analysts, technical configurators to consultants, students to any person interested in understanding S&OP processes, SAP IBP, supply chain digitization, and supply chain management.

An existing SAP IBP business user can use this book to enhance her knowledge of S&OP in SAP IBP, and business managers or analysts who want to gain from the S&OP process and technology can use it to get detailed knowledge for generating business value.

Consultants working in S&OP process improvement and SAP IBP implementation can refer to this book to multiply their knowledge of the process and system applications aligned to industry best practices and guidance from SAP to utilize the SAP IBP tool.

Knowledge of supply chain processes and SAP IBP offers multitudes of career opportunities with exciting work. The student community and anybody interested in the supply chain as a subject can refer to this book for knowledge required to become successful in the marketplace.

How to Read This Book

The chapters are logically sequenced to build knowledge and utilize the same while introducing different topics. The logical sequence and detailed nature of the text allow readers with different backgrounds to benefit from this book. However, a reader interested in a particular topic or configuration reference for her day-to-day job can refer directly to the text in the relevant chapter.

We recommend starting with the introductory chapter for the basics of the S&OP processes and SAP IBP application. The building blocks illustrated in this chapter are used throughout the book. If you have a technical background and want to jump into system configuration, you might jump directly to Chapter 10 on system configuration and follow the chapters after that one to gain technical knowledge before building process and functional skills. For a reader with business or functional background, following the chapter sequence from the start will be helpful.

How This Book Is Organized

This book is divided into sixteen chapters. Chapters 1 and 2 introduce the details of S&OP processes, along with values, challenges, and opportunities for the application of SAP Integrated Business Planning for sales and operations to manage and optimize the S&OP processes.

Chapter 3 to Chapter 6 then move into the details of S&OP processes involving different review cycles associated with these processes. Chapter 4 to Chapter 9 are based on the tools provided by SAP IBP to efficiently manage the S&OP process.

Chapters 10 and 11 discuss the technical configuration for building the SAP IBP model. They cover both basic and advanced configuration, along with the steps to build the planning views in SAP IBP. Analytics is covered in detail in Chapters 12 and 13. Chapters 14 and 15 are based on the data integration, business roles, and security management in SAP IBP The last part of the book is entirely focused on the use cases from different industries, as described in Chapter 16.

The content of the different chapters can be summarized as follows:

- **Chapter 1: Introduction to Sales and Operations Planning**
  The first chapter begins by explaining why S&OP is important in today's global economy from market, process, and technology perspectives. It closes with an introduction to SAP Integrated Business Planning for sales and operations: how S&OP fits with other planning processes, how SAP HANA improves planning data, how SAP Fiori provides a better user experience, and how the cloud increases IT agility.

- **Chapter 2: SAP IBP Model and Navigation**
  This chapter dives into the SAP IBP model, introducing the key concepts that govern the solution across planning applications. Then the chapter focuses on S&OP models, which are built from time profiles, planning levels, key figures, and so on. The chapter closes by explaining how various users will access the SAP IBP model depending on their roles (through Excel planning views, SAP Fiori applications, and/or the SAP Jam Collaboration platform).

- **Chapter 3: Demand Planning**
  Demand forecasting and planning is the first step of S&OP; a small error or improvement in the demand planning process can substantially impact the cost and efficiency of an organization's supply chain processes. This chapter explains how to perform demand planning in SAP Integrated Business Planning for sales and operations, beginning with a high-level overview of the business process. It gives step-by-step instructions for the demand planning process: using historical data, creating a statistical model, financial modeling, and finalizing the organization's demand plan.

- **Chapter 4: Unconstrained Supply Planning**
  The output of demand planning is a consensus demand. Supply planning propagates that demand throughout the supply network. This chapter explains the

unconstrained S&OP heuristic and guides the business/key user on how to use the supply planning solution in S&OP. This chapter explains how to perform unconstrained supply planning with step-by-step instructions, from propagating demand and supply through rough-cut capacity planning.

- **Chapter 5: Constrained Supply Planning**
  The default supply planning method in SAP Integrated Business Planning for sales and operations is unconstrained supply planning, but some SAP IBP customers will use the S&OP optimizer available in the SAP Integrated Business Planning for response and supply module (which requires a separate license). This chapter explains how to perform constrained supply planning with the S&OP optimizer tool. It begins by describing the process in general and introduces the tool itself. The chapter then dives into the process of using the tool for financial modeling and optimization. It closes with an explanation of distribution planning.

- **Chapter 6: Consolidation**
  S&OP is a tactical planning process that connects the strategic plan to the operational plan. Once a demand plan has been generated and subsequently propagated through the supply network, it needs to be consolidated into views for operational and executive review. Users must define concepts for margin and profit. In addition, the agreed-upon plan becomes an input in operational planning processes like demand planning, inventory optimization, and response and supply planning. This chapter explains the consolidation phase with step-by-step instructions.

- **Chapter 7: Collaboration and Management by Exception**
  Collaboration allows companies to finalize a single, organization-wide demand and supply plan based on teamwork from production, purchasing, logistics, finance, sales, marketing, product development, and account management teams. It's critical that users collaborate across departments when they need to respond to exceptions in the planning process; this chapter introduces the SAP IBP tools (custom alerts, tasks, etc.) that facilitate collaboration and management by exception.

- **Chapter 8: Planning Simulations**
  SAP IBP has revolutionized the simulation and scenario capabilities in supply chain planning, especially for S&OP. This chapter discusses what-if scenarios, simulation applications, and version comparisons in SAP Integrated Business Planning for sales and operations.

- **Chapter 9: Process Management**
  Managing an effective global and local S&OP process requires that the cross-functional planning teams are tightly connected and coordinated. This chapter explains how SAP IBP process management functionality breaks the S&OP process into a coordinated workflow.

- **Chapter 10: Configuring SAP IBP for Sales and Operations**
  SAP IBP's status as a cloud application makes configuring each customer's business processes straightforward—but this is the domain of in-house experts and consultants, rather than the average SAP IBP planner. This chapter explains the most common SAP IBP configuration steps for supporting an S&OP process.

- **Chapter 11: Building Planning Views**
  Because supply chain planners traditionally love Microsoft Excel, SAP included an Excel user interface in SAP IBP. This chapter teaches readers how to design and build Excel planning views; it gives step-by-step instructions for using planning view templates, optimizing the EPM formatting features, charts, and using Visual Basic for Applications (VBA) to build state-of-the-art planning views.

- **Chapter 12: Key Performance Indicators and Performance Monitoring**
  Analytics is an essential part of an effective S&OP process. This chapter explains how big and small sets of data are used to monitor performance at various stages in the S&OP process.

- **Chapter 13: Dashboards and Analytics**
  SAP IBP's analytics and dashboard capabilities have revolutionized the usage of KPIs and application reports in S&OP processes. This chapter explains how to set up, use, and manage advanced analytics and dashboards to control the input and output of the S&OP process.

- **Chapter 14: Integrating SAP IBP for Sales and Operations**
  The S&OP process consolidates data from external systems to arrive at a tactical plan that can then be sent to operational and execution systems. The primary master data and transactional data for S&OP comes from SAP ERP, SAP S/4HANA, or other SAP and non-SAP systems. This chapter covers the integration mechanism for inbound and outbound data from SAP IBP, the required master and transitional data entities, and standard templates that can jump-start the integration process.

- **Chapter 15: Roles and Security**
  The S&OP process involves employees and data input from multiple cross-functional teams and across different regions and business units. SAP Integrated Business Planning for sales and operations provides a robust security model with user

management, roles, visibility filters, and permissions so each user can only view and modify appropriate and authorized data. This chapter gives an overview of role management and user provisioning in SAP IBP.

- **Chapter 16: SAP IBP Case Studies**
  This chapter uses two industry-specific case studies to show how SAP Integrated Business Planning for sales and operations can be used effectively at actual (though unnamed) organizations. It calls attention to the organizations' market drivers, their implementation processes and key capabilities, and the benefits received from implementing SAP Integrated Business Planning for sales and operations.

Conclusion

This book will provide you with comprehensive knowledge of S&OP processes and SAP Integrated Business Planning for sales and operations. This book is uniquely developed to cover the detailed aspects of three important categories: knowledge of best-in-class S&OP processes, advanced simulation, automation, analytics, and collaboration tools to optimize the process, and implementation of SAP IBP to harness value. The breadth and depth of the topics will help a business user understand the applications and a technical user implement the solution. In essence, this is your one-stop solution for SAP Integrated Business Planning for sales and operations implementation and related knowledge.

Acknowledgments

It's great to see the success of SAP Integrated Business Planning for sales and operations in the market and see it transforming the digital supply chain for many companies. I have been involved with this product from its very beginnings in 2012, starting with early release of the product to pilot customers through where it is now, the core application module of SAP IBP and a driver for many customer success stories. It's an honor to work with multiple customers, partners, consultants, and industry thought leaders and finally write down our knowledge and expertise gained in the form of a book. I especially would like to thank my coauthors, Pramod, Amit, and Jeroen, for their outstanding efforts in bringing together the broad domain, industry, functional, technical, and implementation expertise in the form of this book that others will benefit from. Also, my special thanks to Meagan White and Emily Nicholls from

SAP PRESS for their guidance in keeping the content relevant for the audience in mind and helping us stay on target for the completion of the book.

My special thanks to SAP IBP senior management for encouraging and motivating us to write this book and to all the great customers who helped make this product a success and giving us the opportunity to work with them to transform their business. Last but not least, a special note of thanks to my family, especially my wife, Pallavi Sridhar, for keeping me motivated and passionate about this journey to contribute to the community.

Raghav Jandhyala

After having worked for years with Raghav, Pramod, and Amit on various SAP IBP projects and codevelopments, it was a great experience to continue this working relationship by building a comprehensive overview of SAP IBP. Working with SAP PRESS was an exciting journey, putting our SAP IBP thoughtware into a physical form, hoping to help companies and integrators in the field add value in their S&OP processes. I'm excited by the result, a book that provides enough depth to kickstart any SAP Integrated Business Planning for sales and operations implementation and to drive companies to use SAP IBP effectively.

I'm coming up on working with SAP IBP for five years, and both the solution and our understanding of it have come a long way. Without my core teams throughout various client engagements in this period, none of this would be possible. I would like to thank my colleagues Akshay, Sanchit, and Vishvanath for their excitement in building our Deloitte IBP Practice with me, and my mentors Deb, Vadhi, and Darwin for getting me to where I am today. Finally, none of this would have been possible without the continuous support, motivation, and understanding of my wife, parents, and brother. Thanks all for making this possible!

Jeroen Kusters

I am first thankful to my coauthor team members, Raghav, Jeroen, and Amit, whose deep supply chain management knowledge, industry expertise, limitless enthusiasm, and collaboration made this book a reality. Special thanks to Meagan White and Emily Nicholls from SAP PRESS for their support, patience, and guidance through various stages of the book and for keeping us on track. I am thankful to Rheinwerk Publishing for providing us the opportunity.

I am also thankful to many colleagues from the SAP Product Development team, who should be recognized for building this successful SaaS product from the ground up. I especially would like to thank Rajwinder Singh, Goutam Chatterjee, Sudhir Thambala, Eduard Korat, and Volkmar Soehner, without whose efforts SAP Integrated Business Planning for sales and operations would not be where it is today. My special thanks to SAP IBP senior management for providing strategy and direction, and to all the customers who helped make this product a success for giving us the opportunity to work with them in a true partnership.

Finally, I am thankful to my family—especially my wife, Vidya, for her continuous support and motivation.

Pramod Mane

First and foremost, I'm thankful to my coauthor team members, Jeroen, Pramod, and Raghav, for the work collaboration that made this book possible. Working with SAP PRESS was a great experience. Special thanks to our editors, Meagan White and Emily Nicholls, for their support and guidance from the conceptual phase to the end product.

I'm thankful to my career mentor, Chris Verheuvel: his guidance has been instrumental to my learning growth and helps me be able to efficiently manage my professional and personal life. I would also like to thank Vadhi Narasimhamurti for his continuous support and guidance. Special thanks to my colleagues and friends Chandra Balasubramanian, Sanchit Chandna, and Shishir Dwivedi for helping me develop this text.

Gratitude is due to my family, my parents, my wife, Surabhi, and my kids, Ivan and Anaya, for their support and encouragement.

Amit Sinha

Chapter 1

Introduction to Sales and Operations Planning

In a continuously globalizing world, with change as the only constant, an integrated business planning solution is more important than ever. SAP Integrated Business Planning can play a pivotal role in bringing supply chain planning processes to the next level.

In this first chapter, we'll explain the importance of the sales and operations planning (S&OP) process in today's global and volatile business environment. We will discover what drives companies to evaluate their integrated business planning from market, process, and technology perspectives. Once the need for a solid sales and operations planning platform has been established, we'll introduce the SAP Integrated Business Planning (SAP IBP) solution. The chapter will conclude by showing how SAP HANA improves planning performance; how SAP Fiori and the SAP Integrated Business Planning, add-in for Microsoft Excel provide better user experience; and how the cloud increases IT agility.

1.1 Market Drivers

Companies operate in a constantly evolving world. In this first section, we will discuss the market trends that drive companies to rethink their supply chain processes. This will provide the foundation for defining the sales and operations planning process as a key tool to manage complex businesses operating in this globalizing and volatile world.

1.1.1 Globalization

Over the past decades, the business environment in which companies are operating has continuously become more global. Facilitated by evolutions in communications, technology, and infrastructure, globalization has impacted all the aspects of business operations today.

Amid this change, supply chain management has been the domain most affected by globalization. While offering opportunities to reach customers in new markets, building relationships with partners and suppliers on a global scale, and diffusing manufacturing operations to new regions, companies need to continuously reinvent their supply chain management processes.

Traditional companies often have grown out of a local business model and over the years opened their supply network to yield the benefits of the globalizing economy. In many cases, the processes supporting this global model have evolved little from when the company was very locally oriented. During the globalization process, small changes to the existing local processes reduced the time-to-value to benefit from the opportunities, which often results in a very complex process structure. Compounding those minor changes, companies find themselves with a monstrous process complexity, inadequate for operating within the new business reality.

Companies that have seen the light of day only in more recent years, on the other hand, have been growing in this global environment. Yet in many cases, due to benefiting from the opportunities the global economy brought, those companies have grown so quickly that their processes are still aligned to an early start-up instead of a company equipped to face today's challenges.

In both cases, building an integrated sales and operations planning process is the key to sustainable success in this global business environment. Before diving into the process transformation required to thrive in this global business environment, we'll go deeper into the opportunities and challenges globalization poses.

Like most things in life, globalization offers a great deal of opportunities but at the same time poses some challenges to companies, as follows:

- **Opportunities offered by globalization**
  - *Access to new markets*
    A globalized world provides businesses access to previously untapped markets. Customers can source their products globally, opening new markets to companies. This increases the market potential substantially, especially for companies that had a specific regional focus before.
  - *Increased sourcing opportunities*
    Just as customers have the ability to procure products anywhere in the world, organizations can expand the search for raw materials globally, allowing them

to find the best product at the best price. This gives organizations access to better products at a better price, thus leveraging a globally competitive landscape.

– *Decentralized manufacturing*
Some countries are more suitable for specific manufacturing processes than others. In a globalizing world, companies can locate their manufacturing processes in proximity to critical production resources. Whether close to a pool of qualified labor, such as locating high-tech companies' research facilities in Silicon Valley, or proximity to critical resources, like oil refineries in the Middle East, globalization allows companies to produce with the best quality for the best price.

– *Increased specialization and outsourcing*
Providing a global reach for output products allows companies to increase their level of specialization. Although specific niche products do not have a broad enough market on a local scale, opening to a global arena allows companies to specialize deeper. The trend toward deeper specialization fuels the opportunities of outsourced manufacturing, allowing companies to spin off activities that aren't at the core of a company's business.
A good example is Apple: though leading the world of smart devices such as iPhones and MacBooks, manufacturing those same devices is not Apple's core business. Apple has been incredibly successful, but the news sometimes exposes some of the challenges this global model brings—even for market-leading companies such as Apple.

- **Challenges with globalization**
  – *The complexity of supply networks*
  With increasing opportunities to source, manufacture, and distribute globally, the complexity of the supply network increases exponentially. Having to ship raw materials all over the world and consider differences in legislation, tax, and cultures drastically increases the complexity of the supply chain, requiring a solid process for its management.

  – *Global competition*
  Opening products to the entire world immediately means companies will be *competing* with the whole world at once as well. This increased competition puts a lot of pressure on companies to manage their supply chains meticulously. Building a global reputation takes years, but it can be damaged in an instance. For example, the exploding battery problem in the Samsung Note 7 put a dent in the fast-growing Samsung smartphone business.

- *Increased risk*

  Having suppliers, partners, and customers all over the world puts companies at the mercy of global events, from natural disasters to port closures. These global events become a thread contributing to supply disruptions in a global company. Although it is impossible to know every region as well as your own, uncertainty adds to the challenges to master when aiming to become a successful global player.

- *Legal and cultural implications*

  Every country operates differently, with its own laws, tax regulations, and culture. To successfully do business on a global scale, all intricacies of global trade must be assessed and considered in all the aspects of a company's process.

Companies that have proven successful in this global playing field all actively manage these challenges while trying to find new ways of reaping the opportunities globalization brings. At the same time, for companies to remain relevant, they must consider increasing market volatility.

1.1.2 Market Volatility

The phrase "change is the only constant" has long been a cliché when talking about markets. Volatility is the new normal under which supply chains must operate. The traditional approach of looking at a supply chain in a static way, spending weeks or months "optimizing" production processes and stable transportation routes, is over. Today, supply chains need to be dynamic to cope with rising customer expectations, shorter product lifecycles, and supply disruptions.

Let's look at the key aspects that require companies to become very agile in their supply chain processes:

- **Rising customer expectations**

  With increased opportunities to source any product from anywhere, customers have been empowered to be more specific in expressing their desires and to enforce those expectations from their suppliers. Traditionally, it was the standard for organizations to build products and then take them to market; this approach is no longer sufficient to exceed customers' expectations. To stay ahead of competition, companies need to get ahead of the customer expectations curve.

  Rising customer expectations can be experienced in various domains. In customer service, companies like Amazon have played a pivotal role in changing customer expectations and behavior and have thrived on it. After starting as an online book-store, today Amazon can get virtually any product to any customer in any part of the world, with delivery times often expressed in hours instead of days.

Continuing in the product realm, more and more companies are obliged to move toward more configurable materials so that clients can choose the product that matches their preferences exactly. The complexity of configurable materials dras-tically adds to the complexity of managing supply chains because the number of finished products rises exponentially with the number of configurable features.

- **Shortening product lifecycles**
Not only do products become more and more configurable, they also have shorter lifecycles. With the pace of technology evolution in the high-tech industry, for example, it becomes hard for companies to bring products to market before they become obsolete. New technologies and global competition forces companies to develop solutions faster, bring them to market as quickly as possible, and launch them globally before the products reach end-of-life.

Vizio disrupted the US television market in 2002 by bringing low-priced TVs to the market at an incredible pace. Vizio was not organized like other manufacturers: the company had no internal manufacturing capability, and its focus was purely on the design of new products being produced by contract manufacturers. This allowed Vizio to maintain an incredible speed to market, forcing competitors to follow the same model.

To deliver on these rising customer expectations, companies must reinvent them-selves and their products continuously. Companies like Apple announce new products multiple times a year and come up with new versions of virtually every product every year. To maintain this speed, leveraging a global market and a global supply model is critical to ensure enough output during the short time the prod-uct is relevant.

- **Supply volatility**
With the increasing pressure from the customer side and the limited mature life-time products have, it's critical for companies to closely manage their supply. The global environment in which companies operate, however, poses a higher risk of supply disruptions. Having suppliers in every corner of the world and manufactur-ing operations distributed across various countries increases the risk of stock-outs, both in the manufacturing process (raw materials) and in distribution to cus-tomers. This requires supply chains to become much more responsive to those supply disruptions and use bigger buffers for safety.

The actual availability of products isn't the only factor that impacts the company's bottom line; the cost to acquire those products does so as well. Commodity prices have seen a lot of instability for the last few years, requiring clear management and a view into what's required in the mid- to long term to effectively hedge against the adverse impact of volatile markets.

With increasing market volatility in a globalizing economy comes a great array of opportunities, but to succeed in this highly complex environment, companies need well-established processes to be successful.

The next section will introduce the key elements of a strong sales and operations planning process as a tool to manage complexity and drive value.

1.2   Process Drivers

Although sales and operations planning is a well-documented process in managing complex supply chains, many companies still do not use it effectively. Even companies that have been running an established S&OP process for years often do not reap the full benefits. This section will start with the definition of the sales and operations planning process and provide an overview of the steps typically included. This will serve as a process basis for the remainder of this book, in which we will explain the details of how SAP Integrated Business Planning for sales and operations can support every step of the process in detail.

1.2.1   S&OP Process Definition

Sales and operations planning processes have always been at the core of companies' planning processes. APICS defines S&OP as follows:

> *A process to develop tactical plans that provide management the ability to strategically direct its business to achieve competitive advantage on a continuous basis by integrating customer-focused marketing plans for new and existing products with the management of the supply chain. The process brings together all the plans for the business (sales, marketing, development, manufacturing, sourcing, and financial) into one integrated set of plans.*

> APICS Dictionary, 14th edition

If we consider profit maximization the core objective of most commercial companies, then the objective of S&OP is to provide the best possible customer service at the lowest cost. Pricing decisions often are not considered key decisions in the S&OP process; the immediate focus is on minimizing inventory, transport, and production costs while planning to meet customer demand.

During the S&OP cycle, companies focus on answering key questions like the following:

- What is the capacity required over the coming months to expand my business to a new region?
- In case of supply constraints, is producing in an alternate location more beneficial to producing earlier and stocking more product, considering the demand planning uncertainty?
- What is the impact of new product introductions on my supply chain?
- What is the impact of an additional distribution center in Central America?
- Which contract manufacturer would be the best partner based on its specific supply network?

Before diving into the details of the S&OP process, it's important to distinguish the different horizons relevant in the business planning process. This allows us to frame where the S&OP cycle fits in the broader organization planning processes.

1.2.2   Planning Horizons

It's important to understand sales and operations planning in the context of various planning functions in the organization, as depicted in Figure 1.1. Traditionally, planning processes in an organization are organized into three planning horizons:

1. **Strategic planning**
   Long-range planning, often related to financial objectives, at a very high level in the organization (e.g., yearly plan for 10 years on the product group level)

2. **Tactical planning**
   Medium-range planning, mostly in volumes and values, typically made up out of an annual operating plan that provides the budget for the year and a monthly refreshed sales and operations plan for the next 18 to 24 months rolling

3. **Operational Planning**
   Short-term planning, on a detailed product mix level (e.g., day-to-day planning for three months at the SKU level)

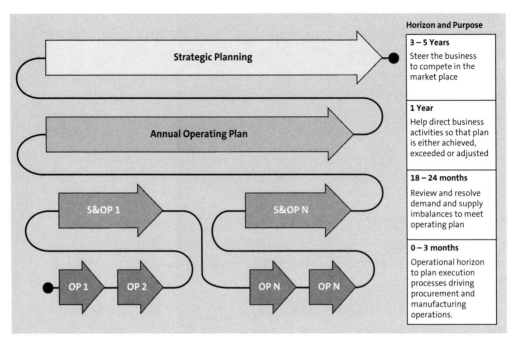

Figure 1.1 Planning Horizons

Although S&OP is defined as a tactical planning capability, it has ties to strategic planning via incorporating strategic objectives into sales and operations plans. It ties into operational planning because to become executable, the agreed-upon sales and operations plans need to transfer to the shop floor to become effective.

1.2.3   S&OP Process Decomposition

A typical S&OP process follows the steps depicted in Figure 1.2. The remainder of this section will provide more background on each of these steps.

Figure 1.2 S&OP Process

Product Review

The S&OP process, though interdependent, typically starts with a product review in which the magnitude and impact of new products is assessed. New products cannot be planned in the same way as mature products due to the lack of historical information. The impact of new products on supply chain operations can be significant, however, so this step shouldn't be omitted. During the product review, the performance of the current product portfolio and its strategic alignment will be confirmed. The output of the product review step is an initial forecast for new products to be launched during the six- to 18-month S&OP horizon.

Demand Review

Complementing new product planning, the demand review step will complete the unconstrained demand plan for the S&OP horizon. The objective is to provide an unconstrained demand picture agreed upon by various functions in the organization, including sales, marketing, and finance.

The consensus demand plan resulting from the demand review step is unconstrained in nature. It represents the volume the organization can realistically sell in the market without considering any capacity or supply constraints.

The unconstrained consensus demand is an unsourced plan; it's considered based on a combination of product and customer. From a product perspective, demand planning can be performed at various levels of the product hierarchy. The objective is to provide input to the supply review process on the level relevant for the S&OP decisions to be made. For example, for packaged goods manufacturers, the individual unpackaged product might be the right level; for pharmaceutical companies, it might be the level of the active ingredient that's critical for S&OP. A consensus demand plan typically involves a customer dimension, which could be individual customers on the ship-to level or sold-to level, regions, or global accounts. The key is to allow the right level of granularity to make optimal S&OP decisions.

The demand review process starts with demand history management. The sales history often is used to forecast the future statistically. Based on the statistics, sales representatives will get an opportunity to enrich the forecast with customer-specific information. The marketing department will provide insights with respect to planned promotions and marketing initiatives. Finally, all forecasts will be provided to the demand planner, who often has a facilitating role in the demand review meeting, during which all stakeholders sign off on the unconstrained consensus demand plan that will serve as an input to the supply review.

Supply Review

Based on the consensus demand plan, the supply review requires a propagated supply plan. Propagation of the consensus demand plan can be performed using various calculation techniques, from simple, rule-based heuristics (covered in Chapter 4) to advanced supply network optimization algorithms (covered in Chapter 5). The supply propagation step results in the following:

- Sourced demand plans, determining the facing location for all customer demand
- High-level production plans, depicting where which finished products and subassemblies will be produced
- Component requirement plans typically focused on requirements for critical components
- Capacity utilization plans typically focused on critical resource loads
- Transport plans

Although detailed production processes are very complex in most organizations, the S&OP process can abstract some of the complexity by focusing on critical components and resources, depending on the industry and the approaches a company wants to take to meet its S&OP objectives. For example, for a PC manufacturer, critical components could include the processors, memory, and hard drives, but not cabling and fixings. This approach makes sense when there's a likelihood of supply constraints on the critical components but an abundance or low risk of constraint for noncritical components. Focusing planning activities on those high-risk factors will help an organization pay more attention to those components that will impact S&OP decisions without cluttering its view by focusing on too broad a collection of products.

Operational S&OP Review

After the supply review step provides the propagated demand, high-level production and transport plans, and (critical) component requirements and capacity loads, the operational S&OP review aims to resolve the issues introduced by the constraints in terms of capacity or supply.

In the operational S&OP review, representatives from sales, marketing, demand planning, supply and operations, and finance will evaluate and analyze constraints and resolve them by considering various scenarios. For example, if there is a capacity constraint in one of the production facilities, options such as producing in a different facility or producing earlier in time to overcome the overload might be viable. The cross-functional team will assess the risks and impacts, often determined as financial measures, and suggest a plan for going forward.

To ensure efficient decision-making, the plans which have been in volumes until this step of the S&OP process are translated to values. In the S&OP cycle, cost and revenue values are only considered relevant if they allow stakeholders to make better decisions. For example, variable manufacturing costs, transportation costs, and inventory carrying costs mostly are deemed relevant costs. However, the fixed costs related to the production capacity available in the organization for tactical decisions is not considered a relevant S&OP cost because it doesn't differ with the different decision options at hand.

The operational S&OP review participants will conclude the meeting by determining one or more viable options, which might require executive decision-making.

Executive S&OP Review

The executive S&OP meeting ensures executive buy-in to the agreed-upon operating plan. In stable business scenarios, this decision-making might consist merely of a sign-off on the plans agreed upon during the operational S&OP meeting. However, sometimes various options can be proposed for executive decision-making. This can be the case if the S&OP decisions to be made are more in the strategic realm or incur a higher risk. For example, if capacity overload is dependent on an uncertain situation, like a big sales opportunity that hasn't yet materialized, an option such as producing earlier in time would expose the organization to a bigger risk. Producing in an alternate location might be less financially viable, but might not incur the risk of producing prior to winning the sales opportunity.

Although the concepts and objectives of the sales and operations planning process are not new, there is still a lot of room for improvement in a lot of companies to run a best-in-class supply chain. In this section, we covered the main steps of the S&OP process. In the next section, we'll look at the impact technological changes have on the S&OP process.

1.3   Technology Drivers

Traditionally, companies have managed their sales and operations planning processes by manually combining information from various sources. Data from the various domains involved in the sales and operations planning process—demand, supply, finance, sales—typically is stored in separate systems. As such, S&OP planners have been forced to consolidate the information manually by extracting data from the various systems and combining it in offline spreadsheets and databases. This is a very time-consuming process, resulting in a S&OP process that often takes the whole month.

To significantly speed up the process, S&OP tools have taken a more prominent place in the supply chain planning technology portfolio. The key purpose of these solutions is to provide S&OP users with consolidated information to build one shared version of the truth: one operating plan. In recent years, advancements in technology have allowed S&OP platforms to become more suited to performing a wide array of tasks in the supply chain planning process, resulting in completely integrated business planning platforms.

In this section, we'll cover some of those improvements that are pivotal in the context of S&OP solutions, setting the stage for introducing the SAP IBP solution in the next section.

1.3.1   Interactive Planning with In-Memory Computing

The latest generation of supply chain planning solutions has been characterized by improvements in advanced planning algorithms. Planning solutions have always had planning algorithms, such as statistical forecasting and supply planning heuristics and optimizers. However, in most cases those algorithms were not fast enough, not allowing planners to use them interactively. Planners mostly had to rely on nightly batch jobs for the to create forecasts or supply plans in case of changes.

Although the rise of in-memory computing can hardly be called a recent trend in 2018, it has taken a certain amount of time for big supply chain planning packages to be able to fully adopt this new way of processing. Even in the time of SAP APO, actual planning operations were typically executed in an in-memory database called live-Cache. The big change in recent years is that the size of the memory that can be used has increased drastically, making it possible to perform full planning in memory.

In the SAP realm, the in-memory computing revolution has been driven by SAP HANA database technology. SAP HANA is an in-memory, column-oriented relational database. As shown in Figure 1.3, an in-memory database keeps the complete application data in memory at any time. This cuts down on the time spent reading and writing from the (traditionally external) relational database, thus speeding processing up significantly.

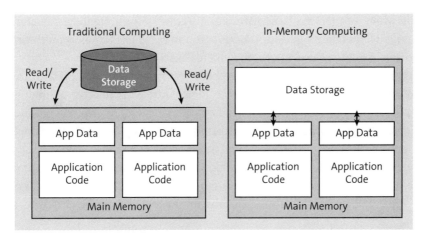

Figure 1.3 In-Memory Computing

Discussing the exact details of why in-memory databases outperform traditional ones isn't in the scope of this book; here, we're mainly interested in what value this can bring in the context of S&OP solutions.

The first and perhaps biggest impact of the increased processing speed of algorithms is the opportunity to start planning interactively. Running planning algorithms over an in-memory database typically reduces the runtime of those operations from hours to minutes. This allows planners to start planning interactively, rather than relying on long batch jobs.

In the S&OP world, this could go as far as starting to use the S&OP platform during operational S&OP meetings to validate impacts on the plan from possible changes.

The biggest new feature that interactive planning brings is the capability to perform scenario planning. Scenario planning in older planning systems, though often a technical possibility (e.g., planning versions in SAP APO), wasn't practical to use because running the baseline plan would probably take up the complete nightly batch window.

If it's possible to plan a supply network in a couple of minutes, that frees up time for planners to add more value to the planning process by considering different scenarios. To address typical S&OP questions (like those raised in previous sections), the planner now can model them in the system as scenarios and assess the implications of the different scenarios to make a more educated decision about which one to pursue.

For example, when planners are faced with capacity constraints in their manufacturing environments, there are typically various solution options. Planners could consider producing in a different plant, thereby increasing the transportation costs but still delivering to the customer. If the capacity constraint presents itself in the future, production could be performed earlier in time, hence increasing the cost of holding inventory but perhaps not incurring the transportation cost of alternative production locations. Finally, planners could opt to fulfill customer demand late, which might come at a cost. Without the opportunity to model these scenarios in the solution, it would be a very time-intensive exercise to make the right choice and thus only viable for big decisions. Allowing these options to be modeled in the system opens this capability to most decisions, improving the overall value of S&OP decision-making.

1.3.2   Data Visualization

The S&OP process involves users across various levels in the organization. Different users, however, use reporting capabilities slightly differently. We can distinguish between operational reporting, which is used by planners in their day-to-day planning activities, and executive reporting, used by executives during S&OP reviews.

Operational Dashboards

With the rise of in-memory databases, one of the first domains been impacted has been the analytics and data visualization space. Historically, technology platforms would have a dedicated reporting database used to store the data and visualize it in custom reports. The main driver for having a separate system for reporting was the speed of aggregation and slicing and dicing the information. When running dashboards, users would like to see the data rendered immediately and have the option to interactively change the level they're looking at—drilling up and down through hierarchies, for example. To allow acceptable response times, most planning environments had to store the data at an aggregate level to ensure it could be visualized quickly.

Using in-memory databases removes the need to store this data in a separate system, making it possible to report on the planning data from the planning system directly. This totally revolutionizes how data can be visualized during the planning process: it's no longer required to wait for batch replication jobs to send data from the advanced planning system to the reporting system. This allows users to report in real time on their planning data, visualize the impact of their actions immediately, and then put that information to use.

For operational reporting, not only is the speed of reporting important, but flexibility also plays an important role in operational reporting. Planners, while visualizing data, generate reports as a means of analysis. This requires almost infinite flexibility to drill into data, starting at higher levels and moving to details where problems might arise.

Executive Dashboards

Just like operational dashboards, effectively using executive dashboarding during the sales and operations planning process is predicated on having real-time access to the planning data. However, with executives spending less time in the technology solution, executive dashboarding adds extra expectations from a usability perspective. For executives to be able to interact with them easily, dashboards need to be concise, use the correct visualization techniques, and be accessible from any device. Executives don't often log into backend SAP systems and instead use mobile devices like tablets and phones to connect. This requires reports to be available in web browsers and provide real-time information in easy-to-understand visualizations.

The rise of better visualizations also drastically changes the application of the technology platform during the S&OP cycle. Having executive dashboards visualizing real-time planning data in a way that's easy to interpret makes it possible to use the dashboards during operational and executive S&OP meetings. This takes away a lot of time-consuming manual work creating PowerPoint presentations based on manually generated Excel charts, thus allowing the planners to use their time to perform value-adding planning activities instead.

1.3.3   Collaboration

Collaboration is a central component of the sales and operations process. Both internal collaboration—having the different functions involved in the S&OP cycle communicate effectively—and external collaboration—working with suppliers and customers to build an integrated plan—are crucial for an effective S&OP cycle. Hence, the S&OP process requires a technology platform that's capable of much more than just providing the functionality of an advanced calculation model. We'll cover the exact requirements for internal and external collaboration in the next two subsections.

Internal Collaboration

The S&OP process is cross-functional, involving stakeholders from almost every domain in the organization. To facilitate an efficient S&OP process, a platform for collaboration has become a critical component. Although cross-functional collaboration takes a lot of different forms, some key elements are as follows:

- Have a common view on the phase in the S&OP process. For example, in a multinational manufacturing organization, there are various demand planners per region per business line. To effectively plan supply, planners often start without necessarily having all demand plans signed off. Having good visibility into the completeness and status of all demand streams is important to provide better coordination.

- During the S&OP process, a lot of documents can support the different steps of the process. The ability to store this information in a common repository can be beneficial to ensure everyone has access to the information at the right time.

- Typical S&OP processes involve a series of meetings and sign-offs. Although some of those meetings provide a true value addition to the process, some are more routine in nature. The ability to virtualize non-value-adding meetings might speed the process and leave more time for the value-added activities.

In Section 1.4.3, we'll cover how the SAP IBP solution can support the internal collaboration processes by leveraging process modeling and SAP Jam.

External Collaboration

Performing S&OP requires an organization to look beyond its own borders, looking both upstream to suppliers and partners and downstream to clients.

Upstream collaboration often refers to sharing plans with your partners and suppliers to increase the reliability of their supply. Opening the planning process to suppliers implies that you share your unconstrained requirements plan with your suppliers. This allows your suppliers to use this extra intelligence in their planning efforts, increasing the commitment they can give and hence reducing the supply disruptions your company might suffer. Suppliers, in turn, can communicate their constraints, allowing you to consider those constraints in time in your planning process, hence further increasing the predictability of those disruptions.

Downstream collaboration refers to the reverse side of this process: you behave as the supplier, receiving unconstrained requirements plans from your customers. These plans can be used to compare against your own forecast for your customers and feed into the consensus demand process. Typically, there is a certain horizon at which those plans from your customers become firmer, giving you more visibility into the near-term demand.

Both processes can drive organizations towards expanding how they look at planning by starting to plan for an "extended organization." More and more business-to-business solutions support this process with technology platform planning for networks. In the SAP realm, the Ariba Network is the solution that supports this process.

1.4   SAP Integrated Business Planning

SAP IBP provides tools that give sales and operations planning a technology foundation and help companies be successful. In this section, we'll show how SAP IBP delivers a completely new and innovative technology platform for companies to correspond to market, process, and technology trends. We'll focus on the broader context of what SAP IBP enables, above and beyond pure sales and operations planning.

Although the sales and operation planning process is the focus of this book, this section will provide a broader introduction to the SAP IBP solution. The approach will be process- and functionality-driven in the first sections, showing the integrated nature of the solution. In the last section, we'll tie back to the modules available in the SAP IBP licensing model.

1.4.1   An Integrated Approach

The key to a successful sales and operations planning process is to deliver an integrated platform. In the previous section, we touched upon the need to deliver a solution that brings together information from various domains in an organization. In the following subsections, we'll look at the evolution of integrated business planning over time in SAP solutions before moving on to how SAP IBP's integrated approach helps optimize different elements of your supply chain. Aligned with traditional S&OP methods, the first versions of the SAP solution focus on propagating a supply plan from the consensus demand throughout the supply network, leading to a production and raw materials plan.

History of SAP Integrated Business Planning

The SAP IBP solution facilitates integrated planning by operating on a single data model: from product review to demand and supply planning to the S&OP meetings, all information is available in that single data model. This is a key differentiator compared to traditional supply chain planning tools, both in the SAP realm (e.g., SAP APO did not share a data model between demand planning and supply network planning) and in best-of-breed environments in which different applications are supported mostly by separate systems.

That integrated data model applies inside of the S&OP process steps, but even more importantly to all the processes adjacent to those traditional S&OP steps. Although the focus of this book is on the traditional steps in the S&OP process, in this section we'll take the time to describe the different functionality SAP IBP brings beyond S&OP.

SAP IBP provides a platform that enables a company to mature its S&OP process into a true integrated business planning process. We'll use the evolution of the SAP solution to describe the path from an S&OP tool into a true integrated business planning solution.

Year	Solution	Capabilities
2012	SAP S&OP 2.0	▪ SAP IBP for sales and operations ▪ New cloud-based SAP HANA platform for advanced planning ▪ New Excel and HTML user experience ▪ Unified architecture ▪ Comprehensive data model ▪ Support for internal collaboration
2013	SAP S&OP 3.0	▪ New SAP HANA Cloud Integration model ▪ Integration content for SAP, SAP APO, SAP Enterprise Inventory and Service Level Optimization ▪ S&OP optimizer ▪ Extended S&OP functionality: modeling, planning, analytics ▪ Planning area templates
2014	SAP IBP 4.0	▪ SAP Supply Chain Control Tower ▪ SAP IBP for inventory ▪ SAP IBP for supply ▪ Gartner MQ Leadership Quadrant

Table 1.1 History of SAP IBP

Year	Solution	Capabilities
2015	SAP IBP 5.0	■ SAP IBP for demand ■ SAP Cloud Platform Integration templates ■ Functional enhancements to each solution
2016	SAP IBP 6.1	■ SAP IBP for response and supply delivering an integrated executional platform in the SAP IBP solution ■ Order-based data model allowing order prioritization, constraint planning, and gating factor analysis
Present	SAP IBP	■ Strong improvements of the SAP IBP for response and supply functionality and data model ■ Paving the way to SAP ERP Integration ■ Native SAP IBP/SAP Ariba integration
Future	Future plans for SAP IBP	■ Major functional investments in SAP IBP for demand and SAP IBP for response and supply ■ Supply chain execution and financial planning integration ■ Integration with SAP Trade Promotion Planning

Table 1.1 History of SAP IBP (Cont.)

When SAP's integrated business planning solution was released in 2012, it was called SAP Sales and Operations Planning powered by SAP HANA, with version 2 the first commercial version based on the SAP HANA in-memory database. The functionality of the solution in 2012 to 2013 was specifically focused on the S&OP process, providing basic demand planning capabilities like statistical forecasting and consensus building. The first versions provided supply planning functionality by leveraging a rule-based S&OP heuristic, which was complemented in 2014 with the S&OP optimizer functionality.

With the upgrade to version 4 in 2014, SAP released SAP Integrated Business Planning, which coincided with the extension of the solution beyond traditional S&OP capabilities. At that time, the SAP Integrated Business Planning for inventory module was born, which allowed companies to leverage the SmartOps multiechelon inventory optimization engine in their integrated business planning processes. Version 5, released the next year, deepened the demand planning capabilities for demand sensing. The next major release followed in 2016 with version 6, in which the first version of SAP Integrated Business Planning for response and supply was launched, completing the planning capabilities by integrating more operational planning into the environment.

Currently, SAP delivers quarterly releases with rapidly evolving new functionality. Since 2016, the naming conventions for releases have changed to adopt the naming conventions of other SAP solutions: two digits for the year (e.g., 18 for 2018) followed by two digits for the month (e.g., 01 for January). This book was completed using the 1802 system as a reference.

Aligned with the evolution of the SAP solution itself, integrated business planning can be looked upon as the next phase in the sales and operations planning maturity. This book will focus on the sales and operations planning capabilities, but we want to use this opportunity to explain some of the more advanced capabilities of SAP IBP, which facilitates more than just S&OP. We'll briefly cover the different supply chain optimization engines available in SAP IBP, then discuss the demand sensing and response management capabilities. We'll spend a little bit of time on the supplier collaboration capabilities available via the connection to SAP Ariba. The rest of this book will then focus on elements within the traditional S&OP scope.

Supply Network Optimization

Supply network optimization optimizes the flow of products throughout the network. This function was released in SAP Sales and Operations Planning powered by SAP HANA version 3 in 2013 and has received a lot of attention ever since. Chapter 5 will explore all the details of S&OP optimization, but first this section will highlight how optimization fits into integrated business planning processes.

S&OP optimization is a profit-optimization-based technique in which revenue and costs drive the objective function. The algorithm will use variable costs only, as depicted in Figure 1.4. The following elements are included:

- **Raw material costs**
  The cost of (critical) components used in the production process

- **Transportation costs**
  Both finished goods and components, from a supplier to an internal location, between internal locations, and to a customer

- **Inventory carrying costs**
  Cost impact of storing inventory

- **Production costs**
  For producing a finished product or intermediate product at a specific location

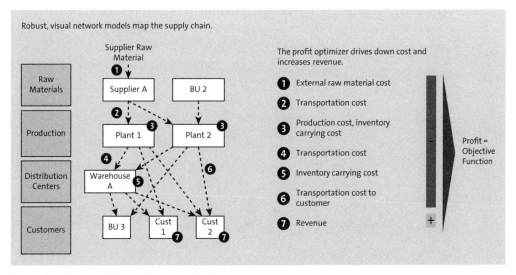

Figure 1.4 Financial Model for Optimization

The objective of supply network optimization techniques is to determine the most appropriate good flows, minimizing costs while trying to achieve maximal demand fulfillment. Besides leveraging the costs, various hard constraints can be introduced in supply network planning, such as the following:

- **Resource capacity constraints**
  The maximum volumes of finished products or subassemblies a resource can produce in the set time granularity
- **Supply constraints**
  The maximum amount of product that can be procured externally
- **Transportation constraints**
  The maximum amount of product that can be pushed through a specific leg of the network

The S&OP optimization engine aims for the highest fulfilment of customer demand possible, at the lowest cost, maximizing profit margins.

Inventory Optimization

Inventory optimization, on the other hand, determines the optimal safety stock to be carried to meet customer demand, while understanding that customer demand forecasts are inaccurate and transportation duration is variable. It calculates the amount of inventory required to meet a target service level for groups of customers. If the supply network has multiple levels, then multiechelon inventory optimization iden-tifies the most advantageous node in the network to store the inventory in. The key elements are depicted in Figure 1.5.

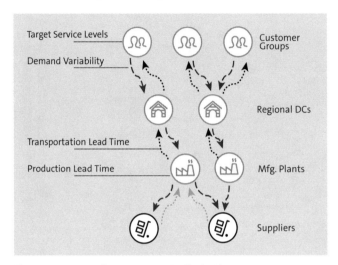

Figure 1.5 Inputs for Inventory Optimization

The following inputs are required to perform multiechelon inventory optimization:

- Supply network and sourcing rules depicting the physical flow of goods through-out the organization
- Target service levels defining what the intended level of service to customers should be
- Demand and demand variability, which often translate into a forecast accuracy indicator; the higher forecast accuracy, the lower the required safety stock to impact the service level
- Lead times and their variability, accounting for the uncertain nature of real life, which can be divided into two categories:
  - Production lead time: the time it takes to produce products
  - Transportation lead time: the time it takes to transport goods; applies to raw materials, finished products moved between internal locations, and finished products moved to the customer
- Periods between review, as the ordering process typically isn't a continuous pro-cess (e.g., a weekly ordering pattern would require inventory to cover the full week on top of lead time)

Although inventory optimization often focuses primarily on determining the optimal inventory of finished products to carry, advanced inventory optimization algorithms also calculate the right amount of raw materials to keep to build an end-to-end inventory picture.

In the SAP IBP platform, the multiechelon inventory optimization algorithms have received a jumpstart via the acquisition of SmartOps by SAP in 2013. This has opened more than a decade of experience in building supply chain optimization engines to SAP, allowing it to incorporate this experience in its new environment and putting SAP directly at the top of the league in inventory optimization.

Global Optimization

Although supply network optimization and inventory optimization are carried out individually for the most part, there is a dependency between the types of optimization. With supply network optimization, changing the sourcing logic inside of the supply network is an input to inventory optimization. Inventory optimization might change the level of inventory, which implies an inventory carrying cost, impacting the profit optimization in supply network optimization in turn. This implies there is some thought required when trying to implement optimization in supply chain planning, considering the dependencies of various calculations. This can be further complicated by minimum order quantities, optimized (economic) order quantities, and the step functions often introduced in raw material pricing.

This is where SAP IBP delivers its biggest leap in effectiveness. Traditionally, companies have adopted distinct technology platforms to carry out S&OP optimization and inventory optimization. This makes it tremendously more difficult to reap the benefit of a combined optimization. In every iteration, data needs to be transferred from one environment to another, making it practically impossible to reach a global optimum.

Demand Sensing

Demand sensing is a forecasting method that leverages new mathematical techniques and near real-time information to create an accurate forecast of demand based on the current realities of the supply chain. As opposed to traditional statistical forecasting techniques that leverage time series, analyzing past sales to create a forecast of future sales, demand sensing uses various demand signals to better predict the very near future.

Gartner defines *demand sensing* as "a capability used to gain real-time visibility and insights from consumption and order data to improve short-term statistical forecasts and drive short-term supply chain operations."

This focus on the very near term makes demand sensing one of the techniques that goes well beyond the tactical nature of the traditional S&OP cycle, typically considered in months. It is, however, a key technique that allows organizations to become more demand-driven. In the integrated business planning processes, demand sensing can play a key role in operationalizing S&OP results and making them available for downstream consumption in detailed planning and scheduling. Understanding that the S&OP process doesn't exist in a vacuum often raises questions about operationalizing the results. Demand sensing can play a critical role in that link, acting as an advanced consumption approach to provide consumed information that's directly usable for operational planning while considering the S&OP decisions that have been made.

Just as in inventory optimization, SAP has had the opportunity to leverage the SmartOps demand sensing algorithms to deliver an impressive starting version of demand sensing.

Response Management

Another technique gaining increasing attention in the context of SAP IBP is response management. The response management functionality is the latest big addition to the SAP IBP platform, introduced in 2016.

Response management is an ex post process, happening after the SAP IBP process. Even with the best processes in planning, the future can never be predicted perfectly. Response management aims to limit the adverse impacts of disruptions in the supply chain by quickly and effectively assessing real-life events and their impacts and generating options for mitigation. As an example, an organization can use supply network optimization and inventory optimization in a mature integrated business planning process but still be faced with a delayed vessel at a port. This delayed vessel might carry critical components that have been carefully planned for, putting the organization in a reactive mode. Response management allows you to determine the impact of this event on the current state of the supply chain and provide various options both for direct execution (e.g., ordering products from a nearby supplier) and for the longer term by adjusting the S&OP plans with this new information.

Just like demand sensing, response management plays mainly in the shorter time horizon, bridging the gap between tactical supply chain planning processes and day-to-day operations.

Response management is the only module in the SAP IBP solution that works on an order-level data model. This is a substantial change from the traditional period-based data model on which the other modules in SAP IBP are based. This also calls for a separate integration model.

Supplier Collaboration

In Section 1.3, we touched upon the need to take planning beyond company borders. To facilitate collaboration in supply chain planning with partners and suppliers, SAP IBP connects natively with the SAP Ariba Supply Chain Collaboration solution.

Since SAP IBP release 1705, it's possible to connect SAP IBP to SAP Ariba without any middleware. This provides a giant leap forward in the ability to deploy supplier forecast collaboration solutions. Traditionally, to collaborate with suppliers companies had to build a unique technological pipeline for their data from their advanced planning system to their supplier, often via Electronic Data Interchange (EDI) protocols. This was a very cumbersome and expensive IT endeavor requiring a substantial investment.

The Ariba Network has grown out of the SAP acquisition of Ariba (now SAP Ariba). It was originally a sourcing and procurement platform focused on indirect procurement, and it has now completely revolutionized supplier collaboration. The Ariba Network allows companies to publish their entire unconstrained requirements plan in one go and count on the Ariba Network to distribute it to the right suppliers.

In this section, we provided an overview of SAP IBP as an extension of the traditional S&OP process thinking and introduced how SAP Integrated Business Planning for sales and operations can be a great starting point for more advanced supply chain planning in the long run.

1.4.2   Better Algorithms

In Section 1.3, we touched on how in-memory computing makes it possible to start planning in real time, leverage scenarios, and speed the S&OP cycle. In this subsection, we'll give an overview of the different algorithms SAP IBP brings to perform better planning:

- **Demand planning algorithms**
  Demand planning algorithms in SAP IBP are mainly on the statistical forecasting side. Statistical forecasting models in SAP IBP are split into three main components:

- *Preprocessing algorithms* allow you to manage the transactional data that feeds into the statistical forecasting engine. Outlier correction and missing value substation algorithms are available.

- *Forecasting algorithms* calculate a statistical forecast from the demand history (possibly corrected by preprocessing algorithms).

- *Postprocessing algorithms* calculate the forecast accuracy based on the ex post forecast.

The combination of these algorithms produces a statistical forecast that feeds into the consensus demand process. Chapter 3 will provide an in-depth overview of the demand planning capabilities in the SAP IBP solution.

- **Supply planning algorithms**
Based on the consensus demand, which is typically on the customer product level, supply planning algorithms calculate all the internal demand flows in the supply network. SAP IBP offers two main algorithms, and each has a variety of settings to fine-tune its behavior:

  - The *S&OP heuristic* is an unconstrained, rule-based, decision-supporting algorithm with a sourcing rule as its basis. The heuristic will calculate the flows in the network in an unconstrained fashion, representing the loads on resources and suppliers without cutting back when overloads are observed. This makes it a true decision-support algorithm, leaving making the decision of how to constrain the demand to the manual intervention of the planner.

  - The *S&OP optimizer*, on the other hand, is a profit-maximization decision-making algorithm. It will use a financial model as the basis of a profit optimization and will make decisions for the planners about which demands to pursue and what flows to utilize in the supply network.

  Both the heuristic and the optimizer will be covered in depth in Chapter 4 and Chapter 5 of this book.

- **Inventory optimization algorithms**
Calculating the optimal safety stock levels can be done by leveraging the inventory optimization engine. SAP IBP comes with two essential inventory optimization algorithms:

  - *Single-echelon inventory optimization* calculates the safety stock for every location independently

  - *Multiechelon inventory optimization* is where the true power comes into play, calculating the inventory for all the locations in the supply network. Considering strategic placements and inventory-pooling opportunities, it's the multieche-lon inventory optimization techniques that drive substantial value and prove the strength of SAP IBP as a completely integrated planning solution.

- **Response management algorithms**
When moving more toward the operational planning space, response manage-ment delivers order-based algorithms that allow SAP IBP to complete the planning cycle with a completely operational plan. Response management can be consid-ered an operational planning engine itself, generating supply elements on an order level, like planned orders, purchase requisitions, and stock transfer requisi-tions. On the other hand, response management algorithms also can be used to rapidly respond to supply disruptions via replanning the network, leveraging a prioritized demand. In that way, response management will help improve a com-pany's margins by allocating the available constrained supply to the prioritized products and customers.

There are various response management algorithms:

- *Constrained planning* will use the open forecast, combine it with open supply elements to build a constrained operational plan, and generate purchase requi-sitions, planned orders, and stock transfer requisitions.

- *Order confirmation* will consider the open sales orders and the forecast in a prior-itized fashion and generate the same supply elements. The order confirmation run will also support a recalculation of the order confirmation date, ensuring that upon supply disruption a new order confirmation date can be communi-cated to customers.

- The *deployment algorithms* will generate deployment stock transfer requisi-tions to improve the internal distribution of stock aligned with the prioritized demands.

> **Note**
> Both inventory optimization and the details of the response management algo-rithms are outside of the scope of this book.

1.4.3   New User Experience

Although SAP IBP offers an integrated approach and an impressive array of algo-rithms, perhaps the biggest plus is its user experience. Traditional SAP advanced planning solutions have focused strongly on power and performance in the planning cycle, sometimes at the cost of the user experience. With SAP IBP, those days are over. The user experience has been revolutionized completely, giving planners the tools and experience they know best. Most S&OP is performed in Microsoft Excel, leveraging the SAP Integrated Business Planning, add-in for Microsoft Excel. Other activities, like reporting and alerting, are performed in a web browser via SAP Fiori.

Excel-Based User Interface

Planners have always relied on Excel as their planning solution of preference. Advanced planning solutions in package software have always fought an uphill battle against the ease of use of a "simple" spreadsheet. Even today, many planners will still extract data from their advanced planning solution, load it into Excel, manipulate the data, and load it back into the advanced planning solution. The biggest downside of this approach, of course, is the emergence of various versions of the plan throughout the organization.

With SAP IBP, those days are over. Excel and the advanced planning solution have become one, merging the user experience of Microsoft Excel with the backend consolidation of one plan of record in the organization. This is achieved via SAP Integrated Business Planning, add-in for Microsoft Excel, a small piece of software installed as an add-in in Excel to allow the planner's personal computer to connect to the SAP IBP database.

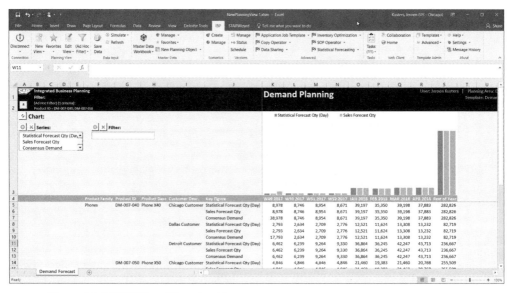

Figure 1.6 SAP IBP Excel Planning View

Figure 1.6 shows an example of what an Excel planning view in SAP IBP. You can see that it looks like a standard Excel sheet, but with an extra tab added in the ribbon in Excel. This **IBP** tab allows you to interact with the SAP IBP application. Upon connecting to the system, the add-in receives the data from the SAP IBP solution and renders it in a tabular format. From that table, all standard Excel functions can be used. This means that the chart shown in Figure 1.6 and the formatting performed leverage all the standard Excel capabilities.

Chapter 2 will provide a deeper overview of the navigation in the SAP IBP solution, and Chapter 11 will talk more about building planning views.

SAP Fiori Applications

A lot of the actual sales and operations planning activities are performed using the SAP IBP Excel planning views, but other activities are rendered in a web browser via SAP Fiori applications. This makes it possible to access SAP IBP from almost any device by using HTML5 web pages.

The SAP Fiori launchpad is the main landing page for users (Figure 1.7). The launchpad contains active tiles, which themselves can display information. You also can click any tile to open its application.

Figure 1.7 SAP Fiori Launchpad for SAP IBP

Types of SAP Fiori applications include the following:

- Dashboards (see Figure 1.8)
- Custom alerting monitors and case management apps
- Forecast model maintenance and assignment apps
- Demand prioritization, gating factor analysis, and project stock apps

Figure 1.8 SAP IBP Advanced Dashboard App

SAP Fiori applications have all been designed in SAPUI5 with a focus on simplification and usability.

SAP Jam

The third user experience innovation comes with the SAP Jam platform, which is integrated into the SAP IBP solution. SAP Jam is based on the performance management software SAP acquired with SuccessFactors. In the context of integrated business planning, SAP Jam adds a social media-like experience to facilitate internal collaboration during the S&OP cycle.

SAP Jam comes with a web browser-based user interface, accessed via an SAP Fiori tile or with an Apple or Android app. The web browser-based version is shown in Figure 1.9 and the iOS-based version in Figure 1.10.

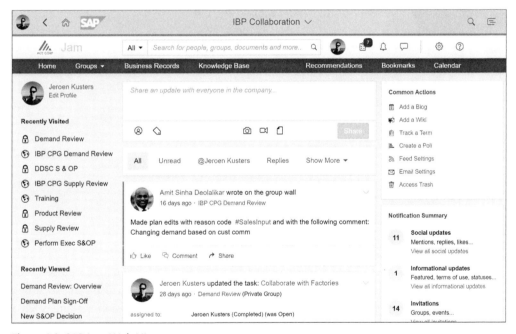

Figure 1.9 SAP Jam Web UI

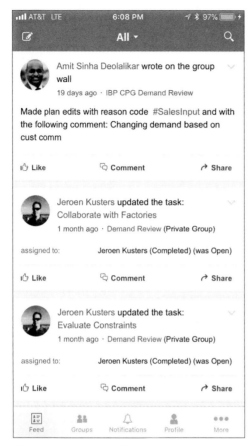

Figure 1.10 SAP Jam iPhone App

The user experience of SAP Jam is comparable to that of modern-day social media apps like Facebook. It provides a stream of updates people have made, either to the plan in Excel, via cases and tasks, or via direct updates. SAP Jam also adds document management capability and delivered content for virtual decision-making, such as pro and con tables, decision sign-offs, and the like.

With this overview of three key new user interfaces, we've touched on perhaps the biggest innovations of SAP IBP. However, before concluding this chapter, it's important that we demonstrate how SAP IBP can provide more agility in supply chain planning technology.

1.4.4   More Agility

To lighten implementation complexity and make advanced planning solutions more accessible, more and more solutions have been deployed by leveraging a cloud-based infrastructure. SAP IBP has been offered via a cloud-based subscription model since 2013 with the introduction of SAP Sales and Operations Planning powered by SAP HANA version 3, and today it's only available in the cloud. In this section, we'll look at what the cloud model means and it helps to provide better planning capabilities.

Using a cloud-based solution means that the hardware server that runs the software is not maintained in the IT department of your own company but is hosted by the cloud provider (such as SAP in the case of SAP IBP) and provided to you as a service. This means that the maintenance of the physical hardware, upgrades to the core operating system and core application, and the network via which the application connects to the Internet are managed by SAP as a service.

When connecting to the application, users do not connect to a local solution but rather connect over the Internet to the SAP data center that hosts SAP IBP. For SAP IBP, solutions are single-tenancy, which means that one IBP solution operates for one customer only.

One of the biggest advantages of operating a cloud-based solution is that the burden of upgrades is performed by SAP on a regular basis. For SAP IBP, which is aligned with the release schedule of other SAP solutions such as SAP S/4HANA, there is a quarterly upgrade process. Upgrades are backward-compatible, ensuring that functionality deployed in prior releases will continue to work seamlessly while every new release gives planners the opportunity to start leveraging new functionality faster.

Having SAP IBP available as a cloud-based solution, combined with the fact that the solution comes with a set of predefined planning models (see Chapter 2 for more on sample planning areas), makes SAP IBP uniquely fit for more agile implementation methodologies.

Agile implementation methodologies try to provide an answer to the common thread in IT projects that there is a gap between business requirements, understanding of solution engineers, and the delivery of the solution; they do so by providing users an early view into the solution. Rather than waiting months after delivering business requirements for a solution, end users follow the journey of building the solution in a very interactive way.

Combining the quarterly upgrade cadence with the move to more agile implementation methodologies drives SAP IBP solutions to be considered for continuous improvement. Every upgrade exposes new functionalities that can contribute to improvements in integrated business planning processes. With the sample planning models, it's possible to test the impact of the new functionality directly, which drives companies to keep the SAP IBP solution much more up-to-date than was possible with more traditional advanced planning solutions.

1.4.5   SAP Integrated Business Planning Modules

Until now, we have not talked about SAP IBP modules, which make up the licensing of SAP IBP. We explicitly chose to focus on the business processes facilitated by the solution rather than starting from a licensing perspective.

However, to complete the introduction to the solution, it's useful to look at how the different functionalities fit into the SAP modules and what this means for potentially investing in an SAP IBP license.

The boxes in Figure 1.11 list the different modules available in SAP IBP. The solution typically is licensed by buying one or more modules, which each provide specific capabilities. With functionality being added on a quarterly basis to the solution, the SAP Help web pages (go to *help.sap.com/ibp-ref* and navigate to **What Is in the SAP IBP Applications**) are the best source of information to find exact licensing information. Moreover, your SAP account representative definitely will be happy to help you out with the details. In this section, we'll give a short functional overview of the content and function of each module.

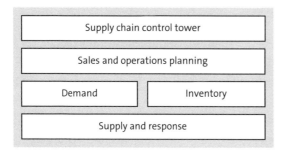

Figure 1.11 SAP IBP Modules

SAP Integrated Business Planning for Sales and Operations

As we described earlier in this section, SAP IBP really matured out of SAP Sales and Operations Planning powered by SAP HANA. To date, SAP Integrated Business Planning for sales and operations is still the most adopted and central component of most SAP IBP deployments. SAP Integrated Business Planning for sales and operations contains the basics to perform an end-to-end S&OP cycle, from demand planning to baseline statistical forecasting capabilities to supply planning to the rule-based heuristic we'll cover in detail in Chapter 4. Building a financial model on top of the demand and supply processes is enabled via the flexible key figure model, which will be covered in detail in Chapter 2. SAP Integrated Business Planning for sales and operations also includes the process management capabilities that are core to the internal collaboration process, which will be covered in Chapter 9.

Having capabilities to support the entire S&OP process means that SAP Integrated Business Planning for sales and operations is often looked upon as the best starting point for companies looking to invest in SAP IBP.

SAP Supply Chain Control Tower

SAP Supply Chain Control Tower complements SAP IBP for sales and operations by delivering some critical management-by-exception capabilities.

The most notable capabilities in this module begin with the custom alerting capability, which delivers users an excellent dashboard to manage flexible, user-defined alerts. In SAP Supply Chain Control Tower, you can select any key figure and perform any comparison, either relative or to an absolute number. You can also define if a user should be alerted of an anomaly, what the priority is, and the like. These alerts then can be managed as cases using the case management apps, allowing you to start a functional workflow from an alert.

Next, for alerting and case management capabilities, SAP Supply Chain Control Tower gives you access to a predefined supply chain operations reference (SCOR) model with metrics and analytics aligned to industry best practices scorecards. This can be valuable, helping to bring your reporting capabilities to the next level with an out-of-the-box repository of leading best practices key performance indicators (KPIs). Chapter 12 will go deeper into creating KPIs in SAP IBP.

Finally, as a new capability introduced in SAP IBP 1705, SAP Supply Chain Control Tower contains business network collaboration capabilities required to connect SAP IBP to SAP Ariba without the use of middleware.

SAP Integrated Business Planning for Demand

SAP Integrated Business Planning for demand deepens SAP IBP's demand planning capabilities by adding to the pre- and postprocessing algorithms available in SAP Integrated Business Planning for sales and operations. SAP Integrated Business

Planning for demand extends the number of statistical forecasting techniques from the four available in SAP Integrated Business Planning for sales and operations to over a dozen in SAP Integrated Business Planning for demand.

The most important addition, made available via the extension of statistical forecasting techniques, is the demand sensing algorithms, which allow you to "sense" demand and thus improve the very near-term forecast accuracy.

Finally, SAP Integrated Business Planning for demand delivers a promotion analysis capability that can be connected to a trade promotion environment. This gives SAP IBP users the ability to assess the base and lift forecasts based on the promotion information available in the SAP IBP solution.

Chapter 3 will provide the details of the demand planning capabilities that are part of SAP IBP.

SAP Integrated Business Planning for Inventory

SAP Integrated Business Planning for inventory adds multiechelon inventory optimization algorithms that make it possible to calculate the optimal safety stock levels to meet customer demand while minimizing inventory investment. In addition to calculating the optimal inventory level, SAP Integrated Business Planning for inventory also adds algorithms to classify the projected inventory in different buckets, such as cycle stock, stock in transit, safety stock, and the like.

SAP Integrated Business Planning for Response and Supply

The SAP Integrated Business Planning for response and supply module essentially is composed of two distinctly different capabilities. On the one hand, this module delivers the S&OP optimizer, which will be covered in more detail in Chapter 5. On the other hand, response management refers to the operational planning engine, which operates on an order-based data store. This latter model is out of the scope of this book.

SAP IBP, Edge Edition

SAP Integrated Business Planning, Edge edition is aimed at mid-market companies and delivers a combination of some key capabilities of the SAP Integrated Business Planning for sales and operations module (basic statistical forecasting, the S&OP heuristic, and the process modeling) with some features out of SAP Supply Chain Control Tower (custom alerting and the SCOR-based KPI model). This allows medium-sized companies to leverage key capabilities to successfully perform their S&OP processes with management-by-exception capabilities while offering an attractive licensing model.

1.5   Summary

In this ever-changing world, in which market volatility and globalization dominate the organizational agenda, the need for an integrated sales and operations planning process has never been more important. In this chapter, we covered the market, process, and technology drivers that point to the need for an integrated business planning platform. With the rise of in-memory computing, planning functionalities have become available that could not be imagined a decade ago, especially in the domain of interactive planning and scenario capabilities.

The remainder of this book will go into detail about how SAP Integrated Business Planning can bring the sales and operations planning process to the next level. In this chapter, we went a little bit beyond the traditional S&OP scope, showing how the SAP IBP solution seamlessly integrates recent supply chain trends like demand sensing and response management. We have shown how the different modules in the solution relate to building the foundation for a best-in-class S&OP process and how the new generation of user interfaces supports adoption across a broad array of stakeholders.

In the next chapter, we'll introduce the key elements of the SAP IBP model and basic navigation, setting the stage for a deep-dive into the functional domains in the remainder of the book.

Chapter 2
SAP IBP Model and Navigation

SAP Integrated Business Planning provides a flexible planning structure to model various business requirements and an easy, intuitive user interface for accomplishing business processes.

In this chapter, we'll introduce the key concepts that enable planning processes across SAP IBP applications. We'll focus on the building blocks used to construct the planning models, such as attributes, time profiles, planning areas, planning levels, key figures, and versions. After we've detailed the planning model, we'll cover the various ways in which super users or planners can interact with or navigate through the planning model and applications depending on their role. This includes SAP Fiori web applications, Excel planning views, and the SAP Jam collaboration platform.

2.1 SAP Integrated Business Planning Architecture

In this section, we'll cover the high-level solution architecture of SAP IBP. Figure 2.1 illustrates the high-level solution architecture of SAP Integrated Business Planning for sales and operations.

On the right-hand side are the cross-functional stakeholders that participate in the sales and operations planning process, ranging from sales/marketing, demand planning, finance, and supply chain to executives.

The primary way for participants to access, analyze, and modify the plans is via the familiar Excel interface. There is an Excel add-on that provides a tab in the Excel ribbon to access various functions for planning. In addition, participants also can access the web interface for embedded real-time analytics, which are user-defined. The social collaboration aspect of the S&OP process is enabled by SAP Jam. All shared content is available not only from the web interface but also from Excel.

To support the S&OP process cadence, SAP IBP supports process modeling a process dashboard that is socially enabled to better engage participants. There is also an admin interface both for managing user roles and permissions and for reconfiguring the SAP IBP planning data model and calculations.

At the core, all data is stored and calculated in the in-memory SAP HANA database. This includes dimensions, attributes, key figures, calculations, versions, user-defined scenarios, and simulations.

On the left side of Figure 2.1 are different data sources from which data can be brought into SAP Integrated Business Planning for sales and operations securely using SAP Cloud Platform Integration.

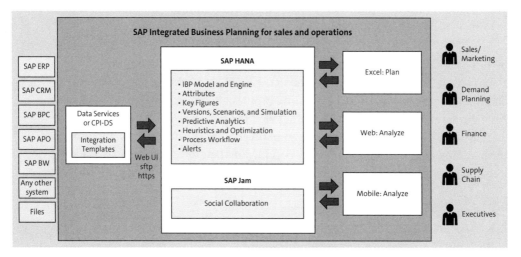

Figure 2.1 SAP IBP Architecture

2.2   Planning Model

When a company implements SAP Integrated Business Planning, the first task is to define and configure the planning model based on business requirements and populate it with data. Then, based on the planning model, planners and analysts can create planning views so they can work on the data using SAP Integrated Business Planning, add-in for Microsoft Excel.

SAP IBP requires a model to describe the data structures that the plan operates on. A planning model allows you to represent your business plan. It describes the structure of your business plan in terms of data and calculations. It defines how data is stored, calculated, and aggregated in the system. You can also think of the planning model as a master plan that defines how the information is stored and aggregated in the system.

From a technical perspective, a planning model is a collection of master data and time series data that is organized in dimensions and enhanced with specific calculations. SAP IBP lets you configure and customize your own planning models to address your unique business requirements.

In this section, we'll cover the various entities that comprise the planning model. We'll cover the key concepts about the entities and the relationships between them. In Chapter 10, we'll also go over how the entities in the planning model are configured in SAP IBP using SAP Fiori apps.

All planning models in SAP IBP are based on the following entities:

- Attributes
- Master data types
- Time profiles
- Planning areas
- Planning levels
- Key figures
- Versions and user-defined scenarios

2.2.1 Attributes

Attributes are the fundamental elements that carry information about a business entity. A logical grouping of attributes is used to model master data types, which represent supply chain or business entities. Attributes describe the characteristics of master data types; for example, a product entity is represented by a unique product identified, description, product family, brand, category, and so on. Hence, the first step in the design phase of a project is to identify all relevant attributes.

Based on the property of the attribute, it can be defined as either numeric or non-numeric.

The following data types are supported for attributes in IBP:

- **String or varchar**
  This data type is the most widely used and represents character information such as product description, product family, customer name, and so on.

- **Decimal**

  The decimal data type is used to maintain numerical information that typically remains the same across the planning horizon. It's also used for modeling attributes as key figures. The information generally considered for decimal attributes includes costs, exchange rates, unit of measure, capacity supply, capacity consumption rates, components, and so on.

- **Integer**

  The integer data type is used to represent information such as lead time, periods of coverage, or demand category, or system settings such as lot-size policy.

- **Timestamp**

  Date or time information is represented using timestamp attributes. Phase-in and phase-out date and product availability date are examples of timestamp attributes.

2.2.2   Master Data Types

Master data contains main categories of information. Master data is used to segment and organize planning information. For example, customer, location, product, and resource are some of the main or simple data categories within the data model. You can also combine the main data categories to create compound data categories—for example, if you want to understand the sales history based on a combination of product, customer, and shipping location.

Master data types generally have many attributes or supporting data. Attributes are characteristics of master data types that can be numeric or non-numeric. For example, an attribute of the location master data type could be the country or location type or region.

SAP IBP supports the following master data types:

- **Simple master data types**

  These represent foundational business objects or entities such as product, customer, location, and resource.

- **Compound master data types**

  These are used to represent characteristics of combinations made of two or more simple master data types. For example, if you have a business requirement to analyze data by a combination of product and customer characteristics, then you need to create customer-product compound master data, made of the primary keys of two simple master data types: customer and product. The compound master data type can have attributes such as market segment.

- **Reference master data types**
  A reference master data type refers to a simple or compound master data type so that you don't have to upload the same data more than once. For example, you can create the *locationfr* (location from) reference master data type that uses the location master data type as a reference. You can't load data into a reference master data type.

- **Virtual master data types**
  Virtual master data types define joins between two or more master data types that otherwise have no connection to each other. The join conditions you define between these referenced master data types determine the set of data the virtual master data type uses. You can only use simple and compound master data types to define virtual master data. Also, you can't load data into a virtual master data type.

- **External master data types**
  Lets you manage master data integrated from an external database into predefined static tables in SAP IBP. The prerequisite to define external master data is to integrate the data from the external database in a predefined format into SAP IBP. When you set up your planning model, you define an external master data type referring to a predefined table that contains the content. You can't manually load data into external master data types. The data is loaded into them from an external database via periodic-based integration.

2.2.3   Time Profiles

A time profile is the time component of the dimensions; it defines the various time levels (days, weeks, months, quarters, years) of time buckets, each with a unique number, in which data can be managed. Each level is made up of periods, which are identified by a number, and each has a start and end of the time period. In SAP IBP, the time profile levels are customizable, which allows for the flexibility to organize data.

To aggregate and disaggregate on time dimensions, hierarchies on different time levels need to be defined. Figure 2.2 shows an example of a time hierarchy. In this example, the time profile levels have multiple parents, and there also can be time profile levels without a parent level.

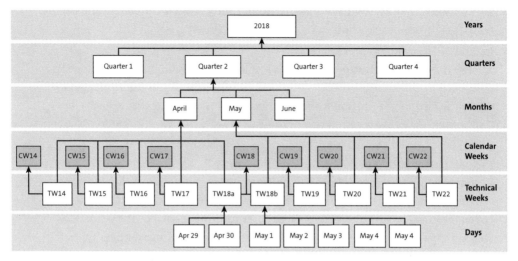

Figure 2.2 Time Profile Levels Hierarchy

2.2.4   Planning Areas

A planning area describes the structure of an SAP IBP for sales and operations plan and is the foundation of the planning model. It's a planning model entity defined by a set of other planning model elements that includes attributes, master data, time profile, planning levels, key figures, and versions.

Figure 2.3 illustrates the relationship between the planning area entity and other planning entities.

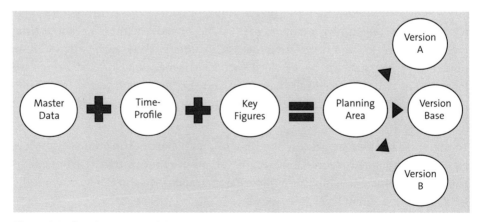

Figure 2.3 Planning Area Entities

The planning areas may contain many plan datasets: one actual or baseline dataset and many version datasets for storing alternate plans for what-if analysis. An organization may have multiple planning areas to enable the sales and operations planning process in different business units.

2.2.5 Planning Levels

It's very important in the SAP IBP or S&OP process to slice, dice, and analyze data by different dimensions. A planning level is based on any set of attributes that is a function of dimensions (such as product, customer, or location).

A planning level entity lets you analyze planning data at an aggregation level, which is different than the storage or calculation level. Key figures in SAP IBP are calculated or stored at specific planning levels.

Planning levels have two types of attributes:

1. **Root attributes**
   They form the keys to independently identify the key figure values. Typically, root attributes are also the keys of the master data, but this isn't always the case.

2. **Nonroot attributes**
   They can be thought of as supporting data. They are characteristics (or sometimes hierarchies) that help to aggregate the key figure values.

For example, if the consensus demand stored key figure is defined and stored at the week-product-customer planning level, then this key figure can be aggregated by other non-root attributes of the time dimension, such as month, quarter, or year; of the product dimension such as product family or brand; and of the customer dimension such as customer region or key customer.

A planning area typically includes key figures of multiple planning levels, and these can be linked with calculations, often resulting in key figures at additional planning levels.

2.2.6 Key Figures

Key figures are measures that hold transaction data. Key figures are series of numbers over time, and each number corresponds to a time period value.

They are associated with a key (of the planning level), which is a combination of attributes from one or more master data objects. Some examples of key figures include sales forecasts, marketing forecasts, consensus demand plans, projected inventories, capacity plans, or actual data such as sales orders and order history.

SAP IBP has the following types of key figures:

- **Stored**

  Data is stored in this type of key figure at the base planning level. The base planning level is the lowest, most granular (key) planning level at which the value of that key figure is defined. Data in a stored key figure is either edited or imported directly.

- **Calculated**

  Values in this type of key figure are always calculated based on a formula. Formulas are user-defined—for example, *Revenue = (Quantity × Price)*. This type of key figure is not editable.

- **Alert**

  These are key figures with user-defined criteria that monitor and manage execution of business plans. They can only have values of 0 or 1, meaning that the alert itself is either true or false—for example, you can have it alert you if *(Target Revenue – Consensus Revenue) ÷ Consensus Revenue > 10%*.

2.2.7   Versions and User-Defined Scenarios

Versions let you maintain alternate global plans. Planning areas can contain many plan datasets: one baseline dataset and alternate plan datasets. Versions let you perform what-if analysis on different versions of data.

There are two types of versions:

1. Versions that share master data with a base version
2. Versions that have their own master data (also called *version-specific master data*)

The type of version is defined in configuration. It can't be changed once the planning area is activated. A planning area can have a combination of the two types of versions.

In addition to versions, you can also create user-defined scenarios. As the name suggests, these are created by business users to enable what-if/simulation analysis. These are private to a user by default but can be shared with other business users for collaborative decision-making. User-defined scenarios use delta logic, as opposed to versions, which are complete copies. Delta changes in key figure values on top of versions and can be published back to versions.

Figure 2.4 illustrates the relationship between versions and user-defined scenarios. The versions are alternate plans. The figure shows that the planning area has three versions: Base, Optimistic, and Pessimistic. The optimistic version shares master data with the base version, whereas the pessimistic version has its own master data. The master data and key figure data can be copied from other versions.

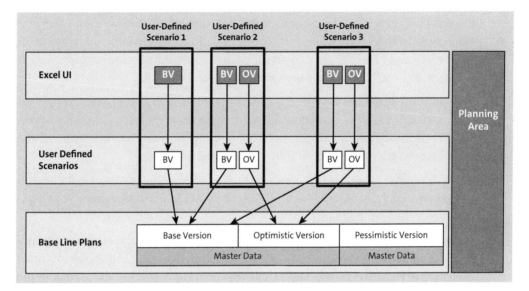

Figure 2.4 Versions and User-Defined Scenarios

The user-defined scenarios are on top of the versions and can be based on one or more versions. Only the delta transaction data is stored in the user-defined scenarios. The data is visible via shine-through logic from the underlying versions.

2.3   Navigating the Planning Model

The ability to navigate through SAP IBP is one of the most important aspects of using it to its best abilities. In this section, we'll walk through how various participants, including business users, administrators, and configuration experts, can access various UIs offered by SAP IBP to accomplish their business objectives.

Once the planning model as described in the previous section is configured, activated, and loaded with master data and transaction data, the planning process can start.

In this section, we'll cover how users can utilize the various interfaces: Excel, web-based SAP Fiori applications, and SAP JAM Collaboration.

2.3.1 Excel User Interface

The primary way for participants to access, analyze, modify, and simulate plans is via the Excel interface. SAP Integrated Business Planning, add-in for Microsoft Excel provides a tab in the Excel ribbon for viewing and changing planning information in Microsoft Excel. The add-in supports localized date and number formats, and it selects your local date and number format automatically.

The add-in also provides advanced planning functions such as supply planning algorithms, statistical forecasting models, and disaggregation and copy planning operator functions depending on the applications your company has licensed and the business role you're assigned.

Before business users can use the add-in, it needs to be installed. The installation can be done manually, or the add-in can be installed via silent installation by your company's SAP IBP administrator.

Before you can start working with your data in Excel, you need to establish a secure connection between Excel and SAP IBP. A connection will establish access to a planning area in a specific system and enable the different buttons in the **IBP** tab in the Excel ribbon.

Now, let's go over the different groups in the **IBP** tab (see Figure 2.5) and their functions:

- **Connection**
  Allows you to logon to an SAP IBP planning area in the system or log-off from the SAP IBP planning area.

  The default method of logging on is via a SAML-based connection. When you log on to the system using this connection, you're redirected to an identity provider and asked to submit your credentials.

  Figure 2.6 illustrates the connection elements that need to be populated in the connection manager.

Figure 2.5 IBP Tab in Excel

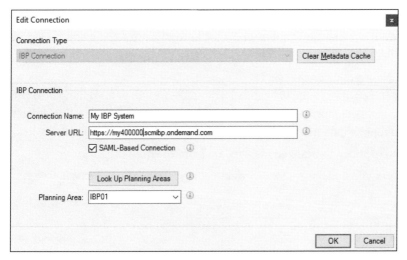

Figure 2.6 SAP IBP Connection Manager

When logging off, you can choose to logoff from the planning area; if you choose this option, you log off from the SAP IBP system, which means that the **Remember Me** setting is deleted, along with your credentials for the identity provider used by your company. Alternately, you can choose to disconnect from the SAP IBP system.

- **Planning View**

  Planning views let you perform planning tasks in SAP IBP. A planning view is a user-defined report that allows for viewing, editing, and sharing information directly from/into the SAP IBP system. The **Planning View** group in the **IBP** tab allows you to create and customize planning views. The created planning views can be stored as favorites. The **Planning View** group also provides quick access to edit the planning views and the filters. An Excel workbook can contain multiple planning views in each sheet.

- **Data Input**

  Once you have the planning views created, the **Data Input** group in the **IBP** tab lets you edit the data, run simulations, and save the data as per your business needs. The **Simulate** drop-down lets you perform what-if analysis. It also provides the ability to simulate advanced planning functions such as time-series supply planning algorithms or inventory optimization functions.

  The **Refresh** button lets you discard any unsaved changes you've made in simulation mode or otherwise and refreshes the latest data from the persistent or database layer.

- **Alerts**

  The **Dashboard** option shows the number of exceptions for the alerts added in your favorite planning view.

- **Master Data**

  The **Master Data** group in the **IBP** tab lets you make minor ad hoc changes to the master data in your system, which is helpful for what-if/scenario planning. It isn't designed to replace data integration. It also allows you to create planning objects.

  There are two options to manage master data from the master data group:

  - Single: Lets you add, copy, edit, or delete single master data records (see Figure 2.7).

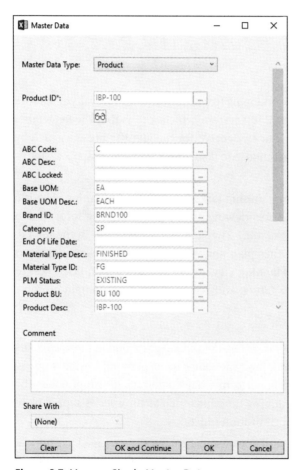

Figure 2.7 Manage Single Master Data

– Mass: The mass maintenance function lets you download master data records from a master data type to a Microsoft Excel worksheet to view or edit the data (see Figure 2.8). If your planning model supports version-dependent master data, the system allows you to specify the version. The mass maintenance function also lets you create new planning object combinations. You can save the Excel workbook as a favorite.

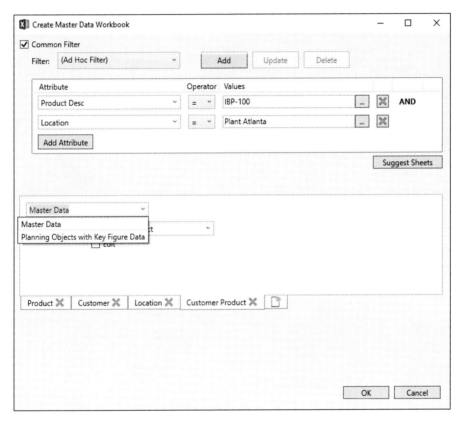

Figure 2.8 Manage Mass Master Data

- **Scenarios**
  As we discussed in earlier, user-defined scenarios are created by business users to enable what-if/simulation analysis. The **Scenarios** group in the **IBP** tab lets you create and manage user-defined scenarios.

Figure 2.9 shows the creation screen for user-defined scenarios. Here, you can create a new scenario and share it with selected users or user groups.

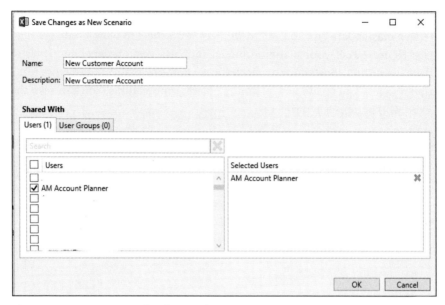

Figure 2.9 Create User-Defined Scenario

Figure 2.10 shows the **Manage Scenarios** screen. From this screen, you can promote a user-defined scenario to the underlying version; reset the scenario, which basically initializes it; delete the scenario; or duplicate or copy an existing scenario.

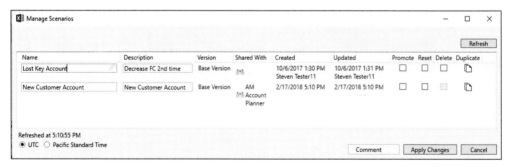

Figure 2.10 Manage User-Defined Scenarios

- **Versions**

  The **Versions** group in the **IBP** tab lets you manage the transfer of master data and transaction data between versions. The base version comes standard with the system; you'll need to configure any additional versions and activate them. The master data can only be copied between versions if a version has its own master data.

- **Advanced**

  From the **Advanced** group in the **IBP** tab, you can run advanced planning functions such as time-series supply planning algorithms, inventory optimizations, and statistical forecasting functions in background mode.

- **Tasks**

  From the **Tasks** group, you can directly display tasks that you have set-up in the Process Modeling SAP Fiori app and change their status to **Completed**. When you click the **Tasks** button, it opens the **Processes and Tasks** dialog, containing a list of your open tasks (see Figure 2.11). You can choose to group your tasks based on **Priority**, **Process**, or **Due Date**.

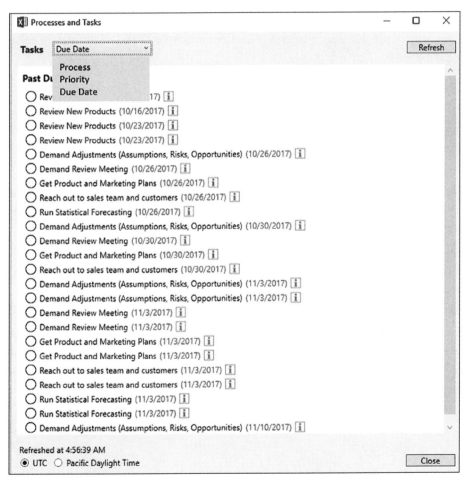

Figure 2.11 Task Management

- **Web Client**

  From here, you can open the Collaboration app or navigate to the web interface home page.

- **Template Admin**

  A *template* is a stored planning view that allows you to create planning views based on your planning tasks and role. When you create a planning view based on a template, the default settings such as time periods, key figures, and planning levels are inherited. The new planning view is based on the template's Excel workbook, so any items stored in the workbook itself, such as formatting, charts, or EPM local members, are also part of the new planning view. However, the system does not save the filter criteria as a template setting.

Users with appropriate permissions can add new templates and edit or delete existing templates.

2.3.2   Web-Based SAP Fiori Applications

In addition to the Excel interface, SAP IBP offers a web UI for web-based SAP Fiori applications. SAP Fiori applications are supported for desktop and tablets. The SAP Fiori launchpad is the access point for all web-based applications for SAP IBP.

SAP Fiori applications are displayed as tiles, and you can launch any app by clicking the corresponding tile from the launchpad. Figure 2.12 shows the SAP Fiori launchpad screen for SAP IBP.

The tiles displayed on your launchpad are arranged into groups, with the group title displayed above each group. The tiles can be rearranged within the group by dragging and dropping them. You cannot add tiles or remove tiles from the tile group.

The set of tiles visible to you in the launchpad is determined by the business catalogs assigned to the business roles that your business user is assigned to. The business catalogs and the corresponding tile groups are delivered as part of SAP IBP. A few examples of SAP Fiori groups and tiles available based on the roles assigned are **Demand Planner**, **Inventory Planner**, **General Maintenance**, and **Model Configuration**. The language for the text is determined by the preferred language defined in your web browser. You can change the language in the SAP Fiori launchpad by changing the default language of your web browser.

When you log in, the first SAP Fiori group you'll see is called **My Home**, which you can customize to include your most commonly used functions. The SAP Fiori launchpad also provides a quick way to edit your home page, find SAP Fiori apps, edit settings, and provide feedback by clicking on the user or person icon.

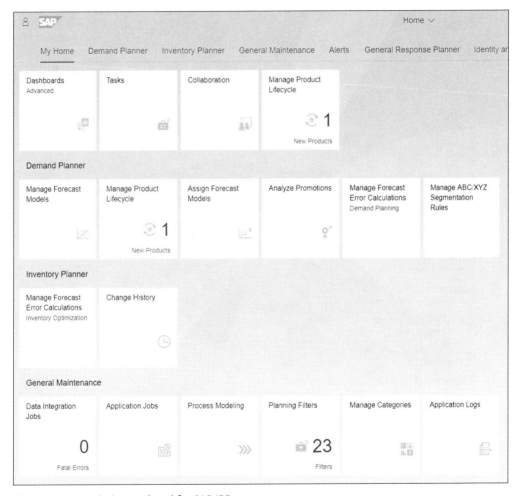

Figure 2.12 SAP Fiori Launchpad for SAP IBP

Figure 2.13 illustrates how to access the edit home page, find SAP Fiori apps, edit settings, and provide feedback. The left panel becomes available after clicking the user or person icon at the top-left corner.

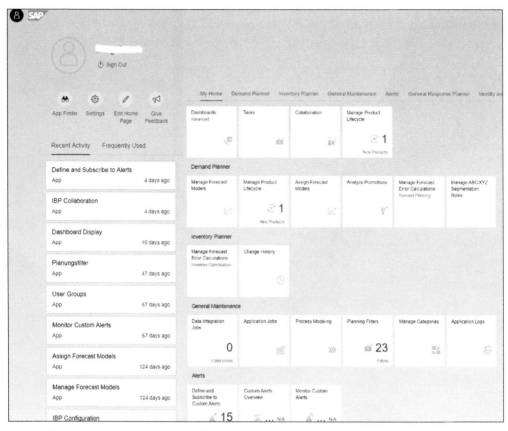

Figure 2.13 SAP Fiori Launchpad: Edit

In the left-hand panel, you can click the **App Finder** icon to find SAP Fiori apps. Figure 2.14 illustrates the **App Finder** page. It lists the available apps on the left and shows the existing SAP Fiori groups to which you can add apps on the right.

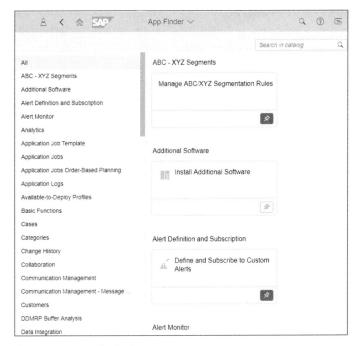

Figure 2.14 App Finder Page

You can also edit your settings by clicking the **Settings** icon. Figure 2.15 shows the settings that can be changed.

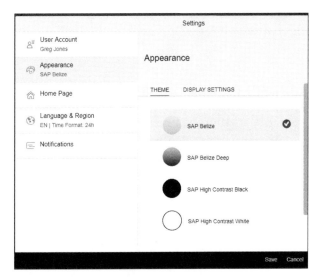

Figure 2.15 Edit Settings

In addition, you can also quickly edit your home page by clicking the **Edit Home Page** icon. This lets you add SAP Fiori apps to existing SAP Fiori groups, including **My Home**; create new SAP Fiori groups; and rearrange the order of SAP Fiori groups.

Figure 2.16 shows the screen from which you can edit the home page.

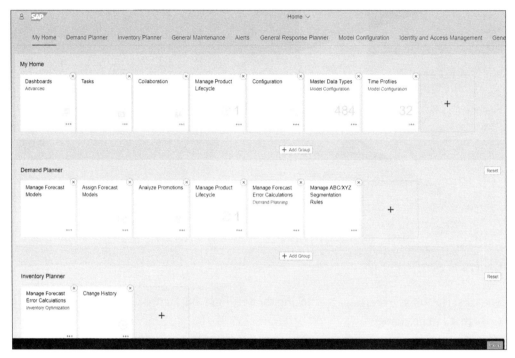

Figure 2.16 Edit Home Page Screen

2.3.3   SAP Jam Collaboration

The social collaboration aspect of the S&OP process is enabled by SAP Jam. As you plan and respond, you might want to share with and get input from your colleagues. The integration of SAP IBP with SAP Jam lets you collaborate with other members of your team and track your processes and process-related tasks.

The SAP Jam application can be accessed from the launchpad using the Collaboration SAP Fiori app (see Figure 2.17) when a direct link to SAP Jam is available and from the SAP Integrated Business Planning, add-in for Microsoft Excel by clicking the **Collaboration** button in the Excel ribbon (see Figure 2.5).

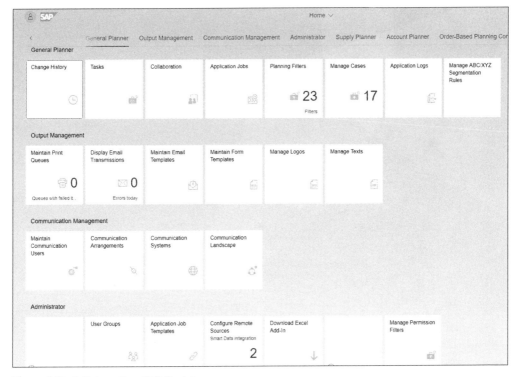

Figure 2.17 Collaboration SAP Fiori App

The SAP Jam home page (see Figure 2.18) lets you view your home feed, enter status updates, and start a discussion with colleagues; it also provides many other tools that make collaboration easier.

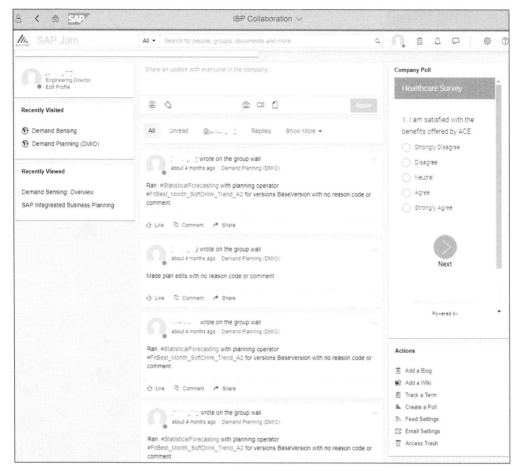

Figure 2.18 SAP Jam Home Page

With SAP Jam Collaboration, you can perform the following actions:

- You can view and create tasks and assign the tasks to SAP Jam groups for each process step from the Manage Process Templates application. Figure 2.19 shows a list of tasks, which are assigned to the process steps from the process template. When a process instance is created, tasks are also created for each user assigned to the SAP Jam group (see Figure 2.20) in that process step.

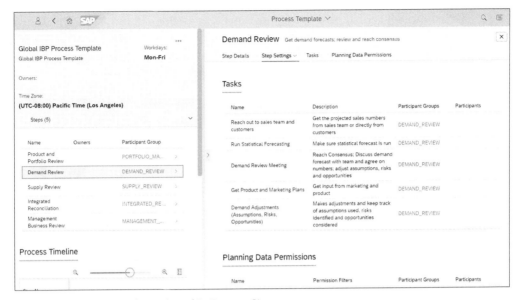

Figure 2.19 SAP Jam Tasks Assigned to Process Steps

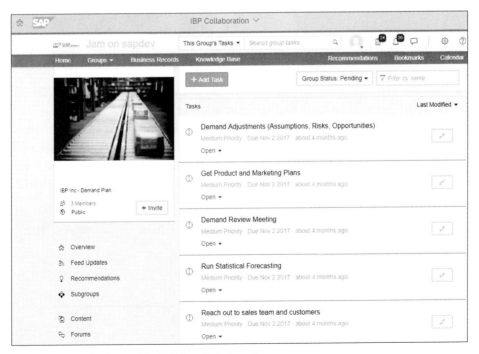

Figure 2.20 Tasks Created in SAP Jam Collaboration

- You can collaborate with cross-functional users on an ad hoc basis. This can be accomplished by creating tasks from the SAP Jam group directly (see Figure 2.20). These tasks also are displayed in Microsoft Excel under the **Tasks with No Process Assigned** category (see Figure 2.21).

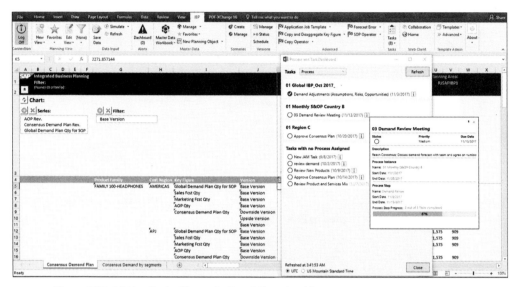

Figure 2.21 Ad Hoc Tasks Shown in Excel Planning View

- You can share business data and other information with members of a SAP Jam group by using the **Share in SAP Jam** button in the apps in which it's available. For example, you can share an application job template, a custom alert, an analytics chart, a dashboard, or information about a transportation lane with members of a specific SAP Jam group. Figure 2.22 shows how an analytics chart can be shared using the **Share** icon at the right-hand bottom corner and choosing **Share on SAP Jam**.

- You can also share business data such as an analytic chart with comments directly with SAP Jam group members (see Figure 2.23).

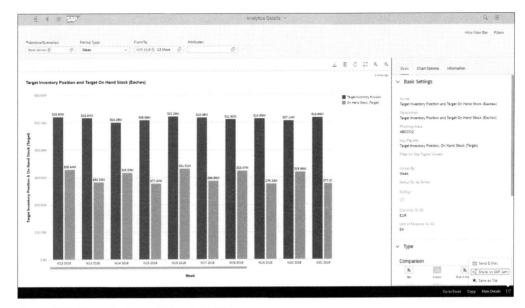

Figure 2.22 Share Business Data via SAP Jam

Figure 2.23 Share Business Data with SAP Jam

2.4   Summary

In this chapter, we covered the key concepts that enable planning processes across SAP IBP applications. We focused on the building blocks used to construct the planning models, such as attributes, time profiles, planning areas, planning levels, key figures, and versions. Finally, we went over the various ways in which super users or planners can interact with or navigate through the planning model and applications depending on their roles. These options include the web application interface via SAP Fiori apps, Excel planning views, and the SAP Jam Collaboration platform.

Chapter 3
Demand Planning

This chapter explains demand planning functionalities in SAP Integrated Business Planning for sales and operations. It covers the concepts of demand forecasting and managing and automating the demand planning process. It also delves into the statistical forecasting, demand review, forecast error, financial modeling, and collaboration for demand planning processes.

Demand forecasting is among the initial steps for the S&OP process as part of the demand review. A relatively small change in the forecast error or forecast accuracy can have a significant impact on the cost and efficiency of an organization's supply processes. This chapter explains how to perform demand planning in SAP Integrated Business Planning for sales and operations, beginning with the overview of the business process of demand planning and associated parameters. It provides step-by-step instructions for the demand planning process in SAP IBP: using data, creating statistical models, financial modeling, and use of collaboration for finalizing a demand plan.

3.1 Demand Planning at a Glance

Through demand forecasting, an organization predicts the future demand of its customers. Based on the industry type of the organization, this demand can be for products or services. Irrespective of the industry segment, size, product output, service nature, or geography, every organization performs a demand planning process to equip itself to satisfy customer demand.

Serving customer demand is the reason for the existence of any firm. The demand planning and forecasting process is the initiation of most of the other business processes of the organization, like procurement of products and services, labor planning, utilization of assets, and movement of the products, information, and money in the supply chain network.

There are a few instrumental parameters for the demand planning processes, which together define the process and help to map it in SAP IBP. These parameters are as follows:

- **Time horizon**

  The time horizon decides the time duration of the demand forecast. Different horizons are considered for the nature of the decision. The time horizon is categorized as short-term, mid-term, or long-term. Different units of time are used for different horizons. For example, it's common to have the demand forecast in weekly or daily time buckets for the short-term horizon; mid-term units usually are weekly or monthly buckets; and the long-term demand forecast is generally represented in monthly, quarterly, or sometimes yearly buckets. The exact duration for the time periods is finalized based on the industry sector and the organization's preferences. For S&OP decisions, it's common to have the forecast time horizons in weekly, monthly, and quarterly time buckets for a period ranging from two to five years.

- **Demand nature**

  It's essential to understand that the aim of demand planning should be to predict customer demands, also known as planned independent requirements (PIRs). Some organizations with less mature demand and supply processes confuse demand planning with internal and external demands, and the demand planners aim to predict the internal network demand, which may be misaligned to the external demand. This is the divide between the demand planning and the supply planning processes. Demand planning processes should be focused on independent external demands, whereas supply planning for PIR demands and multiple other factors (lead time, safety stock, network flow, etc.) should plan for the internal demand.

  The external and internal demands in a mature supply chain (and in SAP IBP) are known as *independent demand* and *dependent demand*, respectively. In this chapter, we'll focus on independent demand; dependent demand elements will be analyzed in Chapter 4 and Chapter 5.

- **Hierarchy levels for aggregation and disaggregation**

  An organization's enterprise level is represented by multiple attributes of products, locations, and customers. Different teams use these attributes for analysis, review, and making managerial decisions. For example, a demand planner may work with product hierarchy levels of product family and product category for analyzing demand, whereas a sales manager can consider grouping, reviewing, and editing the demand plan based on customer segment, customer geography, and sales manager hierarchies.

It's of paramount importance to finalize the product, customer, and location hier-archies before or while designing SAP Integrated Business Planning for demand and SAP Integrated Business Planning for response and supply. SAP IBP inherently provides natural aggregation and disaggregation of data while working across the hierarchy levels. Data consistency is also maintained automatically by the solu-tion. Hence, if the demand plan is updated at one hierarchy level (say, product family), it's automatically updated at all the other product hierarchy levels.

- **Product lifecycle**
  Different lifecycle phases of a product impact its demand in the market. The prod-uct lifecycle phases are introduction, growth, maturity, and decline, as shown in Figure 3.1. The impact of the demand in each phase must be considered when pre-dicting the demand.

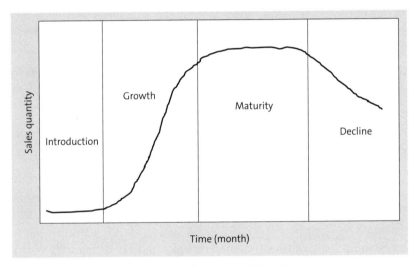

Figure 3.1 Product Lifecycle Phases for Demand Planning

For products in the introduction phase, history is not a good indicator, which may require the demand planner to opt for a qualitative forecast or to forecast through like modeling, in which the historical data of a similar product is used for statistically forecasting the new product. For the growth, maturity, and decline phases, a statisti-cal forecast model with the right consideration of base, trend, and seasonality is required. SAP Integrated Business Planning for sales and operations includes double and triple exponential algorithms, which can be used to model products for different lifecycle phases. However, detailed functionalities of lifecycle planning, as well as advanced models with automatic selection of forecasting parameters, are part of SAP Integrated Business Planning for demand.

A demand forecast can be generated through different methods as applicable for an organization. We'll discuss the details of the forecasting approach next.

3.1.1   Demand Forecasting Approach

The demand forecasting approach is used to adopt a methodology and follow the required steps to generate the demand plan. Different organizations adopt different approaches for forecasting customer demand. These approaches can be categorized as quantitative or qualitative at the macro level. Qualitative approaches are judgment-based, whereas quantitative approaches are based on statistical modeling of data to generate a baseline demand forecast. SAP Integrated Business Planning for sales and operations can be used for both approaches, though it is most widely used for quantitative demand forecasts.

Qualitative and quantitative demand forecasting approaches can be described as follows:

- **Qualitative demand forecast**
  A qualitative demand forecast uses a judgment-based approach in which demand is projected through manual expertise or by conducting a survey. This method is appropriate for new products for which past sales data is not available or for products for which sales history isn't a good representation of future demand.

  Qualitative demand forecasting can be performed through the following methods:

  - A *sales estimate* is a traditional method in which individual sales representatives provide the demand forecast for the products and customers for which they are responsible. This is based on information received from the customer and the sales rep's information about the market. Demand for all the sales rep's forecasts put together provides the demand plan for the organization. SAP IBP can be used to collect these forecasts and run them by the sales team, and then the analysis, review, and update of the forecasts can be performed in SAP IBP to finalize the demand plan. In an environment in which the quantitative method is used for the demand forecast, the qualitative method can be added in the solution design for forecasting the new products or for the review and comparison of the statistical forecast with the sales force estimate.

- In a *market research method*, surveys are performed following the market research methodology to predict the demand for a product or service. This is usually used for a new or disruptive product or service. Although SAP IBP is not a tool you can use to perform the market research, the result of the research can be put together in SAP IBP to generate the baseline forecast.

- *Panel consensus* is performed for a group of experts to agree on the demand forecast of a product or product group. Another variety of panel consensus is called *expert opinion*, in which the opinion is marked as the demand forecast and is used for further analysis and review.

- In the *Delphi method* for a demand plan, the goal is for a consensus to be achieved through multiple rounds of information collection. A group of experts independently provide the forecast and the reasons for their numbers. The facilitator summarizes the values and the judgment basics and shares it with the group, asking members to refine their numbers based on the information. The process attempts to achieve consensus through two to four rounds of analysis and review. The principle is that a structured expert group can generate a good forecast by getting help from the information and knowledge of other experts. SAP Integrated Business Planning for sales and operations can be used to facilitate this process through devoted key figures; the experts can provide the information, the facilitator can review all the information together, can summarize it through analytics, and can share the summary and reasoning with the group through SAP Jam Collaboration.

- **Quantitative demand forecast**
  In a quantitative approach, data is fed into a statistical model to generate the baseline forecast for review and edit. The most important data for the input to the statistical model is past sales or shipment data, though for some advanced and causal models, expected future data also can be provided to the statistical model.

  There are multiple statistical models used for generating a demand forecast. A model is selected based on data availability, the pattern of past sales, and the nature of the organization.

  Based on the data usage, the models may be categorized as either intrinsic or extrinsic. Intrinsic models are time series models for which internal data is used for generating the demand forecast—for example, using the past sales data as the input to generate the future sales through a time series model. For an extrinsic model, external data is used in addition to the organization's internal data for generating the forecast—for example, a regression model for generating the forecast based on past market information and while considering future information in the statistical model. Details of statistical models for demand forecast are illustrated in Section 3.3.

It's typical for an organization with new product segments or an innovative product to adopt a qualitative approach, moving to a quantitative approach with maturity and once the available data set becomes bigger. Supply chain digital transformation and newer technologies like machine learning in demand planning are highly dependent on quantitative approaches.

3.1.2   Demand Planning Strategy

A planning strategy decides the approach of the organization to fulfill customer demand. There are mainly two varieties of planning strategy: make-to-stock (MTS) and make-to-order (MTO). In the MTS strategy, demand is predicted at the customer fulfillment location and the product is made available to the location in advance of the actual demand. This strategy is adopted for most consumer products with regular demand and limited or no customization. Products like milk, toilet paper, books, and numerous other products we buy either in a retail store or from e-commerce stores are planned with an MTS strategy. In the MTO strategy, a product is made for the unique requirements of a customer. Specialized products with irregular demand and a higher level of customization use the MTO strategy.

The most important reason to perform demand planning is to plan for lead time. Consider the following case: After getting an order from Walmart for tomato ketchup, the ketchup manufacturing company places an order for tomatoes and starts planning the machine schedules. However, the order for the next day or next week can't be met even after a month! The demand planning process factors in lead times to help make products available when they're needed.

A similar concern also applies to the MTO strategy. Some time lag is expected from order placement to product delivery for specialized products, but planning is important for this case, too; starting from scratch isn't a feasible option. For example, consider a specialized construction machine from Caterpillar: Although the final machine will be made based on customer requirements, it's vital to plan the components, labor, and machines in advance to deliver the product in a reasonable time. Hence, even for the MTO strategy, it's essential to perform demand planning to plan for the input materials, labor, and machine time.

Variations of the MTO strategy can be used for different industry and products segments. Typical examples include assemble-to-order (ATO) and engineer-to-order

(ETO). A laptop assembled with a processor and memory size based on a consumer's requirements represents an example of ATO, whereas an industrial robot used to perform automatic packing in a manufacturing plant using the same input and output is an example of ETO. As suggested earlier, demand planning is vital for these products segments to make the final products in the expected time after confirmation of customer demand requirements. The move from MTS to MTO in the process happens at a *decoupling point*. For example, for a laptop manufacturer, processors, storage disks, and outer bodies can be planned via an MTS strategy, but the assembly of the laptop is performed via an MTO strategy after receiving a customer's order.

3.1.3 Demand Planning Process

Most companies practice a quantitative approach to generate and finalize a demand plan. For new products, a quantitative application can be used by referencing an existing similar product. If a qualitative forecast provides extra value, then this can also be integrated with the quantitative method for result review, comparison, analysis, and adjustments. SAP Integrated Business Planning for sales and operations can support this end-to-end demand planning and forecasting process.

The demand planning process commonly used in a quantitative approach is represented by Figure 3.2. The process starts with the identification of the relevant historical data, usage of the information to generate the statistical forecast, and then reviewing and updating the baseline forecast to finalize the unconstrained forecast. These steps are described in detail later in this chapter.

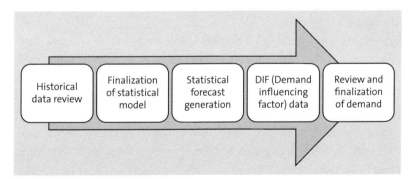

Figure 3.2 Demand Planning Process Steps

SAP Integrated Business Planning for sales and operations provides basic functionalities of demand planning, as illustrated in Figure 3.2. In SAP Integrated Business

Planning for sales and operations, historical data can be used to analyze, review, edit, and cleanse manually before usage for generating the base statistical forecast. The generated forecast is further reviewed, analyzed, and enriched with management knowledge and data analytics to improve the demand plan accuracy in SAP IBP.

Although the process is supported in SAP Integrated Business Planning for sales and operations, it's important to understand that the advanced functionalities of demand planning are part of SAP Integrated Business Planning for demand. For a business user and SAP IBP system adopter, it's essential to understand the demand planning–relevant functionalities differences between SAP Integrated Business Planning for demand and SAP Integrated Business Planning for sales and operations, as highlighted in Table 3.1. Although the primary end-to-end demand planning and forecasting can be performed in SAP Integrated Business Planning for sales and operations, a sophisticated, advanced use of demand planning requires SAP Integrated Business Planning for demand. The comparison is further discussed for individual functionality areas in Table 3.1.

The following are the recommended steps for the quantitative demand forecasting process:

1. **Preprocessing for automated data review and correction**
   Preprocessing algorithms are used to analyze and correct (either automatically or via user action) historical data before it's used in the forecast model. SAP Integrated Business Planning for demand has multiple algorithms to support automated review and data correction; in SAP Integrated Business Planning for sales and operations, this process needs to be done manually.

2. **Statistical models**
   SAP Integrated Business Planning for demand has a wide variety of demand planning and demand sensing algorithms. Demand sensing functionality isn't available in SAP Integrated Business Planning for sales and operations and only limited statistical models are available. However, SAP Integrated Business Planning for sales and operations still has single, double, and triple exponential algorithms, which can plan the demand for the base, trend, and seasonality factors. Details of the available models in SAP Integrated Business Planning for sales and operations are discussed in Section 3.3.

3. **Postprocessing for forecast errors**
   Postprocessing algorithms automatically calculate forecast errors and can use this information for improving forecasts through an ex post forecast approach. In such an ex post forecast approach, history data is divided into two parts: one

for generating a statistical forecast and reviewing errors, and the other for final-izing the best forecasting model. SAP Integrated Business Planning for demand has built-in metrics for forecast errors; SAP Integrated Business Planning for sales and operations has only root-mean-square error (RMSE) for a built-in met-ric. However, other forecast error metrics can be configured by users in SAP Inte-grated Business Planning for sales and operations by following the calculation approach and making the required data available through key figures.

4. **Promotion planning**

   Automated promotion planning functionalities are only available in SAP Inte-grated Business Planning for demand. Manual reviews, edits, and additions for the promotion's impact can be achieved in SAP Integrated Business Planning for sales and operations with user configuration. Do so by creating a promotion key figure and using the logic to update the sales or unconstrained forecast.

5. **Product lifecycle planning**

   Product lifecycle planning is only available in SAP Integrated Business Planning for demand, not in SAP Integrated Business Planning for sales and operations.

Functionality	SAP Integrated Business Planning for Demand	SAP Integrated Business Planning for Sales and Operations
Preprocessing for automated data review and correction	Available algorithms: ■ Outlier detection ■ Substitute missing values ■ Promotion elimination	Not available
Statistical model	Wide range of simple to highly sophisticated models: ■ Simple average ■ Simple moving average ■ Weighted average ■ Weighted moving average ■ Single exponential smoothing ■ Double exponential smoothing ■ Triple exponential smoothing	Basic algorithms capable of forecasting using base, trend, and seasonality: ■ Simple average ■ Simple moving average ■ Single exponential smoothing ■ Double exponential smoothing ■ Triple exponential smoothing

Table 3.1 Demand Planning Functionalities Comparison

Functionality	SAP Integrated Business Planning for Demand	SAP Integrated Business Planning for Sales and Operations
	■ Automated exponential smoothing ■ Croston method ■ Multiple linear regression ■ ARIMA model ■ Demand sensing algorithm	
Postprocessing for forecast errors	Automated generation of several varieties of forecast errors: ■ Mean percentage error (MPE) ■ Mean absolute percentage error (MAPE) ■ Weighted mean absolute percentage error (WMAPE) ■ Root-mean-square error (RMSE) ■ Standard error (SE) ■ Mean absolute deviation (MAD) ■ Total error (TE) ■ Mean absolute scaled error (MASE)	Limited set of automated forecast error: ■ Root-mean-square error (RMSE)
Promotion planning	Available	Not available
Product lifecycle planning for demand	Available	Not available

Table 3.1 Demand Planning Functionalities Comparison (Cont.)

3.2   Forecasting Input with Historical Data

Most mature organizations use a quantitative forecasting approach for most finished materials to predict customer demand. SAP Integrated Business Planning for sales and operations supports a time series statistical model in which historical data is used to generate the statistical forecast.

Sales history and shipment history are commonly used historical data elements for generating the customer demand forecast. Historical data is stored at the lowest level (product-location-customer) in SAP IBP, allowing aggregation at the required level for generating the demand forecast.

You can review, correct, and finalize historical data in SAP IBP before it's used in the statistical model. The reason for the review and edit can be to remove causal variations, which either positively or negatively impact the sales of a product due to an internal or external event. Causal variations can include past promotions, or natural disasters, such as a hurricane that impacted the sales of products in a particular region. These causal variations can skew the demand forecast and hence should be removed from the historical data before using the same in the forecast model. Deviations due to a planned event—for example, a future promotion—can be added to the statistical forecast.

Figure 3.3 shows an example of the historical data in which the deviation occurred due to an event. This is an example of a unique promotion that enhanced the sales of the product in a particular region. The uplift in the sales history can be removed to use an average value before using the data to generate the statistical forecast.

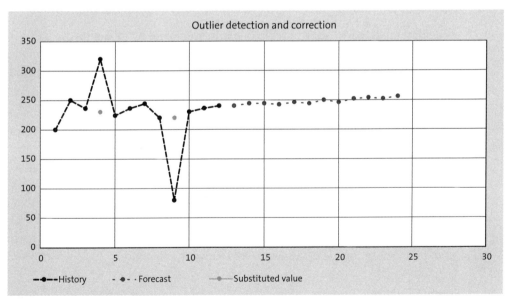

Figure 3.3 Past Deviation Corrected Manually in SAP IBP

Note that in SAP Integrated Business Planning for sales and operations, identification of the deviation and correction of the data can be performed through a manual process; SAP Integrated Business Planning for demand, however, has functionalities to identify and correct the historical data automatically.

For an organization that makes heavy use of promotion data, you may want to consider using two different sets of data elements to generate the forecast. This approach is common in the consumer products industry, in which promotions are planned only in the short to medium term, not the long term. The historical data sets both with and without promotions are used to generate the demand forecast. Statistical forecast output with removed promotion can be used as the baseline forecast for the short to medium term, whereas the historical data with the promotion is used as the baseline forecast for the medium to long term. Promotions are added in the baseline demand for the medium to long term, and because the promotion values are part of the historical data for the long term, the baseline value is robust if the past promotions are a good indicator of the future promotions.

We recommend finalizing your historical data collection, editing, and cleaning strategy for using the statistical model during SAP IBP demand planning design.

3.3   Forecast Generation through Statistical Modeling

Statistical models are used to predict the future demand by modeling the past data. In SAP Integrated Business Planning for sales and operations, five statistical models are available to use, from which one or more can be selected for demand forecasting, based on the properties of the historical data and the organization's business nature.

In the following sections, we'll walk through the statistical models that can take the historical data as the input and then, based on the data properties, generate a forecast value.

3.3.1   Statistical Models

As summarized in Table 3.1, there are five models available in SAP Integrated Business Planning for sales and operations to generate a demand forecast. Model properties and their application are discussed in the following subsections.

Simple Average

Mature products with stable demand can be forecasted using the simple average method. The simple average method is a constant forecast model generating the same values for all future horizons.

Figure 3.4 illustrates the formula to calculate the simple average forecast in SAP IBP along with an example of output in which the average value of the last 12 months of sales is calculated as the demand forecast for the future periods.

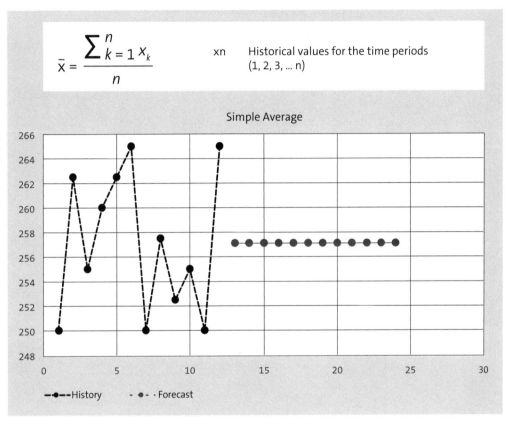

Figure 3.4 Simple Average Forecast Calculation and Output

Simple Moving Average

The simple moving average is used for mature products with stable demand for which the average of last few periods (typically three to five) is used to generate the demand forecast for the future. The simple moving average method is also a constant algorithm the generates the same value for all the future periods. In every period, the forecast value is updated based on the update of the last actuals. Figure 3.5 illustrates the formula to calculate the moving average forecast and an example of the output. In this example, an ex post forecast is represented to illustrate that with passage of time the moving average forecast value changes with updates of the actuals, though the forecast is always a constant value for the future as calculated based on the past values and the number of periods selected for the moving average forecast calculation.

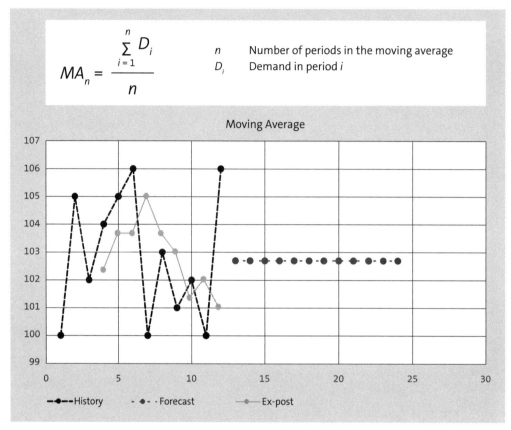

Figure 3.5 Moving Average Forecast Calculation and Output

Single Exponential Smoothing

A single exponential forecast is used for mature products with stable demand with no trend and seasonality variation. It takes care of the base data and exponentially smooths it with the selected factor (alpha, α) to generate the demand forecast for future periods. The value of α can range between 0 and 1. In this method, the weight attached to the past data decreases exponentially as we go back in time—hence the name *exponential smoothing*. A larger value of α (close to 1) provides more weight to the recent observations. Figure 3.6 shows the calculation formula and an output example of single exponential forecasting algorithm.

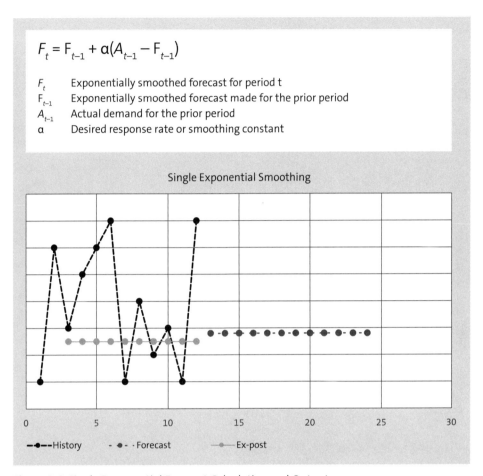

$$F_t = F_{t-1} + \alpha\left(A_{t-1} - F_{t-1}\right)$$

F_t Exponentially smoothed forecast for period t
F_{t-1} Exponentially smoothed forecast made for the prior period
A_{t-1} Actual demand for the prior period
α Desired response rate or smoothing constant

Figure 3.6 Single Exponential Forecast Calculation and Output

Double Exponential Smoothing

A double exponential forecasting model is used if the past data has trend. The name *double exponential* comes from smoothing of both base and trend values and adding them to generate the forecast. Double exponential smoothing is a variable method and generates different forecasted values for different periods in the future.

Figure 3.7 represents the calculation formula and an output example of a double exponential forecast. Smoothing factor α is used to smooth the base value and another smoothing factor, beta (β), is used to smooth the trend. Values of both α and β lie in the range of 0 to 1, with more weight given to recent values for a higher smoothing factor. Generally, values of α and β are between 0.1 and 0.4.

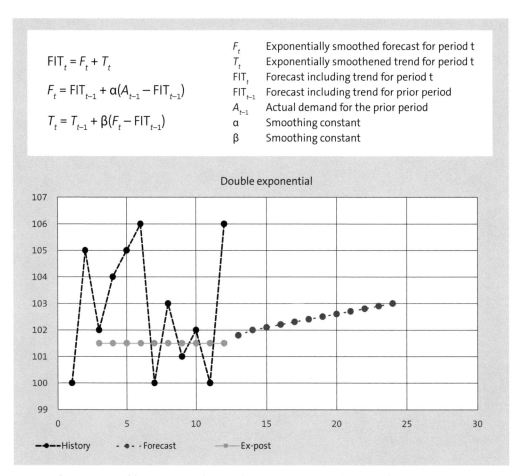

$$\text{FIT}_t = F_t + T_t$$

$$F_t = \text{FIT}_{t-1} + \alpha(A_{t-1} - \text{FIT}_{t-1})$$

$$T_t = T_{t-1} + \beta(F_t - \text{FIT}_{t-1})$$

F_t	Exponentially smoothed forecast for period t
T_t	Exponentially smoothened trend for period t
FIT_t	Forecast including trend for period t
FIT_{t-1}	Forecast including trend for prior period
A_{t-1}	Actual demand for the prior period
α	Smoothing constant
β	Smoothing constant

Figure 3.7 Double Exponential Smoothing Forecast Calculation and Output

Triple Exponential Smoothing

Triple exponential smoothing takes care of trend and seasonality in addition to the base through three different smoothing factors—hence the name *triple exponential smoothing forecast*. At least two full seasonal cycles of history data must be used for generating forecasts with a triple exponential method.

In addition to values used in the double exponential forecast, triple exponential method requires three more elements, as follows:

■ **Seasonality smoothing constant (Υ)**

The gamma coefficient is used as a multiplier to smooth seasonality value; its value lies between 0 and 1, with a normally used value in the range of 0.1 to 0.5. A relatively larger value leads to faster reaction of seasonal indices to changes in data.

■ **Period in season**

The period in season represents the length of the cycle in a season. For example, for a check of yearly seasonality, if the forecasting is done in the weekly bucket, then the period in season will be 52.

■ **Seasonality type**

Seasonality type for a triple exponential smoothing can be additive or multiplicative. In additive seasonality, the trend is considered independent of the seasonality and the seasonality value is added to the trend value; in multiplicative seasonality, the trend is considered to have a multiplicative impact on the seasonality.

3.3.2   Configuring and Executing Forecasting Models

For SAP Integrated Business Planning for sales and operations, the Manage Forecast Models and Assign Forecast Models SAP Fiori apps in the **Demand Planner** group are used for demand planning model configuration.

The Manage Forecast Models app is used for creating and managing the statistical algorithms for demand forecasting. Figure 3.8 shows an example of this app for creating a forecasting algorithm. The name of the profile and the time settings are established under the **General** tab. **Periodicity** represents the time periods used for reading the historical data and generating the forecast. The most commonly used periodicities are week and month for demand forecasting.

Historical Periods in Figure 3.8 represents the number of time periods for which past data is used for generating the forecast: if the periodicity is set to **Week**, then a value of 156 for the past period means that three years of past data is used to generate the demand forecast. The number of **Forecast Periods** indicates the time period for which the forecast is generated: a value of 156 represents that the forecast is calculated for 156 weeks in the future (i.e., three years in the future).

The offset and frozen options here provide additional functionalities for model enhancements and new products. **Offset for Historical Periods** allows the division of past data to generate the forecast for actuals comparison. For example, for a weekly periodicity, a value of 52 for past offset moves the current horizon to 52 weeks in the past, and thus it will generate the forecast for the last 52 weeks, too. This will let you compare actual values with the forecasted values to fine-tune the model.

Offset for Forecast Periods can be used for planning new products. For example, if a new product is planned to be launched after 24 weeks, a value of 24 can be provided as the offset for the future; in this way, SAP Integrated Business Planning for sales and operations will still calculate the forecast of the product, but its values will be saved only after 24 weeks. The value in **Frozen Forecast Periods** impacts the value generation of the forecast in SAP IBP: the system still calculates the forecast value for this time period, but it isn't saved. This can be used for special scenarios such as new products, analytics, or simulation.

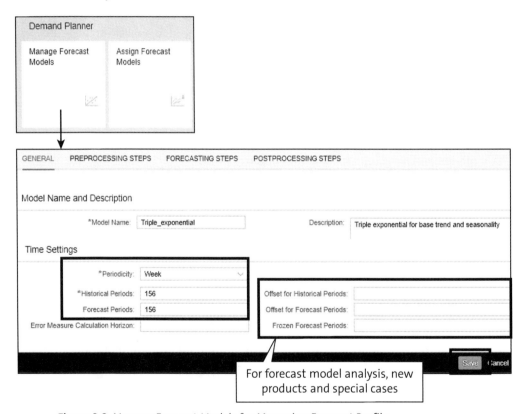

Figure 3.8 Manage Forecast Models for Managing Forecast Profile

The **Forecasting Steps** area is used to detail configuration elements of the forecast profile. A forecasting model is selected from available options. Then, based on the selected model, required values are provided. Through this configuration step, input and output key figures for the forecasting model are provided. A forecasting algorithm can be selected by pressing the **+** button, as shown in Figure 3.9. Based on the algorithm selected, fields will appear on this screen for the input. In the example in Figure 3.9, coefficient factors and seasonality values are provided for a triple exponential smoothing forecast algorithm.

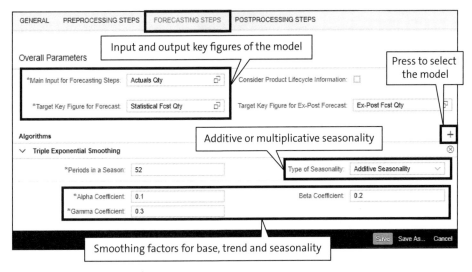

Figure 3.9 Algorithm Configuration

An SAP IBP model can use either one model for an entire data set or different models for different master data groups. Assignment of a forecast model to master data is performed through the Assign Forecast Models app.

Assignment of a forecast model can be performed through selection of master data attributes. Normally used values are based on customer groups, product groups, or locations. Figure 3.10 shows an example of forecast model assignment to a master data group. The **Filters** button shown here provides the master data attribute options for selection. If you click the **Edit Assignment** button, all the available forecasting models appear for the selection, from which one model can be selected with an option to provide the reason code and a comment for the selection.

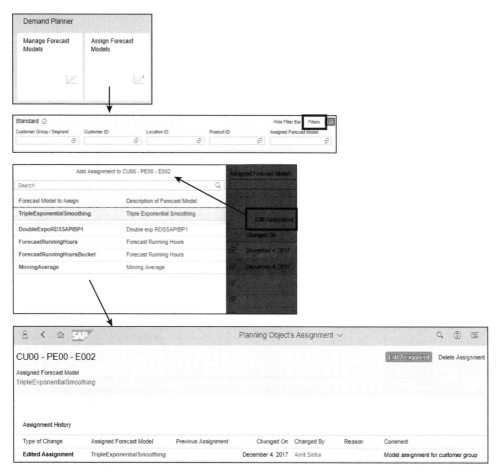

Figure 3.10 Forecast Model Assignment

Statistical forecasting algorithms as discussed in this chapter can be executed in SAP Integrated Business Planning for demand through Excel planning views or by executing a background job. These can be executed manually on demand, scheduled as one-time job executions, or modeled to be executed periodically as batch jobs.

Like other application jobs in SAP IBP, the statistical forecast operator job is managed through the Application Jobs app in the **General Planners** group. Figure 3.11 shows an example of statistical forecast job creation. Click **New** to create a new job, and select **Statistical Forecasting Operator** from the **Job Template** dropdown. Different scheduling options along with forecast parameter selections are available as per requirements to execute the forecast operator.

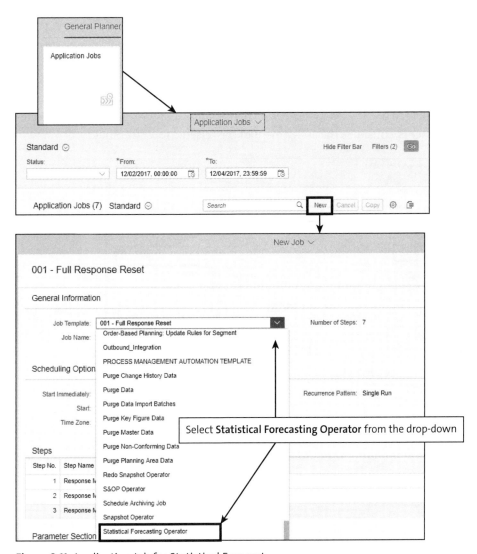

Figure 3.11 Application Job for Statistical Forecast

Figure 3.12 shows the scheduling and parameter selection options for the forecasting job. **Scheduling Options** lets you execute the forecast job as a periodic job or on a one-time schedule. A periodic schedule is used as part of the S&OP cycle, whereas a single execution can be performed for exceptions. Versions allow you to run the forecast for the base version data or for a simulation version, and filter criteria are used if the job execution needs to happen for a selected group of master data objects.

The aggregation level for the forecast execution is selected on this screen as well. With the advanced computation capabilities of SAP IBP, it's possible to perform the forecast at the lowest level, though a better forecast value can be generated at a different aggregation level, such as at a product group or customer group level. The time profile level and planning levels are also selected for this template. Either a forecasting model can be selected for execution of the forecast or the selection of field **Model Assignments**, considers the assignment of the selected forecast model.

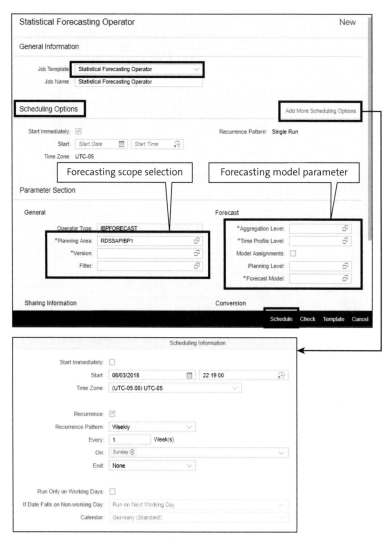

Figure 3.12 Forecasting Schedule and Parameter Selection

In addition to executing the model through an application job, a statistical forecast model can be executed through an Excel planning view. Figure 3.13 shows the execution of a statistical forecast through an Excel planning view. Attributes and filters (if any) for the statistical forecast are provided in the pop-up screen as shown in Figure 3.13. Forecast model selection or selection of the model based on the master data assignment happens here. A confirmation message appears after execution of the job. The status of the forecasting job can be viewed through the same Excel planning view.

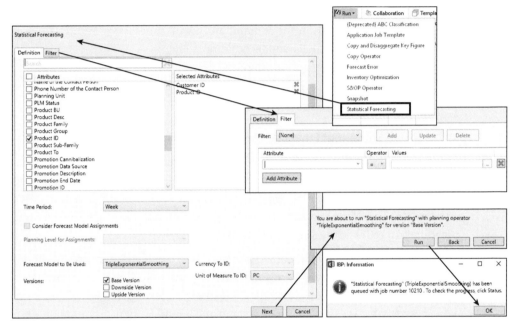

Figure 3.13 Planning View Forecast Execution

Forecast error calculation and demand review analytics can be used to select the right statistical model and to enhance forecast accuracy. There are multiple KPIs based on forecast errors, which are discussed in detail in Chapter 12 (Section 12.1.1). RMSE calculation is provided in the standard SAP Integrated Business Planning for sales and operations license; other forecast error calculations, if required, can be implemented through user configuration.

3.4 Collaborative Financial Modeling of Demand Forecast

Financial alignment and collaboration are the essential elements of a mature S&OP process. SAP Integrated Business Planning for sales and operations fills the gap of previous SAP planning solutions and provides an edge over competing S&OP applications by integrating financial numbers in its applications. Financial modeling related to the S&OP cycle is performed in SAP Integrated Business Planning for sales and operations and can be considered the demand review, operating review, and executive review cycles of the S&OP process. However, it's also important to understand that though SAP Integrated Business Planning for sales and operations provides the financial integration for demand and S&OP processes, SAP IBP is not an application for detailed financial model building.

The next two subsections will explain the use of income statements and financial ratios in SAP Integrated Business Planning for sales and operations.

3.4.1 Income Statement Financial Model in SAP IBP

The inherent consistency of the SAP IBP solution provides the ability to use the cost or price data at the lowest level (e.g., SKU level) and then generate the financial models at different levels (product category, business unit, etc.) as required to make S&OP decisions. The mentioned consistency is derived through the aggregation and disaggregation properties of the SAP IBP model (Section 3.1).

Table 3.2 is an example of an income statement that can be used for the S&OP process. It represents a summary of revenue with expenses, leading to gross profit and operating income. This example is at the organization level; separate income statements based on business units can be created and analyzed for decisions at different levels. SAP IBP can be used to model this as a planning view for use in operating and executive review.

Income statement analytics	Year		
	2019	2018	2017
Revenue	210,000	198,000	196,000
Cost of goods sold (COGS)	44,100	39,600	39,200
Gross profit	**165,900**	**158,400**	**156,800**

Table 3.2 Income Statement Example for S&OP Decisions

Income statement analytics	Year		
	2019	2018	2017
Research and development (R&D) expenses	10,500	10,000	9,500
Sales, general, and administrative (SG&A) expenses	70,200	69,600	69,100
Total operating expense	80,700	79,600	78,600
Operating income	85,200	78,800	78,200

Table 3.2 Income Statement Example for S&OP Decisions (Cont.)

Financial analytics for reviewing the S&OP plan can be modeled easily in SAP IBP. A business spread across geographic areas and using different currencies can be modeled and analyzed by the inherent capability of currency conversion in SAP Integrated Business Planning for sales and operations. Cost and price data can be provided at the SKU level in local currency, and the projected demand plan quantity can be multiplied by the cost and price data in SAP IBP to generate the past revenue and the projected revenue. Via a drop-down button, all values can be represented in one currency—say, USD—which allows for correct addition, subtraction, and multiplication of the numbers for an apples-to-apples comparison and mapping. The numbers can be aggregated by selecting the relevant planning levels to generate the past and projected finance plan.

This flexibility and ease of use allows planning goals to work on one version of truth, removes the silo approach, and facilitates decision making. Figure 3.14 shows a planning view in SAP IBP, with the integrated financial model used in the demand review cycle. As presented in the planning view, a common currency of USD is used for this view, along with pounds (LB) as the common unit of measure (weight). This planning view is used for the review of the annual operating plan (AOP) in SAP IBP during the demand review cycles.

Finance data can also be used in the collaborative planning view to have the detailed information for the plan review. Figure 3.15 shows a planning view for the demand review cycle in which marketing and demand planner quantities, along with price, revenue, and profit data have been represented. This combined view multiplies the efficiency of the S&OP process and eliminates work duplication for the finance, marketing, and planning team to refer to and integrate the financial numbers with the quantities in the plan.

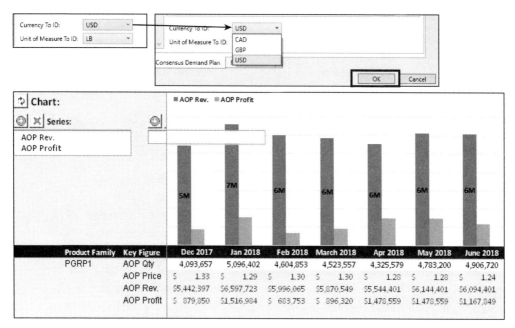

Figure 3.14 Planning View with Integrated Financial Information

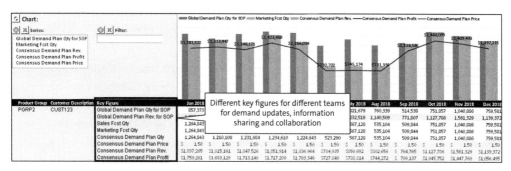

Figure 3.15 Collaborative Planning Views with Finance Data

3.4.2   Financial Ratios and Analytics in SAP IBP

Further higher-level financial modeling can be performed in SAP IBP by using financial ratios.

The following margins at the product-location level can be used by calculating the average values in a high-level calculation for a financial year:

- COGS margin: *COGS ÷ Revenue*
- R&D margin: *R&D expense ÷ Revenue*
- SG&A margin: *SG&A expense ÷ Revenue*

These margin values can be used at the detail level in SAP IBP to calculate the gross profit and operating income for future years based on the projected demand.

Figure 3.16 shows a planning view in IBP with information at the product group level. In the planning views of financial ratios and income projection, yearly time buckets are used for actual and planned numbers. Average price for past years can be calculated for the actual numbers for sales quantity and sales revenue. Then, a planned price for future years can be used in combination with the projected sales quantity to generate the projected sales revenue. On the same principle, COGS can be used and projected. The logic can be based on calculating the financial ratios for the past year, planning the ratios for the future, and then projecting relevant financial numbers for the future based on the ratios for usage in demand planning and the S&OP cycle.

Product Group	Key Figure	2016	2017	2018	2019	2020
PGRP2	Actual Sales Quantity	857,373	901,220			
	Actual Sales Revenue	1,140,306	1,189,610			
	COGS	319,286	321,195			
	COGS margin	0.28	0.27			
	Average Price	1.33	1.32			
	Projected Average Price			1.32	1.30	1.30
	Projected Sales Quantity			921,240	927,340	936,100
	Projected Sales Revenue			1,216,037	1,205,542	1,216,930
	Projected COGS margin			0.26	0.26	0.25
	Projected COGS			316,170	313,441	304,233
	Actual Gross Profit	821,020	868,416			
	Projected Gross Profit			899,867	892,101	912,698
	Actual R&D expense	57,015	59,600			
	Actual R&D margin	0.05	0.05			
	Projected R&D Margin			0.05	0.05	0.05
	Projected R&D expense			60,802	60,277	60,847
	Actual SGA expense	387,704	392,650			
	Actual SGA margin	0.34	0.33			
	Projected SGA margin			0.33	0.33	0.33
	Projected SGA expense			401,292	397,829	401,587
	Projected Operating expense			462,094	458,106	462,433
	Projected Operating income			437,773	433,995	450,264

Figure 3.16 Planning View for Financial Ratios and Income Projection

Note that this analysis is directionally correct but does not contain accurate values due to the average percentage value used for the expenses of all the products of the firm. However, this information helps in making crucial demand planning and S&OP decisions in a collaborative environment with one version of truth for the organization.

This financial modeling functionality in SAP IBP serves as an excellent tool for work integration of the planning and finance teams. Finance guidance and AOPs created through the higher-level organization strategy can be compared and reviewed with the detailed demand and supply work being performed by sales, marketing, operations, and planning teams. A difference can be highlighted quickly through a custom alert or user-friendly analytics, then the teams can collaborate to achieve the goal of aligning the operating plan with the strategic plan.

3.5   Review, Collaboration, and Finalization of the Demand Plan

The demand planning process in the demand review cycle starts with the statistical forecast as the output of the statistical model, which is reviewed and cleaned to produce the baseline forecast. This then is updated with sales, marketing, and account intelligence to develop the *unconstrained forecast*, which is the representation of the market demand without massaging or updating to reflect supply capacity.

In a traditional or old-world planning system, collaboration is an issue that has handicapped team productivity and accuracy. SAP IBP is equipped with easy-to-use Excel planning views and a user-friendly collaboration platform to remove this issue. The SAP Jam Collaboration platform in SAP IBP is also connected with the system database, allowing for dynamic and efficient collaboration.

Different teams can be assigned individual key figures with edit access; other relevant key figures can be provided with the view access to the information. Based on the nature of the work, a particular team reviews the number at the required level. For example, a marketing manager might review the demand plan numbers at the product group and customer region levels, whereas a category manager might review the same numbers at the product category and customer segment levels. Figure 3.17 shows an example of planning views used for the demand review collaboration. A value edited at any level is automatically aggregated or disaggregated based on the inherent consistency of the SAP IBP model.

Figure 3.18 shows an example of a case in which a sales manager updates the forecast for a customer and shares the reason for the update through the collaboration tool. This sharing is updated in real time as a social media message delivered to the relevant group. This activity can be supported further through added collaboration applications for decision-making and task management. Details of these collaboration applications will be provided in Chapter 7.

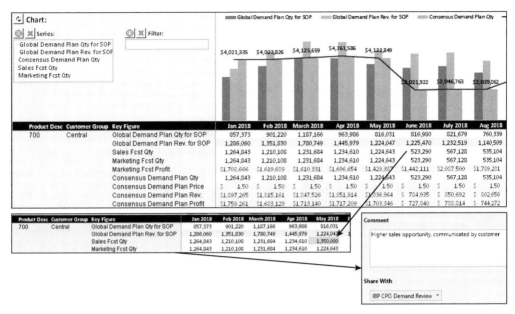

Figure 3.17 Planning Collaboration through Planning Views and Updates

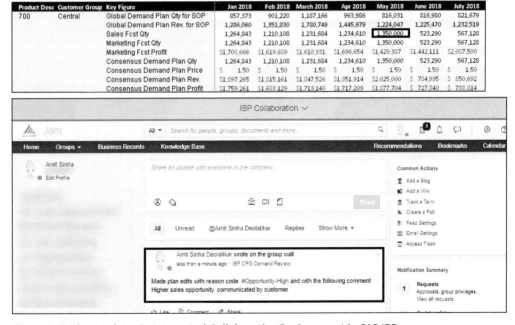

Figure 3.18 Plan Updates in Integrated Collaborative Environment in SAP IBP

There are multiple KPIs based on forecast error that are used to control and enhance the demand forecasting output quality. Details of the demand planning analytics are covered in Chapter 12.

3.6   Summary

Demand planning and forecasting is the first step of supply chain planning and S&OP. The efficiency of the supply chain processes and subsequent processes of production, purchase, inventory storage, and material transfer is highly dependent on the forecast accuracy. SAP Integrated Business Planning for sales and operations has the capability to map and optimize the demand planning processes associated with S&OP. This capability is supported through statistical forecast modeling, demand finalization, and collaboration.

Now, you're ready to navigate into the supply planning area of S&OP in the next chapter.

Chapter 4
Unconstrained Supply Planning

In this chapter, we'll discuss unconstrained supply planning, which will propagate the consensus demand plan throughout the supply network, resulting in a master production plan, distribution plan, and rough-cut capacity insights.

In this chapter, we'll build on the consensus demand plan generated by the demand planning process and cover the inputs to the supply review step in the S&OP cycle. The main objective of this chapter is to provide the full calculation scheme that forms the basis of the S&OP heuristic. We'll try to provide this insight by weaving in practical implications for the choices to be made. After the definition and objectives, the steps in building the unconstrained requirement plan will be detailed. Once we have the basic scenario explained, the different parameters influencing the results of the heuristic will be covered, together with their business use. The chapter will close with an overview of rough-cut capacity planning in the context of the unconstrained S&OP heuristic. This will lay the foundation to move toward constrained planning algorithms in the next chapter.

4.1 Unconstrained Planning at a Glance

The supply planning process starts from the consensus demand plan validated by the product and demand review process steps. The objective of the supply planning process is to agree on a feasible supply plan that meets as much demand as possible while taking supply constraints and profitability into account.

Determination of the feasibility of the plan is typically orchestrated by the supply chain function, for which the key stakeholders are manufacturing, procurement, logistics, and distribution. In organizations in which products are heavily customized for specific orders, the engineering unit may be an important stakeholder as well. Each function faces the same question: Can the demand be supported by the existing capacity?

In the first chapter, the focus of the S&OP process was been established as tactical planning, in which the period from three to 18 months out is being evaluated. We established, however, that there are links to the strategic planning process, giving an overview of how constraints behave in the longer term. This allows companies to perform analyses to determine if strategic changes to capacities are required. For example, extending the time horizon to multiple years makes questions like "Should we open a new production facility or distribution center?" relevant.

Key questions for each function are as follows:

- *Manufacturing:* Is there enough capacity to support the demand plan?
- *Purchasing:* Do the suppliers have enough capacity to support the manufacturing plan?
- *Logistics and distribution:* Can the current logistics network support the transportation volume, and is there enough space to hold the inventory?
- *Engineering:* Can the engineering department support the anticipated changes to the products in an engineered-to-order business?
- *Finance:* How does the current supply and fulfillment plan align with the organization's financial goals?

To answer these questions, the plan needs to be brought to a lower level of granularity compared to the demand review process. Whereas the demand review process focuses on an unconstrained demand plan at a sellable product or product family and customer or customer group level, the supply review process focuses on all types of products, manufacturing locations, vendors, and resources across the network. The supply review process determines how each product's customer demand is fulfilled, where and when the products are manufactured, the capacity required, the material requirements plan, and the distribution plan.

This determination is referred to as *demand propagation* because it traces the path for a given product from a customer to its ultimate supply source through the internal distribution network, up to exploding the bills of material for production processes, resulting in raw material requirements coming from suppliers. At each stage, inventory levels and key supply constraints are considered. This enables manufacturing, procurement and logistics, and distribution to see where there's an inability to supply the required amount of product. These functions then evaluate alternate means to meet demand.

For example, if a given manufacturing plant is unable to produce the required volume of product, it may be possible to outsource manufacturing to a third party, prebuild inventory in less busy periods, or move production to an alternate plant. Each of these scenarios has associated impacts on costs and margin, which should be considered when proposing the preferred supply plan. The final stage of the supply review is for the proposed plan to be agreed on by the organization's leadership.

Once a supply plan has been agreed upon, it's possible to confirm which demand can be satisfied, referred to as *supply propagation*, taking the potentially constrained volumes and pushing them back through the supply network. The relationship between demand and supply propagation is shown in Figure 4.1.

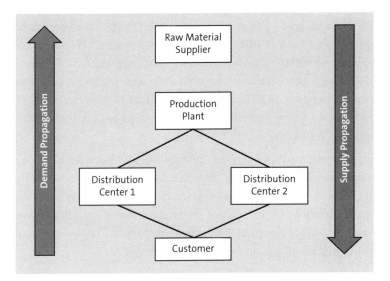

Figure 4.1 Demand and Supply Propagation

This process of demand propagation, evaluation, and confirmation of supply scenarios followed by supply propagation enables an organization to find the answers to the following questions:

- Where do inventory surpluses or shortages exist?
- Which supply capacities (production, handling) are over- or underutilized?
- Which demands will be met, and which will be dropped or delayed?
- What is the approximate revenue, cost, and margin associated with the agreed-upon plan or various versions of the plan?

4.2   The Sales and Operations Planning Heuristic

The SAP IBP solution delivers two time series-based algorithms to propagate the consensus demand plan through the network. In this chapter, we'll explain the operations of the S&OP unconstrained heuristic, called the *time series-based supply planning heuristic* since version 1708, delivered as part of SAP Integrated Business Planning for sales and operations. As the name suggests, this algorithm is an unconstrained or infinite supply planning engine, which doesn't automatically restrict the supply plan based on resource capacities or material constraints.

The heuristic is often referred to as a *decision support algorithm*, leaving the decision with the planner. The heuristic itself will not make decisions about which demands to meet and which not; instead, it will follow the rules defined in the structure of the supply chain network modeled in SAP IBP. It assumes that all resource capacities are infinite and that there are no material constraints. It's a good practice to configure an alert to help identify capacity bottlenecks or material shortages, making it easier for planners to take necessary actions. In Chapter 5, we'll introduce the S&OP optimizer, a decision-making algorithm using financial information to provide a constrained plan without manual intervention.

Both demand and supply propagation in an unconstrained S&OP heuristic are based on simple rules. In demand propagation, the consensus demand plan will be propagated throughout the supply network based on sourcing rules. In supply propagation, the propagated demands will be confirmed by receipts. Either the full demand will be confirmed automatically (unconstrained supply propagation) or by fair-share rules, propagating potential shortages up to the customer level.

For many organizations, the S&OP heuristic is the most appropriate starting point to perform supply network planning. It leverages a very transparent calculation scheme based on user-defined rules, providing the user with visibility of the demands, receipts, inventories, and capacity implications at every level of the supply network. Moreover, visibility into a completely unconstrained plan can be of utmost importance. For example, in supplier collaboration scenarios, planners provide a long-term unconstrained forecast of raw materials to the suppliers using the unconstrained heuristics.

Because the heuristic is a rule-based solver, we'll start by looking at the structure of a supply chain network and the sourcing rules. Once the supply network design is well understood, the demand propagation and supply propagation calculation scheme will be covered in detail.

4.3   Supply Network Design

The supply network is the core structure used by the S&OP heuristic. It depicts the key entities relevant for supply planning, such as customers, locations (distribution centers, production facilities, and suppliers), and BOMs. As noted in Chapter 2, the supply network is depicted via master data types. The key master data types that make up the supply network are as follows:

- Simple master data types
  - Product
  - Customer
  - Location
  - Resource
- Compound master data types
  - Customer product (optional)
  - Location product
  - Location resource
  - Location product resource
  - Sourcing rules (customer source, location source, production source)

In the remainder of this section, we'll dive into each of the supply network elements in groups, starting with the simple and compound master data types, followed by sourcing rules. We'll cover how supply network accuracy can be checked and validated and briefly discuss the impact of subnetworks on the supply network.

4.3.1   Products, Location, and Customers

The supply network in the SAP IBP solution is a very flexible concept: it can be extended easily and can be arbitrarily deep. It consists of master data elements and doesn't require any configuration changes to the system to extend, modify, or restrict it.

To build the supply network in real life, there are various considerations that play an important role. It's uncommon to consider all products the organization uses in the S&OP process. Although most finished products will be accounted for, components that go into the production processes can be reduced in scope. Often the focus of the S&OP process will be on the critical components and resources that will make a difference in the tactical planning processes. Although the selection of critical components depends on the industry and the organization, typically it includes those products subject to a capacity constraint or a significantly higher cost if not planned effectively. This is typically the case for more expensive components or subassemblies or components with a limited number of suppliers.

For example, in a high-tech company, processors used in the finished products can be considered critical, whereas the fixings used for assembly are plentiful in supply and don't need to be considered in the medium- to long-term supply planning processes.

For customers, similar considerations apply to the S&OP process. For some industries, it's of the utmost importance to model all the individual customers as part of the supply network, but other companies sell to individual end users who don't exhibit any structure in their demand patterns. Consequently, for some organizations, all customers can be considered in the S&OP process, but for most a customer grouping can be considered. The modeling of customers in groups also becomes one of the important considerations in other subprocesses of S&OP such as demand planning and inventory planning.

Locations in SAP IBP cover all the entities in the supply network that aren't customers and for which supply (inventory, production, lead times, and supply constraints) needs to be considered. Hence, both internal locations, such as manufacturing facilities and distribution centers, and external locations, such as suppliers, contract manufacturing, and ports, can be modeled as locations. The model can be extended as necessary to support the S&OP process. Usually, locations are differentiated by location type in SAP IBP. Typical key locations in a supply network include the following:

- Manufacturing locations, often with resources (production, handling), production processes, and raw material requirements
- Distribution centers, for storage and distribution of finished products
- Suppliers, for modeling key constraints and/or collaboration around likely requirements

The usage of the compound master data types for location products and customer products allows modeling attributes at the combined level. For example, for a location product, the subnetwork is a key attribute (which will be covered in Section 4.3.4). At a customer level—though the customer-product combination is optional— a sales planner name could be modeled as an attribute, or perhaps the market segment the customer sells this product in.

4.3.2   Sourcing Rules

The relationships among the various aspects of the supply network are defined by sourcing rules. At each location, sourcing rules answer the question, "Where does this product come from?" There are three types of sourcing rules in the standard heuristic, which we'll discuss in the following sections. The network is said to be *closed* if, for every product at every location, this question has an answer.

Customer Sourcing Rules

Sourcing rules start from the level at which the unconstrained consensus demand is defined: typically, a specific product at a specific customer or customer group. Customer sourcing rules define the customer demand fulfillment location for each product. The customer sourcing rule is captured in the source customer master data type.

There is a sourcing ratio (with the attribute CRATIO) which establishes the split between possible sourcing locations. The sourcing ratio for a specific product customer should add up to 100 percent to ensure consistency. This means single sourcing scenarios (i.e., those in which a customer sources all of a given product from only one source) should have a customer sourcing ratio of 1 (100 percent) from a single location, whereas multisource scenarios will require multiple ratios that sum to 1. Sourcing ratios can be reflected as a single value, set up in the master data type; this indicates a constant ratio over all periods. Alternatively, the sourcing ratio can be time-phased, allowing it to vary over time. In that case, the time series flag will be set in the master data type (with the attribute RATIOTS = 'X'). Based on the time series flag, the heuristic will not consider the constant sourcing ratio but will use the customer sourcing ratio key figure for its calculations.

Customer sourcing ratios have a lead time assigned, which marks the time it takes to transport products from a location to a customer. Because lead time provides the only opportunity to capture the time differential between availability of stock at a customer-facing location and receipt of stock at the customer, various factors should be considered when modeling customer lead time. Some examples of components of customer lead times are as follows:

- Time required to pick, pack, and load the product and make it customer-ready
- Time required to process product through customs
- Physical transportation time between fulfillment location and customer site

If, as is typical, customers in SAP IBP are modeled as groups of customers, average lead times should be used.

It's generally not a good practice to add buffers in customer lead times to hedge for uncertainty in customer transports. A better approach is to account for lead time uncertainty in the determination of safety stock targets.

The lead time is set up as a whole number and expressed in the planning bucket the heuristic will operate in; for example, if you're planning in weekly buckets, a value of 1 represents a one-week lead time. Lead time acts as an offset in the demand and supply propagation processes.

Location Sourcing Rules

The next level of sourcing rules determines how the demand is fulfilled at a location other than the customer. A first potential answer to this question could be modeled as a location sourcing rule, or transport rule, which maps this location product demand to be supplied by a different location. Location sourcing rules are used to represent the stock movement between different locations—for example, stock transfer from a manufacturing location to a distribution center.

Location sourcing rules also have a location sourcing ratio, which, just like customer sourcing ratios, can be constant or time-phased. To depict a constant location sourcing ratio, the location transport ratio in the master data type can be maintained (TRA-TIO). If the location sourcing ratio should vary over time, the time series flag will be set in the master data type (RATIOTS = 'X'), resulting in the use of the transport ratio key figure by the heuristic.

Lead times are also available in location sourcing rules to account for the transportation time between the sending and receiving locations. Because lead time provides the only opportunity to do so, you must capture the time offset between availability of stock at a source location and receipt of stock at the destination location. Various factors should be considered while modeling transportation lead times. Some examples of times that may add up to overall transportation lead times are as follows:

- Time required to pick, pack, and load the product at the source location
- Physical transportation time between source and destination locations
- Other time considerations for receiving the product at the destination location, such as time at customs

Aligned with customer sourcing lead times, the lead time is expressed in the planning bucket the heuristic will operate in.

Production Sourcing Rules

The last category of sourcing rules is production sourcing rules, which are applied in two distinct scenarios:

1. **Type P (for production)**
   Reflecting production and a bill of material

2. **Type U (for unspecified)**
   Depicting the end of the supply network

The various ways of depicting BOMs in the supply network are as follows:

- **Standard BOMs**

  At the manufacturing location at which products are produced using other components, production sourcing rules of type P will be applied (SOURCETYPE = 'P'). The production sourcing rules are defined using two simple master data types: production source header and production source item.

  The production sourcing header assigns a source ID to an output product at a specific location. Production sourcing headers, just like customers and locations, have a sourcing ratio: the production sourcing ratio. This can be either a constant and maintained in the production sourcing header master data (PRATIO), or time-phased, which will be modeled as the production ratio key figure. The latter option requires the production ratio time series flag to be set to X in the master data (PRATIOTS = 'X').

  To control the output quantities in the production process, production sourcing items have an output component coefficient. These are used to provide the number of products becoming available after performing the production operation. Just like sourcing ratios, they can either be constant over time and be modeled in the production source header (OUTPUTCOMPONENT) or vary over time, which requires the time series flag to be set (OUTPUTCOMPONENTTS = 'X'). When the time series flag is set, the system will use the output component coefficient key figure (OUTPUTCOMPONENT) to model the output of the production process. This functionality can be applied, for example, to model yields, which might be constant or improving over time.

  To assign components to a BOM, the production source item assigns components to the source ID, which is set up in the production source header. Production source items have a source ID item attribute, which acts as a counter to make the records unique.

The production source item contains the component coefficient, which specifies the number of input products required to produce the output product. Like sourcing ratios, the value of the component coefficient can be constant over time and be assigned to the source production item master data type (COMPONENTCOEFFICIENT). Setting the time series flag in the master data (COMPONENTCOEFFICIENTTS = 'X') will result in using the *quantity per* key figure (COMPONENTCOEFFICIENT).

- **Multilevel bills of material**
  It's possible in the S&OP heuristic to model multilevel BOMs using the rules that have been introduced. A multilevel BOM is modeled by assigning a component of the BOM, a production sourcing rule of type P. There is no documented limit to the levels in a BOM that can be established as such.

- **Unspecified rules**
  Unspecified rules (U-rules) are a specific subtype of production sourcing rules that depicts the end of the supply network. They are used to model product sources the planner doesn't plan. Unspecified rules only require a production source header, in which the source type is set to U (SOURCETYPE = 'U'). The production sourcing ratio should be maintained. When setting up unspecified rules, typically the production ratio is set to 1 in the master data type directly. Although a U-rule still requires specifying a source ID, there is only a production source header and no production source item required.

  Traditionally, U-rules are used to depict the incoming supply at the vendor. Since SAP IBP release 1705, however, it's possible to set the location type to V for *vendor*, which makes it clear that no incoming supply is expected at this location and it is the end of the supply network.

- **Coproduct planning**
  The production process may not necessarily output only one product at a time. Many times, a production process generates multiple output products. Such output products can be thought of as by-products in chemical industry manufacturing processes or coproducts in semiconductor manufacturing processes. In SAP IBP, you model such situations by assuming production for one key product accompanied by several secondary products or coproducts.

  Such coproduct situations can be modeled by setting the source type to C (SOURCETYPE = 'C'), which is tied to the production source of the main product's production process through the source ID. For example, consider a consumer company selling chicken meat. The main demand is for chicken breasts, and for every two chicken breasts produced, there are two chicken wings produced as a side-product. This gives the production sourcing rule laid out in Table 4.1, in which the output coefficient defines the number of products created because of the process.

Source ID	Product	Source Type	Output Coefficient
Chicken_Breast	Breasts	P	2
Chicken_Breast	Wings	C	2

Table 4.1 Example of Coproduction

4.3.3   Supply Network Accuracy and Check Mode

To compute supply plan accurately, the supply network needs to be consistent. A consistent network can be defined with the following two important characteristics:

1. For every product at each customer or location, the question of where the product comes from can be answered completely; that is, at a customer, the customer sourcing ratios for a product need to add up to 1 (100 percent). Similarly, at all other locations, the sum of the location sourcing ratio and the production sourcing ratio for a given product need to add up to 1 (100 percent).

2. The supply network shouldn't exhibit cyclic paths; that is, two locations within the network can't share a receiving and a sending relationship with respect to the same product.

To validate whether the network is consistent, the *check mode* algorithm can be used. This algorithm will simulate the supply planning runs and produce a log, without storing the results of the supply planning run in the output key figure. The log messages should be checked upon completion of the algorithm, and corrective action can be taken. If you are using time series for any of the ratios, then limiting the time period selection during the check network prevents checks for the entire horizon for the same product.

4.3.4   Subnetworks

Using subnetworks, it's possible to limit the run of the S&OP operators to only a limited set of data. Because supply operators are intended as network planning algorithms, they always plan a complete network, independent of what's selected in the planning view. Subnetworks allow you to reduce the scope of planning—for example, to a business unit or a region.

Subnetworks are assigned to the product location master data type, and from there they take effect throughout the supply planning activities. It's possible to run the heuristic for one, multiple, or all subnetworks. If multiple subnetworks are planned together, then the S&OP algorithms will consider them one integrated planning unit.

From a business perspective, the use of subnetworks allows for an array of advanced planning capabilities via which different business units can be planned independently and use the intersubnetwork planning capabilities to barter limited supply across the receiving business units.

For example, imagine a chemicals company in which there is a business unit producing raw chemicals that go into downstream derivative products. If the raw chemicals business unit is specified as a separate planning unit, it's possible to run the S&OP algorithms for this planning unit alone. The demand will come from the downstream business units. If the heuristic would run for all planning units, it would calculate the whole network and give the basic chemicals business unit an unconstrained picture of the total demand.

Using intersubnetwork planning capabilities thus allows for more control over how the potentially limited supply from the basic chemicals business can be distributed over the downstream business units. Adjustment key figures, which will be introduced in Section 4.5.6, can be applied to manage this distribution.

4.4   Propagating Demand

With the supply network established, the heuristic can be run to populate demand and supply plans. In general, demand propagation starts at the customer level and uses the sourcing rules framework to propagate the demand through the supply network. Another starting point for demand propagation can be independent demand for a particular product at a specific location. The use of independent demands as a starting point for demand propagation is recommended when the product is planned to satisfy different needs that aren't all modeled up to the customer level. For example, service part forecasts in automotive industries can be added as an independent demand stream because they're often planned in a dedicated service parts planning solution.

There are a lot of factors that influence the results of the heuristic. This section will start with a simple model, then add complexity step by step to build a deep understanding of the calculation scheme in the heuristic. There are a lot of parameters that can influence the results from the heuristic; those are covered in Section 4.7.

4.4.1   Sample Supply Network

To cover all the key figures that play a role in the S&OP heuristic, the sample network shown in Figure 4.2 will be used in this chapter.

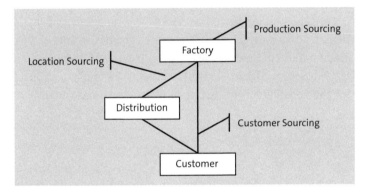

Figure 4.2 Sample Network

The minimal network to explain all the flows in the heuristic can be represented as the graphical model shown in Figure 4.2, consisting of nodes and arcs. The nodes are as follows:

- Customers represent the starting node in our example; the consensus demand from customers can be fulfilled from various locations of the network using the customer sourcing rules.
- Distribution centers act as pass-through locations in the network, fulfilling customer demand while ordering from the factory.
- Factories represent production facilities where an organization produces its main products. Factories fulfill customer and distribution center demand while producing and hence require raw materials.

The arcs connecting the nodes are the customer sourcing or location sourcing rules that represent the material flow between different nodes.

This network allows for covering all the calculations that occur in the heuristic. It's possible to extend the network in every dimension, and the same calculations will be used. For example, raw materials can be ordered from a supplier, which establishes a location sourcing or transportation rule from the factory to the supplier. The calculation schedule will be similar to the location sourcing happening at the distribution center.

4.4.2   Consensus Demand

Consensus demand represents the starting point for a heuristic-based planning process. The consensus demand is an outcome of the demand review process, which was discussed in Chapter 3. Consensus demand (CONSENSUSDEMAND) is a node-based key figure that represents a demand for a particular product from a given customer at a particular time. Consensus demand is defined at the planning level period, product, and customer levels, and it's a stored key figure. Figure 4.3 shows an example of a consensus demand of 100 for the considered product at the considered customer in the month of March.

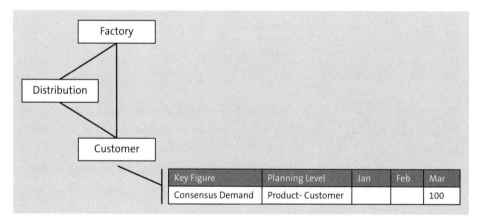

Figure 4.3 Consensus Demand

4.4.3   Customer Sourcing

The information that allows a heuristic to propagate demand further lies in the source customer table, which defines the customer sourcing. It's at this point that the heuristic identifies all connected locations for a customer, along with the corresponding lead times, sourcing ratios, and lot sizes. In the network shown in Figure 4.4, this ratio is split over the factory and the distribution center.

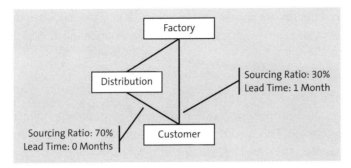

Figure 4.4 Customer Sourcing

The practical decision for how customer sourcing ratios are split is often defined by the demand fulfillment model. In many cases, there will be a single sourcing of customers to locations, based on their geographic proximity. It's important to keep in mind that planning should be for the best-case scenario, ensuring the most cost-optimal route is planned for. Emergencies should be accommodated by a response management solution, which might change the rules.

For example, if customers are supposed to order from the distribution center, this needs to be maintained as the primary customer transportation lane. Direct factory shipments can be considered only if the distribution center is out of inventory. Note that in cases in which customers are represented as a group, multisourcing scenarios are more likely. However, it might be possible to organize the groups of customers in such a way that a single sourcing could be maintained.

In the heuristic, the calculations are performed based on the established rules. The optimizer, on the other hand, will consider the transportation costs to fulfill the customer demand, which are likely higher for infrequent shipments from the factory compared to regular shipments from the distribution center. Hence, the optimizer will make the decision to ship from the factory only when required. To demonstrate the calculation model in the heuristic, we'll continue with the multisourcing scenario, which splits the demand between the distribution center and the factory.

The customer transports are made up of two arc-based key figures, as follows:

- **Outbound customer demand** (DEPENDENTCUSTOMERDEMAND)
  This represents a portion of demand for a product in a particular period from a specific customer to the supplying location. This demand quantity is based on the receipt date at the customer; therefore, no lead time offset is considered while computing this demand.

When defining the key figures, we always try to show how you can calculate the number the system provides yourself. For outbound customer demand, the calculation looks like this:

Outbound Customer Demand = Consensus Demand × Customer Sourcing Ratio

- **Dependent customer demand** (DEPENDENTCUSTOMERDEMANDDS)
  This key figure represents the supplying-location-side key figure corresponding to outbound customer demand. This quantity is exactly same as that of outbound customer demand, based on the ship date at a supplying location. Hence, lead time offset is accounted for in the calculation of this key figure. The calculation is as follows:

  Dependent Customer Demand = Outbound Customer Demand with Backward Lead Time Offset

This will result in key figure calculations shown in Figure 4.5 for the sample supply network.

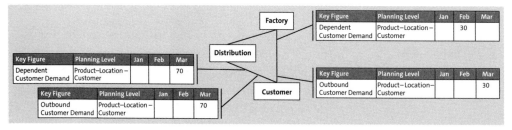

Figure 4.5 Dependent Customer Demand

In this example, the impact of the lead time can be observed between the customer and the factory, for which one month of lead time is applied. Between the customer and the distribution center, there is no lead time, so the demand appears in the same period.

4.4.4   Net Demand Calculation

The next step in the calculation chain zooms into the distribution center fulfilling customer demand. At the distribution center, the complete fulfillment model is calculated with the following key figures:

- **Dependent demand** (DEPENDENTDEMAND)

  A node-based key figure that adds up all the dependent demands at a location. Defined at period, product, and location levels, the dependent demand aggregates the dependent customer demand, dependent location demand, and dependent production demand (the latter two are explained in subsequent sections):

  Dependent Demand = Dependent Customer Demand + Dependent Location Demand + Dependent Production Demand

  In our example, the distribution center only gets demand from customers; however, a distribution center can fulfill other locations (dependent location demand) and possibly could manufacture products (imagine kitting at distribution center), resulting in dependent production demand.

- **Independent demand** (INDEPENDENTDEMAND)

  A node-based key figure representing demand available directly at the location-product combination. This key figure will be added to the dependent demand in the net demand calculation. It can be selected during the implementation to build a solution without a customer dimension, which would imply modeling all demands as independent.

- **Stock on hand** (INITIALINVENTORY)

  A node-based stored key figure that stores the initial inventory available to fulfill demand. This key figure is typically integrated with the operational system and would provide all usable inventory.

- **Inventory target** (INVENTORYTARGET)

  A node-based stored key figure that stores the inventory target considered for a specific product at a location. In a simple S&OP solution, this key figure can be maintained by users manually.

- **Net demand** (NETDEMAND)

  A node-based key-figure that defines the demand that needs to be satisfied for a product at a given location in each period. The net demand is a key calculation in the context of the S&OP heuristic. Net demands are one of the few key figures in the heuristic that go beyond a time period. The calculation for the initial time period (call it time period 1) is different from that for any other time period because there is no "previous" calculation to start from. Therefore, the definition of the initial time period could look like the following:

  Net Demand (1) = Dependent Demand (1) + Independent Demand (1) + Inventory Target (1) – Stock on Hand (1)

The definition of all later period periods would then look like the following:

Net Demand (t) = Dependent Demand (t) + Independent Demand (t) + Inventory Target (t) – Projected Inventory (t-1)

The use of the projected inventory key figure in cases in which it takes a negative value is covered in more detail in Section 4.7.5 during a discussion of carry forward shortage behavior.

In the first period, the net demand uses the stock on hand as the inventory available. As of the second period, and for all subsequent periods, the previously resulting inventory will be used in calculations.

- **Projected inventory** (PROJECTEDINVENTORY)
  A node-based key figure that reflects the inventory that will be available at a certain moment in the planning horizon, at a location for a specific product. Just like the net demand calculation, the projected inventory considers a lot of key figures and lies at the core of the S&OP heuristic. The calculation of the projected inventory will be covered once all the required key figures are introduced.

In the first period, the net demand calculation considers the complete target inventory. In all later periods, depending on the parameterization of the heuristic (which will be covered in Section 4.7), only the difference between the target inventory in the current period and previous period will be used to ensure that no double counting occurs.

The projected inventory key figure can take positive and negative values. A positive value implies there is remaining inventory at the end of the planning period. A negative inventory signifies there is a shortage in this period. The shortage in the heuristic is always locally reflected in the location where it occurs.

Considering all the key figures in the sample network would result in Figure 4.6.

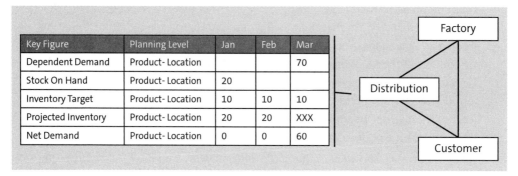

Key Figure	Planning Level	Jan	Feb	Mar
Dependent Demand	Product- Location			70
Stock On Hand	Product- Location	20		
Inventory Target	Product- Location	10	10	10
Projected Inventory	Product- Location	20	20	XXX
Net Demand	Product- Location	0	0	60

Figure 4.6 Net Demand at Distribution Center

In the example with only one customer for the distribution center, the dependent demand is equal to the dependent customer demand. The stock on hand is only considered in the current period. The net demand calculation, in this case, considers the available inventory (20) when trying to fulfill the dependent demand (70), ensuring the inventory target is met (10) and resulting in a net demand of *70 + 10 – 20*.

The resulting net demand will be sourced using the sourcing rules applied for locations, including location sourcing rules and production sourcing rules. Considering the distribution center doesn't produce, the net demand will be propagated to the factory using a 100 percent sourcing ratio on the location sourcing rule.

4.4.5   Location Sourcing

Location sourcing applies to locations with a location sourcing rule applied. Location sourcing rules provide information about the sourcing ratio and the lead time to transport products from one location to another.

In the sample network, as shown in Figure 4.7, location sourcing is a single-sourcing model, in which all the distribution centers' demand comes from the factory. It takes two months for the factory to deliver the products to the distribution center.

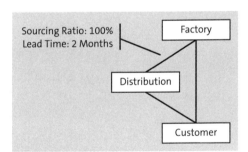

Figure 4.7 Location Sourcing Rules

Like the customer sourcing key figures, two arc-based key figures can be considered:

- **Outbound location demand** (DEPENDENTLOCATIONDEMAND)
  The demand based on the date that required supply is to be received by the location. This key figure is available on the period, product, location, and ship-from location planning levels.

  Outbound Location Demand = Net Demand × Location Sourcing Ratio

- **Dependent location demand** (DEPENDENTLOCATIONDEMANDDS)
  This key figure reflects the corresponding key figure of the dependent location demand at the supplying location, calculated back over the location sourcing lead time. This key figure is available on the period, product, location, and ship-to location planning levels.

  Dependent Location Demand = Outbound Location Demand Offset over Location Sourcing Lead Time

Although the planning level for the outbound customer demand is same as that for the dependent customer demand—that is, period, product, location, or customer— this is not true for the outbound location demand key figure. Outbound location demand is defined for a period, product, or location with its *ship-from* location, whereas the dependent location demand is defined for a period, product, or location with its *ship-to* location. This will have an impact on how the key figures can be viewed in a planning view. It's possible to visualize the dependent customer demand and its downstream key figure easily in one planning view. For the location demand, the location is not consistent. Hence, you often need two separate planning views to visualize the dependent location demand and the outbound location demand key figure.

In the sample network, the resulting dependent location demand key figures are reflected in Figure 4.8.

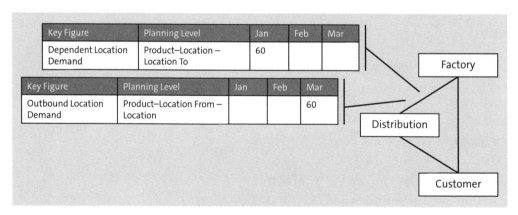

Figure 4.8 Dependent Location Demand

With a lead time of two months, the dependent location demand of 60, which is the full net demand in the distribution center for March, needs to be shipped from the factory in January.

4.4.6 Production Sourcing

At the factory, the same net demand calculation will be performed as documented previously for the distribution center, as shown in Figure 4.9.

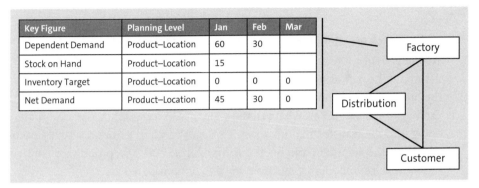

Key Figure	Planning Level	Jan	Feb	Mar
Dependent Demand	Product–Location	60	30	
Stock on Hand	Product–Location	15		
Inventory Target	Product–Location	0	0	0
Net Demand	Product–Location	45	30	0

Figure 4.9 Net Demand at Factory

For the factory, the dependent demand is the sum of the dependent customer demand (30 in February) and the dependent location demand (60 in January). Just like the net demand calculation for the distribution center, the stock on hand and the inventory target are considered to calculate the net demand.

The answer to the location sourcing, however, is different because the factory fulfills the net demand via production sourcing rules. Production sourcing rules, as introduced in Section 4.3.2, define which and how many specific components go into the production of a finished product.

In the sample network, the product is considered produced based on one component. This leads to the production sourcing rule shown in Figure 4.10.

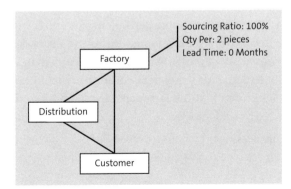

Figure 4.10 Production Sourcing Rule

Although the proposed production provides the supply element for the net demand of the finished product at the factory, per the production sourcing rule of type P, it creates a dependent demand for the components. Production sourcing rules, just like customer and location sourcing rules, have a main and a downstream key figure:

- **Outbound production demand** (DEPENDENTPRODUCTIONDEMAND)
  This key figure represents the dependent demand on the component and is defined at the period, product, location, component, and source levels. In this case, the product in the planning level refers to the finished product coming out of the product transformation, whereas the component represents the raw material going into the transformation, on which the dependent demand actually occurs. To define the requirements on the components, both the production sourcing ratio and the component coefficient need to be considered:

  Outbound Production Demand = Net Demand × Production Sourcing Ratio × Component Coefficient (Quantity Per)

- **Dependent production demand** (DEPENDENTPRODUCTIONDEMANDDS)
  This key figure represents the dependent demand on the component product level, at which the component now is identified as product (not as a component), which makes the finished product represented as *product-to*. Therefore, this key figure is defined at the period, product-to, location, product, and source levels. In this key figure, the product refers to the raw material, whereas the product-to is used to identify the finished product. The period for the dependent production demand is calculated using the production lead time available in the production source record:

  Dependent Production Demand = Outbound Production Demand Offset over Production Lead Time.

The dependent production demand number represents a dependent demand key figure for which the product is the raw material, thus adding up to the dependent demand calculation of the raw material. Remember that the dependent demand is made of the dependent production demand, dependent location demand, and dependent customer demand, which shows that the raw materials that go into finished products also can be distributed or sold directly.

In the sample network, this looks like Figure 4.11.

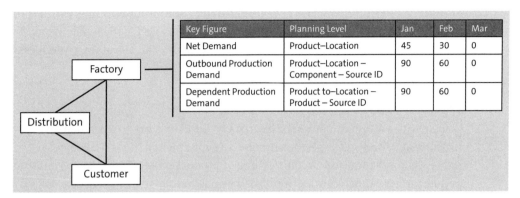

Figure 4.11 Dependent Production Demand

Both the outbound production demand and the dependent production demand will take the *quantity per* into consideration, resulting in a requirement on the raw material of two times the net demand requirement.

Finally, for the components, the same net demand calculation will occur based on the sum of all demands. This will result in a requirement that could be fulfilled further upstream from a supplier. Suppliers can be modeled in SAP IBP just like other locations. Assigning them location type V will result in external demand being populated at the supplier level. In this example, we'll directly assume an unspecified rule at the factory reflecting that we aren't interested in calculating requirements on the suppliers. This allows us to start the supply propagation section from the requirements on components that are being fulfilled externally.

4.4.7 Lot Sizes

Before closing the section on demand propagation, it's important to provide more background on the lot-sizing approach. Currently, in all the provided examples, we've considered lot-for-lot planning. However, in many realistic business scenarios, there are requirements to account for more advanced lot-sizing procedures. The S&OP heuristic can account for the following scenarios:

- Lot-for-lot planning
- Periods of supply, as follows:
  - Static periods of supply
  - Dynamic periods of supply
- Production cycle lot size

As noted, all examples thus far have been based on lot-for-lot planning, which is the default behavior of the heuristic. Other cases will be covered in the remainder of this section. Lot size policies are applied both to the customer and location in production sourcing rules.

Periods of Supply

Using periods of supply allows the heuristic to build up stock to cover demands over the current period and a specified number of subsequent periods. The objective typically is to bundle transport requirements or production requirements to run in one period for a volume covering multiple periods, rather than having a lower value every period.

The number of subsequent periods can be specified in the key figure target subperiods of supply, which will be considered by the heuristic on the period, product, and location levels. Because it's often required to consider partial subperiods, the number of subperiods key figure can be used to specify the total. Imagine planning in weekly periods, but with a requirement to cover the next 10 days. In such a case, there's a requirement to cover partial periods. In this case, the number of subperiods key figure can be set to 7 for every week (the number of days in a week), and the target subperiods of supply key figure can be set to 10. This will mean that the heuristic will consider the demand for the current period and for 3/7 of the demand of the next period in the calculation of the net demand for the current period.

Static periods of supply calculate the number of future periods that could be covered, regardless of the value of the current period. Dynamic periods of supply do exactly the same thing, with the one difference: if the current period has no demand, the logic doesn't apply.

The example in Table 4.2 provides a comparison between lot-for-lot and static periods of supply. In the case of lot-for-lot, every period will cover the demand in the current period with the corresponding supply elements. In the case of static periods of supply, the calculation is based on the number of future periods to be considered. Looking at Week A in the example, the net demand (40) is the sum of the net demand for the current week (10) and the next two weeks because the target subperiod of supply is set to 14 (days), and there are 7 (days per week), so you add another 30 (10 for Week B, 20 for Week C). To find the additional demand caused by the lot-sizing procedure, the heuristic can write back the *additional lot-sizing procedure demand* key figure.

Lot for Lot					
Key Figure	**Planning Level**	**Week A**	**Week B**	**Week C**	**Week D**
Dependent Demand	Product – Location	10	20	10	20
Target Subperiods of Supply	Product – Location	0	0	0	0
Number of Subperiods	Product – Location	0	0	0	0
Projected Stock	Product – Location	0	0	0	0
Net demand	Product – Location	10	20	10	20
Total Receipts	Product – Location	10	20	10	20
Static Periods of Supply					
Key Figure	**Planning Level**	**Week A**	**Week B**	**Week C**	**Week D**
Dependent Demand	Product – Location	10	20	10	20
Target Subperiods of Supply	Product – Location	14	14	0	0
Number of Subperiods	Product – Location	7	7	7	7
Projected Stock	Product – Location	30	30	20	0
Net demand	Product – Location	10 + 20 + 10 − 0 = 40	20 + 10 + 20 − 30 = 20	10 − 30 < 0 → 0	20 − 20 = 0
Total Receipts	Product – Location	40	20	0	0

Table 4.2 Lot-Sizing Policies

To switch on the periods of supply lot-sizing procedure, the LOTSIZEPOLICY attribute can be set to the following:

- 0 for lot-for-lot
- 1 for static periods of supply
- 2 for dynamic periods of supply

Periods of supply are often considered as an alternative to inventory targets. Although the heuristic considers both separately, the periods of supply have an advantage in that they consider the next period in their calculation. Hence, if the demand drops suddenly, periods of supply wouldn't build up unnecessary inventory.

Production Cycle Lot Sizes

This lot-sizing procedure only applies to production sources of supply and defines how often a product is produced. Specifying the time between different production runs for a specific product allows the heuristic to ensure the amount produced is sufficient to cover the demand until the next production cycle. After setting the LOTSIZEPOLICY attribute on the product and location levels to 3, the PERIODSOFCOVERAGE attribute on the production source can be used to specify the number of future periods.

For example, if a product is produced only every five weeks, in a heuristic running in weekly periods, setting the PERIODSOFCOVERAGE attribute on the production source to 5 ensures that the heuristic covers the next five periods and thus produces enough product to last until the next production run. To control the period in which the production starts, you can use the *first period of production* key figure to indicate the start of the production cycle of five weeks.

Parameters of Lot Sizing

Finally, these lot-sizing procedures all can be complemented by minimum lot sizes and rounding values. Maximum lot sizes also can be defined, but they only apply to the S&OP optimizer, so they'll be covered in Chapter 5.

Minimum lot sizes and rounding values are defined in the sourcing rules and apply on customer, location, and production sourcing levels. A minimum lot size ensures that the demand for a certain period is, at a minimum, the quantity specified. Rounding values force the heuristic to round the planned quantity to multiples of the value. For example, a minimum lot size of 120 with a rounding value of 50 allows the heuristic to plan for 0, 150, 200, 250, and so on in increments of 50.

This section on lot sizes closes our overview of demand propagation. In the next section, we'll cover how the heuristic propagates back supply as a confirmation of the demand numbers.

4.5   Propagating Supply

In demand propagation, all the requirements throughout the supply network have been propagated, resulting in the dependent demand and net demand calculations at every level. In the sample network, this results in a net demand for the raw materials, which will be fulfilled by the undefined sourcing rule, depicting the edge of the supply network. Supply propagation will start at this point and confirm all the relevant demand items.

The default operation of the heuristic is a complete, unconstrained supply propagation. This implies that all demands will be confirmed in the quantity with which they have been raised. With the S&OP heuristic defined as a decision support tool, it provides visibility to the planners on the plan but expects the planners to manually adjust it if the plan proves to be not feasible. This differs from the operation of the optimizer, via which demands will only be confirmed to the extent they support the optimal plan.

Because providing a complete unconstrained plan at every level in the network might prove difficult for planners in the real world to manage, a fair-share supply propagation algorithm has been introduced. This fair-share supply propagation allows planners to make adjustments at any level in the supply chain and have the supply propagation logic carry them downstream to the customers. This will be covered in Section 4.7.

The remainder of this section will introduce, just as we did for demand propagation, the various elements the supply propagation process goes through, starting from external receipts from suppliers and moving through production supply elements both on components and finished products. Next, the transport elements and customer demand elements will be confirmed. We'll close the chapter with a short overview of minimum and adjusted key figures to alter or manually overwrite the behavior of the heuristic.

4.5.1   External Receipts

The demand propagation ends when the raw material demand has been raised against the undefined production rule, marking the edge of the supply network. This is where supply propagation starts, providing external receipts for those demands.

Fulfilling the dependent demand on the raw materials in the simple network example in this chapter is performed via the undefined production rule. This will result in external receipts and will thus close the demand propagation process, closing the network.

External receipts (RECEIPT) correspond to a U-rule, defined at period, product, and location levels. External receipts indicate the edge of the supply network. The calculation is as follows:

External Receipts = Net Demand × Production Sourcing Ratio with Source Type U

External receipts represent the incoming supply from the edge of the supply network. This can be considered the start of the supply fulfillment of all the demands that have been propagated. Often, these external receipts are where the supplier gets their products from, which is outside of the scope of typical planning processes. See Figure 4.12 for an example.

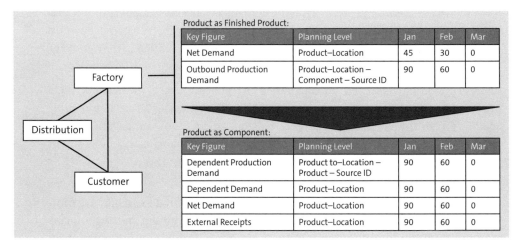

Figure 4.12 External Receipts

In the sample network used so far, the raw materials aren't planned from a supplier but are considered to be received via a U-rule. In this case, they enter the network in external receipts key figure. Considering there was no inventory nor any planned receipts, Figure 4.12 shows the net demand on the components. This demand is being fulfilled by the external receipts. Note that though the component is the product of record, the planning level for the external demand is still period-product-location.

4.5.2 Production Component

With the external receipts providing the raw materials, the dependent production demand (and dependent production demand) key figures can be fulfilled. Their fulfillment counterparts are as follows:

- **Component supply** (PRODUCTIONCOMPONENTDS)
  This is the arc-based key figure that fulfills the requirements at the product (which is a component), location, source, and product-to (which is the finished product) levels:

  Component Supply = Dependent Production Demand

- **Component usage** (PRODUCTIONCOMPONENT)
  This is the arc-based key figure that's the complement of the dependent production demand key figure; it's defined at the product (which is the finished product), location, source, and component levels:

  Component Usage = Outbound Production Demand

This can be visualized as shown in Figure 4.13.

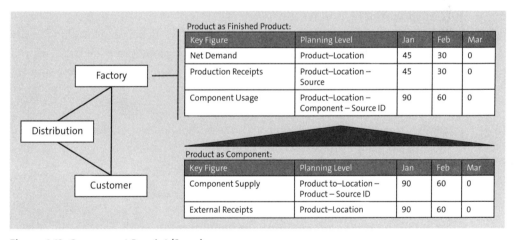

Product as Finished Product:

Key Figure	Planning Level	Jan	Feb	Mar
Net Demand	Product–Location	45	30	0
Production Receipts	Product–Location – Source	45	30	0
Component Usage	Product–Location – Component – Source ID	90	60	0

Product as Component:

Key Figure	Planning Level	Jan	Feb	Mar
Component Supply	Product to–Location – Product – Source ID	90	60	0
External Receipts	Product–Location	90	60	0

Figure 4.13 Component Receipt/Supply

Because the heuristic in its base operations is unconstrained at every step, the main operations of the heuristic results in the supply propagation legs (e.g., component receipt/supply) always being equal to the demand propagation legs (e.g., outbound production demand/dependent production demand). The exception to this process is the fair-share supply propagation, which will be covered in Section 4.7.

4.5.3   Production Receipts

After the external receipts provide the input products for the production process, the requirements of the finished product now can be confirmed. This is done via the production receipts (PRODUCTION) key figure, a node-based key figure computed by the heuristic at the product-location-source ID level. In a situation in which the product is production-relevant, the heuristic computes a proposed production plan using net demands and the production sourcing ratio, as follows:

Production Receipts = Net Demand × Production Sourcing Ratio with Source Type P

Production receipts are shown in the calculation scheme in Figure 4.13.

4.5.4   Transport Receipts

From the proposed production key figure, which confirms the receipt of the supply of the finished product, the next step to be fulfilled is the transport receipts. In the baseline work of the S&OP heuristic, the following transport key figures will be equal to the dependent location demands:

- **Transport supply** (TRANSPORTDS)
  This key figure represents the confirmation leg of the dependent location demand key figure, on the same planning level as the dependent location demand, which is the product, location, and ship-to location. In the example, the transport supply is based on the sending date basis of the factory.

- **Transport receipts** (TRANSPORT)
  Similarly, transport receipts align with the outbound location demand key figure, both at the planning level and on a date basis.

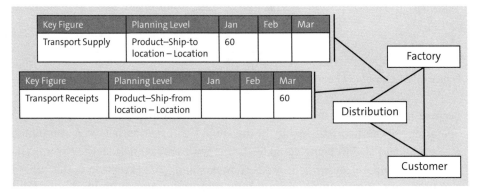

Figure 4.14 Transport Receipts and Supply

4.5.5   Constrained Demand

The constrained demand, though still an unconstrained key figure in the context of the S&OP heuristic, is the final step in the supply propagation logic. The key figures involved in this step are as follows:

- **Customer supply** (CONSTRAINEDDEMANDDS)
  This key figure corresponds to the dependent customer demand as its confirmation leg, and in the context of the S&OP heuristic it will be equal to the baseline setup.

- **Customer receipts** (CONSTRAINEDDEMAND)
  Similarly, customer receipts refer to the outbound customer demand.

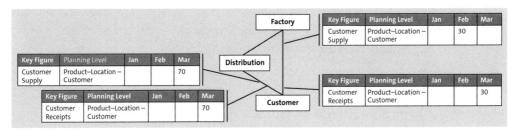

Figure 4.15 Customer Supply and Receipts

In the running example, we've modeled the requirements in such a way that they're nicely outside of the lead times. In practice, however, there could be changing requirements in the short term, which might result in shortages. With the heuristic being an unconstrained planning engine, in which the customer receipts and supply are equal to the dependent customer demands, the shortage isn't propagated downstream. In other words, if there isn't enough supply to fulfill the dependent demands at the distribution center or the factory, this will result in a negative projected inventory. In general, a key figure will be created to represent this as a shortage, ensuring that planners understand the implications well.

This completes the overview of the baseline key figures in the normal heuristic operation.

4.5.6   Minimum and Adjusted Key Figures

SAP Integrated Business Planning for sales and operations accepts planning elements from external systems. This is quite useful, particularly because SAP Integrated

Business Planning for sales and operations isn't a detailed operational tool and hence doesn't generate the planning elements such as purchase orders, stock transfer orders, or production orders. However, it generates the period-based quantities that provide guidance to other operational systems, enabling them to generate detailed order elements.

SAP Integrated Business Planning for sales and operations accepts several minimum key figures that can store the confirmed supply data, such as firm production orders, purchase orders, and transport orders. Typically, those key figures come from the external operational planning environment, like SAP S/4HANA. These values can be modeled as minimum key figures. Minimum key figures provide a lower bound to the heuristic planning algorithm such that the heuristic planning operator can then plan receipt elements higher than minimum key figures, but not lower. Further, such minimum key figures can be allowed to be manually editable and hence provide a good opportunity for what-if and scenario analysis.

The minimum key figures available in the standard operation of the heuristic are as follows:

- Minimum customer receipts (MINCONSTRAINEDDEMAND)
- Minimum customer supply (MINCONSTRAINEDDEMANDDS)
- Minimum transport receipts (MINTRANSPORT)
- Minimum transport supply (MINTRANSPORTDS)
- Minimum production receipts (MINPRODUCTION)

For minimum key figures, the heuristic adopts the following approach:

- The initial (i.e., NULL) value for minimum key figures doesn't impact the heuristic in any way.
- The noninitial value of a key figure is compared to the planned receipts calculated by the system. If the minimum key figure is less than required planned receipts, then planned receipts prevail and the heuristic writes them as output. However, if the minimum key figure value is greater than planned receipt, then the minimum quantity prevails.

The minimum transport key figures behave differently from the minimum customer key figures. If you enter a value for the minimum customer receipt key figure, it will automatically adjust the minimum customer supply key figure by considering the customer lead time. This same logic doesn't apply to minimum transport receipts and supply, for which the system expects to receive both key figures as an input from the operational planning system. The rationale behind this difference in behavior can be found in the relative information available. For internal stock transfers or purchasing activities, reflected in the transport key figures, it's assumed that the organization has perfect visibility into both start and end dates for the transfer. For shipments to customers, however, this information often isn't considered readily available, so the system calculates the corresponding key figure using the stored lead time.

Analogous to minimum key figures are adjusted key figures in that they can be used to influence the heuristic based on external planning elements. However, adjusted key figures differ from minimum key figures in that they provide an absolute value to be adopted as opposed to the lower bound that minimum key figures provide. This property of adjusted key figures makes them useful in capturing activities taking place within the transport horizon or production horizon.

The adjusted key figures available in the operation of the heuristic are as follows:

- Adjusted outbound customer demand (ADJDEPENDENTCUSTOMERDEMAND)
- Adjusted dependent customer demand (ADJDEPENDENTCUSTOMERDEMANDDS)
- Adjusted customer receipts (ADJUSTEDCONSTRAINEDDEMAND)
- Adjusted customer supply (ADJUSTEDCONSTRAINEDDEMANDDS)
- Adjusted demand (ADJUSTEDDEMAND)
- Adjusted production interactive (ADJUSTEDPRODUCTIONRECEIPT)
- Adjusted external receipts (ADJUSTEDRECEIPT)
- Adjusted transport receipts (ADJUSTEDTRANSPORT)
- Adjusted transport supply (ADJUSTEDTRANSPORTDS)
- Inventory correction (INVENTORYCORRECTION)

The heuristic considers the adjusted key figures to have a higher priority than the minimum key figures. Therefore, if there is an adjusted key figure, the heuristic will always adhere to it whether there's a minimum key figure or not. If there is no adjusted key figure, it will use the minimum key figure. If there is neither, then the heuristic will resume normal operation.

In the case of the usage of subnetworks, generally the same key figures can be used to adjust the receipt elements. For example, the use of adjusted transport receipts works just fine, including between planning units. However, to allow maximum flexibility, there are two other key figures that come into play. When we explained the concept of subnetworks in Section 4.3.4, we mentioned that subnetworks allow planning for only part of the network. Consequently, if there are interactions between subnetworks, two pairs of extra key figures can be used to allow planners to overwrite the inputs from the other subnetworks:

- **Intersubnetwork dependent location demand** (IPUDEPENDENTLOCATIONDEMANDDS)
  This key figure models an override of the dependent location demand, looking at it from the perspective of components; it allows the components planner to simulate numbers different from the actual demand of the respective business units.

- **Intersubnetworks transport receipts** (IPUTRANSPORT)
  This key figure models an override of the (confirmed) transport, which the business unit would get from the components planning unit. This allows the planner of the business unit to simulate numbers different from the quantities confirmed by the components subnetwork.

- **Intersubnetwork production component supply** (IPUPRODUCTIONCOMPONENTDS)
  This key figure, similar to the intersubnetwork transport key figure, represents the production component supply in cases in which a BOM encompasses a subnetwork.

- **Intersubnetwork production receipts** (IPUPRODUCTION)
  This key figure is the natural counterpart of the intersubnetwork production component supply key figure, representing the supply of the finished product in cases in which a BOM encompasses subnetworks.

Please note that the **Compute Expected Supply** parameter of the heuristic, which is mentioned in Section 4.7.8, has an altering impact on the operation mentioned.

4.6   Rough-Cut Capacity Planning

In the section on supply propagation, we pointed to the unconstrained behavior of the heuristic, showing that in most cases the supply confirmation is equal to the propagated demand. Although the heuristic is unconstrained in nature, it's possible to leverage the rough-cut capacity planning functionality. The heuristic, as a decision support algorithm, will not reduce the available production quantities to fit the capacities. Nor will it make a judgment on whether to obtain product from different sources. Instead, it will provide an opportunity to highlight the key exception areas and hence will enable planners to choose the correct course of action based on their business needs. A planner will use the adjustment key figures described in the previous section to reduce the plan accordingly.

As a prerequisite to model rough-cut capacity planning, resources will have to be modeled in the supply network. SAP IBP supports three types of resources, which will be covered in the next sections. After covering the resource types, we'll give an overview of the key figures that the heuristic will populate to support the rough-cut capacity planning process.

4.6.1   Production Resources

Production resources are used to manage capacities as they relate to the actual production process. The actual production process constitutes producing new products based on a BOM, thus consuming the components in that BOM. In this case, as we covered in Section 4.3, a production source is defined. Consequently, the capacity utilization is defined on the level of the production source and the production resource.

Production resources are typically defined with type P in the **Resource Type** field of the resource master data type, and they require the following additional master data types to be defined:

- Resource location, as a compound master data type, combining the location and resource. Here you define the available capacity, which can be modeled either in the master data type or as a time series.

- Production source resource, as a compound master data type, combining the production source and the resource. At this level, the capacity consumption can be defined, either as a number in the master data type or as a time series.

Modeling this set of master data types allows for calculating the capacity load that the production process will put on the production resources.

It's very common for most organizations to model only critical resources in the SAP IBP solution, as the solution is not meant to perform detailed production planning and scheduling. Often, a complete facility or production line can be modeled for one resource, measuring the throughput in a planning bucket (e.g., week or month) through this resource.

4.6.2   Handling and Storage Resources

Handling resources allow modeling capacity utilization for resources that don't perform product transformation. In this case, there is no BOM, and the capacity load is calculated by products merely passing this node in the network. An example of a handling resource could be the throughput through a distribution center with a constrained goods receipt process, or a port where the handling capacity is limited to a specific time bucket. Any location products flow through and which are limited in capacity without performing an actual production process could be good candidates for modeling via handling resources.

Because handling resources don't use a production source, the master data model is slightly different. Just like production resources, the resource is typically defined with its type, H for handing resources, and the resource location for modeling the available capacity. The extra master data type to model the capacity consumption is handled via a compound master data type of product, location, and resource.

4.6.3 Capacity Key Figures

As mentioned while defining master data types for resources, the available capacity and the capacity consumption both can be defined either in the master data types or as key figures by setting the master data time series attribute flag to X. This enables the following key figures:

- **Capacity supply** (CAPASUPPLY)
  This is a stored key figure defined at the location-resource level, without a predefined unit of measure.

- **Capacity consumption**
  The key figure for the consumption rate depends on the type of resource:
  - *Capacity consumption rate* (CAPACONSUMPTION) is used for handling and storage resources and is a stored key figure at product, location, and resource levels. It's expressed in the same units as the capacity supply.
  - *Capacity consumption rate of production resource* (PCAPACONSUMPTION) is used for production resources, and hence is a stored key figure defined on the resource-production source level.

  The heuristic will use the available capacity and the capacity consumption to determine the demand and usage of the key figures. The capacity demand is defined as the capacity required to fulfill the complete net demand; the capacity utilization is the resulting capacity from what's been received/produced. In the heuristic, an unconstrained algorithm, the two are typically the same.

- **Capacity demand** (CAPADEMAND/PCAPADEMAND)
  For storage and handling resources, this is defined as a stored key figure on a

product-location-resource level, calculated as the multiplication of net demand with the capacity consumption rate.

For production resources, it's defined as a stored key figure on resource and production source levels, calculated as the multiplication of the net demand on a specific production source with the capacity consumption rate of the production resource.

- **Capacity usage** (CAPAUSAGE/PCAPAUSAGE)

  For storage and handling resources, this is defined as a stored key figure on a product-location-resource level, calculated by multiplying the total receipts by the capacity consumption rate.

  For production resources, it's defined as a stored key figure on production source and resource levels, calculated by multiplying the production receipts by the capacity consumption rate of the production resource.

In most implementations, though not a real output key figure of the heuristic, the resource utilizations are calculated. The capacity utilization (UTILIZATIONPCT) key figure is calculated as the capacity usage divided by the total capacity of the resource. This implies that the calculation results in a key figure on production source and resource levels for production resources, and on product, location, and resource levels for handling and storage resources.

Because the heuristic is an unconstrained algorithm, it won't constrain the plan based on the resources. It's very common to use either custom alerts, which will be covered in Chapter 7 or key figure alerts. Key figure alerts, as described in Chapter 2, are typically defined based on loading capacities above 100 percent. More flexibility can be obtained via comparison with a threshold key figure, which can be defined. This means that the planner will have to perform manual rough-cut capacity planning, using the adjustment key figures available. In practice, two key figures can be used for manually adjusting the plan based on the capacity consumption overloads:

- For handling and storage, *adjusted receipts* can be used to adjust the receipts into the node.

- For production resources, *adjusted production* can be used to reduce the amount which is produced.

The optimizer, which will be covered in Chapter 5, will automate this process by considering the capacities as a hard constraint.

4.7 Parameters of the Heuristic

The heuristic comes with a set of parameters to more finely control the exact calculations. In this section, those parameters will be covered together with the altering behavior they produce on the previously explained calculation model. The parameters are set in the configuration of the heuristic, which since SAP IBP release 1802 has been drastically simplified as shown in Figure 4.16.

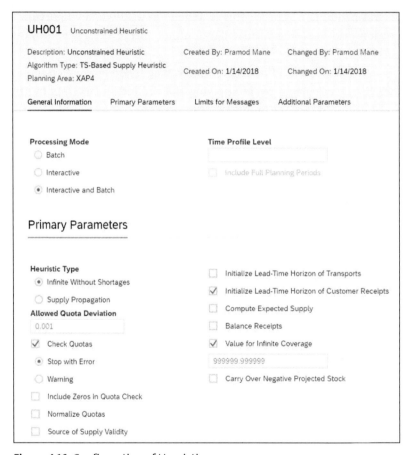

Figure 4.16 Configuration of Heuristic

The remainder of this chapter will guide you through the different settings to be made for the heuristic.

4.7.1   Processing Mode

The heuristic can be set up to run interactively in the planning view, in batch mode, or both. If the interactive run is allowed, the heuristic operator setup will become available in the simulation dropdown in the data input pane of the Excel add-in, as shown in Figure 4.17.

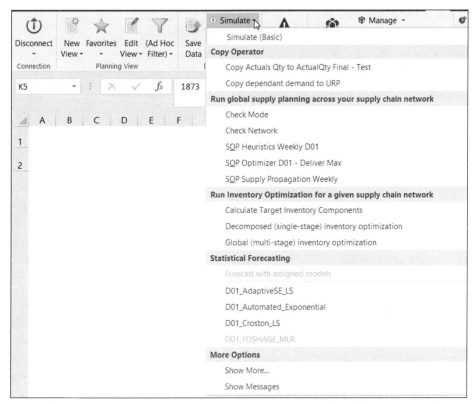

Figure 4.17 Interactive Planninging Operators

Running the heuristic interactively brings tremendous added value as the Excel workbook you're working in becomes a *simulation version*. The numbers in all the sheets will be updated per the latest results of the heuristic run, but they're not saved back to the SAP HANA database yet. This means as a planner you can simulate the plan, making adjustments in the adjustment key figures until you're satisfied, and only save the results back once.

Batch mode allows operators to be included in background runs. It's considered a good practice to run the planning operators at least daily, ensuring all planners are looking at the most recent version of the plan, whether or not the supply planner ran and saved his simulation runs.

4.7.2   Heuristic Type

As of release 1802, there are two supported heuristic types. In the previous sections of this chapter, we covered the infinite heuristic without shortages extensively, but it has traditionally been very challenging for users of this heuristic to construct a feasible plan. The heuristic following the calculation scheme treats shortages as negative projected inventory in the location to occur. This means that the next step in the supply propagation process isn't impacted if a shortage occurs.

For example, imagine a shortage of raw materials not allowing a certain production to be performed. In this case, the heuristic will generate a negative projected inventory for the production facility on the component but still consider the next step in the supply propagation, the production process itself, as feasible. This means that to deliver a feasible plan, the planner should leverage the adjusting key figures at every step in the network. In the case of a shortage of the raw material, this means production needs to be adjusted, and consequently the transport supply and receipts, as well as the customer supply and receipts.

Fair-share supply propagation, new functionality released in version 1802, makes this process significantly more practical by providing a rule-based logic in which only available supply will be propagated downstream. Because this often requires the heuristic to make decisions in case the demand needs to be split over different origins of the demand, a fair-share approach will be taken, as the name suggests. In practice, the fair-share supply propagation leverages a set of fixed rules, which listed in order of in decreasing priority as follows:

1. Adjusted key figures and minimum key figures will always be fulfilled, even if there is no supply (with other words, the projected inventory will still go negative in this case).

2. Inventory correction is an adjustment to the inventory, which will be considered in all cases.

3. Independent demand provides the opportunity to enter a demand signal, added to the dependent demand, at product location level.

4. Dependent customer demand will be the lowest level of priority considered by the fair share supply propagation logic.

With fair-share supply propagation, there are restrictions on other parameters, which will be covered in this section:

- Carry-over of negative inventory isn't supported.
- Periods of coverage aren't supported

Finally, it's important to note that the fair-share supply propagation logic should be tested carefully in business scenarios in which it will be applied because it can drive suboptimal supply plans. In an effort to ease the workload of the planner in propagating constraints throughout the network, the fair-share supply propagation heuristic is still a rule-based algorithm and can't be considered a constraint planning algorithm such as the supply optimizer (covered in Chapter 5).

4.7.3   Planning Level of the Heuristic

In Chapter 2, the time profile and the corresponding planning granularity were introduced. When running the heuristic, it's possible to select a planning granularity that allows you to specify at which level the heuristic should run. For example, if the time profile contains technical weeks, calendar weeks, months, and quarters, then it's possible to select the granularity **Months** in the heuristic. This would mean that the following is true:

- The heuristic would run in monthly buckets, meaning all the input key figures to the heuristic would be aggregated up to months
- The heuristic would provide the output key figures on a monthly level, and the figures consequently are disaggregated down to technical weeks per the disaggregation rules
- The lead times for the heuristic are considered at the monthly level

The **Planning Level of the Heuristic** setting is used to set the granularity, and the value should be equal to the level determined in the time profile (see Chapter 2 for a detailed explanation of how the planning level can be determined). If the parameter isn't set, the base planning level of the stored input key figure for the heuristic will be used.

If aggregation and disaggregation along the time levels are used in the heuristic—in other words, if a level is selected that isn't the base planning level—then there is a parameter that controls whether all time periods at the start or at the end of the planning horizon should be used. For example, if you run the planning operator in months, but don't select all the weeks of the beginning or ending month, the algorithm will complete the planning horizon to include all weeks for the starting and ending month. This is required for the selection of the planning in the execution UI to be in technical weeks, which makes it easy for users to select only partial months. This parameter can be set using the **Including Full Planning Periods** flag.

4.7.4   Quota Check Parameters

In Section 4.3.2, we covered establishing the sourcing rules of the supply network. We noted that in a consistent supply network, the sources of supply add up to 100 percent. When the planner runs the S&OP heuristic, as a first step the system will check if this requirement is met. In the standard operation, without any parameter, the heuristic would fail upon the first inconsistency and not provide any results. Using the right settings, however, it's possible to alter this behavior to avoid a full failure. There are three key mitigation methods, which will be covered in this section:

1. Allow for small deviations
2. Provide a ratio check policy
3. Normalize the ratios

Allowed Quota Deviation

In many cases, the sourcing ratio split can be a calculated key figure. For example, imagine that the consensus demand produced by the demand planning process already contains the location, on top of the customer and product dimensions, and the planners want the heuristic to still start from the consensus demand, ensuring the supply propagation ends up at the customer level. In such cases, the customer sourcing ratio can be calculated, which might result in small deviations from 100 percent when adding the ratios back up for a customer product.

To make sure the heuristic does not fail upon such small deviations, the **Allowed Quota Deviation** setting can be used. If this parameter is set to, for example, 0.01, this would mean the heuristic would consider all sourcing ratios acceptable between 99 percent and 101 percent. Note that if the ratio doesn't add up to exactly 100 percent, neither will the resulting customer demand or net demand. For example, if you use a parameter as mentioned of 0.01 and the sourcing ratio adds up to 99 percent, in a case of a demand of 200, the heuristic will only source 198 (200 × 0.99). The ratio will be applied as is.

Ratio Check Policy

You can select whether, upon failing a ratio check, the system issues an error or a warning. This can be done via setting the **Check Quotas** and using the radio buttons to select either of the following:

- **Stop with Error** to issue an error and stop the operation of the heuristic
- **Warning** to issue a warning and complete the calculations of the heuristic

Although it's often considered pragmatic to use the warning setting, note that if the ratio check policy is switched off or set to **Warning**, the demands will not add up to 100 percent. It will use the ratios as is. Therefore, if the parameter is set to **Warning**, it's of the utmost importance to follow up on the warnings daily. In a productive environment, it's best to use the error setting, ensuring consistency issues in the network are highlighted immediately and corrective action can be taken.

There is a special case for the ratio policy check, which applies if the sourcing ratios add up to zero. In such a case, the normal operation of the heuristic does not generate a warning or error, even if the parameter is correctly set. This stems from the fact that the original heuristic did not have advanced policy checking, and a zero sourcing quota would just depict the end of the network the user was willing to propagate to. To ensure full consistency, it's possible to set the **Include Zeros in Quota Check** checkbox, making sure zero sourcing ratio entries will follow the same rules as other incomplete sourcing ratios.

Normalization of Sourcing Ratios

Both parameters covered so far help users in establishing what should happen if the sourcing ratios don't add up to one. However, neither of the two options corrects the issue, and in all cases, if the heuristic operates, it won't source the demand to 100 percent.

Normalizing the sourcing ratios allows users to ensure the sourcing ratios always add up to 100 percent. If the original values don't add up to 100 percent, the **Normalize Quotas** dropdown can be used, set to one of the following values:

- **Equal** will make sure the planning algorithm calculates the sourcing ratios by giving equal weight to all options. For example, four sources of supply for a customer sourcing rule will give each of the sources 25 percent, independent of their prior value.

- **Proportional** will consider the prior value. For example, if there are two sources of a supply for a customer with values of 40 and 20 percent, the new sourcing ratios will become 66.67and 33.33 percent.

Be aware that if either of these parameter values is adopted, the heuristic will not consider the quotas originally entered by the planner (if they don't add up to 100 percent). Also, note that the heuristic will not overwrite the old values with the newly calculated ones; it will use them at runtime but not write them back to the database. Because of this behavior, we advise you not to use this parameter in a productive environment.

Like the check policy parameter, sourcing rules adding up to 0 percent are considered a special case. To normalize also the zero value cases, the **Include Zeros in Quota Check** parameter can be set. If zeros are included, this means that for a case in which there are two customer sourcing ratios of 20 and 0 percent, respectively, in the case of equal split, the heuristic will calculate 50 percent each. Including zeros is the default value. If you want to ensure zero value sourcing rules are kept out of the logic, the flag should not be set. This will, in our example, result in the heuristic calculating with 100 and 0 percent, respectively.

This section covered various ways of overruling the sourcing checks in the heuristic. However, having a consistent supply network in which all the sourcing rules add up to 100 percent is a critical part of supply network design and a prerequisite of any consistent supply network planning solution. Hence, the options for not using the check can be useful during the build of the initial solution, but shouldn't be relied upon as a long-term solution. We strongly advise only leveraging the allowed ratio deviation as a small number to correct for rounding errors (e.g., 0.001) and using the **Error** setting in the ratio check policy.

4.7.5   Carry Forward Negative Projected Inventory

In the operation of the heuristic, it's possible that the projected inventory shows negative. This means that if for some reason it's impossible for the heuristic to fulfill all demands in a particular bucket, the projected inventory shows negative. This could be the case, for example, if there's no shipment in transit and the lead time is greater than one. Other examples imply the usage of adjusted receipts, adjusted transport, or adjusted production to force the receipt elements, making it impossible for the heuristic to fulfill the demands.

In the traditional launch of the S&OP heuristic, the calculation schema started from a lost sales paradigm. This implies that when the demand in a specific planning bucket is not consumed, it is lost. In other words, the negative projected inventory was not carried forward, as is illustrated in Table 4.3, in which the net demand in February doesn't consider the fact that January closed with a shortage of 50.

Traditional Behavior			
Key Figure	Planning Level	Jan	Feb
Dependent Demand	Product – Location	50	20
Net Demand	Product – Location	50	20
Projected Inventory	Product – Location	-50	40
Adjusted Transport Receipts	Product – Location	0	60

Table 4.3 Not Carrying Forward Projected Inventory

Setting the **Carry Over Negative Projected Inventory** checkbox makes it possible to adjust this behavior, ensuring the demand from January isn't lost. In Table 4.4, you can see that the net demand for February now adds up to 70 by adding the 50 carried forward from January to the 20 for dependent demand in February. This means that at the end of February there is still a shortage of ten, which is consequently carried forward to March.

Carry Forward Project Inventory			
Key Figure	Planning Level	Jan	Feb
Dependent Demand	Product – Location	50	20
Net Demand	Product – Location	50	**70**
Projected Inventory	Product – Location	-50	**-10**
Adjusted Transport Receipts	Product – Location	0	60

Table 4.4 Carrying Forward Projected Inventory

4.7.6   Balanced Receipts

In the section on demand propagation, we covered the fact that the heuristic generally starts with the consensus demand and sources it to a location. From that location, the source of supply is based on the production sourcing or location sourcing rules. On determining which location or production sourcing rule is applied, the heuristic relies on the quota (sourcing ratios).

However, if the heuristic were to use a strict approach to demand propagation sourcing ratios, when coupled with externally planned receipt elements such as firm purchase orders, transport orders, or production orders, it could lead to suboptimal supply planning and result in unnecessary excesses or shortages in the network. For example, consider the sample network shown in Figure 4.18. At a factory, a certain part is supplied by two suppliers, Supplier 1 and Supplier 2. The quotas for Supplier 1 and Supplier 2 are 0 and 100 percent, respectively. There is no lead time for the product to move from suppliers to a factory.

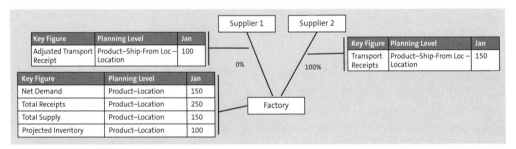

Figure 4.18 Balanced Receipts Turned Off

In the month of January, there is a demand for 150 units at the factory. However, there is a firm incoming receipt of 100 units from Supplier 1, represented as a firm purchase order. This firm purchase order will be implemented either as an adjusted transport receipt or a minimum transport receipt. However, because of the quota of 100 percent, the heuristic strictly plans all 150 units of demand to be procurable from Supplier 2. This results in 250 units incoming at the factory—that is, 150 units of planned transports and 100 units of firm purchase orders. After satisfying the original net demands of 100 units, the factory still has an excess of 100 units at the end of the month of January.

Such suboptimal planning situations get even worse when we have additional factors in supply planning, such as the following:

- Different lead times across multiple suppliers
- Carry forward of shortages in planning where shortages from a previous planning period are added to the net demands of future planning periods

A balanced receipt policy of a heuristic-based planning method helps avoid such excesses or shortages in the planning situation. This policy is activated by setting the **Balance Receipts** heuristic checkbox.

As soon as the balanced receipt parameter is activated, the heuristic treats the sourcing ratio as a pseudo-hard constraint, allowing for flexible replenishment plans. For example, Figure 4.19 shows a planning situation in which the balanced receipt policy is at work. Instead of propagating demands for 150 units to Supplier 2, the heuristic accounts for firm incoming receipts and propagates the remainder of the demand, 50 units, to Supplier 2 instead. This avoids an excess inventory situation at a factory location toward the end of January.

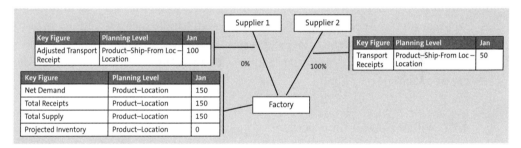

Figure 4.19 Balanced Receipts Calculation

When considering the balanced receipt functionality for an implementation, the following considerations can be important:

- The concept of balanced receipt is relevant for all different combinations of sources of supply. That is, in the example, we used the transport source of supply, but it's possible to apply the policy across production and external sources of supply, too.
- Balanced receipt can be used for customer sources.
- One undesired side-effect of balanced receipts is that when demands can't be satisfied by active sources of supply, the heuristic violates the quota rule and tries to satisfy demands from inactive sources of supply. That is, it propagates demands to sources even when they are set to 0 percent of the sourcing ratio. This situation

can be avoided by setting up the scope for balanced receipts. The following attributes are relevant to set the balanced receipt scope:

- CBALANCERECEIPTSCOPE for source customer
- TBALANCERECEIPTSCOPE for source location
- PBALANCERECEIPTSCOPE for source production

As soon as the value of these attributes is set to 1, corresponding sources don't participate in receipt balancing. If the attribute is set to 0, or not assigned, the sources do participate in receipt balancing.

The fact that receipt balancing flexes the sourcing ratio rules, although useful in many planning situations, can be undesirable in certain business arrangements. For example, certain supplier contracts are forged in such a way that a manufacturing firm is contractually obligated to procure a certain percentage of demand from suppliers for a given period. The fact that another supplier has excess is irrelevant in such a context. This might mean treating sourcing ratios as a strict method of demand propagation at the cost of excesses. Another way to handle such a situation can be to model alerts that constantly track the percentage of procured parts over a considerable period, like a quarter or year, and provide planners the ability to change the course of action accordingly.

4.7.7   Initialize Lead Time Horizon

In the standard behavior, when running the heuristic, the algorithm starts by clearing all the key figures out of the planning horizon specified. This means all the key figures the heuristic writes as an output will be initialized. The exception to his behavior is the transport receipt and supply key figures, which aren't initialized during the lead time horizon. In practice, this means the heuristic expects the previous cycle planning run still to be relevant with respect to the current cycle. For example, if the heuristic plans in weekly buckets, and in the previous week it planned to receive 100 units in a distribution shipped from a factory (with a one-week lead time, for example), it expects in the current week that those 100 units will arrive.

In general, it's good practice to integrate the open stock transfer orders from the execution system. This would mean that the minimum transport receipt key figure can be used to model the open stock transfer orders, which are in transit. Inside the lead time, the minimum transport receipt would act as an adjustment, overriding the transport receipt key figure. Outside of the lead time, it would act as a minimum.

However, if for some reason it's impossible to integrate the open stock transfer orders, there are two behaviors that can be modeled. The default behavior of the heuristic is to consider the transport receipt key figure within the lead time, as previously planned. In other words, the heuristic doesn't initialize the transport receipt key figure and expects the plan to have been executed. The alternative is setting the **Initialize Lead-Time Horizon of Transports** parameter, which will wipe out the numbers from the transport receipt within the planning horizon selected. Because it's impossible for the heuristic to plan a new transport supply within the lead time, there will be no receipts within the lead time (and possibly shortages can be accumulated, which will be reflected as negative projected inventory).

The parameter we just discussed works for location sourcing rules, and the **Initialize Lead-Time Horizon for Customer Receipts** parameter can be set for customer sourcing rules. Doing so will serve to initialize the customer supply and receipt key figures within the customer's lead time.

4.7.8   Compute Expected Supply

Using the **Compute Expected Supply** parameter can influence planning with subnetworks. In Section 4.3.4, we covered how subnetworks allow for separating the planning network into smaller units, to distinguish, for example, between business units of different geographical locations that need to be planned independently. Setting the **Compute Expected Supply** parameter will prevent the heuristic from considering fixed supply from other subnetworks. In Section 4.5.6, we covered how, in the case of subnetworks, it's possible to use either adjusted receipts or the inter-subnetwork transport receipts to fix supply between the subnetworks. Setting the parameter to **Yes** means that those numbers are ignored when planning a specific subnetwork. Note that while the values are being ignored by the heuristic, they aren't initialized.

4.7.9   Use of Validity Dates

Since release 1705, it's been possible for the heuristic to directly consider validity dates in the sourcing rules. Although time series-based sourcing ratios allow for maximum flexibility, setting the **Source of Supply Validity** parameter makes it possible to use master data types for the sourcing rule validity.

Three new master data types can be introduced:

- *Customer source validity*, which has the product, customer, and location as required key fields and uses the CVALIDFR and CVALIDTO attributes to model valid from and to dates.

- *Location source validity*, which has the product, ship-from location, and location as key fields and uses the TVALIDFR and TVALIDTO attributes to model valid from and to dates.

- *Production source validity*, which has the source ID as a required field and uses the PVALIDFR and PVALIDFR attributes to model valid from and to dates.

4.8   Summary

In this chapter, we covered the details of the S&OP heuristic and how it allows planners to build a feasible supply plan. We have defined the S&OP heuristic as a rule-based, unconstrained decision support algorithm that leverages the supply network to calculate production plans, procurement plans, and distribution plans for the consensus demand. The supply network, made of a consistent set of sourcing rules to propagate the demand, defines the rules of the algorithm.

The algorithm starts with the consensus demand and performs a complete demand propagation up to the edge of the supply network, followed by an unconstrained supply propagation. Although the algorithm is unconstrained in nature, it's possible to model resources and provide visibility into the rough-cut capacity planning implications of the sales and operations plan. If there are supply constraints, you should adjust the plan manually, ensuring that the right business decisions are made. The standard operation of the heuristic requires you to make this choice for every step in the network, but with parameterization, a fair-share supply propagation can be implemented.

Although the heuristic is a very powerful algorithm in its simplicity, converting the unconstrained plan into a feasible plan could represent a significant workload for planners. The next chapter will cover the S&OP optimizer, which is a constrained supply planning algorithm. In the optimizer, a lot of the rules from the S&OP heuristic will be replaced by cost parameters that allow the algorithm to calculate a feasible plan that maximizes the profit of the organization. Whereas the heuristic requires you to make decisions in case of constraints, the optimizer will take the best financial alternative and constraints for the plan automatically. This can save a lot of work, but it comes at the cost of significant added complexity.

Chapter 5
Constrained Supply Planning

In this chapter, we'll discuss constrained supply planning. This type of planning takes unconstrained consensus demand as input and generates a feasible production, distribution, and procurement plan while considering supply chain constraints, such as raw material and capacity.

In this chapter, we'll continue to build on the consensus demand plan generated as part of the demand review process, basic master data, and key figures required for supply planning discussed in the previous chapter, and we'll cover the input to the supply review step in the executive S&OP cycle. The main objective of this chapter is to provide understanding of the time series-based S&OP optimizer for generating a feasible production, distribution, and procurement plan. After the definition and objectives, the steps in building the constrained plan will be detailed. Once we have the basic scenario explained, the different parameters influencing the results of the optimizer will be covered, together with their business use.

5.1   Constrained Supply Planning at a Glance

As covered in Chapter 4, supply planning is a crucial step to determine the feasibility of unconstrained demand—that is, how much of what we could sell versus how much will be available considering the resources (machine, labor, etc.) and raw material constraints in the supply chain network.

A supply planner's primary task is to deliver a supply plan that fulfills customer demand on time and covers inventory targets specified in the supply chain network, ensuring that resources are utilized efficiently. A supply planner focuses on integrating the selling side of the business with the making side in an optimal way. On the making side, the focus is on cost-effective production, distribution lot sizes, and minimal changeovers taking into consideration the network resources and material constraints. On the selling side, the priority is to fulfill customer demand in full and on time, meeting inventory targets. The business goals of these two sides often contradict each other, so achieving a plan that's optimized for both aspects is challenging.

Constraining the plan to arrive at a feasible option that balances the selling and making sides can be done either by manually adjusting the unconstrained supply plan results or by using advanced techniques such as the time series-based optimizer.

In the case of an unconstrained heuristic, the consensus demand is propagated through the arbitrarily deep supply network. This provides visibility into the bottlenecks in the tactical planning horizon, which can be in the form of capacity overloads—that is, the required capacity is less than the available capacity—raw material shortages, logistics capacity shortages, and so on. The task of balancing demand and supply—in the form of evaluating options such as prebuilding inventory to meet seasonal demand patterns for a consumer packaged goods (CPG) company, looking for alternative sources of supply, and/or subcontracting—must be performed manually by the planner. The manually adjusted supply plan can then be propagated downstream using supply propagation to arrive at a constrained forecast.

The time series-based optimizer, on the other hand, takes as inputs an objective function in the form of either maximizing profitability or maximizing revenue, the business priorities set by financial key figures, and various hard and soft constraints in the supply chain network to balance demand and supply and generate a feasible supply plan.

5.2   S&OP Optimizer

In this section, we'll explain the time series-based optimizer algorithm, delivered as part of SAP Integrated Business Planning for response and supply. As the name suggests, this algorithm utilizes mathematical optimization techniques to compute the supply plan. The S&OP optimizer will compute a feasible cost-optimized constrained supply plan that considers the various constraints in the supply chain network without any manual intervention. Unlike the heuristic, which follows the rules laid down by the supply chain structure, the decisions for the optimizer are based on the financial aspects defined for the supply chain.

The goal of the time series-based optimizer is to minimize the total costs of the supply chain. This goal is achieved by minimizing the financials aspects of the supply chain, specified in the form of the following fixed and variable costs:

- Revenue lost due to nondelivery or delayed delivery of demand
- Fixed and variable cost rates for production
- Fixed and variable cost rates for transportation
- Fixed and variable cost rates for procurement
- Inventory holding cost rate
- Inventory target violation—that is, going below the set inventory target or going above the maximum inventory level

The objective function contains a sum of all costs, as follows:

- Nondelivery variable costs
- Transportation variable costs and transportation fixed costs
- Production variable costs and production fixed costs
- External receipt variable costs and external receipt fixed costs
- Inventory holding variable costs, inventory target violation variable costs, and maximum inventory violation variable costs
- Minimum capacity usage violation cost rates

We'll discuss the financial information and how it's specified in more detail in Section 5.4.

The optimization is performed by transforming the modeled supply chain specified via master data and key figures into a mixed-integer linear programming (MILP) mathematical model. The output is a feasible master production, distribution, and procurement plan.

The time series-based optimizer supports generating an optimized constrained supply plan in the following modes:

- Profit maximization
- Delivery maximization

In both modes, the objective of the optimizer is still to minimize the total supply chain costs. The difference between the modes is in the interpretation of nondelivery cost rates. An appropriate mode needs to be selected depending on your desired business objectives, as follows:

- **Profit maximization**

  As the name suggests, in this mode the objective of the optimizer is to maximize the overall profit. The profit here is the difference between the total revenue and the total costs.

  The total revenue can be thought of as a summation of the revenue of all the products that can be sold in the market. The revenue is calculated by multiplying the products sold by the nondelivery cost rate. The nondelivery cost rate typically is the revenue lost due to not fulfilling the unit customer demand and is typically modeled as the selling price plus intangible costs for, say, damage to a brand's image due to lost sales.

  The total cost can be thought of as a summation of the costs incurred in the supply chain for all the products that can be sold in the market. The typical costs are production costs, transportation costs, procurement costs, inventory target violation costs, inventory holding costs, and so on.

  Note

  Gross profit is the total of all delivered customer products and location products, multiplied by the non-delivery cost rate that has been defined for these customer-products and location-products, minus all the costs incurred, such as production costs, storage costs, transportation costs, procurement costs, and so on.

  In this mode, demand is fulfilled/delivered for only those products that are profitable. The customer demand for unprofitable products is not fulfilled. This means that if the total cost of a product is higher than the selling price or non-delivery cost rate, then the optimizer plans not to manufacture and transport this product. In addition, because the objective of this mode is to maximize profit, in a scenario in which there's a hard constraint, such as a capacity constraint on a resource, the optimizer chooses to manufacture only the products that result in maximum profit.

- **Delivery maximization**

  The objective of the optimizer in this mode is to maximize customer and independent demand fulfillment for all products, without taking profitability into consideration. Alternatively, the goal of this mode can also be thought of as maximizing revenue. The non-delivery rate is increased to a very high value by the optimizer provisionally so that all products are profitable. In this case, 100% of customer demand is fulfilled unless there is a limiting constraint—for example, insufficient resource capacity, raw material shortage, or lead time.

Which optimization mode to use depends on the business strategy. If the goal of the business is to optimize profits by balancing demand and supply within current constraints and capacities, then profit maximization would be the appropriate choice. However, if a business is new and the goal is to gain market share and reputation at the detriment of profits, then the delivery maximization mode would be appropriate.

5.3   Optimization Constraints

The optimizer generates a cost-optimized constrained supply plan subject to a set of constraints. There are three categories of constraints. In this section, we'll review the different types of constraints.

5.3.1   Hard Constraints

The following constraints must be adhered to or satisfied; otherwise, a solution isn't possible, meaning the optimizer is unable to generate a supply plan:

- **Available or finite capacities of production resources**
  Production resources can be modeled as finite or infinite in the time series-based supply optimizer. The CONSTRAINTTYPE master data attribute on location-resource master data is used to specify whether a production resource is finite (constraint type F) or infinite (blank). This attribute is only relevant for the time series-based supply planning optimizer. The time series-based supply planning heuristic assumes that all resource capacities are infinite.

  If a production resource is modeled as infinite, then the optimizer ignores it.

- **Non-negative projected inventory**
  Projected inventory at end of each period must be greater than or equal to zero.

- **Lead time**
  The lead times for customer source of supply, location source of supply, and production source of supply must be respected.

- **Minimum lot size, rounding value, and maximum lot size**
  The minimum lot size, rounding value, and maximum lot size must be specified for the location source of supply and production source of supply. The rounding or incremental value for customer source of supply are the hard constraints.

- **External source of supply**
  If the boundary of the supply chain network doesn't have an unspecified rule (U-rule) specified, then the optimizer won't be able to get supply to fulfill downstream demand.
- **Maximum key figures**
  The maximum key figures—for example, maximum transport, maximum constrained demand, maximum production receipts, and maximum external receipts—are modeled as hard constraints, except for maximum inventory, which is modeled as a soft constraint.

5.3.2 Pseudo-Hard Constraints

These are constraints for which very high penalty costs are incurred if they are not adhered to. The time series-based optimizer will always try not to violate pseudo-hard constraints to generate a supply plan. However, in certain cases the optimizer may violate the pseudo-hard constraints to compute a supply plan, and the optimizer log will show such violations. These constraints are as follows:

- **Available or finite capacities of storage resources**
  Very high initial inventories can result in exceeding available capacity for storage resources and causing longer run times.
- **Manual adjustments**
  A planner can make manual adjustments via adjusted key figures. Adjusted key figures allow planners to interactively override the output of the computed plan.
- **Minimum key figures**
  The minimum key figures allow the optimizer to consider the supply plan from an external planning or execution system as a lower bound. This is enforced via a pseudo-hard constraint.

5.3.3 Soft Constraints

These are constraints that should be satisfied and are considered in the objective function. Any violations are penalized by the optimizer. Time series-based supply planning currently offers two types of soft constraints, as follows:

1. **Variable cost rates**
   - Variable or cost rates for customer and location transports, production, external receipts

- Nondelivery cost rates for customer demands
- Inventory holding cost rate, inventory target violation cost rate
- Maximum inventory violation cost rate, minimum capacity usage violation cost rate

2. **Fixed costs**
Fixed costs for transports, production, and external receipts

5.4   Financial Modeling of the Supply Chain

As explained in previous sections, the goal of the time series-based optimizer is to minimize the total costs of the supply chain. This goal is achieved by minimizing the financials aspects of the supply chain specified in the form of fixed and variable costs modeled as soft constraints in the objective function. These fixed and variable costs enable the supply planner to model the business priorities that should be considered by the optimizer to generate a feasible supply plan.

In this section, we'll explain the different financial key figures considered as inputs during optimization. In addition, we'll also explain the settings in the optimizer profile.

5.4.1   Financial or Cost Key Figures

The financial key figures in this section represent costs defined in the supply chain network, such as nondelivery costs, transportation costs, inventory holding costs, production costs, raw material procurement costs, and so on. These costs act as a lever to steer the optimizer to compute a supply plan as per desired business objectives.

Most cost or financial key figures are rates or variable costs, meaning that they're defined per unit of quantity and time period. The optimizer computes the total cost for each of these figures by multiplying the quantity (such as a transport quantity or inventory quantity) by the appropriate cost rate key figure.

In addition to cost rates, there are fixed costs, which are incurred if the quantity in each time period is greater than zero. For example, if the transport quantity is greater than zero, fixed transportation costs are incurred. Fixed costs are independent of the quantity in the time period.

> **Note**
> These key figures are ignored by the time series-based supply planning heuristic.

The key figures explained in this section all refer to a cost type, which may include various "real" costs. For instance, the production cost rate key figure should include all costs that are incurred by a production process and that are proportional to the production quantity.

One of the key decisions that needs to be made during implementation of the time series-based optimizer is to determine for which cost key figure types real costs will be used. The use of costs does make sense for certain key figures, such as nondelivery cost rates or production cost rates. However, for other key figures, such as fixed production costs, you don't need to include real costs. The intention of having nonzero costs in fixed production key figures is to prevent the optimizer from planning production in every period. Nonzero values for fixed production costs incentivize the optimizer to group production and not follow a lot-for-lot manufacturing strategy.

Similarly, you could specify that the fixed production costs for all periods are zero but that the inventory holding cost rate key figure has a value greater than zero. In this case, the optimizer is likely to follow a lot-for-lot strategy so that the demand is satisfied (produced) in all periods, but, as a rule, nothing is added to stock to fulfill the demand of subsequent periods (although there may still be other reasons for which the optimizer builds up stock).

The cost key figures, like other time series-based supply planning figures, must have predefined technical names and must be at specific planning levels. You also can use the delivered SAP4 sample model as a reference to view the various cost key figures.

Demand-Related Cost Key Figures

The following are demand-related input cost key figures. Time series supply planning lets you specify demand at the customer-product and/or location-product levels, as follows:

- **Nondelivery cost rate for customer demand** (NONDELIVERYCOSTRATE)
  This input cost key figure contains the lost revenue per unit of a product for the customer. In addition to the lost revenue, you can also model additional intangible costs resulting from image loss due to not fulfilling customer demand. Its planning level is period-product-customer.

This key figure defines the costs per unit of a customer demand quantity per period that isn't met by the supply plan stored in the total customer receipt key figure.

The cost incurred is proportional to the difference between consensus demand and total customer receipt. As an example, imagine the nondelivery cost rate for Product A sold to all customers is maintained as USD 10 in each time period. If the consensus or customer demand in time period N is 100 and the receipt computed is 90, then the nondelivery cost is *(100 – 90) × 10 USD per Unit = 100 USD*.

- **Nondelivery cost rate for independent demand** (INDEPDEMANDNONDELIVERYCOSTRATE)
This input key figure is relevant only when additional demand for a location-product is defined in the independent demand key figure. The optimizer uses the independent demand nondelivery cost rate key figure to calculate penalty costs for nondelivered quantities (by multiplying the value for the key figure by the nondelivered quantity). Its planning level is period-product-location.

Transportation-Related Cost Key Figures

The following input key figures are arc-related key figures: they are defined on the arc between two nodes of the supply chain network. It can be between two location nodes or between a location node and customer node.

- **Customer transportation cost rate** (CUSTOMERTRANSPORTATIONCOSTRATE)
This key figure contains the cost per unit per period to transport a product from a location node to customer node. The cost is calculated by multiplying the constrained demand quantity by the customer transportation cost rate in that period. Its planning level is period-product-location-customer.

- **Fixed customer transportation cost** (FIXEDCUSTOMERTRANSPORTATIONCOST)
This input cost key figure contains the fixed cost for each time period in which the customer receipts are greater than zero. Its planning level is period-product-location-customer.

- **Transportation cost rate** (TRANSPORTATIONCOSTRATE)
This key figure contains the cost per unit per period to transport a product from a ship-from location node to a ship-to location node. The cost is calculated by multiplying the transport supply quantity by the customer transportation cost rate in that period. Its planning level is period-product-ship-from location-ship-to location.

- **Fixed transportation cost** (FIXEDTRANSPORTATIONCOST)
  This input cost key figure contains fixed costs for each time period in which the transport receipts are greater than zero. Its planning level is period-product-ship-from location-ship-to location.

Inventory-Related Cost Key Figures

The inventory-related key figures are defined at the location-product level. Inventory costs are associated with holding inventory of products in stock at various locations throughout the supply chain, as follows:

- **Inventory target violation cost rate** (INVENTORYTARGETVIOLATIONCOSTRATE)
  This input cost key figure represents the costs per unit of product for which the projected stock is below the specified inventory target in a time period. The costs for this key figure are generally penalty costs. For example, let's examine the information from Table 5.1 for a location-product.

Key Figure	Period 1	Period 2	Period 3	Period 4
Inventory target	10	10	10	10
Inventory target violation cost rate (USD)	5	5	5	5
Projected stock	8	10	0	6
Inventory target violation cost (USD)	10	0	50	20

Table 5.1 Inventory Target Violation Cost Rate Example

The inventory target violation cost is calculated as follows: $(10-8) \times 5 + (10-10) \times 5 + (10-0) \times 5 + (10-6) \times 5 = 80$.

Its planning level is period-product-location.

- **Inventory holding cost rate** (INVENTORYHOLDINGCOSTRATE)
  This input cost key figure represents the cost for holding a unit of product in stock for a time period. Typically, this key figure contains storage costs and the cost of capital. The cost of capital is the opportunity cost of holding inventory in stock. It signifies the cost of foregone returns from investment that could have been earned, had capital not been tied up in holding inventory. Its planning level is period-product-location.

The total cost of keeping the products in stock is calculated by multiplying the projected stock key figure for each period by the inventory holding cost rate key figure for each period (see Table 5.2).

Key Figure	Period 1	Period 2	Period 3	Period 4
Inventory holding cost rate (USD)	5	5	5	5
Projected stock	8	10	0	6
Inventory holding cost (USD)	40	50	0	30

Table 5.2 Inventory Holding Cost Rate Example

External Procurement-Related Cost Key Figures

In time series-based supply planning, the external receipts are used to model the procurement of raw materials from an external vendor. The external receipts also can be used for other receipts that aren't specified further via U-rules. The relevant key figures are as follows:

- **External receipt cost rate** (EXTERNALRECEIPTCOSTRATE)
  This input cost key figure defines the cost per product unit and period for external receipts for a location-product. This can be the purchase price of raw material if procured from an external vendor. Its planning level is period-product-location.

- **Fixed cost for external receipts** (FIXEDEXTERNALRECEIPTCOST)
  This input key figure models a fixed cost for each period in which external receipts for a location product are not zero. Its planning level is period-product-location.

5.4.2 Optimizer Parameters

When you configure the S&OP supply planning operator profile for algorithm type **Optimizer**, you need to set optimizer parameters. The settings in the **Optimizer Parameters** section influence the goal of the optimization and set the parameters for optimization runs. In this section, we'll provide an explanation for the settings in each optimizer parameter group.

General

In this section, you can choose the optimization mode. As explained in Section 5.2, profit maximization and delivery maximization are the two available modes. **Profit Maximization Mode** is selected by default (see Figure 5.1).

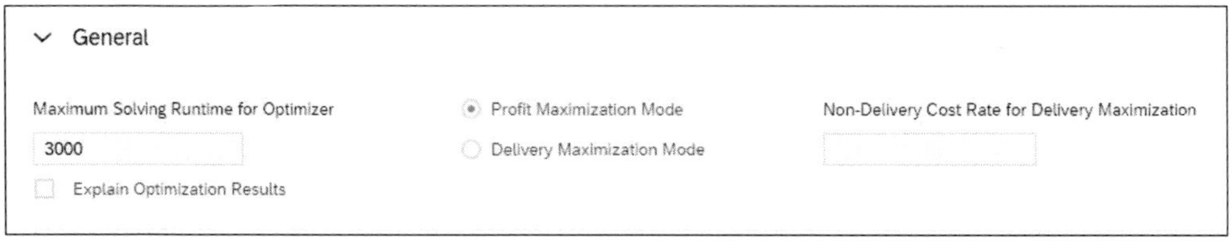

Figure 5.1 General Settings for Optimizer Parameters

You can also enter a value for **Maximum Solving Runtime for Optimizer** (specified in seconds). The default runtime value is 3000 seconds. This setting only limits the MILP solver's internal runtime; it doesn't include the preprocessing and postprocessing steps. If you don't specify a maximum runtime, the optimizer provides a mathematically proven, optimal solution that can take from several minutes to hours, especially if discrete decisions are involved.

If you select **Delivery Maximization Mode**, the cost of not satisfying demands is changed as follows during optimization:

- If you enter a value in the **Non-Delivery Cost Rate for Delivery Maximization** field, the optimizer uses this value as the cost of nondelivery for all demands.
- If you don't enter a value, the optimizer calculates a suitably high cost of nondelivery. This value is set as the cost of nondelivery for all demands. All other costs remain unchanged.

In addition, there is also an **Explain Optimization Results** checkbox in this area. Sometimes, it's difficult to understand why a certain requirement wasn't fulfilled by optimization. When you run the time series-based supply planning optimizer with this checkbox selected, the optimizer provides reasons for unfulfilled requirements. We'll go into more detail on this topic in a later section in this chapter.

Discretization

In this section of the optimizer parameters, you can specify the discrete horizon for areas that require discrete decisions (see Figure 5.2).

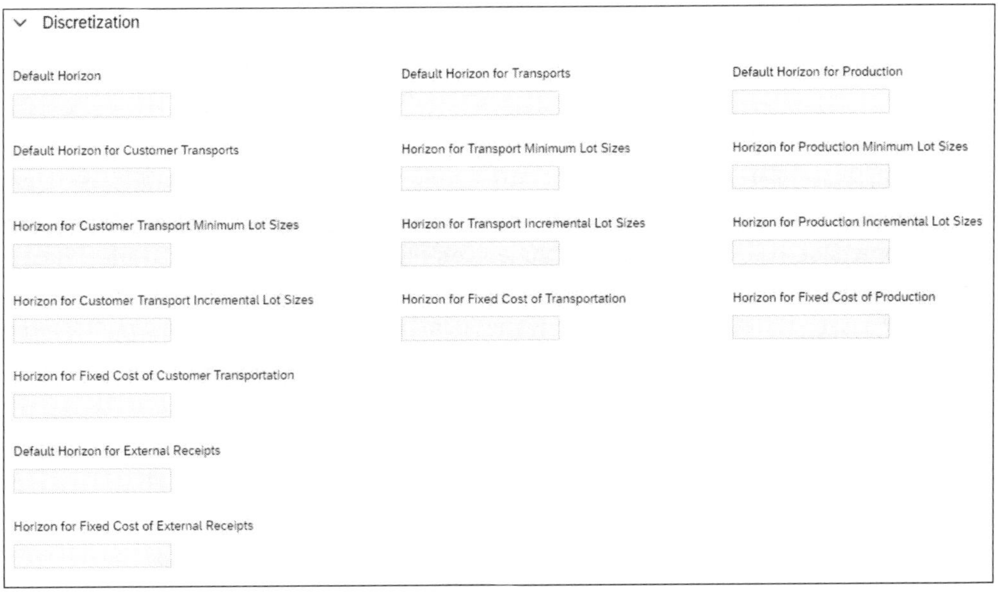

Figure 5.2 Discretization Settings for Optimizer Parameters

There are certain decisions in supply planning that aren't continuous and are discrete/binary in nature. Currently, there are three features that require discrete decisions:

1. Minimum lot sizes for customer transport, location transport, and production
2. Incremental lot sizes for customer transport, location transport, and production
3. Fixed costs for customer transport, location transport, and external receipt

Discrete variables have a big impact on the optimization solver's runtime, so we recommend minimizing their use as much as possible. By setting the **Default Horizon** in the **Discretization** area, it's possible to limit these binary decisions to the first periods in the planning horizon.

If no default value is provided in this section, then the discretization decisions are considered for the entire planning horizon. You can limit the horizon by entering a value in **Default Horizon**. The default horizon applies to all discrete decision areas unless a specific horizon for that area is entered.

You can also provide a default horizon for an area—for example, **Default Horizon for Customer Transports**, **Transports**, **Production**, and **External Receipts**. This then applies to the entire area unless a more specific horizon has been entered for that area—for example, a horizon for fixed costs for transportation.

Fair-Share Distribution

Fair-share distribution allows the time series optimizer to distribute constrained supply in a fair-share manner, such as when the quantity requested by different customers or locations cannot be fulfilled completely. Distribution is calculated based on segmented costs instead of normal cost rates. In the fair-share distribution section (see Figure 5.3), you can specify the **Segments** or tiers for **Non-Delivery**, **Inventory Target**, **Late Delivery**, and **Inventory Holding**.

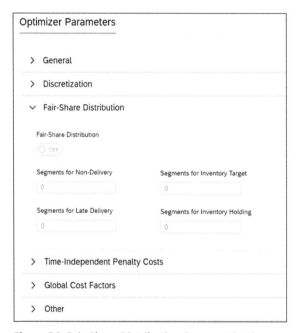

Figure 5.3 Fair-Share Distribution Segment Settings

Fair-share distribution can be used for the following planning features:

- Nondelivery
- Late delivery
- Inventory target
- Inventory holding

More than one segment must be specified to enable this feature. At a maximum, 10 segments are supported. This feature is covered in more detail in Section 5.5.3.

Time-Independent Penalty Costs

This section of the optimizer parameters lets you specify if you want to use time-independent penalty costs (see Figure 5.4).

Figure 5.4 Optimizer Settings for Time-Independent Penalty Costs

By enabling these time-independent penalty costs, the optimizer will set the optimizer costs to values specified in this section. The entered cost value applies to all planning combinations. For example, the value of **Penalty Cost Rate for Non-Delivery** will apply to all customer and independent demands. Time-independent penalty costs let you use the optimizer without defining the cost key figures, especially for testing purposes.

Global Cost Factors

This section of the optimizer parameters is used to specify the global cost factors (see Figure 5.5).

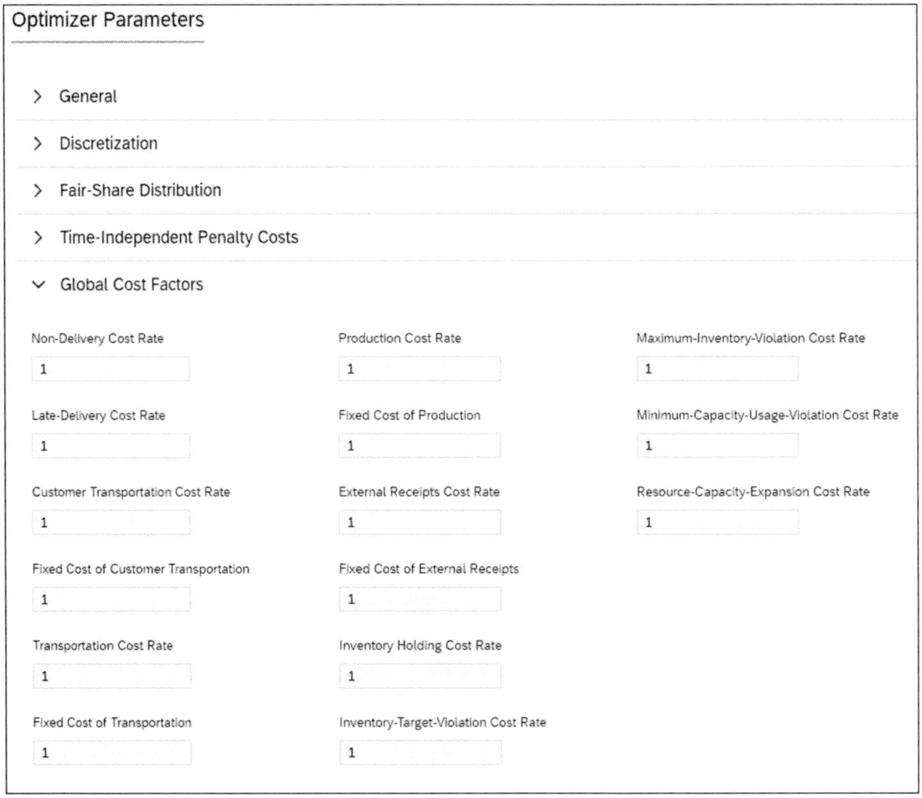

Optimizer Parameters

> General

> Discretization

> Fair-Share Distribution

> Time-Independent Penalty Costs

∨ Global Cost Factors

Non-Delivery Cost Rate	Production Cost Rate	Maximum-Inventory-Violation Cost Rate
1	1	1

Late-Delivery Cost Rate	Fixed Cost of Production	Minimum-Capacity-Usage-Violation Cost Rate
1	1	1

Customer Transportation Cost Rate	External Receipts Cost Rate	Resource-Capacity-Expansion Cost Rate
1	1	1

Fixed Cost of Customer Transportation	Fixed Cost of External Receipts	
1	1	

Transportation Cost Rate	Inventory Holding Cost Rate	
1	1	

Fixed Cost of Transportation	Inventory-Target-Violation Cost Rate	
1	1	

Figure 5.5 Optimizer Global Cost Factors

Global cost factors are used to increase or decrease the impact of certain cost key figures. The cost factor value entered for a specific cost acts as multiplying factor for the corresponding optimizer costs. A cost factor value of 0 allows the optimizer to completely disregard certain costs from its objective function. By assigning a very small value such as 0.001 to the external receipts cost rate, you can determine if external receipt costs are impacting the demand fulfillment rate.

The default value for all cost factors is 1.

Other

This section (see Figure 5.6) lets you specify whether minimum aggregated constraints can be violated. This means they are considered as pseudo-hard constraints by the optimizer.

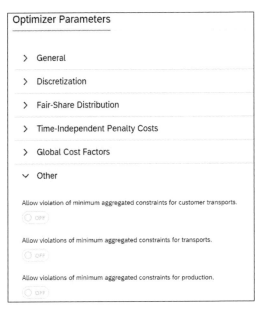

Figure 5.6 Other Optimizer Parameters

5.5   Advanced Optimizer Features

There are industry-specific planning requirements that require advance capability to model in a planning application. In this section, we'll cover features for the time series-based optimizer that allow you to model such advanced business requirements.

5.5.1   Late-Demand Fulfillment

The default behavior of the time series-based optimizer is to fulfill the customer demand and independent demand in the requested time period. This means the optimizer will try to generate a supply plan so that customer receipts and independent supply can fulfill consensus/customer demand and independent demand in the requested time period. If the demand can't be satisfied in the requested time period, it isn't carried over to the next time period and is deemed a lost sale.

However, in certain situations or industries, it's possible to carry over the unfulfilled demand and fulfill it in a later time period.

The time series-based optimizer enables this feature by modeling based on additional optimizer cost input key figures. This feature is supported for both customer and independent demand.

Input Key Figures

As the names suggest, the following input key figures are used by the optimization engine as input:

- **Maximum late-delivery periods for customer demand** (CONSDEMLATEDELIVMAX)
  This cost key figure represents the maximum number of time periods that a customer demand, or part of a customer demand, can be delivered late. If a demand can't be delivered within the maximum number of time periods, it's considered lost demand. Its planning level is period-product-customer.

- **Maximum late-delivery periods for independent demand** (INDEPDEMLATEDELIVMAX)
  This cost key figure represents the maximum number of time periods that an independent demand, or part of an independent demand, can be delivered late. If a demand can't be delivered within the maximum number of time periods, it's considered lost demand. Its planning level is period-product-location.

- **Late-delivery cost rate for customer demand** (CONSDEMLATEDELIVCOSTRATE)
  This key figure represents the cost incurred for a unit of consensus demand fulfilled late per time period. Its planning level is period-product-customer.

- **Late-delivery cost rate for independent demand** (INDEPDEMLATEDELIVCOSTRATE)
  This key figure represents the cost incurred for a unit of independent demand fulfilled late per time period. Its planning level is period-product-location.

Output Key Figures

The following key figures carry the output planning results after the optimization planning run:

- **Total customer demand delivered** (CONSDEMDELIVERED)
  This key figure contains the total customer demand satisfied for a time period, either on time or in a later period. Its planning level is period-product-customer.

- **Total independent demand delivered** (INDEPENDENTDEMANDSUPPLY)
  This key figure contains the total independent demand satisfied for a time period, either on time or in a later period. Its planning level is period-product-location.

- **Customer demand delivered late** (CONSDEMDELIVEREDLATE)
  This key figure contains customer demand for a period that is delivered late. Its planning level is period-product-customer.

- **Independent demand delivered late** (INDEPDEMDELIVEREDLATE)
  This key figure contains independent demand for a period that is delivered late. Its planning level is period-product-location.

- **Average delivery delay of customer demand** (CONSDEMDELIVEREDLATEAVG)
  This key figure contains the average delay in fulfilling customer demand. Its planning level is period-product-customer.

- **Average delivery delay of independent demand** (INDEPDEMDELIVEREDLATEAVG)
  This key figure contains the average delay in fulfilling customer demand. Its planning level is period-product-location.

5.5.2 Minimum Resource Consumption

In certain businesses or industries, it's required to have production resources utilized above a certain minimum threshold even if there isn't sufficient customer or independent demand. This may be due to financial reasons such as return on assets or other business reasons.

The time series-based optimizer allows minimum consumption for a production resource so that production receipts generated can fulfill the specified minimum consumption even if production receipts are more than the requested demands. This feature is only applicable to production resources. The following input key figures need to be specified:

- **Minimum capacity usage** (MINCAPAUSAGE)
  This key figure specifies the minimum consumption value for a resource in each period. This value can be violated and will incur a penalty cost. Its planning level is period-resource-location.

- **Minimum capacity usage violation cost rate** (MINCAPAUSAGEVIOLATIONCOSTRATE)
  This key figure specifies the penalty cost rate for violating the specified minimum resource consumption. You must specify a value to make sure that minimum resource consumption works. In addition, you also need to ensure that this value

is higher than the production cost rate for this resource; otherwise, the optimizer will violate the minimum capacity usage threshold instead, because the violation cost rate is cheaper. Its planning level is period-resource-location.

Using this feature, the optimizer may produce more than required to fulfill customer or independent demands. In this case, depending upon the costs specified for transports, inventory holding, and/or production, the optimizer may hold inventory in projected stock at a manufacturing location, transport it to downstream locations, or use it in another production process.

5.5.3   Fair-Share Distribution

Fair-share distribution allows the time series–optimizer to distribute constrained supply in a fair-share manner when the quantities requested by different customers or locations can't be fulfilled completely. Distribution is calculated based on segmented costs instead of normal cost rates.

You can set a maximum of 10 segments. A minimum of two segments are required to activate fair-share distribution. The segments are specified in the optimizer profile.

Fair-share distribution can be used for the following planning features:

- **Nondelivery**
  When there is insufficient supply to fulfill multiple demands for the same product, the optimizer distributes the available quantity equally relative to the requested quantity. This is supported for customer demand and independent demand.

  Let's walk through an example. Assume the requested demand quantity for Product X for Customer A and Customer B is 100 each, with the same nondelivery cost rate, and the available supply is 100. In this case, the optimizer will decide to fulfill demand for either Customer A or Customer B because from its perspective both incur the same nondelivery penalty costs. However, with fair-share distribution and four segments defined, the optimizer groups the requested quantity for each demand in four equal, fair-share segments of 25. Also, additional increasing linear costs are added for each segment, which ensures that the available quantities will be split into tiers. This results in a fair-share distribution with 50 units for each customer demand as the violation costs in the tiers are increasing.

- **Late delivery**
  Fair share for late delivery ensures that the portion of demand for a product with multiple demands that will be delivered on time is shared fairly. The optimizer

doesn't perform fair-share distribution for the quantity that will be delivered late. This can also be interpreted as on-time delivery fair share.

- **Inventory target**
Fair share for inventory targets is similar to nondelivery fair share. The inventory targets for a product in this case are distributed in a fair-share manner between different locations when their inventory targets can't be met with the available quantity. The fair-share steps are relative to the inventory target at each location.

- **Inventory holding**
Fair share for inventory holding lets you distribute stock between different locations. Maximum inventory must be set to be able to use fair share for inventory holding. The maximum inventory provides the upper threshold for fair-sharing. If there's an inventory target set as well, it will act as a lower point of reference.

5.5.4   Aggregate Constraints

All the constraints (soft, pseudo-hard, and hard) described in this chapter until now were defined at the lowest level—that is, at the product, location, customer, or source ID attribute level. However, aggregate constraints, as the name suggests, enable you to model optimizer constraints at an aggregate level—that is, any aggregation level of product, customer, location, or source ID.

For example, you can specify the following:

- Minimum constrained demand (transports) that needs to be satisfied for the combination of product brand and customer region
- Maximum production allowed for resource family and product group at a manufacturing location

Aggregate constraints are modeled as hard constraints by default. This behavior can be changed to model pseudo-hard constraints in the optimizer profile for minimum aggregated constraint key figures.

SAP Integrated Business Planning for response and supply or for sales and operations supports the following aggregated constraint key figures, which are delivered as part of the SAP4 planning area:

- MINAGGDEMAND (minimum aggregate constrained demand)
- MAXAGGDEMAND (maximum aggregate constrained demand)
- MINAGGDEMANDDS (minimum aggregate constrained demand downstream)

- MAXAGGDEMANDDS (maximum aggregate constrained demand downstream)
- MINAGGPRODUCTION (minimum aggregate production)
- MAXAGGPRODUCTION (maximum aggregate production)
- MINAGGTRANSPORT (minimum aggregate transport)
- MAXAGGTRANSPORT (maximum aggregate transport)
- MINAGGTRANSPORTDS (minimum aggregate transport downstream)
- MAXAGGTRANSPORTDS (maximum aggregate transport downstream)

Aggregate constraint key figures are only stored at the aggregate level at which the values are saved in the Excel planning view; there is no disaggregation. They can also be viewed in the Excel planning view at the exact same level at which they were stored. Aggregate constraints can be defined on multiple levels in parallel for the same key figure.

5.5.5   Multiple Demand Category

Sometimes, you'll need to categorize and prioritize one demand over another—for example, to prioritize the base forecast over promotional forecast or prioritize sales orders over the forecast.

The demand category feature lets the optimizer define a grouping that can be used to prioritize different forecast types. The prioritization is set based on nondelivery costs. This feature is only supported for consensus demand, which is at the customer-product level.

To enable this feature, a new master data type to define demand categories must be created (see Table 5.3), and the base-planning level of consensus demand needs to be extended from customer-product to customer-product-category. In addition, appropriate nondelivery costs must be specified to prioritize demand categories. Currently, you can define up to five demand categories; the category ID must be of the integer data type.

CATID(X)	CATDESCR
1	Base forecast
2	Promotional forecast

Table 5.3 Demand Category Master Data

5.5.6   Product Substitution

Product substitution functionality is applicable when a company offers alternative products that have similar characteristics as the substitutable product and are equivalent or interchangeable from a customer's perspective. These alternative products can satisfy the customer demand for substitutable products. For example, if Product A (substitutable) has alternative products Product B and Product C, then demand for Product A can be satisfied with either Product B or Product C.

This functionality is only applicable for products directly sold to customers—that is, products that have a customer sourcing rule defined. The alternative products can be delivered from location other than that for the substitutable product and can have different nondelivery costs, customer transportation costs, inventory target violation costs, inventory holding costs, and production costs defined. The time series optimizer can decide to fulfill the demand for a substitutable product fully or partially using one or more alternative products if the supplying location of the substitutable product has resource constraints or if it's just cost-optimal to use alternative products.

A product substitution matrix needs to be defined via master data table PRODUCTSUB-STITUTION (see Table 5.4). Here PRDID is the substitutable product and SPRDID is the substitution product.

PRDID (X) (Main Product)	SPRDID (X) (Substitution Product)
Product A	Product B
Product A	Product C

Table 5.4 Product Substitution Master Data

In addition to the entries in Table 5.4, you also need to define the customer sourcing rules for Product B and Product C. Otherwise, the optimizer can't decide to fulfill demand for Product A via alternative products.

> **Note**
>
> Product substitution is relevant only for the time series-based supply planning optimizer and not for the time series-based supply planning heuristic, which always sources customer demands per the quotas defined in the customer sources of supply.

5.5.7   Subnetworks

As described in previous chapters, a subnetwork is a portion of the entire supply chain network for which you want to plan a separate planning run (e.g., all location products in a region or product brand). Subnetworks are typically used for collaboration between several planners who are responsible for a part of a supply chain, like a region or product group.

The following key figures are relevant for planning subnetworks with the time series-based supply planning optimizer:

- **Inter subnetwork nondelivery cost rate** (IPUNONDELIVERYCOSTRATE)
  This key figure is relevant for the upstream subnetwork and specifies the internal sales price when goods are sold to the downstream subnetwork. The value specified is the receipt date at the ship-to location (i.e., the time period during which the products arrive at the ship-to location). The subnetwork nondelivery costs are calculated per period by multiplying the value you define by the number of goods that weren't delivered—that is, by the difference between the outbound location demand and receipts at the receiving location. Its planning level is period-product-ship-to location.

- **Intersubnetwork receipts cost rate** (IPURECEIPTCOSTRATE)
  Use this optimizer input key figure to specify the internal unit procurement cost for goods (e.g., semifinished products) procured from an upstream subnetwork. The value specified is the receipt date at the receiving location (i.e., the period during which the products arrive at the location). Its planning level is period-product-location.

  The subnetwork external receipt costs are calculated per period by multiplying the intersubnetwork external receipt cost rate by the transport receipts period by period.

- **Transport receipts ship-to** (TRANSPORTRECEIPTSHIPTO)
  This is an output key figure that contains the quantity transported from the ship-from location to the ship-to location in a time period. This is only used for subnetworks; this key figure contains the same values as the transport receipts key figure (base planning level product-location-ship-from location); the only difference is the structure of the key. Both key figures are based on delivery times at the ship-to location (because the transportation costs are calculated for the period in which the goods arrive at the ship-to location). Its planning level is period-product-location-ship-to location.

The transportation costs are calculated by multiplying the value of this key figure by the value of the transportation cost rate key figure. The optimizer calculates transportation costs based on this logic when calculating a cost-optimal supply plan.

5.5.8   Optimizer Explanation

The time series-based optimizer is a MILP solver, and sometimes it isn't easy to understand why a certain requirement was fulfilled and another not. This can occur even for a simple supply chain network. Comprehending the results can be even more difficult for a complex supply chain network with various costs and constraints.

To support the planner, the time series optimizer provides an explanation mode, which helps explain the outcome of optimizer runs by providing reasons for unfulfilled requirements.

After running the time series-based supply planning optimizer, you can display explanations for the following types of results:

- Unsatisfied demands (including consensus and independent demands)
- Missed inventory targets
- Missed adjusted values

The possible explanations include the following types:

- Cost-related reasons such as low nondelivery cost rates. Due to these reasons, the optimizer may not find it profitable to fulfill the requirements.
- Resource-related reasons such as missing capacity. The explanation log shows the current values and the amount the capacity needs to be increased for the requirements to be fulfilled.
- Due to lead time reasons—either transport or production—it may not be possible to fulfill the requirements because the product needs to have been sourced in the past.
- If there are adjusted values, they may impede the optimizer from fulfilling requirements.
- Missing sources of supply can be an issue when there are customer-products that don't have customer source or a location source or don't have a production source defined.

- Maximum lot sizes or maximum key figures for customer receipts, transport receipts, production receipts, or external receipts can restrict the fulfillment of the requirements. The explanation log displays their current values and by how much they need to be increased for the requirements to be fulfilled.

- Aggregated constraints might be defined that impede the fulfillment of requirements. Because aggregated constraints aren't referenced directly, only the item of the aggregated constraint is shown as an example.

The explanation function must be enabled in the profile of the time series-based supply planning optimizer. Explanation mode is only available in batch or background mode. In Excel, when you choose an operator with explanation mode, an additional tab appears in which you can choose the requirements to be explained (see Figure 5.7). You also can select the products/locations/customers for which you want to get an explanation and the explanation horizon.

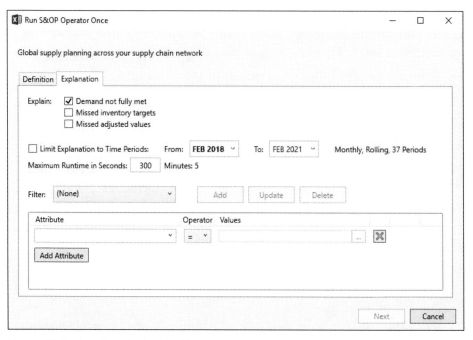

Figure 5.7 Explanation Mode Selection

You can see the detailed optimizer explanation log of the various reasons for not fulfilling the demand or missing inventory targets or missed adjusted values in a separate sheet in the business log (see Figure 5.8).

Issue	Period	Product ID	Custome	L	Reason
Customer demand can't be fully satisfied (Requested amount: 100.0, Fulfilled amount: 0.0, Explair	Sep-17	PRODUCT5	105		Non-delivery cost rate of consensus demand is too low.
Customer demand can't be fully satisfied (Requested amount: 100.0, Fulfilled amount: 0.0, Explair	Sep-17	PRODUCT5	105		Resource Capacity of 0.000000 too low. Increase resource capacity at least by 50.000000.
Customer demand can't be fully satisfied (Requested amount: 100.0, Fulfilled amount: 0.0, Explair	Sep-17	PRODUCT5	105		Resource Capacity of 0.000000 too low. Increase resource capacity at least by 50.000000.
Customer demand can't be fully satisfied (Requested amount: 100.0, Fulfilled amount: 0.0, Explair	Oct-17	PRODUCT5	105		Non-delivery cost rate of consensus demand is too low.
Customer demand can't be fully satisfied (Requested amount: 100.0, Fulfilled amount: 0.0, Explair	Oct-17	PRODUCT5	105		Resource Capacity of 0.000000 too low. Increase resource capacity at least by 50.000000.
Customer demand can't be fully satisfied (Requested amount: 100.0, Fulfilled amount: 0.0, Explair	Oct-17	PRODUCT5	105		Resource Capacity of 0.000000 too low. Increase resource capacity at least by 50.000000.

Figure 5.8 Issue Explanation in Business Log

5.6 Summary

In this chapter, we covered the details of the time series-based optimizer and how it allows planners to build a feasible production, distribution, and procurement plan. We explained the different optimization modes, various types of constraints, the financial modeling of the supply chain via penalty cost key figures, and the optimizer parameters influencing the results of the optimizer. We also covered the more advanced optimizer features such as late demand fulfillment, minimum capacity utilization, fair-share distribution, and so on in a business context. Finally, we also went over the explanation mode, which helps explain the optimizer results.

Chapter 6
Consolidation

In this chapter, we'll discuss consolidation in SAP IBP. The unified planning process is executed in SAP IBP when the constrained supply plan from S&OP is consolidated for executive review; the agreed-upon plan is then output to the operational/execution processes.

After the constrained supply plans are created and reviewed for the unconstrained demand, the last two phases of the S&OP process cover profitably aligning demand and supply and consolidation into a single, agreed-upon tactical plan, which is an input to other operational and execution processes. In the integrated reconciliation phase of S&OP, we evaluate alternative plans and recommend a profitable plan for the executive meeting, a plan which balances supply and demand. In the executive review phase, we decide on a balanced plan that profitably matches supply and demand over the mid- to long-term horizon.

In this chapter, we'll cover how the integrated reconciliation and executive review phases of S&OP are executed in detail. We'll also cover how the agreed-upon constrained tactical plan is operationalized in SAP IBP.

6.1 Consolidation at a Glance

Demand and supply review cycles of S&OP are focused on the unconstrained forecast generation and then constraining the demand while considering the supply element. In the integrated reconciliation and executive review phase, holistic consolidation is performed to analyze the end-to-end demand and supply scenarios with cross-team work and to validate and approve the constrained plan.

Consolidation in the integrated reconciliation and executive review phase allows the organization to review the input from various teams, like supply chain, finance, marketing, key accounts, and so on, and perform some financial analysis and demand-supply simulation to agree on the best, most suitable S&OP plan for the organization. Besides volume-based forecasts and supply plans, the valuations of the plans in terms of revenue, profit, price, and costs are incorporated to get full volume and value-based views across different planning scenarios. In this section, we'll cover an overview of consolidation in the integration reconciliation review and executive review and then discuss how the approved plan is operationalized.

6.1.1   Integrated Reconciliation Review

During the reconciliation review of the monthly cycle, the representatives from sales, finance, marketing, production, and demand planning discuss deviations between constrained demand and consensus demand, agree on executive proposals, and prepare a list of issues for escalation.

The integrated reconciliation review includes the following tasks:

- Collaboration across all stakeholders to select a balanced and profitable sales and operations plan
- Compare revenue and profit targets and compare supply chain costs
- Alternative scenario comparison and analysis
- KPI analysis and gap resolution
- What-if analysis and scenario planning

Subsequently, the executive management will make a decision on an executive proposal during the management business review.

6.1.2   Executive Review

During executive review or management business review, the executive management of the involved business units determines if the presented proposal aligns with the company's financial targets and key performance indicators. Management assesses and makes decisions on the presented list of escalated issues. This results in an approved, final consensus demand and supply plan that should ultimately drive revenue growth and increase market share, optimize product and customer profitability, minimize inventory costs, and overcome capacity constraints.

Thus, the end goal of the management business review process is to achieve executive agreement on a final consensus demand plan across functional business units.

Note

SAP Best Practices content contains information on how to run an integrated reconciliation review and executive review.

Typical charts that are evaluated in the management business review include constrained demand revenue versus AOP, comparing last year to current and future year quarter-by-quarter, as shown in Figure 6.1.

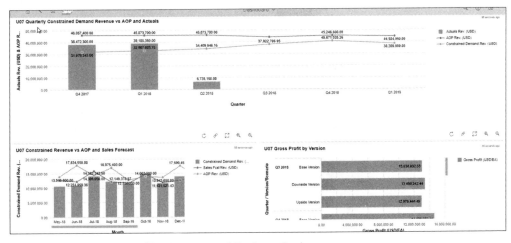

Figure 6.1 Charts Reviewed in Management Business Review

Other charts evaluated are comparisons of gross profit by different plan versions on a quarter-to-quarter basis, as shown in Figure 6.2.

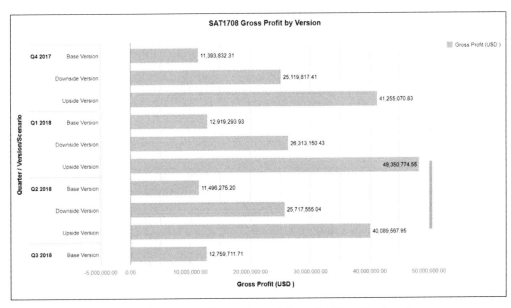

Figure 6.2 Review Quarter-by-Quarter Comparison of Gross Profit by Plan Versions

6.1.3   Operationalize the Approved Constrained Plan

Once the plan is finalized in the executive review meeting, it needs to become operational. Therefore, the constrained plan from S&OP needs to be sent to other operational processes and to SAP ERP or SAP S/4HANA for execution. The results from SAP Integrated Business Planning for sales and operations flow to other SAP IBP modules, like SAP Integrated Business Planning for demand, SAP Integrated Business Planning for response and supply, and so on. This is detailed in Section 6.3.

The integrated data model in SAP IBP allows for running the planning processes with a clear handover of process and data across different levels, different planning horizons, and different planning granularities using one underlying data model and an intuitive user interface, with no need for complex data transformations between planning modules. To get the full value of the digital supply chain, customers implement SAP Integrated Business Planning for sales and operations together with other application modules with specialized functions.

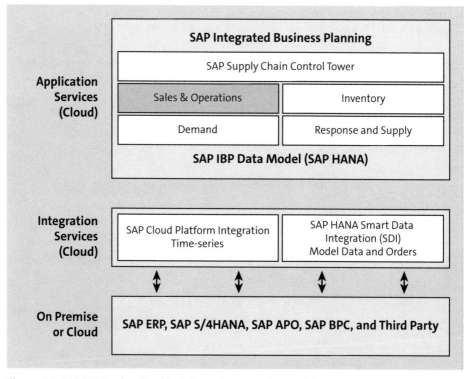

Figure 6.3 SAP IBP Application Modules and Integration Architecture

Figure 6.3 shows an SAP IBP system architecture with internal integrated processes across strategy, tactical, and operational areas supported by SAP Integrated Business Planning for sales and operations, SAP Integrated Business Planning for demand, SAP Integrated Business Planning for inventory, SAP Integrated Business Planning for response and supply, and SAP Supply Chain Control Tower, together with external executional processes and data in SAP S/4HANA or SAP ERP.

This connected and integrated planning process provides robust planning and end-to-end visibility on strategic, tactical, and operational levels. With closed-loop integration, the connected planning process helps you with the following actions:

- Make strategy actionable
- Integrate tactical planning and execution
- Drive visibility and agility
- Create a plan that is feasible and actionable
- Accelerate decision-making process
- Improve operational and financial KPIs

6.2 Financial Projections and Review

In the following sections, we'll go deeper into what financial information is modeled in SAP IBP, how the integrated reconciliation review phase is carried out, and finally how the executive review phase is executed.

6.2.1 Financial Projections of the Plan

Every stage of the S&OP process includes financial elements like revenue, margin, costs, and price calculations for the valuation of plans, in addition to the plan volumes. During the integrated reconciliation review phase, the consensus plan from the demand review phase and the constrained plan from the supply review phase are valuated and several scenarios and versions evaluated to make the best recommendation for the executive review meeting. SAP IBP provides several financial key figures out of the box to calculate the dollar values of key figures from their volumes.

During the integrated reconciliation phase, the finance managers work with the demand and supply planners to valuate the plan by calculating projected revenues, costs, and margins. Figure 6.4 shows an example of an Excel planning view created during the integrated reconciliation phase covering financial key figures.

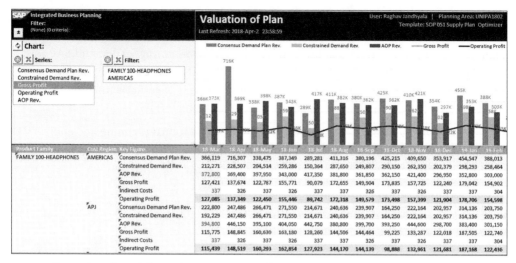

Figure 6.4 Financial Key Figures in SAP IBP for Revenue, Profit, Price, and Costs

If you're using a planning area initially copied from SAPIBP1, a few financial key figures are predelivered in the model. To create a planning view as in Figure 6.4, choose the following key figures:

- Consensus demand plan revenue
- Constrained demand plan revenue
- AOP revenue
- Gross profit
- Indirect costs
- Operating profit

You will also select a monthly time period for the next 18 months and planning levels viewed at product family and customer region levels.

The consensus demand revenue from the demand review phase is compared with constrained demand revenue of the supply phase along with the AOP revenue targets for the year.

When calculating the revenues, typically the planned price or average selling price of the product is taken into account. After the revenue key figures are calculated, these are netted with the costs to get to the gross profit. To calculate the overall gross costs, typically the constrained volumes are multiplied by the cost per unit key figure. Finally, operating profit is calculated as gross profit with deduction of indirect costs.

The financial key figures in the SAPIBP1 model are configured as follows:

- **Planned price**

  This is the planned price for a product customer combination that is typically loaded from SAP ERP or SAP S/4HANA or can be manually maintained in SAP IBP at a base planning level of week-product-customer-currency. This key figure is multiplied by volume key figures like sales forecast quantity, consensus demand quantity, and so on to get the revenue key figures. Figure 6.5 shows the planned price key figure as delivered in the standard model.

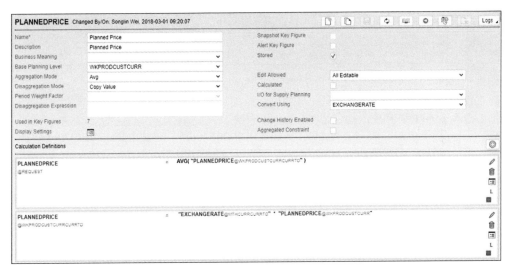

Figure 6.5 Planned Price Key Figure Calculation

- **Consensus and constrained demand revenue**

  These key figures are calculated in SAP IBP by multiplying their corresponding volume key figures by the planned price or custom price key figure maintained in the model. Figure 6.6 shows a configuration of the consensus demand revenue key figure, which is calculated as follows:

```
CONSENSUSDEMANDREV@WKPRODLOCCUSTCURR =
CONSENSUSDEMANDPLANQTY@WKPRODLOCCUST × PLANNEDPRICE@WKPRODCUSTCURR.
```

There is also a calculation considering the exchange rates so that you can view this key figure value based on the user-selected target currency.

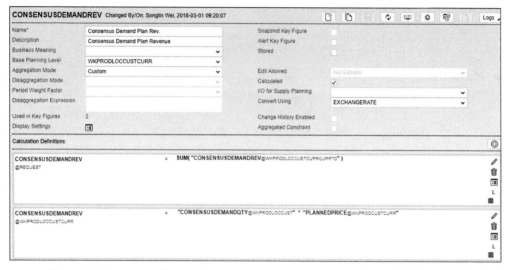

Figure 6.6 Consensus Demand Revenue Key Figure Calculation

- **Cost per unit**
  This key figure is typically the cost of goods sold value imported from SAP ERP or SAP S/4HANA or manually maintained in SAP IBP. This is an input stored key figure that is usually loaded at the week-product-location-currency level. Figure 6.7 shows the key figure definition of the unit cost key figure delivered in SAPIBP1.

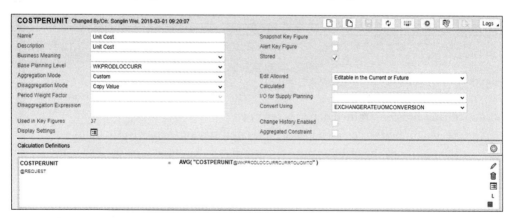

Figure 6.7 Cost per Unit Key Figure Configuration

- **Gross profit**

  This key figure is calculated in SAP IBP by subtracting gross costs from constrained demand revenue, as shown in Figure 6.8, where gross costs (HGROSSCOSTS) is a helper key figure calculated as follows: COSTPERUNIT@WKPRODCURR × CONSTRAINEDDE-MAND@WKPRODCUST.

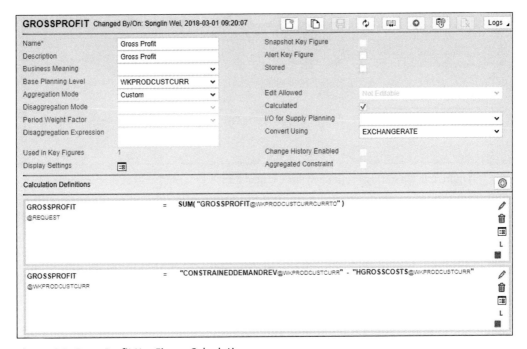

Figure 6.8 Gross Profit Key Figure Calculation

- **Operating profit**

  Operating profit is calculated by netting the gross profit against the indirect costs, as shown in Figure 6.9. Indirect costs is a key figure that is input externally from the SAP ERP or SAP S/4HANA source system or manually maintained in SAP IBP.

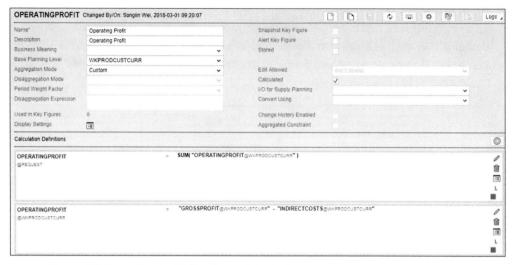

Figure 6.9 Operating Profit Key Figure Calculation

The definition of these financial key figures can be modified further in the SAP IBP model configuration. See Chapter 10 on model configuration for further details on maintaining key figure calculations. These financial key figures are then calculated for different scenarios and versions for the variations of demand and supply plans that need to be evaluated.

6.2.2   Integrated Reconciliation Review

After the demand review and supply review phases of the S&OP process, the integrated reconciliation phase lasts for about two to five days and is attended by representatives of middle management and experts from the areas of finance, sales, purchasing, production, product development, and customer service.

Financial valuations of different demand and supply scenarios are carried out for decision-making and providing recommendations for the executive review meeting. Typically, planning views and charts are created to review deviations between the consensus demand plan and constrained demand plan. Several scenarios are created to evaluate different plans.

For example, we can create scenarios from SAP Integrated Business Planning, add-in for Microsoft Excel by selecting **Create Scenarios** to create the **Increase Capacity** and **Profit Optimization** scenarios, as shown in Figure 6.10, and run a supply planning operator to create the supply plan.

Figure 6.10 Create and Manage Supply Scenarios

We can then compare the resulting demand and supply plans and other financial metrics for profitability. Figure 6.11 shows comparison of the two scenarios, showing that the most profitable scenario is to increase capacity, despite the higher production costs and inventory holding costs. The profit optimization scenario would short-change customer demand, and because of the higher nondelivery cost rate, this scenario is not profitable compared to the increase capacity scenario.

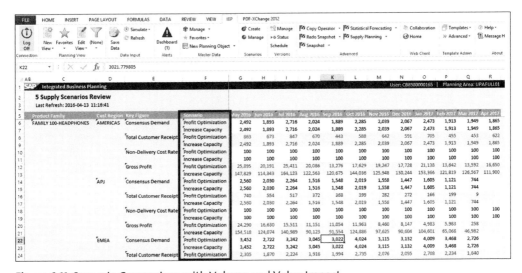

Figure 6.11 Scenario Comparison with Volume and Value Impact

In addition to scenarios, you can create several other versions to evaluate options, like make versus buy decisions (i.e., to check what is the most profitable scenario for demand and supply match: manufacture in house or use an external contact manufacturer). These supply scenarios may also need version-specific master data—for example, to create new transportation lanes for a contract manufacturer or adjust the sourcing ratios between in house and contract manufacturers.

For example, you can have a planning view for version comparison in which you can compare customer demand versus receipts, consensus versus constrained revenue, and constrained demand profit. In this scenario, the upside scenario of using a contract manufacturer is more profitable than other supply scenarios of manufacturing in house or using mixed sourcing.

After evaluating several versions and scenarios along with the business assumptions, these options are made transparent for decision-making to the stakeholders using SAP Jam Collaboration for SAP IBP and its available decision tools.

Figure 6.12 shows an example of supply options created in SAP Jam using the pros and cons table available in the SAP Jam group created for integrated reconciliation. Access it by navigating to **Content • Create • Decision-Making Tool**.

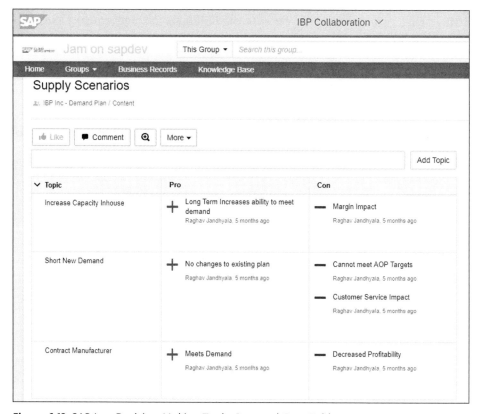

Figure 6.12 SAP Jam Decision-Making Tools: Pros and Cons Table

Here, for example, the evaluated scenarios are listed along with **Pros** and **Cons** for each scenario or **Topic**—namely, **Increase Capacity Inhouse**, **Short New Demand**, and **Contract Manufacturer**. The participants of the process step can add their own pros and cons and collaborate further using the tools available in SAP Jam. Charts and dashboards also can be shared to the user groups and SAP Jam groups for transparency and self-service analysis of the planning results.

SAP delivers SAP IBP Best Practices content with some examples of the charts used in the integrated reconciliation phase. These include the following charts, as shown in Figure 6.13:

- Quarter-to-quarter revenue comparison of constrained demand revenue versus AOP revenue versus actuals revenue
- Consensus versus constrained demand revenue comparison across different versions and scenarios evaluated
- Top product segments by ABC code comparison of consensus versus constrained revenue
- Scenario comparison of projected gross profit for each quarter filtered by key product family

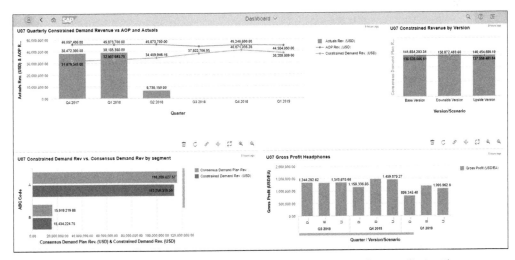

Figure 6.13 Sample Charts in SAP IBP Best Practices Content for Integrated Reconciliation Phase

6.2.3   Management Business Review

All the prior steps of the S&OP process culminate in the executive review meeting, in which management decisions are made and a plan is approved to be operationalized.

The executive review is typically held as a meeting that lasts for one to two hours and is usually held in the last working week of the month. The executive meeting typically is held by the general manager or president of the company responsible for the S&OP process. This meeting is attended by the leadership team, consisting of the senior management from sales, financial, marketing, product, supply, and logistics.

The S&OP coordinator is typically responsible for ensuring the preparation steps for the meeting are completed and the participants briefed on the outcome of the integrated reconciliation phase, the decisions to be made, and the gaps and escalations to be discussed.

The management review meeting is conducted with a sample agenda as in Figure 6.14, created in an SAP Jam Collaboration group created for the participants of the management review meeting.

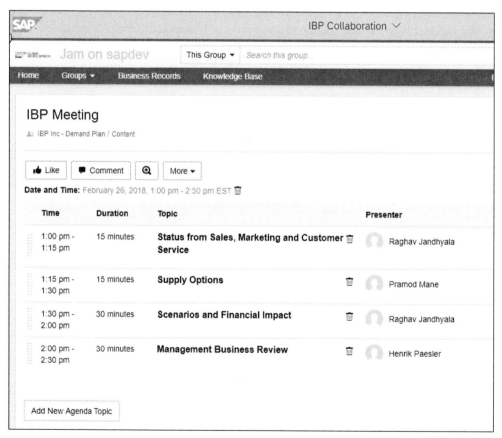

Figure 6.14 S&OP Executive Review Meeting Agenda Created in SAP Jam

The SAP Jam group facilitates collaboration among participants in the executive review phase, including the agenda for the meeting; storage of preparatory documents; content for the review meetings, such as charts, PowerPoint presentations, and documents; documented decisions from the meeting; review of assumptions, risks, and opportunities; and so on.

During the executive meeting, each functional leader—for example, sales, marketing, finance, supply chain, and so on—provides an update on plans, deviations from strategy, or financial targets; a review of the assumptions; both volume and valuation of the projected plans; and highlights of the risks and opportunities. SAP IBP is used to run meetings in real-time to simulate scenarios, analyze results, understand the history of changes to the plan, compare forecasts versus actuals, and so on.

The SAP IBP Best Practices content provides some example charts and business process flows that can be used for the Executive review phase. This can be used as a starting point for the implementation. Typically, each company differs in the way it runs executive meetings because the planning data structures and business drivers may vary by industry and organization.

Some of the charts used in the executive review, as shown in Figure 6.15, include the following:

- Quarterly historical and projected revenue comparison of constrained demand revenue versus AOP revenue and actuals revenue
- Projected month-to-month comparison of constrained revenue versus AOP revenue versus sales forecast
- Gross profit projection for the next eight quarters for each evaluated version/scenario

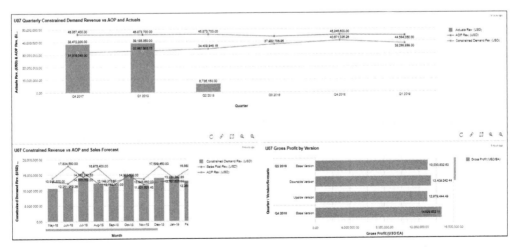

Figure 6.15 Sample Charts in SAP IBP Best Practice Content for Executive Review Phase

These charts are created prior to the meeting or on the fly during the meeting. Typically, there's a need to drill down into details or analyze other data for quick decision-making during the review meetings. This is where the power of SAP IBP analytics comes into play: charts can be created on the fly by business users, taking into account their data permission filters.

Figure 6.16 shows an example of a chart that can be created on the fly for the executive review meeting, showing the dollar value amount of demand, receipts, and projected inventory at the distribution centers and plants. Such a chart can be created from the SAP Fiori Analytics app by selecting **New • Chart** and then providing the required details in the **Basic** tab on the right for the **Planning Area, Key Figures—Total Receipts Value, Total Demand Value**, and **Projected Stock value**. Choose the target **Currency** and **Unit of Measure** and select **Column Chart** as the **Chart Type**. Because you want to view data monthly for the next 12 months, choose **Month** for the **Period Type** and provide the **From** and **To** months. Finally, restrict the **Location Types** attribute to only **Distribution Centers** and **Plants** in the **Attributes** selection.

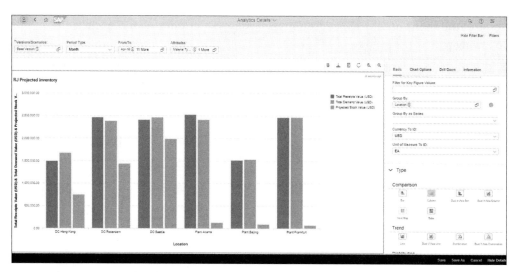

Figure 6.16 On-the-Fly Chart Created in Executive Review Phase

In addition to charts, a waterfall view of the plan is also reviewed to see the different consensus demand plan snapshots compared to actuals along with the forecast accuracy for a three-month lag.

The outcome of the management business review is the agreed-upon plan that will be operationalized. Any new assumptions or changes to assumptions or business drivers are evaluated and documented. Any gaps or escalations from the integration reconciliation meeting are resolved, and finally all the action items from the meeting are well documented and made available to all participants and in SAP Jam collaboration for transparency.

As a final step, the S&OP coordinator promotes the agreed-upon scenario/version to the baseline version. For example, in the executive review meeting, the supply option with external contract manufacture was agreed upon as the scenario to go forward with. This upside version plan needs to be copied over to the baseline version from Excel by choosing **Manage Versions**, selecting **Copy**, and then selecting **Upside Version** for **From:** and **Base Version** for **To:** for selected key figures, as shown in Figure 6.17. Finally, the snapshot operator is run to create a snapshot of the agreed-upon constrained and consensus plans to be able to compare with the prior planning cycle plan.

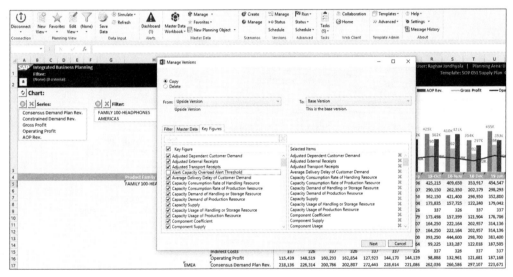

Figure 6.17 Version Copy to Promote Upside Version to Baseline

6.3   Operationalizing the Plan

After the final tactical sales and operations constrained plan is agreed upon and approved, it needs to operationalized by providing the constrained plan to downstream operational and execution processes. For customers running an integrated business plan, it's important that the strategic, tactical and operation planning processes are run in a single planning platform with seamless integration between the processes and the execution systems. In this section, we'll look at integration across strategic, tactical, and operational processes in SAP IBP, along with details of how the sales and operations plan is operationalized and integrated with demand planning, inventory optimization, order-based response planning, and finally execution.

6.3.1   Plan Integration Overview

In SAP IBP, the planning processes are integrated within one unified data model with a clean handover of processes and data across several SAP IBP application modules. The planning foundation offers core functionality like simulation, save, versions, and integration, commonly used across all application modules using the same user interface. Figure 6.18 shows how the application modules in SAP IBP fit into strategic, tactical, and operational planning types.

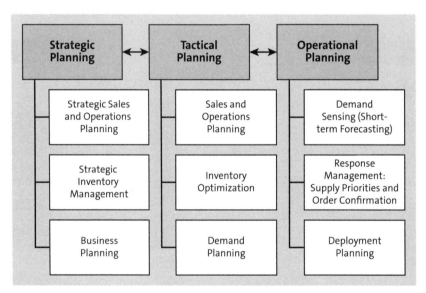

Figure 6.18 SAP IBP Application Modules Scope for Strategic, Tactical, and Operational Planning

The functionality offered in SAP IBP for sales and operations fits into both strategic and tactical planning processes. Similarly, SAP IBP for demand fits into both tactical processes with demand panning and operational short-term processes with demand sensing.

Figure 6.19 shows how SAP IBP for sales and operations integrates with other application modules in SAP IBP.

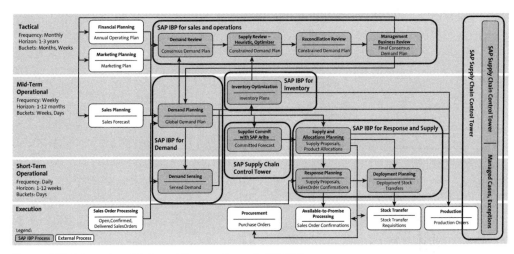

Figure 6.19 Internal and External Process Flows in SAP IBP

In an integrated business planning process, the output of S&OP, which is the final constrained plan, is input into weekly demand planning processes, which are inputs into all the downstream operational and execution processes.

Figure 6.20 shows the outbound integration from SAP IBP for sales and operations to SAP IBP for demand and to operational planning/execution processes. During the global demand plan creation, the output from the S&OP management business review process containing the constrained demand based on rough-cut capacity and material constraints check becomes input into weekly demand planning.

The output of the demand planning quantity becomes input into downstream planning processes—inventory planning, demand sensing, and supply and response allocation—or input into material requirements planning (MRP) processes in SAP ERP or SAP S/4HANA as planned independent requirements.

Even if you don't implement SAP IBP for demand, the output of the S&OP process can still be input for other planning processes. Figure 6.21 shows the management business review process. The output final constrained demand can be input into demand planning in SAP IBP for demand or into other operational processes within or outside of SAP IBP.

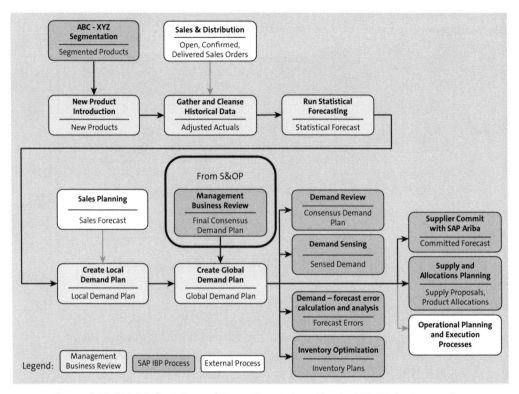

Figure 6.20 SAP IBP for Sales and Operations Integration to SAP IBP for Demand

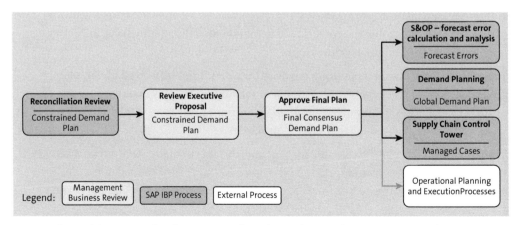

Figure 6.21 Integration from SAP IBP for Sales and Operations to Operational Processes

6.3.2   Integration between SAP IBP for Sales and Operations and SAP IBP for Demand

SAP IBP for sales and operations integrates with SAP IBP for demand as follows: The input for the S&OP process is the weekly demand. During the first week of the month, the weekly demand plan quantity that is planned in SAP IBP for demand is snapshotted and becomes input into SAP IBP for sales and operations. After this, the demand planning quantity can be changed every week. After the management business review is completed in SAP IBP for sales and operations, the final constrained plan becomes an input into demand planning in SAP IBP for demand. In S&OP, the planning is monthly, whereas in SAP IBP for demand the planning is typically in weeks. If the granular levels of data between S&OP processes and demand are different, then they need to be disaggregated.

In the delivered SAP IBP model, the input from SAP IBP for demand to SAP IBP for sales and operations is managed using the disaggregation and copy operator. To see the settings of this operator, in the **Model Configuration** group, choose the Configuration SAP Fiori app. Under **Manage Planning Operators**, choose **Disagg Planning Operator • Copy to Global Demand (SOP)** to copy from key figure DEMANDPLANMNINGQTY to SOPDEMANDPLANNINGQTY, as shown in Figure 6.22.

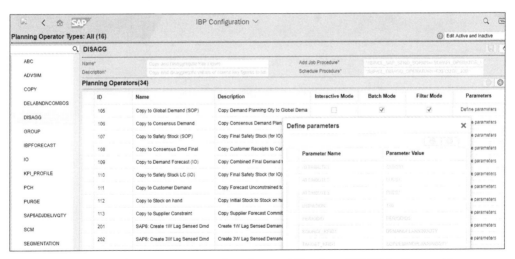

Figure 6.22 Disagg and Copy Operator to Copy Demand Plan from SAP IBP for Demand to SAP IBP for Sales and Operations

6.3.3   Integration between SAP IBP for Sales and Operations and SAP IBP for Inventory

SAP IBP for inventory is typically executed as an operational weekly process to provide an operational inventory target to SAP ERP. This frequency can differ by customers and can run once a week, once a month, or ad hoc. Once a month, the output of the inventory, which is the recommended safety stock, is snapshotted and becomes input into the time series S&OP supply and heuristics. The output of S&OP then becomes input into the weekly demand plan and consequently into SAP IBP for inventory as IOFORECAST, thus forming a closed-loop integration between all the planning processes.

Table 6.1 shows the handover of data and processes between all the application modules and external systems in SAP IBP. The time granularity and the input and output key figures that are mapped as in the SAPIBP1 planning area are shown. This is a best practice guideline, but customers can choose to implement this setup differently based on the business planning processes that fit their needs.

From/To	Sales and Operations	Supply (Time-Series-Based)	Demand	Inventory	Response and Supply (Order-Based)	External System(S)
Sales and operations		Monthly conensensus demand plan	Monthly final consensus demand			
Supply (time-series-based)	Monthly: constrained demand plan					Weekly: unconstrained forecast (if SAP IBP for response and supply isn't implemented)

Table 6.1 Integration between SAP IBP Application Modules and External Systems

From/To	Sales and Operations	Supply (Time-Series-Based)	Demand	Inventory	Response and Supply (Order-Based)	External System(S)
Demand	Monthly: global demand plan			Weekly: demand forecast (global demand plan + final sensed demand)	Weekly: demand forecast (global demand plan + final sensed demand)	Daily: final sensed demand Weekly: global demand plan
Inventory		Monthly: safety stock				Weekly: safety stock
Reponse and Supply (Order-Based	Weekly: constrained forecast Daily: order confirmation run					Weekly: unconstrained forecast
External System(s)	Monthly financial plan, marketing plan	Weekly: committed forecast (if SAP IBP for response and supply isn't implemented)		Weekly: target service levels, forecast error	Weekly: committed forecast	
Master data (when required), sales plan (monthly), historical sales (weekly), sales order data (daily)						

Table 6.1 Integration between SAP IBP Application Modules and External Systems (Cont.)

6

6.3.4   Integration between Tactical Time Series-Based and Order-Based Plans

A system rich in planning functionality is underserved if the plan can't be executed. SAP IBP provides the end-to-end planning process such that the plans can be actionable. This requires integration between time series and order-based planning. If you map the application business processes to the planning models delivered by SAP, then the time series-based planning areas covering SAP IBP for sales and operations, SAP IBP for demand, SAP IBP for inventory, SAP Supply Chain Control Tower, and tactical supply are part of planning area SAPIBP1. Similarly, SAP74 is the planning model covering the order-based planning for SAP IBP for response and supply, as shown in Figure 6.23.

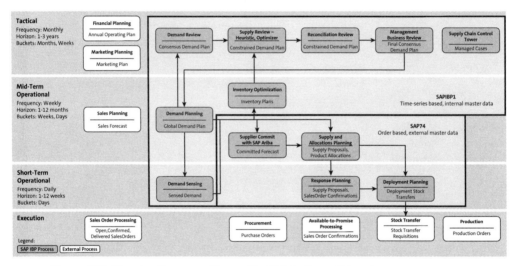

Figure 6.23 Planning Processes Mapped to SAP-Delivered Planning Areas

The integration between tactical time series-based planning and order-based planning is as follows: The weekly global demand plan quantity (from SAP IBP for demand or from SAP IBP for sales and operations) becomes an input forecast for supply and allocations planning. The output allocations plan can then become an input into the S&OP and demand planning processes for the next cycle.

6.4   Summary

In this chapter, we covered how financial key figures are calculated in SAP IBP in depth based on the demand and supply plans across different versions and scenarios.

We then covered how these financial elements are used in consolidation of integrated reconciliation and executive review. We dug deeper into how integrated reconciliation and executive review phases are carried out, along with user roles, inputs, outputs, and planning steps followed in each phase. We ended the chapter by discussing how the final constrained plan in SAP IBP for sales and operations acts as an input to other operational processes and the feedback loop from the operational processes back to the S&OP process. Such an integrated planning process provides a high business value in the following ways:

- Increasing product and customer profitability by given supply and financial constraints
- Developing an optimal business plan to drive revenue growth and increase market share
- Better alignment of strategic, long-term supply chain planning with operational, short-term planning
- Improving the speed, agility, and accuracy of sales and operations planning

Chapter 7

Collaboration and Management by Exception

This chapter covers collaboration, such as with other team members in different departments, and using alerts to notify you of issues— just two of the tools available that will allow you to get more out of SAP IBP.

Collaboration allows companies to finalize a single organization-wide demand and supply plan based on teamwork from production, purchase, logistics, finance, sales, marketing, product development, and account management teams. In particular, it's critical that users collaborate across departments when they need to respond to exceptions in the planning process; this chapter introduces the SAP IBP tools (custom alerts, tasks, etc.) that facilitate collaboration and management by exception.

Specifically, we'll cover the tools you can use for collaboration, with a heavy focus on SAP Jam. We'll also dive into custom alerts, both their creation and monitoring. Next, we'll discuss case management, from how cases are maintained to tracking and closing them. Finally, we'll end by covering tasks in SAP IBP.

7.1   SAP Jam Collaboration

Modern supply chain organizations of the world are becoming truly global, with different teams responsible for various functions like demand planning, marketing, sales, supply planning. A good sales and operations plan can't be achieved by working in functional silos. Many organizations already understand the importance of cross-functional collaboration to achieve a steady demand and supply plan. Collaboration in supply chain planning requires multiple S&OP stakeholders to come together, share a plan, and collaborate in a central environment to achieve the optimum plan.

We live in a digital era; most of the time, it isn't possible to colocate all stakeholders in a physical location. Virtual collaboration tools let the team prepare an initial central plan, share it, incorporate their thoughts, make adjustments, and finalize the plan across distances. Collaboration allows for discussion and interacting with one central plan, as compared to local spreadsheets used by different teams. Let's look at the case of fictional ABC Corporation, which has its demand planning function located at its central office managing all the product groups. However, the sales organization is spread across the geographic regions. Demand planning prepared an initial demand plan and ran it through all the sales organizations. The sales team gathers market intelligence, which is a valuable input to arrive at a consensus demand. We need a virtual collaboration platform in which central demand planners and the local sales team come together and work as one.

SAP Jam is the collaboration and professional social media platform integrated with SAP IBP. This collaboration application is connected with the central planning database of SAP IBP and is integrated with process and task management applications. Tasks can be assigned to members or groups and can be tracked to their due dates. Members can post a message to a private group or a public message to the whole organization. SAP Jam also can trigger email notifications when a task is assigned and when a task is completed.

SAP Jam is accessed by launching the Collaboration app from the **General Planner** group. The SAP Jam Collaboration page is launched within the SAP IBP web GUI frame. Figure 7.1 shows an example of the collaboration page in SAP IBP. There are various sections in the overview page, like the message board, groups and knowledge base area, alerts and notifications, common actions area, and notifications summary. The screen layout of the collaboration page is analogous to that found in user-friendly social media applications.

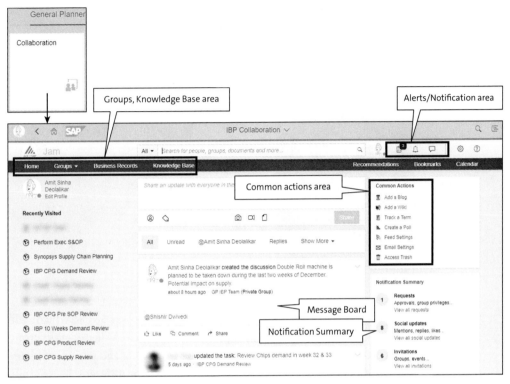

Figure 7.1 SAP Jam Collaboration Overview Page in SAP IPB

In the following sections, we'll look at how to navigate in SAP Jam, how it integrates with SAP IBP, and how it integrates specifically with the Excel planning view.

7.1.1   Navigation

The various sections of the SAP Jam page commonly used in S&OP processes are as follows:

- **Groups/knowledge base**

  This area lets you access various groups of which you are a part; a user can identify some of the groups as favorites as well to access them quickly. As illustrated in Figure 7.2, the **Groups** tab lists both **Favorites** and **Recently Visited** groups. Selecting a group takes you to a group page with specific discussions.

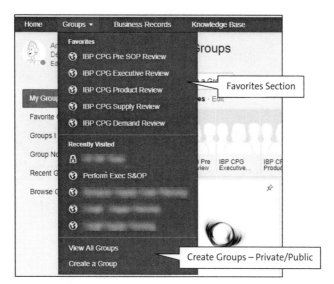

Figure 7.2 Group/Knowledge Base Areas

Separate groups are created for each of the process steps in S&OP, which helps when discussing a specific topic. In a typical S&OP process cycle, separate groups are created for demand review, supply review, S&OP review and executive review. Members of each group and the topics of discussion may be different. These groups can be created directly in the SAP Jam page for ad hoc discussions as well, and members can be invited to the group. The invited members are notified by email to accept the invitation to join the group. The knowledge base area lets you maintain documents, spreadsheets, rulebooks, and the like that can form a repository for the entire organization.

- **Message board**
  This area displays various activities happening in the group that you're a part of, and it lets you share an update, picture, video, or document publicly with everyone in the organization or with a specific audience. Messages also can be hashtagged (with #), and all messages with the same hashtag can be grouped. Hashtags are also updated with reason codes when manual adjustments are made to a plan. We'll look at hashtagging a reason code in later sections of this chapter.

  Figure 7.3 shows what a message board looks like, including tasks that are created by or assigned to the user. In this example, the plant manager plans a plant shutdown due to plant maintenance and assigns a task to the central supply planner with a due date to assess the impact of distribution and steps to be taken to meet the customer demand. The tool sends periodic reminders to the members assigned to the task. The central planner is notified, chooses which action to take, updates the case, and closes the task.

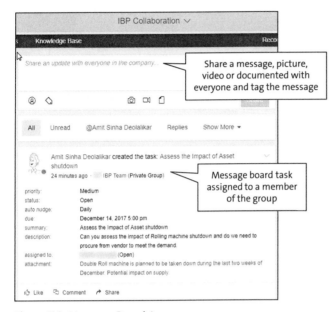

Figure 7.3 Message Board Area

Tasks also can be created while configuring the process steps in SAP IBP so that they can be created automatically within the process step groups when a step is triggered. Task definition in the process steps and the assignment of a task to members of the group are detailed in the next section.

- **Alerts/notifications**

  This area contains the following icons:

  - The **Task** list is a consolidated area where you can see the list of tasks assigned to you, tasks created and assigned to others, and a list of overdue tasks. This page lets you prioritize tasks and take actions.

  - The **Notifications** button opens the list of notifications that you need to be aware of. Some of the notifications that you can see on this page include notifications to join a private group, notifications of actions taken by a member of a group or task, and so on.

- The message center lets you send a message to another user or to a group privately.

Figure 7.4 illustrates the task area, various classifications of alerts, and notifications relevant to the user.

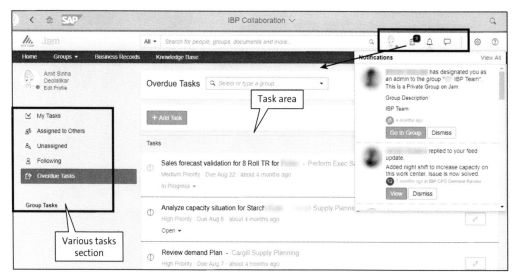

Figure 7.4 Alert/Notification Area

7.1.2   SAP IBP Integration

Now that we've discussed the SAP Jam collaboration page and how it functions, let's get into the details of how SAP IBP integrates with it. There are various integration points between SAP IBP data and SAP Jam, which includes SAP Fiori apps and Excel planning views, as will be discussed in the following sections.

Collaboration with Process Steps

Process steps can be modeled to depict various steps that are to be performed. For example, in the S&OP process, there could be standard steps like demand review, supply review, pre-S&OP review, and executive review. SAP IBP provides the flexibility to define these steps that each organization has in its S&OP process. These steps can be modeled as process steps within an instance; various actions to be performed in these steps can be tracked and a collaborative decision can be made.

The process steps can be modeled by using the Process Modeling app available under the **Administrator** group (see Figure 7.5). We can model multiple steps here and specify a relative start day and end day for each step.

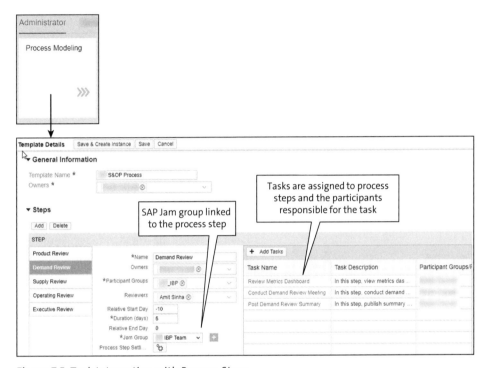

Figure 7.5 Task Integration with Process Steps

Consider an example of a monthly S&OP cycle: demand review and baseline forecast generation steps are planned to be performed starting the fourth day of the month and continuing to the seventh day. This step is followed by the supply review step until the fourteenth calendar day. Final consensus demand numbers are available on the eighteenth of the month, and these numbers will be an input for the downstream planning process. In such cases, SAP IBP can be used to streamline the process without manual reminders and multiple meetings.

Each step has an owner and participant groups assigned. Here, we can define a standard set of tasks that are to be performed in each process step. If each step in a process is required to be performed by a different set of participants, we can assign different groups so that the task can be assigned appropriately and discussion can be restricted to a focused audience.

These process steps can also be collaborated on with an SAP Jam group by assigning the group to the step. If the participants of each step are different, then you can create multiple SAP Jam groups and assign them to the steps. Tasks that are assigned to these process steps are created automatically in the collaboration group.

In an SAP IBP team collaboration group, tasks are created automatically when the process instance is triggered. In the example we discussed for the S&OP cycle, various tasks that need to be performed for demand review are automatically created and posted to the participants with a due date to complete. Integration of process steps with the SAP Jam page enables collaborative decision making, in which multiple participants work on a single platform, share their insights, and have focused discussions.

Task Collaboration in SAP Jam Group

You've see how a predefined process step creates tasks to be performed by participants. You can also create ad hoc tasks in a group and assign them to one participant. In the example in Figure 7.6, one of the rolling machines is planned to be shut down. A task is created for the deployment manager to assess the impact of asset shutdown and the plan of action for demand fulfillment during this period. The task is assigned to a single participant. However, all participants will come to know about this through the group feed.

You can assign a due date to a task and assign a priority to it. Notifications also can be generated for the task assigned to ensure timely action is taken on the task. The tasks can be tagged and a file can be attached.

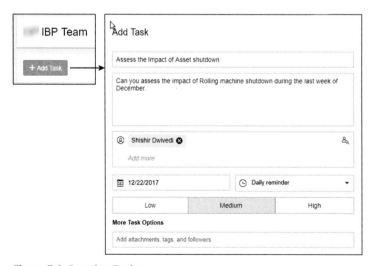

Figure 7.6 Creating Tasks

Creation of User Groups

Process steps specific to collaboration happen within a focused group; it's essential to define the user group and the SAP Jam group in the system. SAP Jam groups can be created directly from the process step definition page by clicking on the **+** symbol next to the SAP Jam group. This opens a window in which you can assign the name of the group, as shown in Figure 7.7.

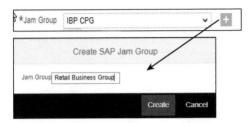

Figure 7.7 Creating SAP Jam Collaboration Group

A user group can be created from the User Groups app available under the **Administrator** group. Clicking the icon to add a new group opens a screen to enter the **User Groups** name and a **Description**. Figure 7.8 illustrates the user group creation process.

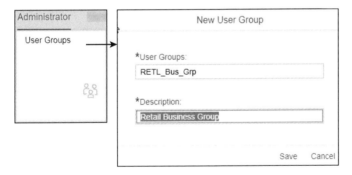

Figure 7.8 User Group Creation

Once the group is created, multiple SAP IBP users can be added to the group. Click the **Save** button to update the changes, as shown in Figure 7.9.

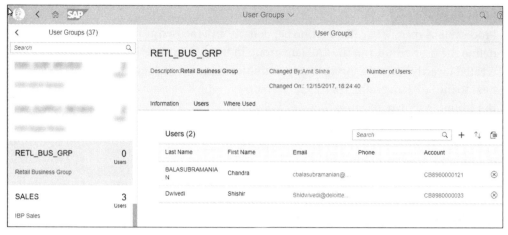

Figure 7.9 Adding Users to Group

7.1.3   Excel Planning View Integration

Excel planning views can be integrated with SAP Jam collaboration. When a change is made to the planning data in an Excel planning view, it can be shared with the collaboration groups in the form of hashtags. The system pops up a window in which you can assign a reason code to the change. There is also an option to share the action with the SAP Jam collaboration group.

For example, a user can make changes to the forecast unconstrained key figure. When the change is saved, a reason code, **Sales Input**, is assigned to it. In addition, you can add a **Comment** explaining why this change is made and share it with the group.

The action is posted on the message board of the SAP Jam collaboration group with the reason code in a hashtag, as shown in Figure 7.10. All messages posted in a group with the same hashtag can be identified together.

Standard SAP IBP has a set of reason codes that you can use. In addition, you can also add customizable reason codes that suit your business needs. Reason codes can be configured in the Reason Code app available in the **Model Configuration** group, as shown in Figure 7.11. In the Reason Code app, click the **New** button to create a reason code. Save the results after the reason code is created.

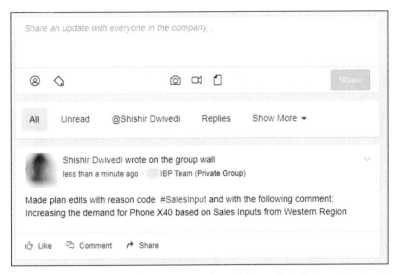

Figure 7.10 Planning Update Message Shared through Collaboration Application

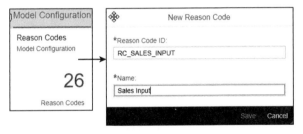

Figure 7.11 Reason Code Configuration

SAP IBP also has a powerful analytics capability and it's user-friendly for building charts. You can share charts with the SAP Jam group and tag participants in the post. This is a great collaboration functionality in which the system is not only providing real-time information, but also is providing a tool to collaborate in order to act on the information.

Figure 7.12 illustrates how a chart can be shared with a group. You can add comments and tag somebody in the message. In this scenario, the category manager observed a drop in utilization of an asset, and he shares that information with the group. He also tags a participant in SAP Jam to assess the impact of demand fulfillment.

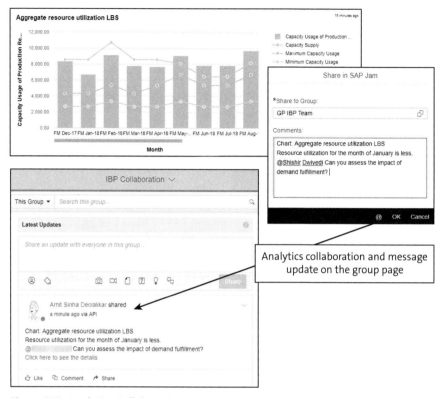

Figure 7.12 Analytics Collaboration

7.2   Custom Alerts

Alert monitoring and analysis has been part of the daily cycle of demand and supply planners since the creation of systematic supply chain planning solutions. Several business situations need users to identify and report exceptions. Managing such exceptions efficiently and in time is critical for supply chain processes in any organization. To facilitate these tasks, custom alert functionality in SAP IBP is advantageous. Using standard custom alert apps, users can define the alert criteria, assign an alert to a user or user group, and monitor the alerts on a regular basis. Users can then perform actions to identify and address the cause of the alert.

7.2.1   SAP Fiori Applications

Custom alerts in SAP IBP are managed via three distinct SAP Fiori apps: Define and Subscribe to Custom Alerts, Custom Alerts Overview, and Monitor Custom Alerts (see Figure 7.13).

Figure 7.13 Custom Alert Apps

Define and Subscribe to Custom Alerts

Alert definition involves identification of data points and rules that should be monitored and reported in case of exceptions. Depending on business needs, users have the flexibility to select one or more key figures that are critical for supply chain processes. For example, a demand planner should be notified if the mean absolute percentage error (MAPE) for a given brand or category is more than the given threshold, and an inventory planner should be notified if the target stock value is more than the expected value. Monitoring and reporting exceptions for essential data points is critical to identify issues within the supply chain.

Users must be careful to define the rules that represent true business needs to identify exceptions. A rule too generic or with too wide a range can lead to generation of several alerts, which may not be helpful. On the other hand, a rule too restrictive may not capture all valid exceptions, and users may miss the opportunity to identify and act on a scenario that requires manual intervention.

As part of alert definition, users can specify multiple parameters, such as alert name, planning area and calculation level, and time horizon for which the alert or rule is to be checked. Alert severity can be defined as high, medium, or low. This helps business users to prioritize the alerts for analysis as part of their day-to-day tasks.

Subscribing to custom alerts ensures that business users receive alerts only for specified filter values—that is, for the products, customers, or locations for which they are responsible.

Custom Alerts Overview

The Custom Alerts Overview app gives planners a consolidated view of all the alerts they've subscribed to. It also provides a single screen from which users can navigate to details of any alert they want to analyze. Alerts shown in SAP IBP are based on real-time data, showing the current status of key figure values. This enables real-time scenario planning and validation of exceptions during different phases of S&OP review. Alerts are categorized based on their severity, which helps prioritize issues to be discussed during S&OP review meetings.

Users have the flexibility to change the display format or navigate to a detail monitoring screen to view individual alerts and take necessary actions. Alert screens in SAP IBP provide a user-friendly view and consolidated alert counts to help identify the overall alert situation after execution of planning processes. The view can be set in graphical or tabular form depending on user preferences.

Monitor Custom Alerts

This app allows users to view detailed information about alerts they've subscribed to. Users can navigate to the Monitor Custom Alerts app from the Custom Alerts Overview app as well. All the information related to alerts can be viewed in this app. This information includes the following:

- Alert name
- Master data for given calculation level specified in alert definition
- Metrics
- Severity
- User and user groups with whom alert is shared
- Quantity and unit of measure (UoM) for the relevant key figures used in alerts

Users can navigate to the SAP IBP analytics page and analyze the alert situation using different filter criteria to identify the best action. Users may also share the alert by adding it to a case or by sharing it with a user group via SAP Jam collaboration. SAP IBP provides flexibility to perform multiple actions, as shown in Figure 7.14, when the alert is generated.

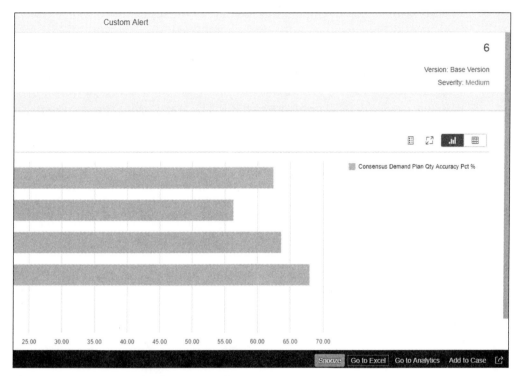

Figure 7.14 Action Examples for Custom Alert

The most important actions are as follows:

- **Add to Case**
  The alert can be assigned to a new or an existing case to notify users to take action on the alert. The person responsible for the alert (**Owner**) and the **Due Date** can also be provided on this screen, as shown in Figure 7.15.

- **Go to Analytics**
  You can go to an analytics page to view the key figure values, filters data, and grouping conditions and decide whether to change the data values to perform root-cause analysis. Narrowing down the data with filters helps you identify possible actions to address issues.

- **Go to Excel**
  You can navigate to an Excel sheet directly from the alert monitor screen. The Excel planning view opens with the planning level, master data, and key figure

selected in the alert definition. You also can edit the key figure values and perform analysis to address the situation that resulted in the alert creation.

- **Snooze**

  An alert can be snoozed to make it temporarily inactive so that it doesn't appear in the active alert list. Such alerts form the snooze list. You can snooze an alert indefinitely or specify the date after which it will be active again. You also can specify whether an alert should be activated if there's any change in master data associated with the alert. Finally, you can manually activate any alert that's part of the snooze list.

- **Share using SAP Jam**

  You can share the alert information with a user or user group using SAP Jam collaboration. Comments can be added along with the alert details to the collaboration page, and a task can be created to track the actions for a given alert.

Figure 7.15 Adding Case to Alert

In the next subsection, we'll discuss how custom alerts can be applied in different business scenarios to facilitate integrated business planning processes.

7.2.2   Using Custom Alerts

Planning key figures within SAP IBP store the data values relevant for planning processes. The key figure values represent the overall health of the supply chain; any exceptions or outliers in these values must be captured and reported.

Custom alerts can be applied on variety of scenarios or key figures to capture exceptions. Key figures available in a planning area can be checked and compared with the threshold values.

Using mathematical operators, key figures can be compared against the absolute value or percentage value of another key figure. These comparisons help business users to identify situations in which key figure values are not as expected under normal business situations and which require user intervention.

There are several possible ways in which alert rules can be set up to meet business requirements using the key figures and operators mentioned previously. Let's look at an example of supply chain in which a business user wants to identify situations in which the projected stock is negative—that is, there isn't enough lead time or capacity available to meet the required demand. Such scenarios can be modeled easily, as shown in Figure 7.16.

Figure 7.16 Alert Rule Application Example

On the other hand, there could be business situations that need comparison of more than one key figure to identify exception situations. For example, imagine a business need to identify situations in which the demand planning quantity is less than fifty percent of sales forecast and thus the sales forecast is significantly overestimated compared to the unconstrained demand planning quantity. Figure 7.17 shows a setup based on percentage comparison of two key figures.

Figure 7.17 Custom Alerts Based on Percentages

Sales and operations planning processes in SAP IBP are data-driven, and real-time visibility into KPIs and metrics is represented by SAP IBP dashboards, which facilitate meaningful S&OP discussions and review meetings.

Custom alerts can be applied to a wide variety of scenarios in S&OP, and alerts that represent situations of concern or require executive input can be considered for discussion in pre-S&OP or executive S&OP meetings.

Now, let's discuss how custom alerts can be used in different business scenarios related to S&OP.

Custom Alerts in Demand Review

A consensus demand plan created during the demand review of S&OP processes acts as a key input for day-to-day operational activities for an organization. Comparison of the consensus demand quantity or its monetized value provides insight into future opportunities and issues that the organization may face. Measuring consensus demand planning with respect to the sales forecast or actual sales helps businesses identify the gaps. This timely identification of gaps then can enable business users to take necessary actions to close them.

Business users can leverage custom alert functionality to assess a demand plan and identify situations in which manual intervention is needed. For example:

- Alert generation if the forecast is significantly lower than targets set in the annual operation plan
- Alert generation if actual sales in the past period are significantly lower than the consensus demand in the previous period
- Alert generation if forecast bias is significant over a given horizon

Depending on an organization's needs, custom alerts can be set up multiple ways to identify the gaps in the demand plan to be addressed as part of the S&OP process.

Custom Alerts in Supply and Operating Review

Custom alerts based on supply planning key figures can provide excellent visibility into situations in which supply can't meet demand or excess capacity exists that can be evaluated for alternative usage.

Supply-based key figures in SAP IBP can provide information related to on-hand inventory, capacity usage, days of supply, projected inventory, and more. Supply planners can set up custom alerts using these key figures to identify issues on the supply side and take necessary actions after performing root-cause analysis.

Typical supply planning custom alerts may include the following:

- Alert generation if the projected stock is lower than the target value or the target safety stock
- Alert generation if the capacity utilization is lower than the target value for the given resources
- Alert generation if the planned procurement quantities are higher than the supplier capacity to provide raw materials

Depending on the business requirements, SAP IBP provides flexibility to model custom alerts in several different ways considering the choice of key figures and threshold values.

Custom Alerts in Financial Review

As part of the S&OP process, different what-if scenarios can be evaluated to determine the financial impact of different options. Custom alerts in SAP IBP can be used to identify gaps between different financial metrics relevant for an organization. For example, if the monetized value of a forecast based on the consensus demand plan is lower than the target set in the AOP, then business users can be alerted about the situation. They can then perform a detailed analysis to identify options and reduce the gap between the AOP and consensus demand. Such options may include running extra promotions to drive up sales and increase the consensus demand number, or adding an additional shift for a given plan to bridge the gap between demand and supply if the consensus demand number is lower due to supply constraints.

Typical custom alerts that can be set up to facilitate financial review may include the following:

- Alert generation if the monetized demand plan is significantly lower than the target set in annual operating
- Alert generation if the gross margin is lower than the threshold value

7.2.3   Configuring Custom Alerts

For custom alert configuration, use the Define and Subscribe to Custom Alerts apps to set up the alerts in SAP IBP. On the new alert creation screen, specify the parameters relevant for the alert by navigating to each tab in the sequence specified ahead.

Information

In this tab, as shown in Figure 7.18, specify the following parameters relevant for alert creation:

- **Name**
  Specify the name for the alert
- **Active**
  Set the alert to active (checked) or inactive (unchecked)
- **Description**
  Specify the description of the alert
- **Category**
  Specify the grouping of alerts used for reporting
- **Planning Area**
  Specify the planning area to be used for alert calculations

- **Calculation Level**
  Specify the aggregation level at which the alert is calculated

- **Aggregate Alerts Over Time Horizon**
  If checked, alerts over the entire time horizon are represented in one chart rather than in an individual chart for each period

- **Time Horizon**
  Specify the periodicity for aggregation of data for alerts

- **From/To**
  Specify the time period within which alert calculations should take place

- **Rolling**
  If checked, the from/to periods are rolling instead of absolute values

- **Severity**
  Specify the severity of the alert based on business impact and urgency

- **Version**
  Specify the version to be used for alert calculation

- **Excel Template**
  Specify which Excel template should be used when you navigate to the Excel planning view

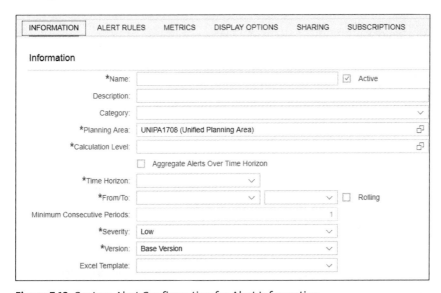

Figure 7.18 Custom Alert Configuration for Alert Information

Alert Rules

After you specify the alert information, specify the rules to be evaluated before generating alerts.

In this step, define the rules for generating alerts in SAP IBP. One or more rules can be defined as part of a rule group. Users can define grouping conditions via which an alert can be generated if all or any conditions within a rule group are satisfied. Rule definition is a key aspect of alert definition.

An alert rule can consist of one or more rule groups. Each rule group has a calculation defined for at least one key figure. When more than one rule group is used, you can generate alerts using one of the following criteria:

- **All Rule Groups Are Satisfied**
- **Any Rule Group Is Satisfied**

For each rule group, you can specify one or more key figure calculations. A key figure's values can be checked against different operators, as follows:

- = (key figure value is equal to)
- < (key figure value is less than)
- <= (key figure value is less than or equal to)
- > (key figure value is greater than)
- >= (key figure value is greater than or equal to)
- <> (key figure value is not equal to)
- **Is Null** (key figure value is null)

If an absolute condition is used in the alert rule, then the key figure value is compared directly with the value specified in the rule along with the operator.

For example, in Figure 7.19, if **Consensus Demand Plan Qty Error (%)** is more than or equal to **40**, then an alert should be generated.

If a percentage condition is used in an alert rule, the key figure value is compared against the percentage value of another key figure.

For example, in Figure 7.19, an alert should be generated if **Consensus Demand Plan Qty** is less than or equal to **70** percent of the **Sales Fcst Qty** key figure.

If, as shown in Figure 7.19, the alert rule is set to **Any Rule Group Is Satisfied**, then an alert will be generated if either of the two rule groups specified is fulfilled.

Figure 7.19 Custom Alert Rule Configuration

Metrics

Under this tab, specify the key figures related to the selected planning area that are to be used for reporting alerts in charts. You can select multiple key figures as metrics.

Display Options

In this tab, specify the display options for the alerts in the Alert Overview app.

Specify the unit of measure ID and currency to be used during display if the selected key figures are relevant for quantity or currency calculation. You should specify the chart type to be used for display. If more than one key figure is selected, then you can use chart types with dual X and Y axes. Figure 7.20 shows a display option for a horizontal bar.

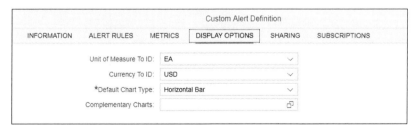

Figure 7.20 Custom Alert Display Options Configuration

Sharing and Subscriptions

In these tabs, you specify a user or user groups to receive and view or act on alerts.

Prior to assigning users or user groups here, the user or group should be created in SAP IBP; only existing users or user groups can be selected. It's possible to specify multiple users or user groups. User groups can include demand planners, supply planners, inventory planners, or others.

The last step in alert creation is to define a subscription. Navigate to the **Subscriptions** tab and click **+** to add a new subscription.

For the new subscription, specify its name and description. You can also deactivate the subscription by deselecting the **Active** checkbox.

In the filter options, select attributes such as product, customer, location, and so on, then select the attribute values relevant for a given subscription. Specifying filter values ensures that users don't receive alerts for products or customers for which they are not responsible. It also limits the number of alerts received by each user, as shown in Figure 7.21.

Figure 7.21 Custom Alert Subscription Configuration

7.3   Case Management

As discussed in earlier sections, monitoring exceptions and acting on them in a timely manner is critical to ensure that supply chain processes are running efficiently and uninterrupted. Most of the alerts generated within a supply chain are not resolved immediately but rather require conscientious focus planners. These planners may act on the alert on their own or assign it to someone more familiar with the issue or who is responsible for addressing the problem. Alert resolution can take from a few hours to a few days—or in some cases, even longer.

Case management functionality in SAP IBP enables planners to monitor the action or set of actions being taken for generated alerts, keep track of alert status and the progress of issue resolution, and finally ensure that the underlying issue is acknowledged and addressed by the personnel responsible.

Standard SAP IBP provides multiple means to create and manage a case. A case can be created by using the Manage Cases SAP Fiori app, or you can create a case directly while analyzing the alert using the Monitor Custom Alerts app.

When creating a case, you can specify the case name, description, and due date and assign it to a user or a predefined user group. When navigating via Monitor Custom Alerts, you also can add alerts to an existing case. This helps avoid creation of duplicate cases for similar issues that need to be addressed.

If a case is assigned to a user or user group, a notification is displayed in SAP Jam once it's shared with the group, as shown in Figure 7.22.

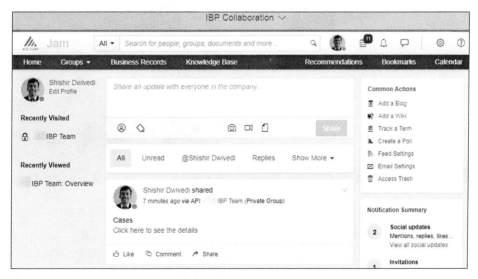

Figure 7.22 Case Management Collaboration

Users can also email a case to an assigned user using the Manage Case app. As the case analysis progresses, users can update the information in the case and share it with other users or user groups. Collaborative problem-solving using alert monitoring and case management tools can add significant value to supply chain processes.

For every case created in SAP IBP, certain mandatory information must be populated, such as **Name**, **Description**, and **Owner**. You should choose a case name and description that makes the case identifiable to assigned users or user groups. The case **Owner** is the responsible person within the organization directly impacted by the underlying issue. The user creating the case may share her understanding of the underlying issue in the case description. Figure 7.23 shows fields relevant for input during case creation.

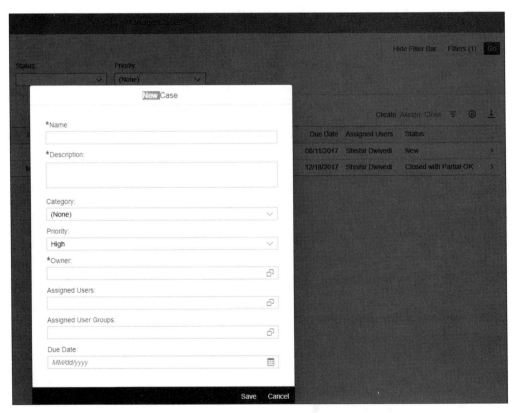

Figure 7.23 Managing Cases

Other than mandatory fields, you should assign a **Priority** to signify the importance of the case and the urgency with which it must be addressed. The **Due Date** can be assigned based on the severity of the issue and user understanding about tentative duration to resolve the issue. The **Assigned Users** or **Assigned User Groups** are the responsible parties involved in resolving the case.

Using the Manage Cases app, you can view all the cases created within the SAP IBP system. You can filter the list to view the relevant cases based on priority, due date, created by, created on date, and so on. You also can download the case information in an Excel file for sharing with other users or groups that have limited access to the Manage Case app. The details of each case can be viewed by clicking on the case's row, as shown in Figure 7.24. From this screen, you can navigate to Monitor Custom Alerts to view the alert details or add a comment and share it with other users using SAP Jam collaboration.

Figure 7.24 Case Details

Other important information that can be added to the case to make it more meaningful and actionable is case categorization and snapshots. Using the Manage Categories app, you can define categories such as sales forecast cases or stockout cases. These predefined categories can be assigned during case creation, which helps track, filter, and report on cases created with SAP IBP.

As the case analysis progresses or new alerts are generated based on changes in key figure values, you can capture snapshots using the Monitor Custom Alerts app. These snapshots then are assigned automatically to the case and are available for users to view and act on. The snapshots are sorted based on creation date. You also can remove snapshots from the case if the values of the key figures in the snapshot are no longer relevant for case analysis. The case creator also can remove the alert from the case if he believes the alert is no longer relevant for the case analysis.

A case can have the following statuses depending on its progress:

- **New**
  A case is created.

- **In Progress**
  A user to whom the case is assigned acknowledges the case.

- **On-hold**
  The case is awaiting a decision and temporarily can't be resolved.

- **Closed**
  Underlying issues are resolved, and no further action is needed.

- **Closed with Partial OK**
  Underlying issues are resolved, but certain actions must be taken to avoid recurrence. Comments should be updated to clarify the conditions under which the case was closed.

- **Confirmed**
  This is the final status of a case. It means that no further action is needed and underlying issues are resolved. Once confirmed, a case can't be reopened.

7.4   Tasks

Process management in SAP IBP is driven by defining tasks while modeling planning processes and assigning responsibilities to users to accomplish these tasks. This helps streamline the process flow from one business function or area to another and enables identification of process bottlenecks for which follow up is needed to drive a task towards completion.

Task management apps within SAP IBP provide multiple capabilities to view and report on progress on predefined tasks and to create ad hoc tasks depending on business needs. Task management integration and partial coverage of apps were also covered in Section 7.1.2.

Tasks are created in SAP IBP during modeling of planning processes. Depending on the process complexity and level at which the process needs to be managed, tasks are created using the IBP Process Modeling app, shown in Figure 7.25. The tasks added to the process steps can be assigned to a user or user group. Users can view the assigned tasks in the SAP Jam collaboration page or in an Excel planning view.

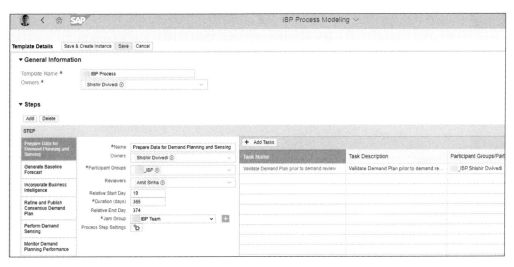

Figure 7.25 Task in Process Step

The start and end dates of tasks are based on the due dates defined in the process step during process modeling. An overdue task appears as an alert on the SAP Jam collaboration screen, and a notification can be triggered to automatically send an email to users when the tasks are due. Figure 7.26 shows an overdue task assigned to a user in the SAP Jam Collaboration page.

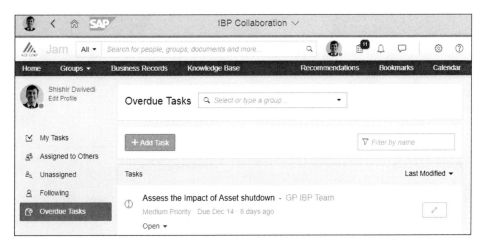

Figure 7.26 Overdue Tasks Viewed in Collaboration Portal

Once tasks are created and assigned to users, users can change the due dates and priority or the completion status either through the collaboration page or through the Tasks app.

Figure 7.27 shows different options for updating a task from the SAP Jam Collaboration page. When the status of a task is updated to **In Progress** or **Completed**, the tasks are updated in the process model as well, and the overall completion progress of the process is updated accordingly.

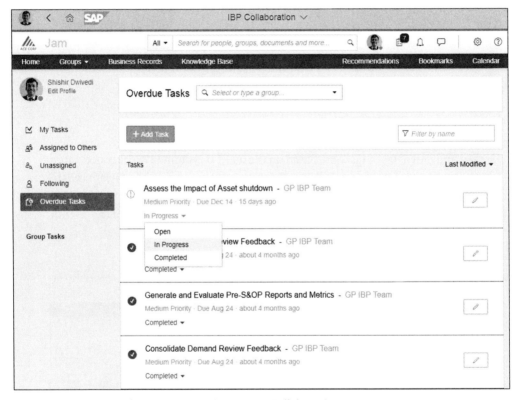

Figure 7.27 Task Management via SAP Jam Collaboration

In some situations, you may need to act on certain tasks that aren't part of the regular process. Users have the flexibility to create ad hoc tasks using the Tasks app.

7.5 Summary

Collaboration is the heart of an efficient S&OP process. SAP IBP provides efficient end-to-end collaboration involving different parties in the S&OP process. Collaboration application is further fortified by integrating information sharing with the central planning database, along with provisions for custom alerts and case and task management. Alerts let planners spend their time on value-adding activities, help predict unwanted situations, and help users take the most appropriate actions. Case and task management help with the visibility and control of the activities of the S&OP process.

7

Chapter 8
Planning Simulations

SAP IBP has revolutionized the simulation and scenario capabilities in supply chain planning, especially for S&OP. This chapter discusses the what-if scenarios, simulation applications, and version comparisons in SAP Integrated Business Planning for sales and operations.

SAP IBP has revolutionized the simulation and scenario capabilities in supply chain planning, especially for S&OP. This chapter discusses the what-if scenarios, simulation applications, and version comparisons in SAP Integrated Business Planning for sales and operations. It starts with the reasons to perform planning simulations and then leads to different capabilities of SAP IBP applications for simulation and what-if scenarios.

8.1   Simulation Planning at a Glance

The performance of a supply chain network is based on the business decisions made by the supply chain and associated professionals. Planning simulation supply chain professionals compare, validate, and analyze the potential future impacts of supply chain decisions being made today. Planning simulations help in making better decisions by predicting possible outcomes. These simulations are immensely beneficial applications for planners, allowing for outcome validation of a decision before the decision is implemented in real life. A bad decision can cost an organization millions of dollars in addition to other negative outcomes, like market share loss and formation of bad relationships with customers. Moreover, good decisions are crucial to an organization's success. A series of consistent good supply chain decisions develops a competitive advantage for a firm. Simulating and comparing the outcomes leads to better prediction of business events, resulting in better decision making and higher supply chain performance.

A crystal ball to see the future impact of current actions has always been a dream of planners. Planning is more important than ever in today's world because the dynamism and complexity of the market dynamism demands such capabilities. Predicting the future impact of current actions is also now technically feasible, made possible through digitization, big data, and analytics, which make this capability available through SAP IBP. In this section, we'll discuss the demand factors that require planning simulations when making S&OP decisions. We'll also discuss the factors which helped make it feasible to perform these simulations through the planning environment.

8.1.1   Demand Factors

Some of the important factors that have enhanced the requirements of performing simulation or what-if analysis when making S&OP decisions are as follows:

- **Short product lifecycle**
  With the growth of technical capabilities and relatively fast change of customer tastes, most industries today face short product lifecycles. This multiplies the decision risks of supply chain professionals. A bad decision can lead to product shortage and missed revenue on the one hand, or an excess of outdated products blocking huge capital on the other.

- **High customer expectation and service rate**
  Most of today's customers, be they retailers for product manufacturers or end consumers, expect excellent service. Leading organizations are aiming for more than a 90 percent (many are aiming for 99 percent) service rate, with an objective to fulfill customer requirements on-time and in full. Consider the complexity of this expectation of being able to supply all products all the time while still being agile and holding minimum inventory to optimize working capital management.

- **Intense competition in a digitized and connected environment**
  With the abundance of options available or a strict service rate policy, a bad decision can lead to loss of potential customers/revenue. In the digitized and connected world, every customer (irrespective of the size) can access information to compare available options and make the best decision. A mismatch of an organization's plan and market reality can be a crucial factor in revenue and profit for the organization.

- **Environmental factors**
  A hurricane that hit Florida in 2017 had a huge impact on customer demand, which impacted the requirements for consumer goods, industrial goods, and services. In addition to impacting the market of the affected area, the impact was felt in other near-by areas as well. A few leading companies that factored this potential impact

into their supply chain decisions were able to better serve their customers and managed the impact internally, too. Many others just reacted to the situation when it hit, had poor customer service, and were affected by shortages and excesses of products in a short span of time.

- **Internal constraints**
  Internal constraints like planning maintenance downtime for production resources, labor planning, production shifts, and so on offer some flexibility for decision-makers. An ability to perform a what-if scenario to identify the best possible actions against these constraints can have a substantial positive impact on the efficiency and realized revenue of the organization.

- **Complex logistics**
  Considering the current market realities, in which most firms own the operations aligned to their core competencies, logistics and transportation functions are being delivered by partner firms of the manufacturing firm. Add to this the complexities of e-commerce, varying transportation costs, driver shortages, and the like. A response to a demand surge from the customer can be to increase production in a short time, but if end-to-end planning wasn't simulated, it might be the case that transportation resources won't be available to supply the finished goods at the demand location. Now imagine a case in which this enhanced demand was simulated in SAP IBP for an end-to-end impact, so the required decisions were made in time.

- **Increased customization**
  Increased customization is the reality of the current market situation. Consider two product types: regular white soda cups at McDonald's and Wendy's, compared with cups on which the names McDonald's and Wendy's are printed. With high customization, even when a cup is available from a producing firm, it can't be supplied during an uptick in demand unless the inventory is available for the customized product. Higher customization takes the aggregation cushion away; every customer situation requires different analysis and action.

All these scenarios are excellent candidates for planning simulations. A what-if situation analysis supported by real data with potential events and an ability to work in a detailed dataset while still not impacting the live production data is a boon to planners. Planning simulations allow the planner to mock up unique situations, review, perform end-to-end analysis through a demand and supply plan, share the results with team members, and finalize the best possible action. Once the best action is reviewed and agreed upon, it can be copied to the active production dataset.

8.1.2   Supply Feasibility Factors

The factors that make it feasible to supply the planning simulation expectations through SAP IBP are as follows:

- **Hardware technological advancement**
  In the last decade, hardware advancements for both end user machines and data servers have exponentially enhanced data-processing capabilities.

- **Cloud computing and high computation speed of SAP IBP**
  SAP IBP is powered by cloud computing and the unique computation capabilities of SAP S/4HANA. This allows millions of dataset calculations to be made in a fraction of a second. This computation power enables the system to create and work in scenarios with huge data sets without impacting the live production data. The system can support multiple scenarios for multiple users without interfering with live data or different unique simulations.

- **External data integration and enhanced collaboration**
  Technical advancements, the Internet of Things (IoT), and data progress have allowed access to external data sets (big data) from the SAP planning and execution system. The additional market intelligence and points of sales data can be crucial input when performing planning simulation event analysis and comparing decisions.

- **Integrated systems and connected SAP landscape**
  The planning system in SAP IBP is connected to the execution system and can be connected to associated landscapes like SAP Ariba, SAP EWM, and so on. This connected system landscape allows for end-to-end analysis. For example, a procurement plan for a supplier can be shared via SAP IBP and SAP Ariba integration, a supplier can provide a commitment, and if the commitment isn't aligned with the requirements, then different procurement options can be mocked up and analyzed through planning simulations to take the best possible action.

8.1.3   Simulation Examples

The goal of simulation planning is to prepare a strategy proposal that helps in making effective decisions in the S&OP process. Uncertainty can arise from both the demand and supply sides of the business. Fluctuation in demand can be due to new product introductions, customer promotions, global impact, and so on, whereas supply-side impact can be from downtime (both planned and unplanned), delivery issues, late transports, and so on.

Through planning simulations in SAP IBP, potential events can be simulated through a what-if scenario, the planning algorithm (forecast, supply, etc.) can be executed, alerts can be generated, and then collaboration and comparison is performed to identify the best action plan while considering the end-to-end impact.

The following are some examples of performing planning simulations:

- **Demand change and customer delivery**
  Consider a business scenario in which, due to a sudden surge in demand at a retailer, the retailer (a customer of the organization) has requested an increase in demand in the short-term—over the next few weeks. The planner can create a what-if scenario by increasing the demand in a planning simulation environment and can execute the supply plan to understand the end-to-end impact. This can lead to options such as increasing a production shift, using an alternate machine, subcontracting, postponing other orders, and so on. The simulation planning in SAP IBP allows for mocking up, comparing, and sharing all these scenarios in the system to finalize and agree on the best course of action and update the customer on the same.

- **Inventory coverage**
  An ability to meet the customer's demand with a minimum cost to the company is highly impacted by inventory policy. Inventory coverages for both short supply and excesses are mocked up for the projected periods based on the market dynamics mapped through planning simulations.

- **Rough-cut capacity planning**
  This measures the impact of demand and supply changes on the approved S&OP, demand, and supply plans. It reviews the impact on resource loads, component requirements, projected revenue, material availability, etc.

- **Production schedule**
  Machine runs, planning for downtimes, alternate machine planning, and the like can have multiple options to be analyzed and compared. The results can determine the best course of action in various demand and supply scenarios.

- **Shelf life**
  In supply planning, one of the problems to be solved is whether to preproduce materials and hold them in inventory or produce only on demand. For organizations with products that have seasonal demand, preproduction may be a necessity; however, if the product has a shelf life, then there's a potential risk. This scenario can be mapped and compared in a planning simulation to finalize the best supply plan.

- **Procurement planning**
  This is a review of the procurement plan, supplier commitments, alternate supply situation, and the produce versus procurement scenario.

The preceding examples are representative simulation examples only. Based on the supply chain network and business requirements, different planning simulations can be identified and used in SAP IBP. SAP IBP provides flexible ways to simulate supply and demand planning, and you can share the scenarios with various stakeholders in real time.

There are three options provided in SAP IBP to perform planning simulations: simulate, version, and scenario. These options together provide cutting-edge planning simulations and what-if analysis. *Simulate* functionality is used to make adjustments in the Excel planning view, execute planning operators, and analyze the results in a simulation environment. A simulation can be used for further analysis and review, can be scrapped, or can be copied to active data. *Versions* are configured in the system, and you can use these versions to simulate a full planning cycle. *Scenarios* are a more local and flexible feature available for simulation. Active master data is used to analyze the what-if scenario transaction data in a scenario application. The planner can create a local version or scenario on the fly and share the results with the group or other users.

8.2   Simulations

Supply chain planners face different situations that contribute to the fluctuation of the demand or supply plan. The situation could be an opportunity or a risk, and it's important to assess the impact of the situation before it occurs. Typically, planners simulate the possible scenarios, assess the impact, and decide on the action to be taken. For example, BEST Corporation produces paper napkins at its facilities located across the United States. A prediction states that the sales of napkins will double six months from now. This scenario provides an opportunity for the organization to realize more sales and it brings a risk to the supply planner to deliver finished goods on time. Various options are available for the planner, like procuring from an external vendor, adding manufacturing capacity to the existing facility, or acquiring a new facility. All these options require extensive simulation planning to project the possible financial impact to the organization. SAP IBP's simulation functionality helps in simulating the defined versions and providing the results to make a quick and informed decision.

The Excel planning view in SAP IBP provides flexibility with ease of use and speed of operations and lets you view and make changes to a plan. Simulation planning is available as a function in the **Data Input** section of the **IBP** tab in the Excel ribbon. Planners can make manual adjustments to some key figures, like capacity or cost parameters, or can manually override consensus demand and execute planning operators on the fly without saving results. Planning operators like a copy operator or heuristics can be executed in a simulation mode without saving the results to the base version. The runs that are triggered in this mode are relevant to the key figures and the time period selected in the view.

Figure 8.1 shows the simulation functionality available in the SAP IBP tab. Clicking the **Simulate** button shows the list of operators that can be executed. The operators include copy operators and planning operators, like those for executing statistical forecasting and heuristics. After making manual changes to the plan, a planner can analyze the results of the planning run and choose to retain or discard the changes. Click **Save** to save the data changes to the backend database. The **Refresh** function reverses all unsaved changes that have been made.

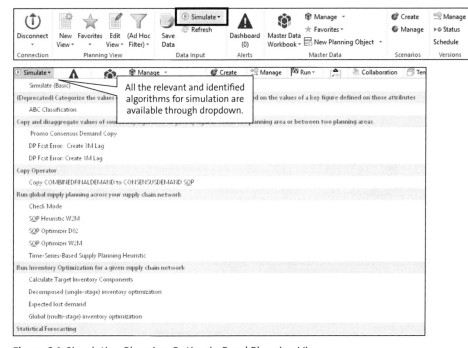

Figure 8.1 Simulation Planning Option in Excel Planning View

In this section, we'll walk through an example showing how to simulate changes and make local planning runs in simulation mode. In this case, say that you open the consensus demand Excel planning view and needs to make changes to the final demand of your SoCal Bikes customer for three weeks, as shown in Figure 8.2. The statistical forecast quantity will be overridden with the desired numbers. In Figure 8.3, you can see that only the statistical forecast quantity has changed; it hasn't impacted other key figures.

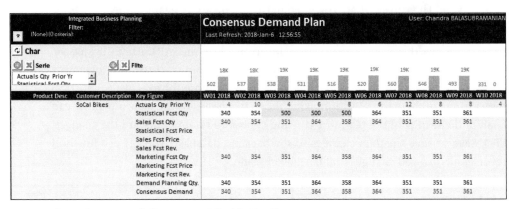

Figure 8.2 Manual Changes to Editable Key Figures

Click the **Simulate** button to open the list of operators to choose from. Select the **Copy** operator; the other key figures are updated automatically. These key figure changes are not made in the backend database. Now, you can review the copy results and even execute downstream functions like supply heuristics and view the results. Once the results are reviewed, they can be saved back to the database, or you can click **Refresh** to remove unsaved changes.

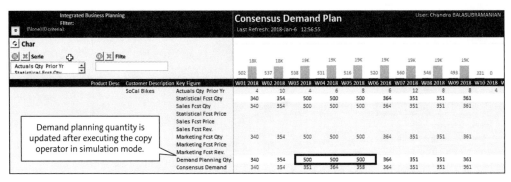

Figure 8.3 Data Copy through Simulation

Simulation functionality lets you simulate and view results before saving changes. Normally, you can take one of three actions after performing simulation planning through SAP IBP:

1. **Retain and save**
   If the simulation results are aligned to your expectations and add value, then you can click the **Save Data** button to copy the simulated data to active plan.

2. **Refresh and delete the simulated changes**
   If the simulation results are unfeasible or don't add value, then you can click the **Refresh** button. The simulated changes will be deleted and the plan refreshed.

3. **Further analysis**
   The simulation results may look promising, but you may have to analyze further or discuss the results with another team member before copying the information to active data. In this case, the results of the simulation can be copied to a scenario and can be reviewed and shared through SAP IBP collaboration. Figure 8.4 shows an example of saving the simulated data as a scenario and sharing the same with a team member. The scenario is further reviewed, analyzed, and managed from the **Manage Scenarios** screen. Details of scenario management are discussed in Section 8.4.

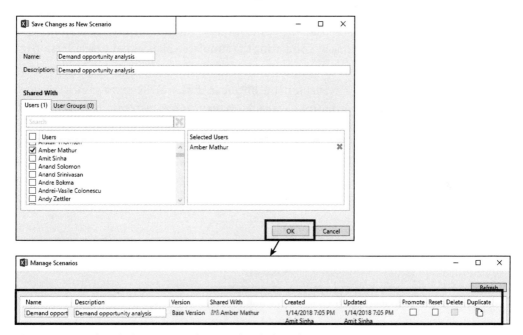

Figure 8.4 Simulated Planning Results Saved and Shared as Scenario

You can only perform simulations and scenarios using the master data values in the active data environment. If the simulation requires its own data set, then the version functionality in SAP IBP is used, which we'll discuss next.

8.3   Versions

A version is the simulation tool that SAP IBP provides to help create and compare alternate plans for what-if scenario planning. A version can be created as a copy of the base version, which is the data integration and base planning version. Changes can be made to the simulation version, and results can be compared in a single planning view. Specific master data and key figures can be copied to the simulation version. Usually, the data is copied before or immediately after the overnight planning run to keep the supply plan up to date with simulation planning.

Versions are configured in the **Planning** area and can be reused for a specific use. You have the flexibility to specify the key figures required for simulation planning. In an organization, multiple versions are created, and they can be used by various planning groups. It's essential to communicate to the users which planning versions they can use for making changes. A simulation version is a powerful tool to let you make changes and compare the base and simulation versions in the same planning view. It's easy to make decisions by comparing the simulated plan with the base version on the same screen.

Versions functionality is available in the **IBP** tab in the Excel ribbon, as shown in Figure 8.5. There are three action buttons available: **Manage** offers two options, either to copy a key figure from the base version to the simulation version or, once the changes are made, to delete the version when it's no longer required. Copying and deletion can be run on an ad hoc basis, or predefined jobs can be scheduled. The **Status** button offers visibility into the execution status of the scheduled jobs. Once the versions are defined and data copied, you can execute planning runs specific to a version.

Figure 8.5 Version Application in Excel Planning View

In the following sections, we will discuss the activities needed to create a version: version management, comparisons, and configuration.

8.3.1   Manage Versions

Figure 8.6 shows the selection screen that pops up after you click the **Manage** button. There are two options available: **Copy** and **Delete**. The copy functionality lets you choose versions to copy data **From** and **To**. In Figure 8.6, we're copying data from the base version to the upside version. The **Filter** options provide the flexibility to choose specific attributes of the version to copy. For example, for the version created for central region planners, it's sufficient to copy data only for the central region if there is no global impact to be studied as part of the simulation. **Key Figures** let you select specific key figures that you're interested in. The copy also can be executed for a specific time period only, as specified in the selection screen.

Once the selection parameters are provided, the **Next** button executes the version copy. A pop-up message shows the job number created for the version copy.

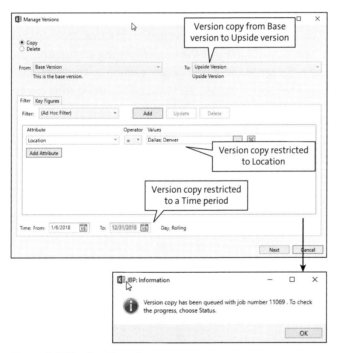

Figure 8.6 Version Copy Screen

You also can copy the simulation version back to the base version if the simulation results are satisfactory. You need to be cautious about doing so, however, because it writes to the active database. There are chances of base version data being overwritten. It's advisable to copy back to the base version by restricting your selections.

Figure 8.7 shows the status of the version copy that's triggered. The status of scheduled jobs can also be seen in this window.

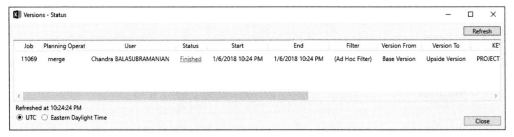

Figure 8.7 Version Copy Status

8.3.2   Version Comparison

Once the version is copied, you can compare the base version and simulation version in the same Excel planning view. Figure 8.8 shows the Excel planning view definition, in which you must select the base version and simulation version to compare both versions. Changes can be made to the simulation version and planning runs can be made. Planning results can be compared to make a decision.

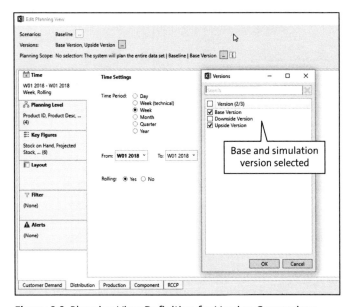

Figure 8.8 Planning View Definition for Version Comparison

There are a few key figures that don't have a simulation version, like the stock on hand key figure shown in Figure 8.9. In Section 8.3.3, you'll see how to restrict some key figures from version planning.

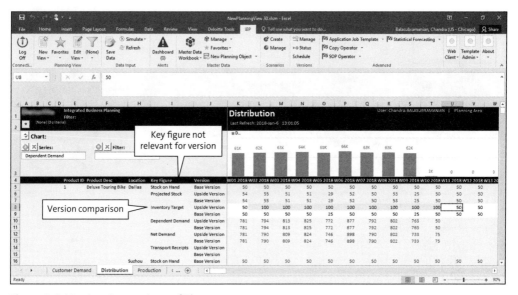

Figure 8.9 Version Comparison of Plan

8.3.3   Version Configuration

Versions must be configured in a planning area and are available for all planners with the necessary authorization to use them. Version configuration can be accessed by launching the Configuration app available under the **Model Configuration** group (see Figure 8.10). From the screen, click **Manage Version** to open the version configuration page. Here, select the planning area for which the version needs to be configured.

In the configuration screen, shown in Figure 8.10, you can create a new version by clicking the **Create New** button. A pop-up window opens in which you need to provide a name for the version (see Figure 8.11). You can select specific key figures only for a version or select all key figures. If a version is created for a specific function, and if the simulation activity doesn't have an impact on other functional areas, then it's best to select only relevant key figures.

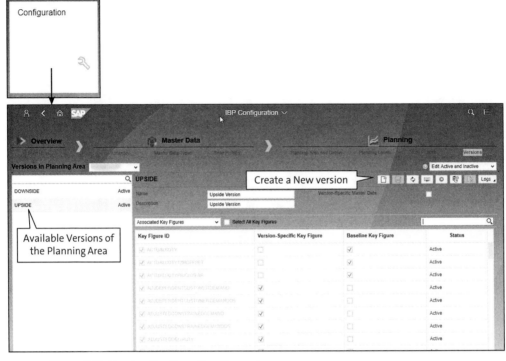

Figure 8.10 Version Configuration Example

Figure 8.11 Version Creation

If a key figure—like inventory on hand or sales order quantity—gets data from an external SAP ERP system or other systems, then we can associate these key figures with a version and mark them as baseline key figures so that version copies don't impact them and the values reflect the current data for simulation planning. Once the parameters are saved, you can activate the version and it's ready to use.

Versions are an effective tool to perform simulation planning. Once the version is created, it need not be shared with other users. All users can access the version.

However, the versions must be configured, and the configuration team has to create the version in SAP IBP before business users can use it. In the next section, we'll explain how scenarios can be more flexible for performing what-if planning on the fly.

8.4 Scenarios

Scenario planning is functionality provided in SAP IBP that's used to perform simulation planning locally and share the results with a group or other users and collaborate on the scenarios. This is a flexible tool via which you can create multiple scenarios on the fly without configuration and promote the agreed-upon scenarios back to the baseline scenario. The baseline scenario contains the data from the active database.

Although versions provide a structured process for simulation planning, they're restrictive in the sense that a version must be configured and initialized from a base version. This creates significant rigidity in terms of creating and using a new version. There are business scenarios that require planners to build various alternatives on the fly and trigger discussion of their impact. Scenarios remove this restriction by enabling planners to use recent planning data and create a local scenario around it without impacting the baseline scenario. Scenarios share master data with the baseline scenario, and transaction data is automatically copied to the scenario.

8.4.1 Scenario Creation

The **Scenarios** group is available in the **IBP** tab of the Excel ribbon. There are two options available to create and manage scenarios, as shown in Figure 8.12. You can create a new scenario by clicking on the **Create** button, which opens a pop-up window to provide the scenario's details. Here, you enter a **Name** and **Description** for the scenario. The scenario must be shared with other users so that they can access the alternative plan. You can share the scenario with specific users individually share with a user group.

Figure 8.12 Scenarios Group in Excel Planning View

A scenario can be created either after making changes to the baseline scenario or without making changes to the Excel planning view. When a scenario is created after making changes to the baseline scenario, the changes are saved directly to the scenario without impacting the baseline version. Figure 8.13 shows an example of scenario creation.

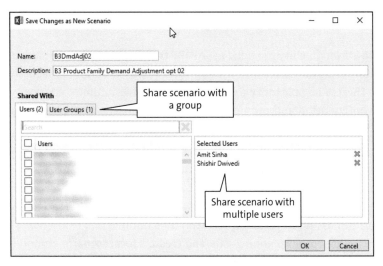

Figure 8.13 Scenario Creation Example

8.4.2 Scenario Comparison

Once the scenario is created, you can make changes to the plan for the available alternatives. Just like versions, scenarios also can be viewed in a single Excel planning view for comparison. In edit mode in the Excel planning view, all scenarios must be selected in order to view them together.

In Figure 8.14, an Excel planning view shows a key figure available in the baseline scenario and two other simulation scenarios. In this example, the demand planner faces a situation in which the demand for a product family is expected to be reduced based on sales intelligence input. The demand planner must make adjustments to the demand for individual products in the product family so that the desired results are achieved. The first step is to identify alternatives that are available. The planner has two options to be evaluated:

1. Adjust the demand for only one product in the family by pushing more products to the distributor with a price cut so that they can be sold to the end customer. To

do so, the planner must reduce the quantity sold to wholesale customers to balance the overall demand.

2. The second option is to increase the sales of low-priced product and reduce the sales of high-priced product.

After identifying the options, they're modeled in the system by creating scenarios. Manual changes are made to the scenarios and shared with users or user groups. This triggers discussion among various stakeholders, and finally a scenario is selected for further processing.

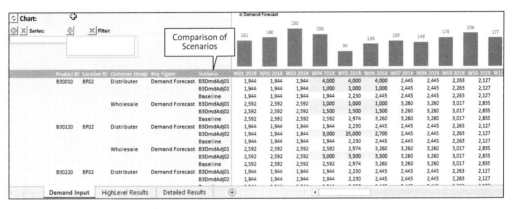

Figure 8.14 Scenario Comparison

8.4.3 Manage Scenario

Clicking the **Manage Scenarios** button opens a pop-up window in which the following options are available for the scenarios created, as shown in Figure 8.15:

- **Promote**
  This option promotes/copies the changes made in the scenario to the baseline scenario.

- **Reset**
  This option resets the selected scenario; the scenario is retained, but the changes made to the scenario are lost.

- **Delete**
  This option deletes the scenario completely; the scenario can't be used for further scenario building.

- **Duplicate**
  This option lets you create a new scenario by copying an existing scenario.

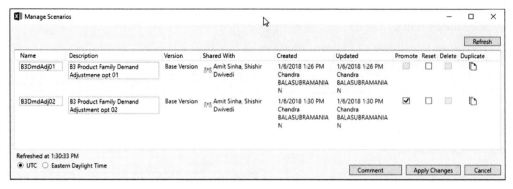

Figure 8.15 Manage Scenarios Options

After selecting the desired action, you can add comments, assign a reason code, and share it with an SAP Jam group (see Figure 8.16). Scenario planning is a great tool for simulation planning, and it integrates well with collaboration as well.

Figure 8.16 Scenario Comment and Collaboration

8.4.4   Version and Scenario Comparison

You've now seen various tools that SAP IBP provides for simulation planning. Each of these has various merits and meets the simulation needs of different demand and supply situations. Version and scenario functionalities are compared in Table 8.1.

Versions	Scenarios
Offer structured method of creating various alternative versions for comparison	Offer flexibility to create, compare scenarios, and promote
Must be configured before they can be used by planners	No configuration required; can be created on the fly by planners
No need to share the versions; all versions are available to all planners who have authorization	Scenarios must be shared with other users who need to access them
Key figures can be restricted to a version	All key figures are included by default in a scenario
Version copies can be restricted to selected attributes	All attributes are selected by default
Versions can be restricted by time period	The entire time horizon is applicable
Data copy to a simulation version is performed by the simulation copy function on an ad hoc basis or by scheduling a version copy job	Data is copied automatically when the scenario is created
Versions can be compared in Excel and can be viewed in a dashboard	Scenarios are restrictive and can be compared only with the Excel planning view

Table 8.1 Version and Scenario Comparison

8.5   Summary

Simulation planning is an important functionality required for supply chain planners to deal with a fluctuating market situation. Various alternative solutions can be built by leveraging the simulation functionalities provided by SAP IBP, and a decision can be made to create the optimum sales and operations plan. The simulation planning functionality in SAP IBP provides great flexibility to build various alternative plans, and it's well integrated with collaboration functions.

Chapter 9
Process Management

In this chapter, we'll discuss process management in SAP IBP, which provides the functionality to automate and orchestrate an S&OP process across cross-functional teams, thus aiding transparency, collaboration, increased participation, and adherence to process.

Sales and operations business processes involve collaboration and orchestration of the tactical planning process across cross-functional teams. For a company, the S&OP process can be executed across different hierarchical structures, such as across countries, market regions, business units, or a combination of these. A typical S&OP monthly process involves process steps such as product review, marketing review, demand review, supply review, and management business review. There can be variations in these steps depending on the type of business.

Each of these process steps has a duration, process owner, participants, collaboration group, and a set of actions or tasks to complete for a planning cycle. Often, a global S&OP process for a company is subdivided into regional/country-specific processes. These processes can vary in their dates, participants, and tasks. The challenge in managing an S&OP process in an organization is to ensure that the process deadlines are adhered to and that participants are completing their required activities on time during each process stage. If there are any delays in completion of tasks, they should be made transparent quickly so that the process step progress isn't blocked, thereby affecting the next steps of the process.

In larger organizations, the most time-consuming and challenging task is to orchestrate the process across several cross-functional teams and ensure all participants are completing activities on time. Process owners today spend most of their time on emails and follow-up activities, chasing the participants who are behind to ensure that they are completing their forecasts, analyses, or other planning activities on time. For example, a company could have about 300 sales planners and 20 demand planners in a demand review process step. It's important to track that the sales fore-casts are entered by all the sales planners and that the demand planners perform the consensus demand planning activities. The process owner should have visibility into the process progress and which users are falling behind schedule to take actions to remedy the process delays.

Another important aspect of process management is ensuring that there is some automation in the process—that is, the processes start automatically based on the dates set and complete when all underlying activities are completed, such that the process owners can focus on more important activities and be informed or take action when there are process delays. Moreover, end users should receive tasks auto-matically when a certain process stage is reached and be notified when they are due to complete their activities.

As will be discussed in the following sections, SAP IBP provides the following func-tionality for process management:

- Defining process templates
- Running periodic processes
- Automated tasks and task completion
- Process automation
- Process monitoring and visualization
- Integration with SAP Jam for collaboration

9.1   Process Management in Practice

In an SAP IBP process, the three main pillars are people, processes, and tools. SAP IBP bridges these three aspects with the process management capabilities connecting the S&OP process, user participation and collaboration, and the planning operations. The benefits of properly executed process management include the following:

1. Workflow of process steps
2. Customization of processes for different regions/business units
3. Transparency into the status of the process
4. Tasks management

5. Automation of processes

6. Process orchestration for batch application jobs

The rest of the section will cover details of process modeling scenarios and examples of how they can be achieved in SAP IBP. For our examples, we'll look at a typical S&OP setup for fictional company ABC, which has two regions for business unit XYZ, North America and Europe, as shown in Table 9.1.

Region	Subregion/Countries	S&OP Process Template
North America	United States	US S&OP
	Canada	Canada S&OP
	Mexico	Mexico S&OP
Europe	Eastern Europe	EE S&OP
	Northwestern Europe	NWE S&OP

Table 9.1 Example S&OP Process

For the North American region, there are three S&OP processes, one for each country; for the European region, there are two S&OP processes, one for each subregion (all countries within each European subregion follow the same S&OP process cadence). There can be different participants for each of the S&OP processes. Also, the process timelines and process steps may vary for each country/subregion.

To manage S&OP processes, SAP IBP provides two SAP Fiori-based applications: Manage Process Templates and Manage Processes, as shown in Figure 9.1. The Manage Process Templates app provides all the functionality to define a structure for a recurring S&OP process with details about its steps, participation, duration, tasks, and automation criteria.

The Manage Processes SAP Fiori app provides visualization, monitoring, and management for the lifecycle of the processes created from a process template. In our example, for the US S&OP process template, a process would represent a monthly instance or planning cycle of the template: for January US S&OP, February US S&OP, and so on.

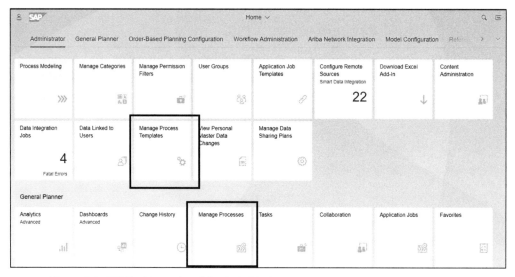

Figure 9.1 SAP Fiori Launchpad for SAP IBP: Process Management Apps

Managing process templates is an administrative function, so the Manage Process Templates app appears under the **Administrator** group in the SAP Fiori launchpad, whereas the Manage Process app is under **General Planner**. The process participants, process owners, and reviewer use this app to view the status of the process. SAP IBP provides the business authorization to control the user's access to perform view or edit actions in the Manage Process Template or Manage Processes app.

Before creating a process template, there are a few organizational questions that need to be answered

1. **Who are the owners of the process template?**
   In general, the S&OP process owner is responsible for the managing the process. There can be more than one owner of a process.

2. **What process steps need to be included in each template?**
   Typically, the S&OP process includes five process steps, as mentioned at the beginning of the chapter. However, some regions/countries may have different process steps and cadence. For example, In the US monthly S&OP process, there could be five steps, whereas the Canadian S&OP process may have four steps starting with demand review (i.e., the product review process could be part of the demand review).

3. **What is the duration of each process step?**
   In a monthly S&OP process, the goal is to start the processes at the beginning of month and end during the last week with a management business review. Therefore, each S&OP process step is about three to five days in duration—sometimes less and sometimes more.

4. **Are the process steps sequential or parallel?**
   S&OP process steps are usually sequential; however, you can model parallel process steps in an S&OP process. For example, in the Canada S&OP process template, the process step for demand review could be split into two parallel steps—sales review and demand review—with some overlapping dates.

5. **Who are the owners and participants in each step?**
   It's common for each process step to have a different process step owner to manage its lifecycle. There can be one or more participant groups in a process step. For example, in US S&OP template, for the demand review step, there can be three participant groups: US sales planners, US demand planners, and US marketing planners.

6. **What are the tasks that need to be executed during a process step and by whom?**
   During each process stage there are several tasks that need to be executed by the planners. For example, during the demand review phase, sales planners need to enter the sales forecast, the sales director needs to approve the forecast, and marketing managers need to enter promotions and pricing information, etc. These tasks need to be completed to move to next stage of the process.

7. **Is automation required for the process steps?**
   Process steps can be automated to always start on a certain date, start when the previous step is completed, end when all tasks are completed, and so on.

8. **What batch processes should be included in the automation?** Sometimes, certain batch jobs can be associated with a process step's start or end state. For example, when a demand review step starts, you may want to run the statistical forecast, or when the management business review ends, run the copy operation and perform a data integration outbound job for SAP ERP or SAP S/4HANA.

Once these questions have been answered for a process template, the process template owner can create the required templates in SAP IBP. The next section walks through some of the common steps performed during template creation.

9.2   Setting Up Process Templates and Automations

The Manage Process Template SAP Fiori app shows a list of all available templates created, as shown in Figure 9.2. For example, the US, Canada, Mexico, and Eastern and Northwestern S&OP templates would be visible in this list when created. This list view also provides the capability to start a process or quickly copy an existing process template to create a new one.

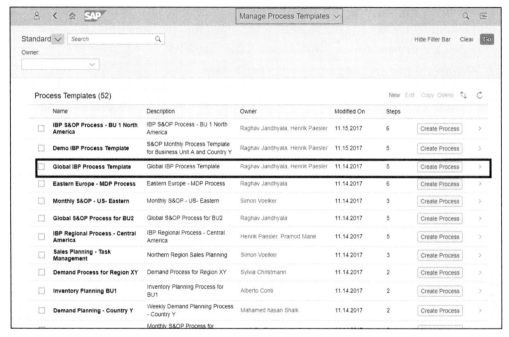

Figure 9.2 Process Template List View

As shown in Figure 9.3, within the process template, a list of process steps created is provided, along with a Gantt chart view showing the steps overview. This allows the process owner a quick view of the process steps, their duration, and whether there are any overlapping steps, along with the automation criteria. The circles indicate that there are SAP IBP application jobs associated with the step, and arrows show whether there are any automation criteria defined for each step.

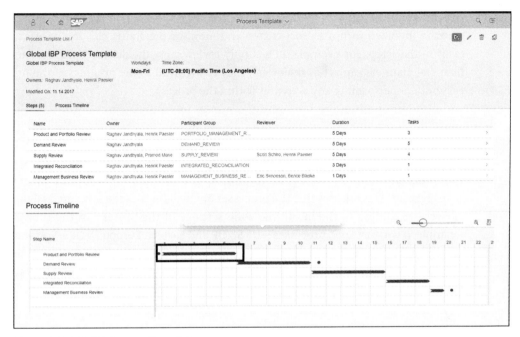

Figure 9.3 SAP IBP Process Template

The following sections cover all the relevant areas of the process template in detail with examples of their usage and setup. We start with the process roles, time zones, and weekday settings, followed by detailed settings of process steps, tasks assignments, process step automations, and process orchestration of application jobs, and finally cover the visualizations of the process template with Gantt charts.

9.2.1   Process Roles

As shown in Figure 9.3, process templates also show the process owners, participant groups, and reviewers associated with each process step. Because SAP IBP manages collaboration across various functional groups, it's important that the right groups of users are assigned to the right process steps. For example, a demand review participant group for the demand review step is a user group consisting of demand planners in the United States. This can be set up in the **User Groups** section of SAP IBP. Typically, participants in the process step are assigned tasks. There can be one or more participant groups for a process. For example, the product and portfolio review step may have two user groups, consisting of product management and marketing planners.

285

Other than the participant groups, there can be reviewers assigned to a process step, who are involved within a process step and monitor the status but don't perform tasks in that step. For example, in a supply review step, the demand planners and financial planners can act as reviewers: they're involved in the progress of the process but not performing any activities within the process.

9.2.2   Time Zone, Workday, and Duration Settings for Process Steps

When the S&OP process is managed globally with several regional and country-specific processes, the time zones and local times are considered by SAP IBP process management. This ensures that the processes are running and the tasks are assigned correctly according to the local time zone settings of the process. In the running example, if you have two processes—US S&OP and Eastern Europe S&OP—you want to ensure that the right time zones are assigned to each so that the automation settings with respect to scheduling application jobs associated with the process or starting/ending the process and assignment of tasks adhere to this setting.

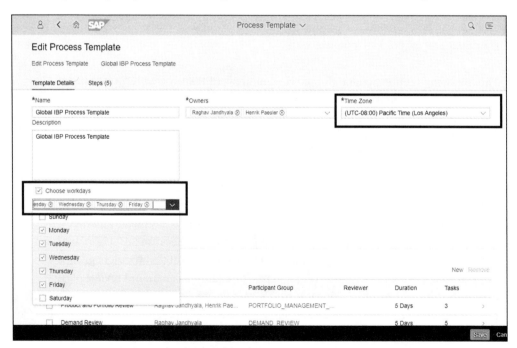

Figure 9.4 Localized Time Zone and Workday Settings for Process Template

SAP IBP process management also provides settings for default workdays as shown in Figure 9.4—for example, for work weeks starting on Monday and ending on Friday each week. These settings are used when creating a process for this template for each month; the template automatically considers the work days for each process step.

In a template, you only define the duration of each process step. When creating a process, the actual dates are calculated considering the step duration and workdays.

9.2.3   Tasks Assignment

A set of template tasks can be defined for each planning step. Usually in a planning process step, different activities are happening and the participant users are responsible for the timely completion of those activities. Figure 9.5 shows a demand review step in which different plans are created and consolidated to reach a consensus demand plan considering the assumptions for the demand changes. In the demand review meeting, this plan is reviewed and approved, along with capturing action items and new sets of assumptions.

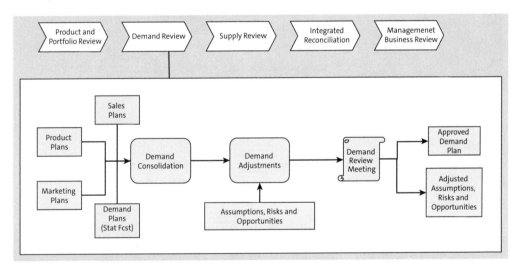

Figure 9.5 Sample Demand Review Process Activities

In SAP IBP, one or more tasks can be defined for a process step and assigned to participant groups and/or users associated with that process step. Task management in SAP IBP will be covered in more detail later in Section 9.4, wherein we'll discuss how tasks are assigned to users, how they are monitored and completed, how to create ad hoc tasks, and more. For example, a demand review step may have a task called Update Sales Forecasts, which is assigned to a participant group, US Sales Planners.

Assume that there are 100 sales planners in the United States. When the process step starts, this single task is then assigned as 100 individual SAP Jam tasks and assigned to each sales planner. Users get notifications when tasks are assigned, and as they complete the tasks, the step progress increases. There is no order sequence for the tasks. All tasks will follow the same duration as the step duration and will start and end based on the step dates. As shown in Figure 9.6, for each process step one or more tasks are assigned.

Figure 9.6 shows the flexible layout for process steps, which increases the ability to view the different process steps and jump to the header and details of each process step. The left part of the flexible layout is the steps overview, showing the step list and Gantt chart. For each step selected, the right side shows the details of the step: participation, duration, automation settings, job templates, and tasks.

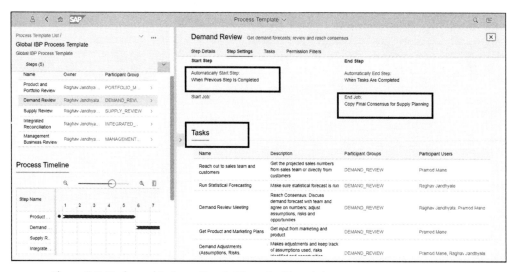

Figure 9.6 Tasks and Automation Settings for Template

9.2.4   Process Steps Automation

As shown in Figure 9.6, the process template owner can assign automation criteria for how the steps should start and end. In the example, the demand review step starts when the previous step, product and portfolio review, is completed; the step ends when the tasks associated with the demand review step are completed—that is, when all tasks are completed and the progress reaches 100 percent.

SAP IBP provides the flexibility to customize the automation criteria for each process step. As mentioned earlier, the step automations can be defined for the start and/or end steps. The default is to not have automation; that is, start and end are activated manually by the step owner. When you select automation criteria, you have several options. For the start step, the standard conditions are **On Start Date**, **When Previous Step Is Completed**, or **When Application Job Associated with the Previous Step Is Completed**. Similar settings are offered for the end condition: **On End Date**, **When Tasks Are Completed** (this selection is only available when SAP Jam is enabled), or **When Application Job of Start Step Is Completed**. You can choose one or more of these conditions and apply and/or conditions for the selection

For example, the start condition of the process step can be defined as follows: to start on the start date and when the ending job of the previous step is completed, as shown in Figure 9.7. This can be the case for, say, an integrated reconciliation step in which you always start on the 16th day of each month, but only when its previous step (supply review) is completed based on the completion of that step's end application job (e.g., a copy operator).

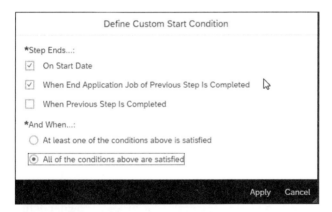

Figure 9.7 Process Step Automation Settings

Other conditions could be set such that the management business review meetings always start on their set start date and end on the end date irrespective of the status completions of the prior steps. Therefore, process automation gives flexibility to define the automation criteria for each step, and this can be different across different process templates. For example, the US process template may have demand review start as soon as the product review step is completed, whereas in the Canada S&OP process, the demand review step may have a criterion to always start on the start date. Note that the automation criteria can be manually overridden; for example, the process step owner can choose to complete the process earlier, thus overriding the automation criterion for that step to end on its end date.

SAP Integrated Business Planning for sales and operations lets you define exception conditions based on certain user-defined criteria, especially when there is an AND condition for the steps. For example, a supply review step can configured in such a way to only end once its end date has been reach *and* when tasks are completed; if there is an exception, then an exception state can be defined by the user as **Delayed**. This is a configurable field in the process settings.

9.2.5   Process Orchestration of Application Jobs

As part of a monthly process cycle, there can be many batch jobs that need to run. For example, when the step starts, you may want to clear the key figures to be ready for planning. When the demand review step begins, you may want to run a statistical forecast job, or when the final plan is confirmed, run a snapshot operator or copy operators.

SAP IBP provides the ability to run application jobs as part of Excel and in the Application Jobs app. In addition, to orchestrate process-oriented scheduling of application jobs in which the application jobs are run not just based on dates, but based on the automation criteria of the steps, these application job templates can be associated with a process step. The step settings let you assign only one application job setting per start and end of the step. In Figure 9.8, for the US demand review step, we've assigned an application job template for when the step ends.

When a process owner manually sets a step to complete, the application job associated with the end step is immediately triggered. The same is true if the process step ends when the automation criteria is reached. Typically, the processes owner defines the application job templates that need to be assigned to a step. In the example, there are five process templates, one for each country/subregion. For each of the demand review end steps, we can assign a country- or subregion-specific custom application job template. These application job templates will run based on the process cadence. In Section 9.3, we'll further discuss how the application jobs are run, their authorizations, and automation criteria.

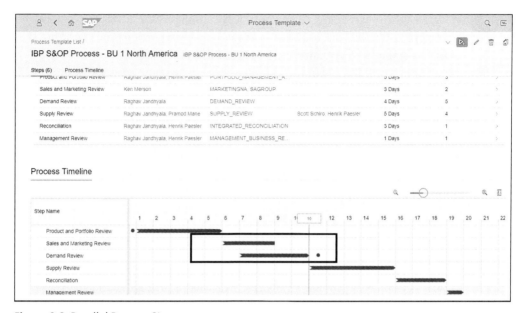

Figure 9.8 Parallel Process Steps

9.2.6   Gantt Chart View of Sequential and Parallel Processes

Gantt charts provide process owners with a good visual overview of the automation associated with each step. Here, a process step with no automation will have no directional arrows. In Figure 9.8, the process shows two parallel steps: Sales and marketing review and demand review. The dates overlap, such that the sales step ends before the demand review step. The circle next to the demand review indicates that there's an application job associated with the end step of the demand review process, and the process bar shows that there are start and end step automations associated with the demand review step. With such a setup, the process owner can quickly understand the overall step dependencies and adjust the settings as needed.

Another capability offered by process management as of SAP IBP version 1802 is making certain key figures editable only when a process stage is active or the process step dates have been reached. The process steps in the process template have settings to assign permission filters to participants/participant groups. When the process step is in progress, the permission filters are applied to the users; when the step is completed, these permissions are removed, thereby effecting the key figure editability for users. This topic is covered in Chapter 15 in more detail.

So far, we've discussed how to create process templates for different countries and subregions. Next, we'll discuss how to create monthly recurring processes from these templates and how to visualize and monitor the processes.

9.3   Manage Processes

The Manage Processes SAP Fiori app provides process monitoring, visualization, and lifecycle management for S&OP processes. Based on their assigned user role, a user can be an owner, participant, or reviewer of a process step. There are three important aspects of managing processes, which we'll discuss in detail:

1. Create one or more process instances
2. Manage the lifecycle of the process
3. View and monitor the status of the process

In this section, we'll provide an overview of what a process is and then walk you through creating a process. We'll then discuss managing and monitoring processes.

9.3.1   What Is a Process?

A *process* is an instance of a process template that runs every recurring period. For example, for the US S&OP template, there can be one process for each month: January 2018 US S&OP process, February 2018 US S&OP Process, and so on. As shown in Figure 9.9, each process has actual dates associated with it and its steps based on the duration and workdays defined in the template.

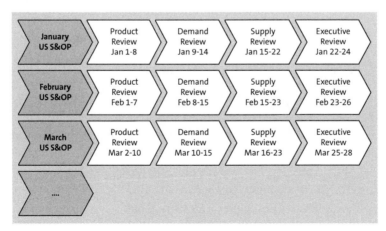

Figure 9.9 Processes for Process Template

The Manage Processes app shows a list view of all the processes on entry with a clear indication of the running processes, closed processes, and processes that are overdue. To get a quick insight into where there are process issues, the manage processes list view shown in Figure 9.10 shows the processes that are overdue and indicates the overall process status completion and if there any exceptions to the process (e.g., the start date was reached and the previous step isn't completed). A quick overview of the current running steps also is shown. In our example, for each of the process templates, there can be one or more processes that can be defined, but typically only one process will be running and others will be closed or not yet started.

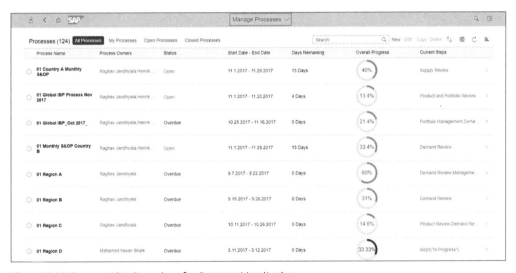

Figure 9.10 Process List Overview for Process Monitoring

Processes in SAP IBP have only three statuses: **Open**, **Overdue**, or **Closed**. The **Overdue** status indicates that the days remaining for the process is zero or the current date is past the process end date.

9.3.2   Creating a Process

In the Manage Processes app, processes can be created for each process template. The only information that needs to be provided is the process name, start date of the process, and any adjustments to the dates. For the sample template, you can define processes for the next planning cycle or as required for the next six months of the planning cycle. When a process instance is created for the process, you can specify a default start date; all other dates of the process steps are adjusted considering the duration of the step and the workdays, based on the default start date set.

For example, if a process step starts on Friday and has a duration of four days, then the dates of the process step will be adjusted such that the four days excludes the non-working days (i.e., Saturday and Sunday); thereby the end date becomes Wednesday of the following week. If there are any fiscal holidays for the region in which the process is run, then they need to be taken into account and the dates adjusted manually for the process step start and end dates along with the dates of the other steps.

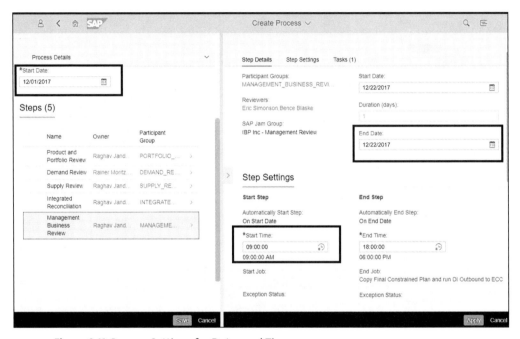

Figure 9.11 Process Settings for Dates and Times

In addition to the dates, the process step owner can choose to enter the start date and time if step automation is included with date-based criteria, as shown in Figure 9.11. For example, you can choose to have the step start at 9 a.m. in the time zone setting of the process so that any application jobs are run at that time, and any tasks are created for the users at 9 a.m. The management business review process step has automation settings to start on the start date with a start time of 9 a.m. and end on the end date with an end time of 6 p.m. When the process step is completed at 6 p.m., the **Copy Final Constrained Plan** job will be triggered immediately.

Process owners can create more than one process for a template (January US S&OP, February US S&OP, etc.). If there are automation settings for the processes defined such that the processes start on a defined date, then these processes will be automatically executed by the system sequentially.

9.3.3   Managing Process Lifecycle

After the processes have been created from a process instance, they're automatically run when an automation criteria is defined for the steps. You can also manually run the process steps for steps that don't have automation defined for them.

The process steps have a lifecycle with **Not Started**, **In Progress**, and **Completed** statuses, as shown in Figure 9.12. By default, the process steps start with **Not Started** and move to **In Progress** either when the process step owner manually changes the status or when the automation criteria is satisfied and the background automation technical job moves the status to **In Progress**. For example, the product review step is configured to start on the start date of January 1 at 9 a.m. When this date and time criteria are reached, the system automatically moves the status to in progress. The status completions are reached either by the process step owner manually changing the status or when the automation criteria are reached; for example, the demand review step is set to **Complete** when all the tasks are completed. If all the tasks are completed, the progress moves to 100 percent.

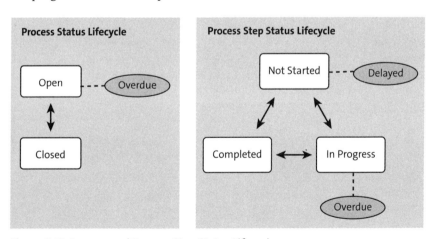

Figure 9.12 Process and Process Step Status Lifecycle

There are a few secondary exception statuses that can be defined by the process template owner for certain automation criteria. For example, when the start date is reached and the previous step is not completed, the step stays in **Not Started** status with a secondary user defined status of **Delayed**. Similarly, when the end date of the step is reached and the step is not completed, perhaps because the tasks associated with the step aren't completed, then the step is still in **In Progress** status with a secondary status of **Overdue**. As stated earlier, the process step owner can manually change the status as required, which will override the automation criteria set for the step.

Only the process step owner has the authority to change the status of the process step. The process step uses the permission filters of the process step owner, which means that any application job scheduled as part of the process step will run with the process step owner's permission filters. This ensures that the jobs are run with the right authorizations. Also, the background process automation job will schedule the application jobs using the permission filters of the process step owner.

As shown in Figure 9.13, the process step owner can manage the lifecycle of the process step within the Manage Process application or from the process chart in the SAP IBP dashboard. Depending on the status of the current process step, the next possible step status is shown for the process step owner to change the status of the step.

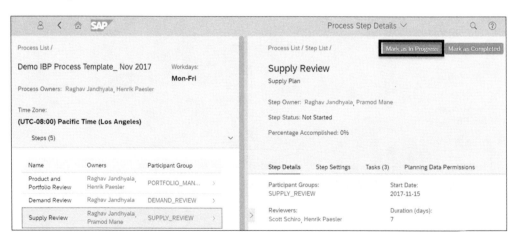

Figure 9.13 Manage Process Lifecycle Status

When a step is set to **In Progress**, the following set of activities happens:

1. Tasks are assigned to participant groups or users.

2. Task notification emails are sent out by SAP Jam.

3. If there are any application jobs that are associated with the start step, they're triggered immediately.

4. As users complete the tasks, the progress of the process increases.

5. Once all tasks are completed, the process step progress reaches 100 percent and the step moves to **Completed** status based on the automation criteria defined for the step. For example, if automation is set to end when all tasks are completed, then the step is set to the **Completed** status once all tasks are finished. If automation is based on the end date and task completion, then the step goes to **Completed** status when the end date is reached and the tasks are completed.

6. If there are any application jobs associated with the end of the step, they're started.

Further details about task management will be covered in Section 9.4.

9.3.4   Monitoring Process Status

The Manage Processes app provides nice visualizations and better usability to quickly get to the information that is most relevant for finding bottlenecks in the process. The visualization and monitoring aspects of the process include the following:

1. Status of each process step

2. Progress percentage of each step

3. Gantt chart view of processes and tasks

4. View status of application job runs and navigate to application job

5. View task completion status for participants

6. Navigation to SAP Jam collaboration group for further collaboration

The Gantt chart view of the process gives a quick visual indication of the progress of the process steps, timelines, and associated tasks with their statuses. As an example, the monthly S&OP process for Mexico is shown in Figure 9.14. It shows that the first step, product and portfolio review, is 100 percent complete. The second step is overdue because the step is not 100 percent complete, but the due date has passed. The reason for this, as shown in Figure 9.14, is that task **03 Demand Review Meeting** isn't completed.

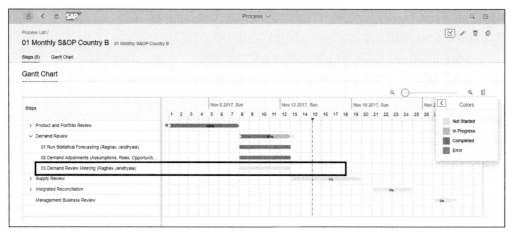

Figure 9.14 Gantt Chart View of Process

Because of this, the next step, supply review, isn't started because it's dependent on the completion of the demand review step, so its secondary status is set to **Delayed**, as shown in Figure 9.15.

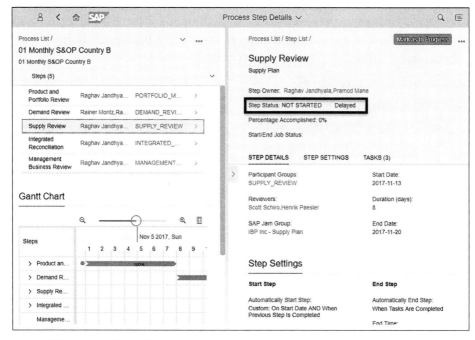

Figure 9.15 Process Step with Delayed Status

In this case, the second step will resume processing as soon as the first step is set to **Complete**, either by manually completing the process step or automatically when the last task associated with the step is completed. It's clear that because of a delay in one step, the consecutive steps are affected, especially if they have dependencies. This is made transparent to the planner and the planner can take necessary steps to either readjust the dates of the dependent steps or let the process continue with the reduced duration.

9.3.5   Process Dashboards

In addition to the list view in the Manage Processes app, where multiple processes can be viewed together, the Dashboard app in SAP IBP provides the functionality to add process-related charts together with other analytical charts, thereby showing the process- and data-related charts together in one view. This also offers the ability to view multiple processes together based on user selection criteria. You can select any open/running processes and include them in the dashboard.

For example, all the running processes for North America—US S&OP, Canada S&OP, and Mexico S&OP—can be included in a process dashboard along with other analytical charts, like revenue per country and profitability by region, as shown in Figure 9.16.

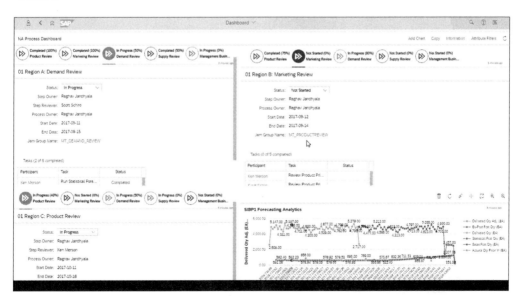

Figure 9.16 View Multiple Processes in Dashbaord

As of SAP IBP version 1705, in SAP IBP dashboards, users can choose to include analytical charts, alerts, and process charts. The controls on the process chart in the dashboard also now provide options to swap the process chart with another chart. The process chart in the process dashboard is interactive, in the sense that you can select different process steps to see the step details and tasks. The process charts display a chevron of the process steps with their statuses and completion percentages. For each process step, the step details, process participation, task assignments and completions are displayed, along with navigation to SAP Jam groups, application jobs, and tasks. By default, the running process step for a process is shown in the chart.

Similar to the Manage Process app, the lifecycle of a process step can be managed from the process chart by setting the step to **In Progress** or **Completed**. The **Tasks** list shows the status for each task associated with the step. If there are tasks that are falling behind, overdue email notifications can be sent directly from the process chart, as shown in Figure 9.17.

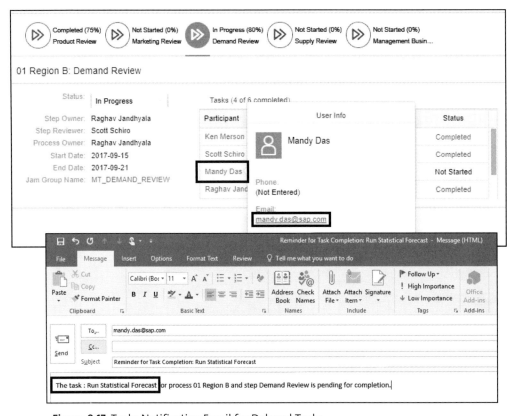

Figure 9.17 Tasks Notification Email for Delayed Tasks

9.4   Task Management

To manage workflow of tasks, SAP IBP process management provides the necessary functionality to create task templates, task assignments, notifications, completions from the web UI and Excel UI, and task monitoring. SAP IBP tasks are realized as SAP Jam tasks.

Planners like to be notified when they have a task and be able to finish the tasks assigned to them easily without navigation to multiple screens. This section covers details about how tasks are created, assigned, and completed in SAP IBP. We'll also cover how task completions can be performed from SAP Integrated Business Planning, add-in for Microsoft Excel, and finally we'll cover how the process progresses to the next stage of completion for the tasks.

9.4.1   Tasks Assignments and Completions

Tasks are created for each process step in a process template with assignments to process step participant groups and/or users, as follows:

1. When a step is set to **In Progress**, SAP Jam tasks are created for each user assigned to the step. If the user isn't yet part of the SAP Jam group, an invitation to join the group is sent first.

2. A notification email is sent from SAP Jam to users about the task assignment and due date.

3. To facilitate ad hoc tasks beyond the standard tasks in the template, the Tasks app lets users create ad hoc tasks and assign them to users in the process step along with due dates. In addition, users can assign a task to be tracked in the process step progress percentage, as shown in Figure 9.18.

4. When logged into SAP IBP, whether from the web UI or Excel, users can view their open tasks and complete them. In the web UI, there is an app called Tasks. In this app, the open tasks for the logged in user are displayed. The user can complete the tasks directly from here or navigate to SAP Jam tasks and complete them from there.

5. When a user is logged in through Excel, the **IBP** tab will show a **Tasks** area that lists open tasks; the user can view and complete tasks from there.

6. After a user completes a task, the process step progress increases accordingly. For example, say there are four tasks for users assigned. If one of the users completes a task, the step progress increases to 25 percent.

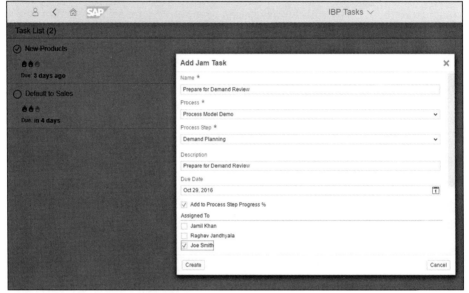

Figure 9.18 Create Ad Hoc Tasks for Process

7. When all the tasks are completed, the process step reaches 100 percent and then can be set to **Completed** automatically if the step completion criteria are reached.

8. Users participating in a process can view the status of the process step and the tasks completion in the Manage Process app to see who has completed a task on time and who has fallen behind schedule.

9. In SAP Jam, further information can be gathered or collaboration can be done for each task. For example, you may want to attach documents to the task. New ad hoc tasks can be created from SAP Jam that aren't part of SAP IBP process management.

9.4.2   Tasks Completion from SAP Integrated Business Planning, Add-In for Microsoft Excel

Since SAP IBP release 1711, SAP Integrated Business Planning, add-in for Microsoft Excel provides the functionality to view and complete tasks from Excel. When a user is participating in an S&OP process—such as a demand planner as part of a demand review step currently in progress—they are notified in the **Tasks** group of the **IBP** tab about the number of open tasks, as shown in Figure 9.19.

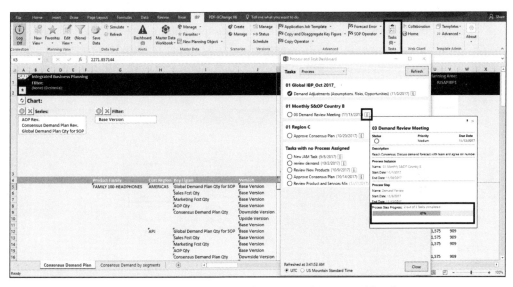

Figure 9.19 Task Management in SAP Integrated Business Planning, Add-In for Microsoft Excel

This demand planner can then click on the **Tasks** icon to see the list of open tasks, which can be grouped by **Due Date**, **Priority**, or **Process**. When grouped by **Process**, the **Tasks** screen will show all the open tasks across different processes to which the user is assigned. When the user selects the information context of the task, it will display the task details along with the details of process steps and the progress percentage. In Figure 9.19, the **Demand Review Meeting** task is open for this planner and is due, as indicated in red. The progress is 67 percent, with two out of three tasks completed; when the user completes this activity, the progress of the process step will reach 100 percent. The demand planner can then perform his final steps, which could include making some planning data changes and/or setting up the demand review meeting and marking the task as **Completed** directly from Excel.

9.4.3   Process Progress Based on Tasks Completion

When the demand planner completes this task from Excel or the Tasks SAP Fiori app, and when all tasks associated with the process step are completed, the demand review process step immediately goes to **Completed** status. Consequently, the following step, supply review, which is dependent on completion of the demand review step, goes to **In Progress** status.

As shown in Figure 9.20, the demand review step is at 100 percent and is set to **Completed**. The end application job associated with demand review—a copy operator to copy final demand to consensus demand for supply planning—is triggered. The supply review step goes into **In Progress** status, and tasks are created for the users participating in this step. As shown in Figure 9.20, the progress of the supply review keeps increasing as tasks are completed by end users.

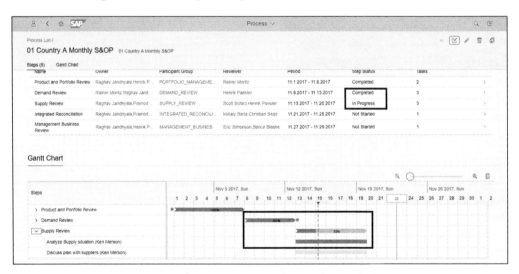

Figure 9.20 Automation of Process Step Based on Task Completion

Thus, process management provides transparency into the process steps that need attention; when the process blockers are handled, the process automatically moves to the next steps. If the supply review step has a delay, it is captured in the status of the step, and such information will be useful in future releases of SAP IBP, in which process adherence KPIs are planned to be tracked, giving process owners the ability to see process improvements over time, process participation, process-to-process comparisons, and so on. Upon completion of all the steps associated with the process, the process automatically is closed and appears under **Closed Processes**, as shown in Figure 9.21.

Figure 9.21 Process List View of Completed Processes

9.5   Process Management with SAP Jam

SAP IBP uses SAP Jam as a collaboration platform to facilitate collaboration across cross-functional teams. An SAP Jam group can be assigned to each process step to provide collaboration across several cross-functional teams. For our example process, you could create an SAP Jam collaboration group for each process step as shown in Table 9.2.

Process Template	Process Step	Participant Groups	SAP Jam Group
US S&OP	Demand review	US demand planners	US Demand Review
EE S&OP	Demand review	EE sales planners, EE demand planners	EE Demand Review

Table 9.2 SAP Jam Group Assignment for Process Step

SAP IBP provides flexibility in creating SAP Jam groups and assigning them to process steps as follows:

- Start by creating an SAP Jam group, such as US Demand Review, and invite several users who are US demand planners to that group (typically users from the participant groups).

Or:

- When creating a process step, define a new SAP Jam group. In this case, you don't need to invite users. When the process step starts, the participant users who are assigned tasks are automatically sent an invitation to join the SAP Jam group.

Additional users can be added directly to the SAP Jam group who may or may not be part of the process. Figure 9.22 shows a SAP Jam group for demand review, which enables collaboration among participants of the demand review process step. SAP IBP uses SAP Jam for task assignments, as we covered in detail in Section 9.4.

Figure 9.22 SAP Jam Group for Demand Review

> **Note**
>
> The process management functionality will work even if you don't have SAP Jam enabled, except for the collaboration aspects, tasks assignment, and progress, which are dependent on SAP Jam. The process automations will continue to work without SAP Jam.

9.6   Summary

In this chapter, we covered details of how to create and run an S&OP process using process management capabilities in SAP Integrated Business Planning for sales and operations. We also detailed setting up process templates with process step roles, durations, task assignments, automation criteria, and orchestration of application jobs. We then covered how to manage and run recurring processes, including creating a process, managing the process lifecycle, monitoring the status of the process steps and exception conditions, and using process charts and dashboards to view and manage multiple running processes.

We next covered details of task assignments and completions, along with how planners can easily complete tasks in Excel and how process steps can progress upon completion of tasks. We finally covered how SAP Jam collaboration and process management are seamlessly integrated. All these capabilities provide robust process orchestration and management of processes across cross-functional organization units, providing transparency, visibility, and adherence to the process.

9

Chapter 10
Configuring SAP IBP for Sales and Operations

In this chapter, we'll discuss sales and operations configuration in SAP IBP. The highly flexible configuration options allow customers to model their unique business processes and consolidate planning across different levels of data.

The planning model in SAP IBP is a set of configurable entities used to model a customer's unique business models. For example, a model defines what key figures or measures are planned or analyzed, the characteristics they belong to (product, customers, etc.), and the hierarchy levels at which they are viewed or planned.

SAP IBP provides very flexible model configuration with a collection of modeling constructs. Model configuration is the foundational activity in SAP IBP, on which several other processes depend. A planning model should be defined before you start loading data, perform planning operations like saving and simulating data, or run planning operators like supply chain planning.

Customer models start with a baseline configuration and evolve over time when new business processes are introduced or merged. Therefore, it's very important that the configuration is highly flexible so that expert business users can define and maintain their models and make changes when the business evolves.

Let's walk through the example Excel planning view shown in Figure 10.1 to understand how this relates to a planning model. An Excel planning view allows the business user to view data in a structure represented by the key elements like key figures, planning hierarchy/planning levels, time level, and time horizon, along with functions like aggregations, disaggregation of data, simulations/save, and running planning operators like supply planning, copy operator, and so on. All these elements of planning are configured in a planning area, which is typically customized for every customer.

Once a planning area is configured, activated, and loaded with data, it can be accessed by several areas of an application, like Excel for planning and simulations, analytics and dashboards for data analysis and visualizations, data integration to load data for custom-defined planning master data, time profiles and key figures, and so on.

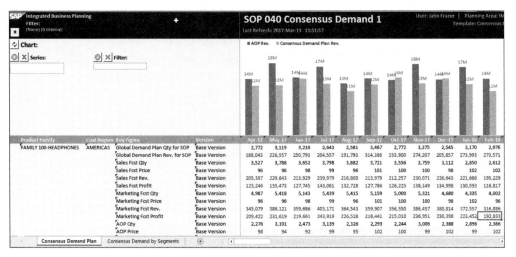

Figure 10.1 Planning View Representing Different Aspects of SAP IBP Planning Model

In this chapter, we'll go deeper into the planning area setup and configuration by covering core elements of the planning area like attributes, master data types, key figures and calculations, planning levels, versions, and planning operators. We'll also cover some of the performance recommendations for planning area configuration.

10.1   Planning Areas and Time Profiles

The **Model Configuration** group in the SAP Fiori Launchpad for SAP IBP (see Figure 10.2) provides the SAP Fiori apps for viewing, configuring, and maintaining SAP IBP models.

The main apps in **Model Configuration** include Attributes, Master Data Types, Time Profiles, Sample Model Entities, Reason Codes, and Transport Model Entities.

The main high-level steps involved in creating a planning model are as follows:

1. Create a time profile.
2. Create attributes.

3. Create master data types and assign attributes.

4. Create planning area.

5. Assign attributes to planning areas.

6. Create planning levels.

7. Create key figures.

8. Create versions.

9. Create planning operators and assign them to planning areas.

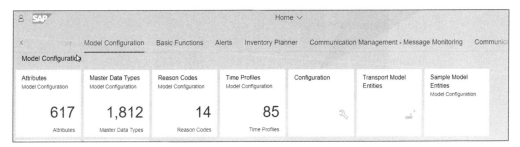

Figure 10.2 Model Configuration SAP Fiori Apps

The following subsections cover details about planning areas and time profiles in SAP IBP. We'll first look at SAP-delivered planning areas and how to go about creating your S&OP planning areas from SAP-delivered models. We'll also cover the general settings of the planning area. We'll then look at time profile setups, the hierarchy of time levels, typical time profiles used in S&OP, and how to load data into a time profile.

10.1.1   Planning Areas

A planning area consists of configurable objects that define the business model. This includes planning attributes, master data types, key figures, time profiles, planning levels, planning operators, and so on. Using the configuration UI, you can define the metadata of the model, which includes the structure of the attributes, master data types, key figures, calculations, and so on. Upon activation, the actual tables, views, authorizations, and other dependent objects are created in the SAP HANA database.

A planning area shows the meta configuration, which upon activation is realized with actual physical entities in SAP HANA. Therefore, these modeling constructs have active and inactive statuses. **Active** status marks objects that have been successfully activated. **Inactive** status is for planning entities that are new or modified.

SAP IBP provides default planning areas out of the box that can be used as starting points for implementation. For running S&OP processes, there are a few planning area options, as follows:

- **SAP2: S&OP planning area**
  This includes sales, marketing, finance, key figures and processes. The time profile level is months.

- **SAP4: Supply planning area**
  This includes a minimal set of key figures with a focus on supply planning. The default time profile is months, but it can be modified to weeks/technical weeks.

- **SAPIBP1**
  This includes S&OP processes, along with integration with other SAP IBP application areas.

If you plan to run SAP Integrated Business Planning for sales and operations and integrate it with other modules like SAP Integrated Business Planning for demand, SAP Integrated Business Planning for inventory, SAP Supply Chain Control Tower, and so on, then you can use SAPIBP1 and take a slice of this planning area for S&OP. SAPIBP1 includes configuration for SAP Integrated Business Planning for sales and operations and allows for easier integration with other modules.

If your demand planning processes with key figures and planning levels are quite different from SAPIBP1, you can start with SAP4, which is the core model for time-series-based tactical supply planning, and add additional configuration as required to support demand planning processes. If you add other modules, then their key figures should be added manually.

Figure 10.3 shows individual application modules for specific planning areas (SAP2 through SAP7) and integrated planning areas such as SAPIBP1 and SAP74.

If you're starting with SAPIBP1, you can choose which application modules to start with. For example, if your business process covers S&OP, demand, and inventory elements, choose the related specific modules when performing an advanced copy.

Application specific planning areas
Used when focusing on implementing **one** application

🎯 *Focus: Depth*

SAP2	Sales and Operations Planning
SAP3	Inventory Optimization
SAP3B	DDMRP
SAP4	Time Series Supply Planning
SAP4C	Business Network Collaboration
SAP5	Supply Chain Control Tower
SAP6	Demand Management
SAP7	Response Management

Integrated planning area
Used when implementing **multiple** applications to allow integrated planning

🎯 *Focus: Integration*

SAPIBP1	Unified Planning Area across all Time Series-Based Planning
SAP74	Response and Supply (Time Series and Order Integration)

Figure 10.3 SAP-Delivered Planning Areas

As an administrator, login to the SAP IBP web UI and access the Sample Model Entities SAP Fiori app under the **Model Configuration** group. Choose **Unified Planning Area**, select **Copy • Create New with Dependencies**, and select the application modules to do a partial copy by deselecting **Demand Sensing** and **Supply Chain Control Tower**.

Figure 10.4 Partial Copy from SAP-Delivered Unified Planning Area

Your planning areas can be accessed from the Planning Areas app under the **Model Configuration** group of the SAP Fiori launchpad. When you navigate to one of the planning areas from the **Planning Areas** list, you can see the main settings of the planning area along with other tabs representing **Attributes**, **Planning Levels**, **Attributes as Key Figures**, **Key Figures**, **Planning Operators**, and **Versions** associated with the planning area. Figure 10.5 shows an example of the **Planning Area** screen with the general settings associated with the planning area. The main settings include the following:

- **Time Profile association**
  Time profiles are defined in the Time Profile app and contains time profile, hierarchy levels of time periods, and time horizon settings.

- **Storage Time Profile Level**
  This is the most granular level of the time profile that can be associated with a planning area. For the SAPIBP1 model, **Day** is the most granular.

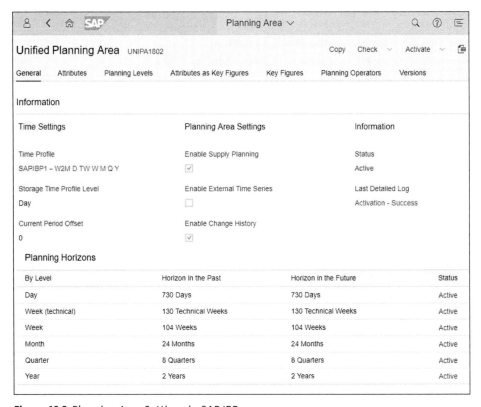

Figure 10.5 Planning Area Settings in SAP IBP

- **Current Period Offset**

  This is the number of periods from the current period of the planning area. For example, for a value of 1 in **Current Period Offset**, the new period is calculated one day from today.

- **Planning Area Settings**

  Here, there are options to check if the planning area is enabled for the following:

  - **Supply Planning** (typically used for planning areas like S&OP, supply, and IO), where time series supply planning functionality is used

  - **External Time Series**, relevant for order-based planning in SAP74 and SAP7 planning areas

  - **Change History**, which allows change tracking of key figures

S&OP planning areas typically have **Supply Planning** and **Change History** settings enabled.

10.1.2   Time Profile

In SAP IBP, several planning processes run at different time granularities and have different planning horizons. For example, S&OP planning is a monthly process and includes key figures that can be maintained and viewed at different time levels, like week, month, quarter, and year. The time horizon of S&OP processes can run from the previous two years to three years in the future.

Depending on the time granularity of the process, which could vary by each customer, the time profiles can be configured in SAP IBP to include the overall duration, time levels, and their default horizons, along with the hierarchy of time levels. For example, an S&OP process can consist of three time levels, month, quarter and year, with their default horizons as shown in Figure 10.6.

It's common for an S&OP process also to have time profiles with weekly time periods. Customers may have 4-4-5 calendars, meaning that a quarter could include months with four weeks, four weeks, and five weeks, respectively.

When your planning area includes several other processes, like daily demand sensing, response planning and weekly demand planning, inventory, and other processes, the time profile can be defined to include daily, weekly, monthly, quarterly and yearly time levels. However, when weekly planning periods need to roll up to monthly levels, then they first need to be split into technical weeks. Figure 10.7 shows a hierarchy of time profile levels that supports a technical weeks setup in which a week belongs to more than one month. In this case, the days roll up to technical weeks and from there to months or calendar weeks. The calendar week doesn't have additional hierarchy levels.

			Time Profile	

1 - 7 Year M, Q, Y 1

Description: Start Date: 31.12.2011   Planning Areas:
7 Year M, Q, Y   End Date: 30.12.2025   3

Time Profile Levels

Levels

Name	Level	Base Level	Period Type	Horizon in the Past	Horizon in the Future
Monthly	1	-	Month	6 Months	11 Months
Quarterly	2	Monthly (1)	Quarter	2 Quarters	3 Quarters
Yearly	3	Quarterly (2)	Year	1 Years	2 Years

Figure 10.6 Time Profile Definition

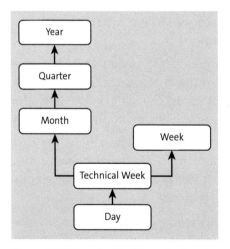

Figure 10.7 Time Profile Hierarchy Levels

The hierarchical relationship between time profile levels is represented in the time profile definition UI of SAP IBP, as shown in Figure 10.8, in which **Level** represents the time profile level and **Base Level** represents the child that rolls up to that level. The lowest level will have the base value set to empty. Thus, the time profile in SAP IBP allows for flexible assignment of time levels to meet customers' business processes. In addition to time levels and their hierarchy and horizons, time profile attributes can be defined and assigned to time profile levels. For example, week weight is an attribute assigned to a time profile level of technical week. This can have a value between 1 and 7, representing the number of days associated with that technical week. Such attributes are used during time profile disaggregation from calendar weeks to technical weeks.

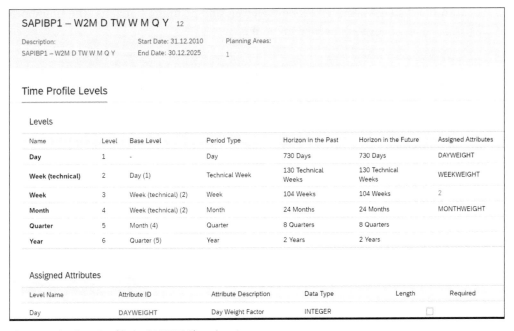

Figure 10.8 Time Profile in SAPIBP1 Planning Area

After a time profile is created, it needs to be activated so that the underlying technical artifacts like tables, views, and so on are generated. Once the time profile is activated, you can load the time profile data.

To create a new time profile or modify an existing time profile, it's first important to know what time profile levels will be managed in your planning area, along with the planning horizons. You can create a new time profile from scratch or copy from SAP-delivered time profiles. Typically customers copy an SAP-delivered planning areas as a starting point using the advanced copy functionality of a planning area, as part of which a new time profile is created.

You can also create a new time profile from Time Profile SAP Fiori app under the **Model Configuration** group of the SAP Fiori launchpad. Click the **New** button (Figure 10.9) and, in the **Select Time Profile Levels** dialog that appears, select the time profile levels. For example, say you're interested in storing some key figures at a technical week level and aggregating across weeks, months, quarters, and years. Choose these levels in the **Select Time Profile Level** screen and click **OK**.

In the last screen that appears, enter the **ID**, **Name**, and **Description**, along with the **Start** and **End Date** of the time profile. The middle section is populated by default with the system-suggested hierarchy levels and planning horizons. The time horizons can be changed as needed for your business.

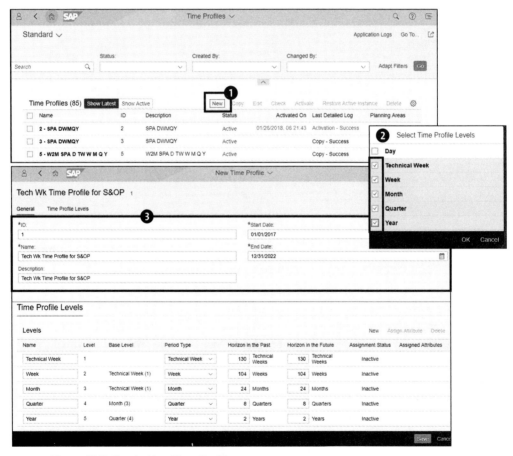

Figure 10.9 Create New Time Profile

All SAP-delivered planning areas come with default time profiles. If you only perform S&OP planning, typically you choose a time profile level that has three levels (i.e., monthly/quarterly/yearly) or a time profile with technical weeks, weeks, months, quarters, and years. If you manage multiple processes in one planning area, you may include days as an additional time level. When you copy SAP-delivered models like SAP4 or SAP2, you get a planning area with time profile 1 by default, which includes months, quarters, and years. If you copy planning area SAPIBP1, you get technical weeks and days, as well allowing for weeks that spread across multiple months.

Once a time profile is activated, you can load data into a time profile in the following ways:

- In the Data Integration app, choose your time profile and download a template. During download, you can choose to prefill time periods. Once you download the CSV file, it can be uploaded from the Data Integration app.

- Generate the time periods for the time profile by running an application job template, Create Time Periods for Time Profile.

The next step in model configuration of the planning area is to define the attributes and master data types that are relevant for your business.

10.2   Attributes and Master Data Types

In addition to the predelivered attributes and master data types, SAP IBP allows you to define custom attributes and master data types that are specific to your business model. There are different types of master data types, like simple, compound, reference, virtual, and external, to model the right types of planning dimensions. In this section, we'll go into detail with examples of how to define attributes and master data types, and we'll look at some of the most common master data types used in S&OP processes.

10.2.1   Attributes

Every planning dimension of a planning model—for example, customer or product—contains one or more planning attributes, which represent the characteristics of the planning dimensions. For example, PRDID is a key attribute of a product and represents a unique product ID, and PRDDESCR is an attribute of a product dimension and represents the description of each unique product.

An attribute can be defined freely in SAP IBP with types integer, decimal, varchar, and timestamp. A customer typically has several planning attributes that need to be added to a model. The first step is to define an attribute with its type and length, followed by assigning it to its corresponding master data types and planning areas.

SAP IBP has a predelivered set of attributes that covers most of the common supply chain attributes, like CUSTID, LOCID, RESID, PRDID, and so on. When you copy an SAP-delivered planning area, these attributes are copied over as well. Note that certain planning operators, like supply planning operators, require a fixed set of attributes, like PRDID, LOCID, and so on.

You can search for SAP-delivered attributes in the Sample Model Entities app. This will show for each attribute its association with other master data types, planning areas, and time profiles. For example, Figure 10.10 shows a **Product Family** attribute with details of its description, **Data Type**, and **Length**, along with lists of **Master Data Types** and **Planning Areas** where this attribute is used.

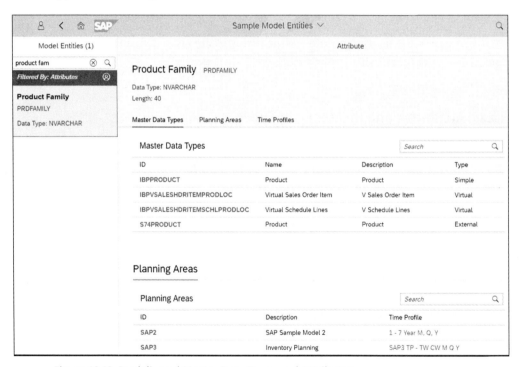

Figure 10.10 Predelivered Master Data Types and Attributes

10.2.2   Master Data Types

Master data types in SAP IBP are planning dimensions representing the primary business data entities—for example, product, customer, location, resource, sales organization, and so on. Master data types contain one or more planning attributes.

Table 10.1 shows the most common master data types used in an S&OP process across demand, supply, and finance areas. These master data types are assigned to planning areas, enabling an integrated S&OP process to profitably align demand and supply.

Note that master data types can be assigned to one or more planning areas; that is, multiple planning areas can share same master data types such that the master data is loaded once and used across multiple planning areas.

Master Data Type	Used for Modeling of...
IBPPRODUCT	Product-related attributes
IBPLOCATION	Location-related attributes
IBPCUSTOMER	Customer-related attributes
IBPCOMPONENT	Definition of a component for bill of materials
IBPCURRENCY	Available currencies (currency from)
IBPCURRENCYTO	Available currencies (currency to)
IBPCUSTOMERPRODUCT	Customer-product-specific attribute values
IBPEXCHANGERATE	Currency conversion factors
IBPLOCATIONFR	Starting location for transport relations
IBPLOCATIONPRODUCT	Location-product-specific attribute values
IBPLOCATIONTO	Ship-to-related attributes
IBPPLANNINGUNIT	Subnetwork
IBPPRODUCTIONRESOURCE	Capacity consumption rate for production resources
IBPPRODUCTIONSOURCEITM	Maintaining BOM
IBPPRODUCTSUBSTITUTION	Product substitution for mapping products
IBPPRODUCTTO	Output product; modeled as reference to product

Table 10.1 Examples of SAP-Delivered Master Data Types Used in S&OP Process

10

Master Data Type	Used for Modeling of...
IBPRESOURCE	Resources
IBPRESOURCELOCATION	Available capacity or capacity supply at resource-location level
IBPRESOURCELOCATIONPRODUCT	Capacity consumption rate for handling resources
IBPSOURCECUSTOMER	Sourcing location for customers
IBPSOURCELOCATION	Defines the transport relation between two locations
IBPSOURCEPRODUCTION	Defines the sourcing (production or external procurement)
IBPUOMCONVERSIONFACTOR	Unit of measure conversion factor

Table 10.1 Examples of SAP-Delivered Master Data Types Used in S&OP Process (Cont.)

SAP IBP provides different master data types to model business data entities, which we'll discuss next.

Simple Master Data Types

Simple master data types are used to model primary master data types—for example, product, customer, location, resource, and so on. These master data types usually include the key, description, and other hierarchical or informational attributes of the primary master data type. For example, the product master data type includes attributes like product ID and product description; hierarchical attributes like product family, product group, product category, and business unit; and other informational attributes like material type, ABC code, active/inactive flag, and so on.

The simple master data types typically have master data types with a single primary key attribute. However, there can also be master data types with multiple primary keys; for example, the production source header master data type includes the LOCID, PRDID, and SOURCEID keys.

SAP provides many predelivered simple master data types, as shown in Figure 10.11. Many master data types are shared between SAP-delivered planning areas. For example, the product master data type is a fundamental supply chain master data type used by all SAP-delivered models: SAP2, SAP3, SAP4, SAP5, SAP6, and SAPIBP1. Note that the order-based planning models SAP7 and SAP74 use external master data types for primary master data types like product.

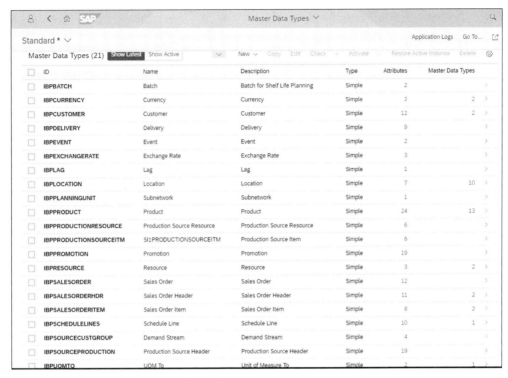

Figure 10.11 Master Data Types Delivered in SAP IBP

For sales and operations planning, the most common simple master data types include those listed in Table 10.2.

Common Master Data Types	Demand-Relevant	Supply-Relevant
Product	Sales organization	Resource
Customer	Channel	Production source header
Location	Division	Production source item
Currency	Promotion	Production source resource
Unit of measure		Customer source validity
		Location source validity
		Production source validity

Table 10.2 Simple Master Data Types in S&OP

Typically, customer implementation projects add several master data types, especially to model different demand planning processes.

Compound Master Data Types

These master data types represent combinations of primary attributes and are composed of two or more simple master data types. For example, a customer product master data type represents a combination of product ID and customer ID as roots along with attributes that belong at product and customer levels, such as market share and market group.

The key attributes of the compound master data types belong to other simple master data types. For example, PRDID, which is a key attribute of the IBPCUSTOMERPRODUCT master data type, is a primary key attribute of the IBPPRODUCT master data type.

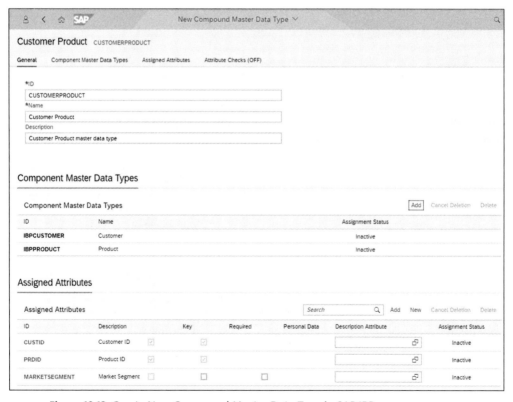

Figure 10.12 Create New Compound Master Data Type in SAP IBP

During data integration, when a compound master data type is loaded, the primary key values are checked against its corresponding master data types. In SAP IBP, all master data types are created and maintained in the Master Data Types SAP Fiori app under the **Model Configuration** group. To create a compound master data type, in the **Master Data Type** screen, choose **New • Compound**.

When you define a new compound master data type, you choose two or more master data types. These are typically simple master data types, but in some cases compound master data types can be used. In Figure 10.12, we chose **Customer** and **Product** as two simple master data types. The keys of these master data types are then assigned to the attributes. Additional attributes can then be added to this master data type, like MARKETSEGMENT.

Table 10.3 shows some of the most common compound master data types used in an S&OP process.

Common Compound Master Data Types	Demand-Relevant	Supply-Relevant
Customer product	Product sales organization	Resource location
Location product	Customer sales organization	Resource location product
Location product currency		Source customer
UOM conversion factors		Source location
		Product substitution

Table 10.3 Example Compound Master Data Types Used in S&OP

Note that sales org, division, channel, and their compounds are not part of SAP IBP-delivered models. These can be added as required during implementations.

Reference Master Data Types

Reference master data types are references to other master data types and use the same master data as the primary master data types. Examples of reference master data types in SAP IBP include components, currency to, location from, location to, and so on.

Currency to is a good example of a master data type that references the currency master data type. Master data for currency is only loaded once as part of the currency master data type. When key figures like exchange rates are loaded, the key structure or base planning level of the exchange rate includes currency ID, currency to ID, and date. The currency to ID comes from the currency reference master data type.

Figure 10.13 shows a configuration for **Reference** master data type **Component**, for which the **Referenced Master Data Type** is **IBPPRODUCT**. When you create a new reference master data type, you choose one referenced master data type. Then you add attributes to the reference master data type and assign its corresponding attributes in the primary master data type. The reference master data type can have fewer attributes than its referenced master data type.

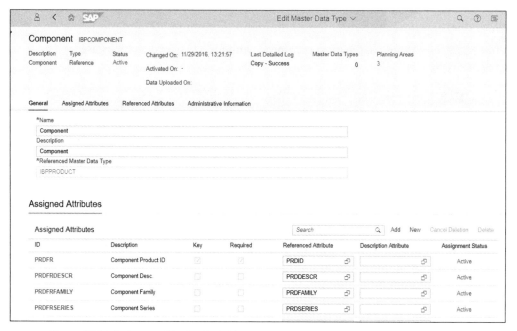

Figure 10.13 Reference Master Data Types

In SAP Integrated Business Planning for sales and operations, the reference master data types shown in Table 10.4 are commonly used.

Common Reference Master Data Types	Supply-Relevant
Currency to	Component
	Location from

Table 10.4 Example Reference Master Data Types

Common Reference Master Data Types	Supply-Relevant
	Location to
	Product to

Table 10.4 Example Reference Master Data Types (Cont.)

Note that data can't be loaded into a reference master data type. When data is loaded into primary master data types, it's also available as part of the reference master data types.

Virtual Master Data Types

Virtual master data types are used to define joins on two or more master data types on attributes that are common to the master data types. The attributes that are being joined need not be root attributes.

Figure 10.14 shows an example of a virtual master data type: brand product, which is composed of two master data types, product and brand. The join condition is specified as *Product→Brand ID = Brand→Brand ID*. The resultant virtual master data type brand product has attributes of both product and brand.

Virtual master data types help in reducing duplication of data by joining on the relevant attributes. The attributes of the virtual master data types can be assigned to planning areas and relevant planning levels.

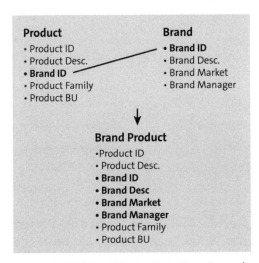

Figure 10.14 Virtual Master Data Type Example

In SAP-delivered sample planning area content, there are a few virtual master data types. For example, the business partner customer master data type used for business network collaboration in SAP Supply Chain Control Tower joins two master data types—IBPBUSINESSPARTNER and IBPCUSTOMER—using the join condition IBPBUSINESS-PARTNER→BUPAID = IBPCUSTOMER→CUSTBUPAID, which is a nonroot attribute of the IBP-CUSTOMER master data type. The resultant master data type has attributes from both IBPBUSINESSPARTNER and IBPCUSTOMER master data types, as shown Figure 10.15.

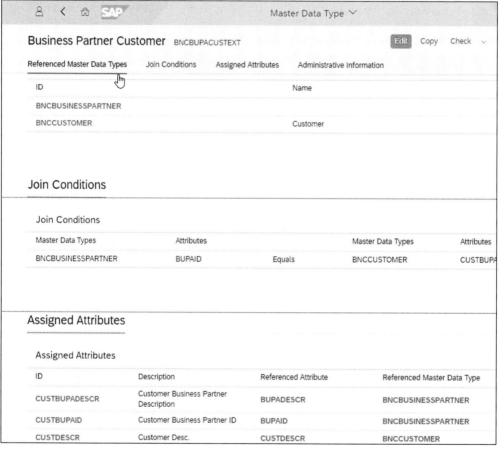

Figure 10.15 SAP-Delivered Virtual Master Data Type

In standard SAP-delivered master data types for S&OP, there are no virtual master data types. However, customer projects may include these types if such data modeling is needed.

External Master Data Types

External master data types are used to model master data structures that are tightly connected to SAP ERP or SAP S/4HANA. Such master data types are typically used in order-based planning, in which there are predefined entities defined on the source system and mapped to SAP IBP external master data structured through mapping. The data in such master data types can be filled through SAP HANA smart data integration (SDI). These master data types have a fixed structure and can't be extended easily with attributes that are not maintained in SAP ERP or SAP S/4HANA.

When you're creating a new external master data type, you first choose an external source from the available predefined external data sources, as shown in Figure 10.16.

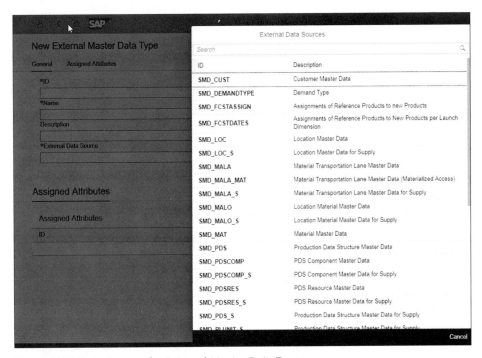

Figure 10.16 Data Sources for External Master Data Types

After selecting a data source, you can define attributes for this external master data type along with a mapping to fields in the external data sources. In SAP IBP, there are several predelivered external master data types, used in SAP7 (response planning area) and SAP74 (response and supply planning area). These master data types have an S7 or S74 prefix depending on the planning areas they're assigned to.

Figure 10.17 shows an external master data type, **Product**, which maps to external data source **SMD_MAT** and has a few product attributes, like **PRDID** mapping to **MATERIAL_NUMBER** of **SMD_MAT**. Note that external master data types can't be loaded through SAP Cloud Platform Integration for data services or the data integration UI of SAP IBP.

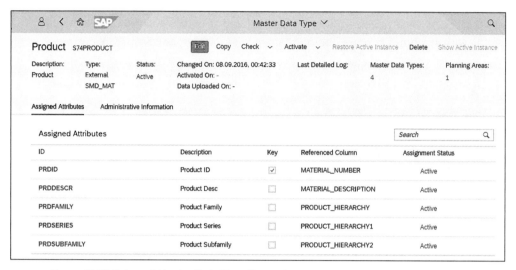

Figure 10.17 External Master Data Type Example

For an S&OP process, it's very common to have models that aren't of type external because of the flexibility required to maintain master data, extend attributes, perform new product introduction-type scenarios, create combinations that aren't in SAP ERP/SAP S4HANA, and so on. However, with SAP74, the tactical supply planning of S&OP can be combined with order-based planning of response to be run in a limited fashion. Some functionality of S&OP tactical supply operators like lot size policy, balanced receipts, and so on can't be run based on external master data types, because the data for such master fields (e.g., LOTSIZEPOLICY in IBPPRODUCTLOCATION) aren't available in SAP ERP or SAP S/4HANA.

10.3   Planning Levels

Planning levels are the hierarchical levels at which the data for the key figures is stored or key figure calculations are defined. A base planning level represents the storage level of stored key figured. The planning levels in SAP IBP are comprised of time profile and master data type attributes. A planning level has one or more root attributes representing the key structure for the hierarchical level along with other attributes of the primary master data types and their compound master data types.

One of the greatest strengths of SAP IBP is the flexibility to define any planning level depending on the key figures that need to be stored or calculated. Because customer planning models vary in terms of the levels at which they plan, the levels at which they store data, and the levels at which they view or calculate key figure values, a flexible planning hierarchy is provided by SAP IBP.

Figure 10.18 shows an example of a planning level in SAP IBP. This planning level, WKPRODLOC, is used by most supply planning key figures in the S&OP process. This planning level is comprised of attributes from the weekly time profile, with the week as the root attribute. The planning level has other root attributes, PRDID and LOCID, coming from product and location master data types. All attributes of these primary master data types, along with attributes of compound master data types using the product and location, are included as part of this planning level.

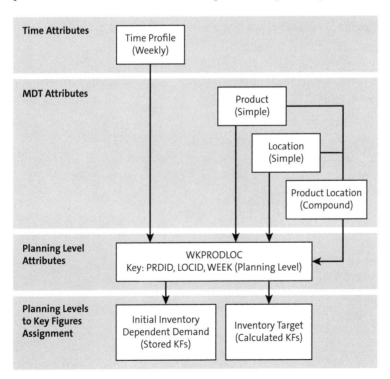

Figure 10.18 Planning Levels Structure

This planning level now can be assigned as a base planning level of stored key figures—for example, initial inventory, dependent demand, independent demand, and so on—or key figure calculations can be defined at this planning level; for example, inventory target is the sum of the targets and manual overrides key figures.

Time independent planning levels can also be defined in SAP IBP for planning levels with no time dependency. For example, the UOM conversion factor key figure does not vary by time and has planning levels with product ID and UOMTOID as root attributes (where UOMID is an attribute of product).

Planning levels in SAP IBP also can be defined on aggregate nonroot attributes of the underlying master data types. For example, the financial targets key figure can be defined at month, product family, and customer group levels, where these attributes are non-key attributes of weekly time profile, product master data type, and customer master data type, respectively. Figure 10.19 shows a monthly product family-customer region planning level in the SAPIBP1 planning area. This planning level, in addition to the root attributes coming from the non-key attributes of the primary master data types, contains additional attributes that are at a product family-customer group or higher level: brand, product business unit, and so on.

Figure 10.19 Planning Levels Definition

The advantage of having a flexible planning level is that you don't need to maintain separate master data types for aggregated attributes (e.g., product family customer group master data type). Also, the data integration of SAP IBP ensures that if there are planning levels at aggregate levels of primary master data types, the data integrity is checked during data load. To illustrate this in more detail, suppose a product master data type has the data entries listed in Table 10.5.

PRDID*	PRDFAMILY	PRDBU
P1	PF1	BU1
P2	PF1	BU2

Table 10.5 Product Master Data Example

At aggregate planning level week-product-family-customer group, the assigned attributes from the product are PRDFAMILY and PRDBU, and PRDFAMILY is root. During data integration, such a batch is rejected because now, when aggregated to the PRDFAMILY level for PF1, there are two unique values for PRDBU—that is, BU1 and BU2, where PRDBU is a nonroot attribute and can hold only one value.

10.4   Key Figures

In SAP IBP, customers can define custom calculations and disaggregation rules using key figures. Key figures are measures of data over time—for example, sales forecast quantity, production quantity, and so on, which have values for characteristic combinations over time. Some key figures can be defined as time-independent—for example, unit of measure conversion factors.

In this section, we'll cover how to create key figures in detail: different types of key figures, their properties, aggregations, disaggregations, and key figure calculations, with several examples that are relevant for S&OP.

10.4.1   What Are Key Figures?

Key figures are the foundation for all planning and analytical functions of SAP IBP. Key figures are defined for a planning area and can be used later in all areas of SAP IBP. Key figures calculation definitions are highly flexible and can be used to model most customer-specific business processes.

All key figures in SAP IBP are either stored or calculated at a certain planning level. For example, marketing forecast quantity is stored at the technical week, product, and customer base planning level, or the WKPRODCUST level. Further key figure calculations can be defined at any aggregate level. For example, you can define a new calculation for marketing forecast quantity @ WKPRDFMLCUSTGRP = SUM (MARKETINGFORECATQTY @ WKPRODCUST). Here, you're adding the WKPRODCUST base level to the WKPRDFMLCUSTGRP aggregated level.

There are several pre-delivered planning areas in SAP IBP. Each one includes several key figures that have business context. There are several key figures that have fixed semantics and are used as input or output for planning algorithms. For example, in SAP Integrated Business Planning for sales and operations' time series-based supply planning, there are several key figures that have fixed usage in supply heuristics or are optimized. These include consensus demand, independent demand, dependent demand, and so on.

A planning area can contain fixed key figures used in algorithms and has fixed semantics. In addition to the fixed key figures, there can be custom key figures with custom key figure calculations. Note that the fixed key figures can have additional calculations defined on top of them. The custom key figures also can flow as input to the fixed key figures.

Key figures are based on different types and have different sets of properties to provide the high level of flexibility required for planning.

Figure 10.20 shows the key types and properties of key figures. We'll discuss these with some examples and show how some of these key concepts are used for modeling S&OP key figures.

Figure 10.20 Create New Key Figure

10.4.2   Creating Key Figures

You create a new key figure in SAP IBP from the Configuration SAP Fiori app. Click the
Key Figure tab, choose a planning area, and click **New** to create a new key figure. Provide
a **Key Figure ID** and **Base Planning Level**. Every key figure definition has two sections. The
Header section contains the key figure types and properties, and the **Calculations** section contains all the relevant calculations for this key figure. The header section of the
key figure definition has several properties and is used to model different types of key
figures. A summary of all the key figure types and properties is shown in Figure 10.21.
These will be explained with examples of key figures used in S&OP.

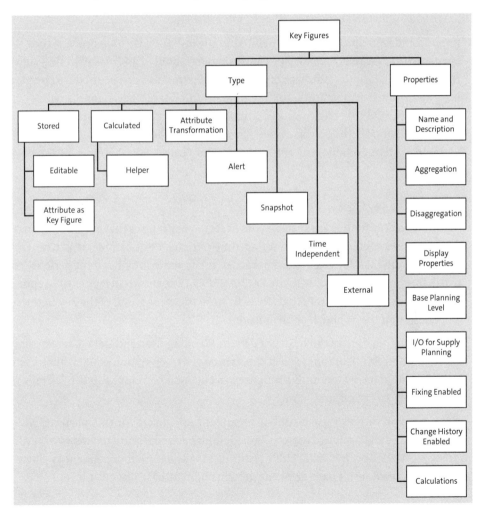

Figure 10.21 Key Figure Types and Properties

10.4.3   Key Figure Types

The first classification of key figures is whether they are stored or calculated.

Stored Key Figures

Stored key figures are stored at the root levels defined in their base planning levels. For example, marketing forecast quantity is stored at the week-product ID-customer ID level. Customers have flexibility to define whatever level the key figure should be stored at. For example, marketing forecast should be stored at the month-product family-customer level by defining the base planning level as such. Stored key figures are usually uploaded using data integration in SAP IBP.

If the stored key figures need to be edited in the SAP IBP planning process, they can be marked as **Editable**. Editable key Figures can be edited in an Excel planning view if the user has the right authorization. These key figures also can be modified by planning algorithms or operators. An example of an editable key figure is SALESFORE-CASTQTY in the SAPIBP1 planning area. This key figure is stored and editable in current and future periods. The configuration allows for the following editable settings: **Not Editable**, **System Editable**, **Editable in Current or Future**, **Editable in the Past**, or **All Editable**.

Attributes as Key Figures

Attributes as key figures are special types of stored key figures that are loaded as master data and have a single value for all time periods. For example, if you're using exchange rate that, for calculation purposes, is the same for all current periods, you can define an attribute as key figure **EXCHANGERATE** as shown in Figure 10.22 and set **From Periods** to **-24** and **To Periods** to **24** to store the same value of the key figure for 24 periods in the past and 24 in the future.

Attributes as key figures can be defined in the **Planning Area and Details** screen of the Configuration SAP Fiori app. Select the **Attribute as Key** option to view the master data types that have attributes configured as key figures, along with the settings for **From Period**, **To Period**, and so on.

Note that you can also use a time-independent key figure for this purpose, which stores only a single value of the key figure independent of time. For example, key figure UOMCONVERSIONFACTOR in SAPIBP1 planning area is a time-independent key figure. This key figure doesn't have any time dimension in its base planning level.

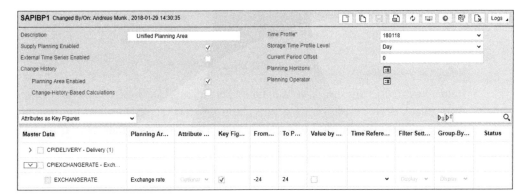

Figure 10.22 Attribute as Key Figure Definition

Calculated Key Figures

Calculated key figures are used heavily in SAP IBP to perform custom calculations. For example, the sales forecast revenue key figure is calculated as *Sales Forecast Quantity × Planned Price*. As shown in Figure 10.23, SALESFORECASTREV is defined as a calculated key figure. It has three calculations:

1. A request level calculation to aggregate the results by sum

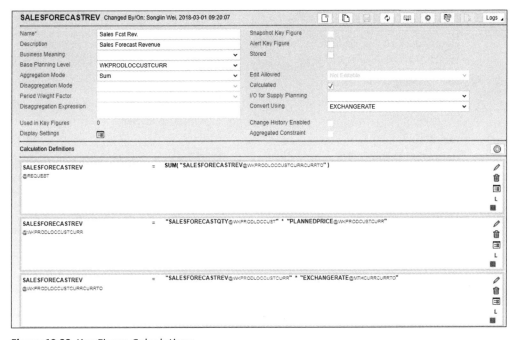

Figure 10.23 Key Figure Calculations

2. A revenue calculation across two different planning levels for quantity and price

3. A currency conversion calculation

Helper Key Figures

Helper key figures are similar to calculated key figures, but they're used for intermediate calculations and not visible in a planning view. The helper key figures don't have the key figure definition section. They just have intermediate calculations. For example, gross costs is a helper key figure used in gross profit calculation. It's calculated as a cost per unit multiplied by constrained demand. Figure 10.24 shows an example of a helper key figure with a calculation across different planning levels as follows: HGROSSCOSTS@WKPRODCUSTCURR = COSTPERUNIT@WKPRODCURR * CONSTRAINEDDE-MAND@WKPRODCUST.

Figure 10.24 Helper Key Figure Calculations

Alert Key Figures

Alert key figures are special calculated key figures with an **Alert Key Figure** flag checked in the key figure configuration. For example, in an S&OP planning area, you can define a capacity overload alert if the utilization percentage goes beyond the defined threshold. These are database-generated alerts and will be visible in the **Alerts** dashboard in Excel. Figure 10.25 shows the capacity overload alert key figure delivered in the SAPIB1 planning area. This key figure has the **Alert Key Figure** checkbox selected.

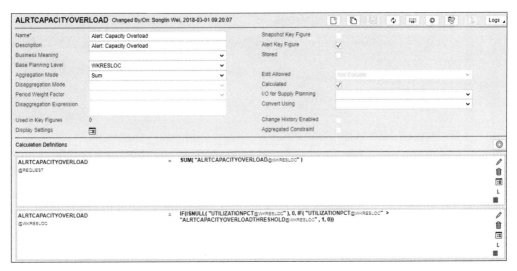

Figure 10.25 Alert Key Figure Definition

Snapshot Key Figures

Snapshot key figures are system-generated key figures created when a snapshot is defined for a planning area for one or more selected key figures. Snapshot key figures are stored key figures with the **Snapshot Key Figure** checkbox selected in the key figure configuration. You can choose up to nine snapshots in the snapshot definition. When the planning area is activated, it creates the snapshot key figures in the planning area according to the snapshot definition.

External Key Figures

An external key figure is a special type of stored key figure for which the data is loaded using SDI in near real time, connected directly to SAP ERP or SAP S/4HANA. Such key figures are usually used in order-based models such as SAP74 and SAP7 used for SAP Integrated Business Planning for response and supply. To enable external key figures, the planning area should be marked as **External Time Series-Enabled** and a data source for the external key figure definition should be selected in the base planning level of the external key figure.

10.4.4   Key Figure Aggregations

Aggregation mode describes how the key figures should be aggregated. The supported aggregation modes are:

- SUM (default)
- MIN
- MAX
- AVG
- CUSTOM

The request-level calculation of the key figure contains the aggregation mode in the calculation definition. Custom aggregation mode is usually used when the request-level calculation has request-level inputs.

For example, AOPPRICE, shown in Figure 10.26, is a key figure delivered in the SAPIBP1 planning area and is defined as a weighted average calculation with the input key figures calculated at the request level. Therefore, the **Aggregation Mode** is **Custom**.

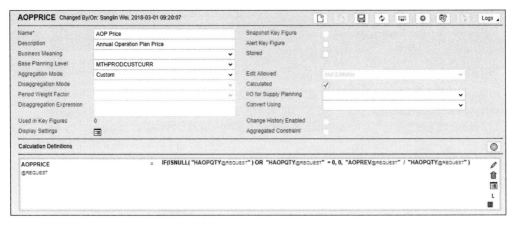

Figure 10.26 Custom Aggregation Mode Definition

10.4.5   Disaggregation

IBP supports disaggregation for stored and editable key figures. Disaggregation in SAP IBP is supported by SAP Integrated Business Planning, add-in for Microsoft Excel when a planner makes changes to key figures at any aggregated level and performs a simulation or saves. The copy and disaggregation operator also performs disaggregation of key figure values. The disaggregation options in SAP IBP include the following:

- Proportional if aggregated value is not zero; otherwise, equal distribution. Typically used for disaggregation of quantity and revenue key figures.
- Copy value.

- Equal distribution.

- Proportional if aggregated value is not zero; otherwise, copy value typically used for price and cost key figures.

In addition to disaggregation based on attributes, SAP IBP also provides disaggregation based on time using the **Period Weight Factor** disaggregation setting in the key figure configuration. This setting typically allows disaggregation for a week to month split. For example, if a key figure is stored at a technical week level and is uploaded at a calendar week level, then this setting can be used to distribute the week to the technical weeks based on the **Week Weight** attribute of the time profile.

Disaggregation expressions can be defined for disaggregating the key figure based on a calculation. For example, in Figure 10.27, the sales manager forecast key figure is disaggregated based on sales forecast quantity, if the stored value of sales manager forecast is empty.

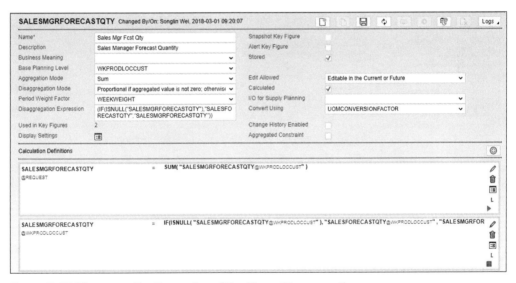

Figure 10.27 Disaggregation Expression of Key Figure Disaggregation

Disaggregation expressions can't be defined for the **Copy Value** and **Equal Distribution** disaggregation modes. Only stored key figures can be part of the disaggregation expression, and they should be at the base planning level of key figure being disaggregated. Note that calculated key figures can't be part of a disaggregation expression. If disaggregation based on calculated key figures is needed, the result of the calculation should first be stored in a stored key figure before disaggregation can be performed. The ADVSIM operator can be used for this purpose.

10.4.6   Key Figure Calculations

SAP IBP model configuration allows for free-form definition of key figure calculations. Every key figure has one or more calculations, of which the request-level calculation is the important because it decides how the key figure is viewed and aggregated.

For example, in our model we define a new key figure, ACTUALSQTY, which holds the sales history loaded from SAP ERP or SAP S/4HANA. The base planning level of such a key figure is WKPRODLOCCUST. Figure 10.28 shows an example of a key figure definition in SAP IBP for the ACTUALSQTY key figure delivered in SAPIBP1. You can see the key figure properties in the top section and the key figure calculations in the bottom section.

Figure 10.28 Key Figure Calculation Definitions

When you create such a key figure, you also provide the calculations. The actuals quantity should be aggregated by SUM. Therefore, define a request level calculation as follows:

ACTUALSQTY@REQUEST = SUM(ACTUALSQTY@WKPRODLOCCUST)

Then, select the input key figure and choose ACTUALSQTY@WKPRODLOCCUST as the stored value.

This is a simple definition of ACTUALSQTY. Now, suppose you want to perform unit of measure conversion calculations so that you can see ACTUALSQTY in the UOM selected by a user.

To do so, first create a new calculation as shown in Figure 10.28:

```
ACTUALSQTY@WKPRODLOCCUSTUOMTO =
ACTUALSQTY@WKPRODLOCCUST * UOMCONVERSIONFACTOR@PRODUOMTO
```

In the **Input Key Figures** section, choose the stored value of each of the input key figures, as shown in Figure 10.29. This is an example of calculation across different hierarchy levels. The join happens on the common attributes—PROD in this case.

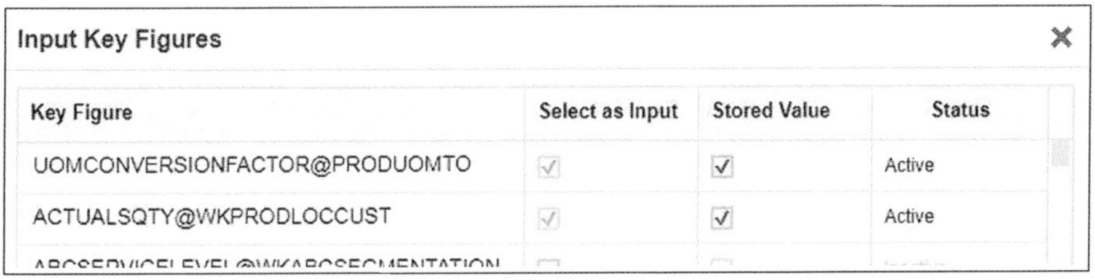

Input Key Figures			✕
Key Figure	**Select as Input**	**Stored Value**	**Status**
UOMCONVERSIONFACTOR@PRODUOMTO	☑	☑	Active
ACTUALSQTY@WKPRODLOCCUST	☑	☑	Active
ABCSERVICELEVEL@WKABCSEGMENTATION	☐	☐	

Figure 10.29 Input Key Figures for Calculation

Note that UOMCONVERSIONFACTOR is a time-independent key figure with root attributes of PRDID and UOMTOID.

After the second calculation is defined, next define a request-level calculation, as follows:

```
ACTUALSQTY@REQUEST = SUM(ACTUALSQTY@WKPRODLOCCUSTUOMTO).
```

In the **Input Key Figures** section, make sure **Stored Value** is unchecked, as shown in Figure 10.30. This is because we just defined this new key figure calculation at the WKPRODLOCCUSTUOMTO level.

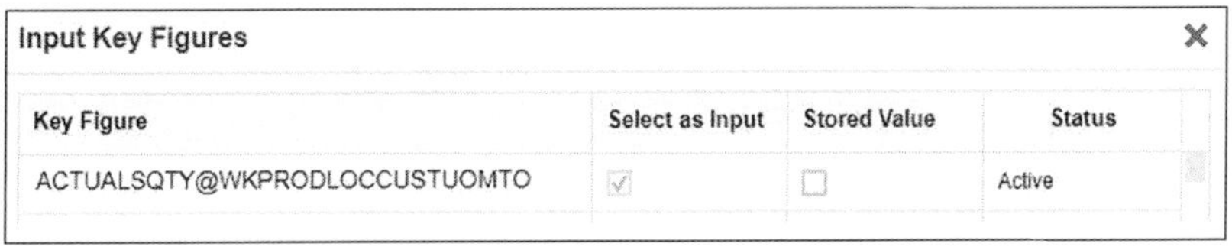

Input Key Figures			✕
Key Figure	**Select as Input**	**Stored Value**	**Status**
ACTUALSQTY@WKPRODLOCCUSTUOMTO	☑	☐	Active

Figure 10.30 Input Key Figure for Calculation at Request Level

When you select the formula/graph view of the key figure calculation, you can see the graphical view of the calculation, as shown in Figure 10.31. In this case, the green-colored key figures are stored input key figures. Every graph should end with a stored key figure. When you hover over the nodes, you can also see the associated calculations.

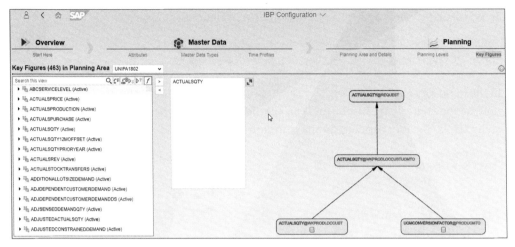

Figure 10.31 Graph View of Calculations

10.5   Planning Operators

For large volumes of data computations, SAP IBP provides planning operators. These operators have specialized functions and run operations like planning algorithms or mass copy of data or data lifecycle management, to give just a few examples. Planning operators can be scheduled as part of application jobs or can be run ad hoc in a planning session. Some operators also offer simulation; for example, you can run the supply heuristic in simulation mode.

There are several planning operators offered in SAP IBP, as shown in Table 10.6.

Operator Type	Operators
Supply planning/SCM	■ S&OP (supply) heuristic ■ S&OP (supply) optimizer
Inventory planning/IO	■ Single-stage inventory optimization ■ Multistage inventory optimization ■ Expected demand loss ■ Forecast error CV calculator ■ Calculate inventory components ■ Forecast error calculation

Table 10.6 SAP-Delivered Planning Operators

344

Operator Type	Operators
Demand planning/SAP IBP forecast	■ Outlier correction ■ Substitute missing values ■ Promotion sales lift elimination ■ Automated exponential smoothing ■ Single exponential smoothing ■ Demand sensing
Copy	Copy between source and target key figures
Copy and disaggregate/DISAGG	Copy and disaggregate key figure values from source to target key figure
SNAPSHOT	Run snapshot operator to copy key figure value to snapshot key figures with cascading
SNAPSHOTREDO	Overwrite most recent snapshot with new snapshot
Forecast error/KPI-profile	Used to setup forecast error calculations
Segmentation	Perform ABC/XYZ segmentation
Order-based planning	■ Order-based planning: confirmation run ■ Order-based planning: constrained forecast run ■ Order-based planning: deployment run ■ Order-based planning: gating factor analysis ■ Order-based planning: copy version data
Data lifecycle management	■ Delete abandoned combinations ■ Purge data (e.g., time series older than a certain date) ■ Archiving jobs
ADVSIM	Preprocessing and postprocessing for simulation
GROUP	A group of planning operators run in a defined sequence

Table 10.6 SAP-Delivered Planning Operators (Cont.)

Of the available planning operators in SAP IBP, the following planning operators are used most frequently in an S&OP process:

- Copy operator
- Snapshots and snapshot redo
- SCM/supply planning operator
- Version copy, to copy from source to target versions (e.g., baseline version to upside version)
- Data lifecycle management

In the following sections, we'll cover how to create planning operators in SAP IBP, using the copy operator as an example, along with data lifecycle management functions to manage the data in SAP IBP.

10.5.1   Creating a Planning Operator

Planning operators are created in the **Manage Planning Operator** section of the Configuration SAP Fiori app. Some generic planning operators are managed here, such as the copy operator, DISAGG operator, IO operator, and so on. There also are dedicated SAP Fiori apps to manage other planning operators. These include Manage Forecast Models, Manage ABC/XYZ Segmentation Rules, S&OP Operator Profiles, and so on.

Suppose you want to create a new copy operator. Choose **COPY** for the **Planning Operator Type** and click **Add Planning Operators** to add details about the operator, including whether it should be in interactive mode, batch mode, or filter mode, as well as the parameters.

In Figure 10.32, we're creating a copy operator to copy the output key figure of the consensus demand planning process as input for the CONSENSUSDEMAND key figure of the supply operator, in case the source and target key figures are at different base planning levels.

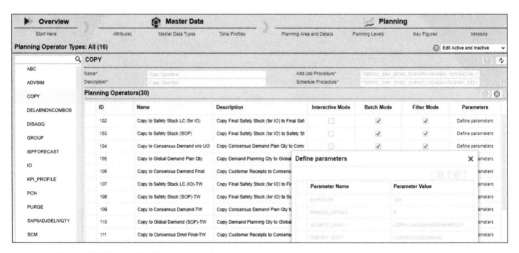

Figure 10.32 Create Copy Operator

Once a planning operator is created, it's assigned to the planning area in the **Planning Area and Details** configuration. A *copy operator* is most commonly used in S&OP processes to handover data between processes by copying data between configured source and target key figures. For example, the output of a sales and operations plan, which is the constrained demand, can be input for other operational processes, like SAP Integrated Business Planning for demand or SAP Integrated Business Planning for response and supply. Copy operators also create target planning combinations if they don't exist. In addition to being able to copy from source to target key figures, the copy operator provides a few other parameters to support additional copy functions, as listed in Table 10.7.

Copy Functionality	Copy Operator Parameter
Clear key figure values between planning cycles.	CLEAR_KF_VALUES
Initialize time periods for target key figures.	CREATE_TIMEPERIODS
Copy key figures with a period shifting for a specified duration. For example, say you want to copy ACTUALSQTY, but shifted by one year. Also, you can offset to start *n* periods before or after the current period.	PERIOD_SHIFT, DURATION, PERIOD_OFFSET
Run in parallel mode if source to target key figures need to be copied without any dependencies.	PARALLEL_MODE

Table 10.7 Copy Operator Functions and Parameters

10.5.2 Data Lifecycle Management

To manage the growth of data overtime and remove unused/unwanted data, SAP IBP provides several data lifecycle management functions. These are delivered as application job templates and can be run in the Manage Application Jobs SAP Fiori app. Table 10.8 lists the application job templates for purge operations in data lifecycle management in SAP IBP.

Application Job Template	Purpose
Purge Key Figure Data	Delete key figure data that is older than a specified period
Purge Change History Data	Delete all change history data that is older than a specified period
Purge Data Import Batches	Delete all batches and data older than a specified number of days

Table 10.8 Data Lifecycle Management Functions in SAP IBP

Application Job Template	Purpose
Purge Planning Area Data	Delete data from multiple planning areas, including key figure data; can also delete master data from the related master data types
Purge Nonconforming Data	Delete obsolete (nonconforming) data from a planning area
Purge Master Data	Delete all master data from given master data types from a planning area together with the associated planning data (planning objects and key figures)
Purge Key Figure Data Outside Planning Horizon	Delete key figure data that is outside the planning area's planning horizon

Table 10.8 Data Lifecycle Management Functions in SAP IBP (Cont.)

To create a new data lifecycle job, open the Manage Application Jobs SAP Fiori app and choose **New Job**, select the **Job Template**, and provide the necessary parameters. In the example in Figure 10.33, we run the Purge Change History Data app for planning area UNIPA07, baseline version, to purge change history records older than 100 days.

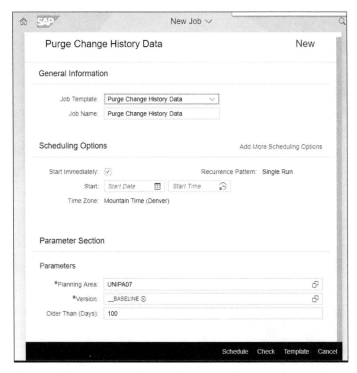

Figure 10.33 Run Purge Change History Application Job Template

10.6   History Report

The change history function in SAP IBP allows for tracking changes to the stored key figure values and any calculated key figures that depend on them. This helps determine which user made what changes to planning data and the reason behind the changes. As shown in Figure 10.34, to configure change history, follow these steps:

1. Mark the planning area as **Change History Enabled.**

2. Stored key figures that need to be tracked should be **Change History Enabled**.

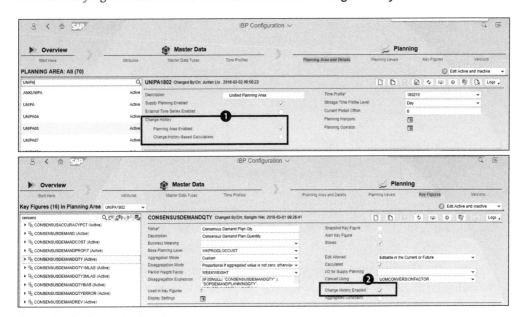

Figure 10.34 Change History Settings

After these settings are enabled and activated, the key figures are change history-enabled. Whenever data is changed for such a key figure as part of Excel planning views, data integration, or operators, the before and after values of the key figure are tracked. Changes can be viewed or reported in the Change History SAP Fiori app in the web UI or in the change history report in Excel.

The Excel planning views provide an option to create a change history report based on two options:

1. **Effect of Changes on Planning View**

2. **Original Changes**

In the first option, you can select the level at which aggregated changes are viewed along with the time range for change history. The system then displays, as in Figure 10.35, a list of changes in the change header and details of the changes, like change by user, change by date, reason code, comment, and so on. In the data section of the change history report, the individual changes with information about before and after values for the key figure at the user-selected planning level are displayed. This view can be further customized with a flexible layout, orienting rows and columns in different orders.

Change History Header (Effects of Changes on Planning View)															
2147483647 3/12/2018 12:56			Songlin Wei			Reason Codes: Sales Input; Commet Monthly Update for Q1									
9321 3/12/2018 12:56			John Frazer			Reason Codes: Promotion ; Category BSN upsell									

Product ID	Change ID	Type of Value	Key Figure	2018 CW07	2018 CW08	2018 CW09	2018 CW10	2018 CW11	2018 CW12	2018 CW13	2018 CW14	2018 CW15	2018 CW16	2018 CW17	2018 CW18
IBP-100	2147483647	Before	Consensus Demand Plan Qty	557	568	445	617	699	681	1127	936	591	1100	854	799
		After	Consensus Demand Plan Qty												
		Difference	Consensus Demand Plan Qty	-557	-568	-445	-617	-699	-681	-1127	-936	-591	-1100	-854	-799
		Difference in Percent	Consensus Demand Plan Qty	100	100	100	100	100	100	100	100	100	100	100	100
IBP-110	2147483647	Before	Consensus Demand Plan Qty	526	575	595	490	819	462	329	546	728	686	462	357
		After	Consensus Demand Plan Qty												
		Difference	Consensus Demand Plan Qty	-526	-575	-595	-490	-819	-462	-329	-546	-728	-686	-462	-357
		Difference in Percent	Consensus Demand Plan Qty	100	100	100	100	100	100	100	100	100	100	100	100
IBP-120	2147483647	Before	Consensus Demand Plan Qty	543	579	441	609	588	245	182	483	455	294	413	553
		After	Consensus Demand Plan Qty												
		Difference	Consensus Demand Plan Qty	-543	-579	-441	-609	-588	-245	-182	-483	-455	-294	-413	-553
		Difference in Percent	Consensus Demand Plan Qty	100	100	100	100	100	100	100	100	100	100	100	100
IBP-130	9321	Before	Consensus Demand Plan Qty							131	129	198	136	225	202
		After	Consensus Demand Plan Qty							195	570	873	603	996	301
		Difference	Consensus Demand Plan Qty							64	441	676	466	770	99
		Difference in Percent	Consensus Demand Plan Qty							49	342	342	342	342	49

Figure 10.35 Effect of Changes on Planning View

Change IDs also can be removed from the planning level section, the effect of which is aggregation of changes where the before and after values of the key figure across all changes are displayed.

The **Original Changes** option shows all the manual changes that were made for the change history key figure, along with the level at which the original changes were made. In this view, you can select the key figures and time range for changes, and the system will display all the planning levels and time levels at which the changes were made.

For example, Figure 10.36 shows that the **Consensus Demand without Promotions** key figure was changed at two different levels, first at the product ID level of PRD_001, followed by the product and location ID level of PRD_001 and LOC_001. The system shows all relevant settings (planning level, filter, conversions) that were used at the time when the change was made, as well as the dates and times when the changes were made, reason codes, comments, and the before/after values of the change. The **Original Changes** view also can be filtered to view changes associated with user-selected change IDs.

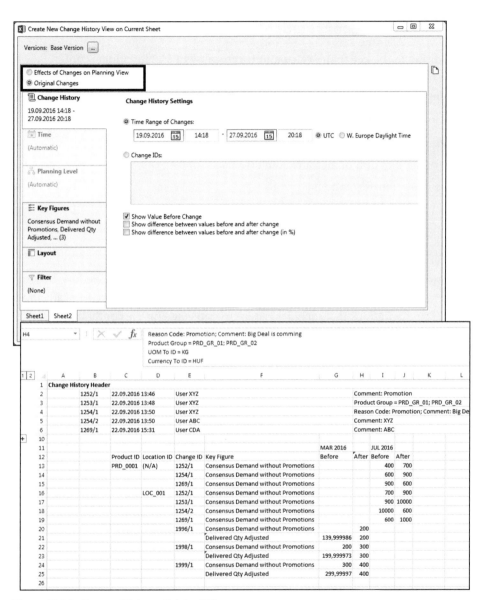

Figure 10.36 Change History: Original View

The change history report in Excel also provides navigation capabilities to navigate from a planning view to a change history view and from a change history effect view to a change history original view.

10.7   Advanced Configuration

In addition to the key figure calculations capability in SAP IBP model configuration, some more advanced modeling capabilities are provided to meet highly flexible customer planning models.

Some of the examples for advanced configurations include the following:

- Period shifting
- Currency and unit of measure conversions
- Attribute transformations
- Last period aggregation
- Weighted average calculations
- L-code for advanced logic

The **Model Configuration** section of SAP IBP provides some details on how to setup these advanced configurations. SAP also provides an SAP Note with a list of advanced model configurations that includes a step-by-step guide on the configurations, sample data, and planning views to test the results: SAP Note 2347105—Master Note for the Configuration of Sample Models.

Some advanced configuration information can be found in the following SAP Notes:

- 2240173—SAP IBP Sample Model Configuration: Calculation of Average and Weighted Value of Price Key Figures (Including Unit of Measure and Currency Conversion). An example of the weighted average is shown in Figure 10.37. The top section shows the planning view at the base planning level of product ID and customer ID for key figures at the monthly level. The bottom section shows the aggregated view at the product ID level. The average price key figure is calculated as the average of the unit price of combinations P1/C1 and P1/C2. The weighted average price is calculated as FORECATREVENUE@ REQUEST / FORECASTQTY@ REQUEST. For January 2018, at the aggregated product ID level, the weighted average price = 250000/ 1500 = 166.67.

- 2240170—SAP IBP Sample Model Configuration: Rolling Sum of the Last Three Periods.

- 2240178—SAP IBP Sample Model Configuration: View Monthly Key Figures at Weekly Level Based on Number of Weeks in the Month.

Base Planning Level				
Product ID	Customer ID	Key Figure	Jan-18	Feb-18
P1	C1	Unit Price	100	100
		Forecast Quantity	500	550
		Forecast Revenue	50000	55000
	C2	Unit Price	200	200
		Forecast Quantity	1000	1100
		Forecast Revenue	200000	220000
Aggregated Level				
	Product ID	Key Figure	Jan-18	Feb-18
	P1	Forecast Quantity	1500	1650
		Forecast Revenue	250000	275000
		Avg Price	150	150
		Weighted Average Price	166.67	166.67

Figure 10.37 Weighted and Average Price Calculation

- 2319165—SAP IBP Sample Model Configuration: Triggering an Alert on First Occurrence.
- 2289617—SAP IBP Sample Model Configuration: Aggregation of Last N Periods in Current and Future Periods. In this configuration, you perform an average of the sales quantity for the last six months and copy it to current and future periods. Figure 10.38 shows an example of average sales quantity for the last six months from current period. For product P1, and current period = March 2016, the average of the last six months (100, 150, 140, 200, 180, 150) is 153. This value is copied to current and future periods.

Product Family	Product ID	Key Figure	Sep'15	Oct'15	Nov'15	Dec'15	Jan'16	Feb'16	Mar'16	Apr'16	May'16	Jun'16	Jul'16	Aug'16	Sep'16	Oct'16	Nov'16	Dec'16
PF1	P1	Sales Qty	100	100	100	100	100	100	100	100	100	100	100	100	100	100	100	100
		Avg Sales (6mo)							100	100	100	100	100	100	100	100	100	100
	P10	Sales Qty	200	200	200	200	200	200	200	200	200	200	200	200	200	200	200	200
		Avg Sales (6mo)							200	200	200	200	200	200	200	200	200	200

Figure 10.38 Average Sales for Last Six Months Copied to Current and Future Periods

An extension to the above configuration is to perform year-to-date and year-to-go calculations, as shown in Figure 10.39.

Product ID	Key Figure	Nov'15	Dec'15	Jan'16	Feb'16	Mar'16	Apr'16	May'16	Jun'16	Jul'16	Aug'16	Sep'16	Oct'16	Nov'16	Dec'16
P1	Sales Qty	100	100	100	100	100	100	100	100	100	100	100	100	100	100
	Sales Qty YTD					300									
	Sales Qty YTG					900									
P10	Sales Qty	200	200	200	200	200	200	200	200	200	200	200	200	200	200
	Sales Qty YTD					600									
	Sales Qty YTG					1,800									

Figure 10.39 Year-to-Date and Year-to-Go Calculations

- 2286684—SAP IBP Sample Model Configuration: Last Period Aggregation for Key Figures.

- 289651—SAP IBP Sample Model Configuration: Last Period Aggregation with Unit of Measure Conversion. In last period aggregation, you show the last period value of the key figure when aggregated at a time level. For example, when inventory is aggregated from months to quarters, you want to show the inventory value of the last month for the quarter (see Figure 10.40).

Monthly

Product	Location	Key Figure	Jan'17	Feb'17	Mar'17	Apr'17	May'17	Jun'17	Jul'17	Aug'17	Sep'17	Oct'17	Nov'17	Dec'17
P1	LOC10	INVENTORY	10	20	30	40	50	60	70	80	90	100	110	120
		INVENTORYTIMEAGG	10	20	30	40	50	60	70	80	90	100	110	120
P10	LOC11	INVENTORY	130	140	30	60	80	100	120	200	100	120	140	160
		INVENTORYTIMEAGG	130	140	30	60	80	100	120	200	100	120	140	160

Quarterly

Product	Location	Key Figure	Q1 2017	Q2'2017	Q3'2017	Q4'2017
P1	LOC10	INVENTORY	60	150	240	330
		INVENTORYTIMEAGG	30	60	90	120
P10	LOC11	INVENTORY	300	240	420	420
		INVENTORYTIMEAGG	30	100	100	160

Yearly

Product	Location	Key Figure	2017
P1	LOC10	INVENTORY	780
		INVENTORYTIMEAGG	120
P10	LOC11	INVENTORY	1380
		INVENTORYTIMEAGG	160

Figure 10.40 Last Period Aggregation Example

- 2288329—SAP IBP Sample Model Configuration: Time as a Dimension (Year-to-Date and Quarter-to-Date Aggregations).

- 2298382—Requesting L-Code from SAP.

- 289248—SAP IBP Sample Model Configuration: Time-Independent Unit of Measure Conversion.

- 2564552—Unit of Measure Conversion for Component Materials (Using Attribute Transformation).

Another advanced model configuration that's listed in the SAP IBP Model Configuration Guide is the use of time profile attributes to model period-to-period comparison. Figure 10.41 shows the result of such configuration, in which you can perform year-over-year comparisons of the actuals quantity key figure by month and grouped to quarters. This can also be used to perform quarter-to-quarter comparisons.

SAP	Sales and Operation Planning										User: sopadmin		Planning Area: STTPATTR	
Y2Y by QtrMo														
Last Refresh: 2016-Feb-22 16:51:45														
			Q1			Q2			Q3			Q4		
Product ID	Key Figure	Time	01-JAN	02-FEB	03-MAR	04-APR	05-MAY	06-JUN	07-JUL	08-AUG	09-SEP	10-OCT	11-NOV	12-DEC
P1	Actuals Qty	2013						80	80	80	80	80	80	80
		2014	90	90	90	90	90	90	90	90	90	90	90	90
		2015	100	100	100	100	100	100	100	100	100	100	100	100
		2016	110											
P200	Actuals Qty	2013						130	130	130	130	130	130	130
		2014	140	140	140	140	140	140	140	140	140	140	140	140
		2015	140	140	140	140	140	150	150	150	150	150	150	150
		2016	150											
P300	Actuals Qty	2013						180	180	180	180	180	180	180
		2014	190	190	190	190	190	190	190	190	190	190	190	190
		2015	200	200	200	200	200	200	200	200	200	200	200	200
		2016	210											

Figure 10.41 Year-to-Year Comparison of Actuals Quantity Using Time Profile Attributes

10.8   System Performance Recommendations

No matter how large you size your system, you can always model your application in a way that the hardware will be brought to its limits. The high flexibility of SAP IBP is a major advantage when it comes to adjusting it to your business model. However, it can be a disadvantage if the performance impact isn't considered. The complexity of the model together with the data volume determine the hardware needed. SAP provides configuration and performance recommendations in SAP Note 2211255, which includes the following guidelines:

- Perform sizing at the beginning of implementation. Verify the sizing assumptions are correct postimplementation, after data is loaded into the system.
- Keep your configuration as simple as possible to balance requirements and performance.

A planning model that contains the right level of data granularity and key figure calculations together with clear data lifecycle management and efficient Excel planning view templates provides the right user experience and adoption of the solution by end users. This section provides guidelines on the modeling of key figures, master data types, global configuration parameters and other modeling constructs along with how to manage the growing data in the system. These include the following:

- **Attributes and master data types**
  - Keep the overall number of attributes and master data types to what is truly required. Too many attributes in master data types and planning levels can affect performance.
  - You can use a non-key attribute of a master data type as a root attribute in planning levels. That way, you don't need to model additional master data types. For example, you can define a planning level with root attributes product family and customer region where they are non-key attributes of product and customer master data type respectively.
- **Key figures and planning levels**
  - Model key figures at the required detail with regard to time and attributes. A finer granularity than needed carries a performance penalty.
  - Minimize the number of root attributes in stored planning levels. More granular data leads to higher data storage and more data processed when used in calculations.
  - Minimize the number of calculations that include different input planning levels wherever possible (but without increasing the number of key figure values you need to store).
  - Avoid on-the-fly attribute transformations in queries frequently used by users. The corresponding queries can be slow because large data will be fetched if filters aren't pushed down. Instead, if possible, try to store the results of attribute transformation to a stored key figure using a copy operator.
  - Check for attributes or key figures that aren't used in planning views or analytics and remove them from planning areas or even from master data.
- **Attributes as key figures**
  - If you use key figures that are filled via a master data attribute as a key figure, use time-independent key figures instead of time-dependent ones.
  - If time-dependent attributes as key figures are required, use the **From Periods** and **To Periods** settings in **Attribute as Key Figure** configuration to limit the number of time periods this attribute needs to be copied to.
  - If an attribute value is not time-independent and needs to vary over time, then load it as a regular key figure.
- **Data integration**
  - Schedule large data loads during off-peak hours.

- Don't load data frequently if not required; for example, avoid loading daily actuals and master data for a monthly S&OP process.
- Use the purge functions to purge data that isn't used in the system.

- **Change history**
  - Only switch on change history for planning areas and individual key figures where it's really required—for example, for key figures that are changes in Excel.
  - Usually it's not required to track changes for key figures loaded from external systems. If you need to make manual changes to such key figures, which you want to track in the change history, it's better for logical and for performance reasons to introduce an additional key figure when you make the change and use an overwrite calculation.

- **Global configuration parameters**
  Make sure the following global configuration parameters are configured to the recommended default settings for better performance. The defaults are available in the system for reference:
  - TRACE->TRACELEVEL
    Make sure this isn't set to D for debugging; otherwise, some parts of the application, like disaggregation, will be slowed down.
  - PLAN_VIEW-> MAX_RESULT_ROW_SIZE
  - INTEGRATION-STAGCLEANUP
  - PLAN_VIEW-> MAX_DIM_MEMBERS
  - SCHEDULER_INTERVAL_IN_MINS
  - SCN_COUNT_MAX

There are also two relevant Excel planning view performance recommendations:

- SAP Note 2153455—Planning View Performance Recommendations
- SAP Note 1790530—VBA-Based Templates for Better Performance, Stability, and Robustness.

10.9   Summary

In this chapter, we covered the most essential aspects of planning area configuration and its core planning elements, like attributes, key figures, master data types, time profiles, versions, and planning operators. We covered these core concepts with several examples, along with the most common configurations for S&OP processes. We also covered sample models delivered by SAP and some recommendations on how to get started with building your S&OP planning area.

Finally, we went over topics like change history, advanced configurations, and system performance recommendations, which are essential for every S&OP project to enable a stable and performant planning model and increase end user usability and adoption. Planning areas in SAP IBP provide a high level of flexibility in modeling different customer business processes. As mentioned, planning areas are the foundation for SAP IBP customer implementations, upon which several other planning processes, planning profiles, end user simulations, analytics, data integration, and so on depend. Therefore, it's important to get the business model right to support all the functional areas of SAP IBP.

Chapter 11
Building Planning Views

In this chapter, we'll discuss one of the most widely appreciated strengths of SAP IBP: its user interface. SAP IBP's UI is especially helpful for the day-to-day planner who can leverage his favorite planning application, Microsoft Excel.

In this chapter, we'll elaborate on the one of the most popular features in the SAP Integrated Business Planning for sales and operations environment: Excel planning views. Chapter 2 introduced the concept of Excel planning views and SAP Integrated Business Planning, add-in for Microsoft Excel. This chapter will go deeper into the advanced capabilities that come with Excel as a key user interface for planners.

We'll start by explaining the logic of templates and favorites, used for planners to store their specific planning views. Then, we'll introduce the formatting capabilities with sheet options, local members, and the EPM formatting sheet, followed by charting capabilities. To manage master data, the latest releases from SAP IBP feature master data workbooks, which allow users to interactively visualize and change data, leveraging the power of Excel. Finally, the chapter will conclude with an overview of how the solution can be elevated to the next level by leveraging Visual Basic for Applications (VBA) to influence how the Excel planning view interacts with the backend SAP IBP solution.

11.1 Planning Views, Templates, and Favorites

An *Excel planning view* is a user-defined, Excel-based data report that allows you to view, edit, and share data from SAP IBP. Excel planning views can be created from scratch in a standard Excel workbook, but they often start from a baseline template that already has the right planning levels, key figures, filters, and formatting. This starting point, called a *planning view template*, is typically made available to end users by power users or originates from the implementation phase of the project. In this section, we'll explore the use of templates and favorites. However, first we'll introduce the different aspects that make up an Excel planning view.

11.1.1   Planning View Creation

Excel planning views are made of five elements that can be managed during creation or editing of the planning view. Creating or changing an Excel planning view can be done from from the **IBP** tab in the Excel ribbon. Figure 11.1 shows the create or change dialog for an Excel planning view.

Keep in mind that a workbook containing planning views can have multiple sheets. Those sheets are shown at the bottom of the edit/create planning view dialog. To create a planning view, follow these steps:

1. Add a sheet to an existing Excel planning view by clicking the **New Planning View** button from an existing template, which will show the option to copy from the current sheet. Although you can copy either with or without formatting, we strongly advise you to copy with formatting rather than get an unformatted worksheet, which is often harder to use (Section 11.2).

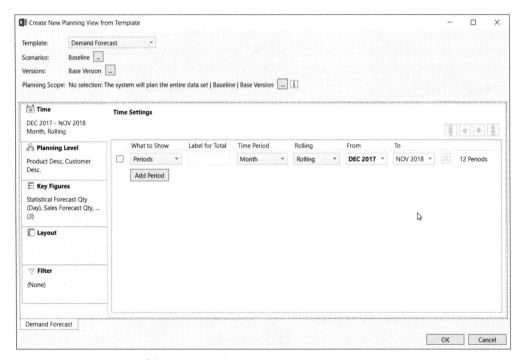

Figure 11.1 Create/Change Excel Planning View

2. Select versions or scenarios (this step is optional). The dialog to create a new planning view shows the key information at the top, consisting of the template this Excel planning view refers to and the scope of data it contains in the context of scenarios, versions, and planning data. This selection delineates the scope that supply planning algorithms, such as the S&OP heuristic and optimizer, will run for. You can select multiple versions and scenarios in the planning scope, but we advise you to do so only if your objective is version or scenario comparison because all the interactively run algorithms will use this full dataset.

3. Select scenarios, versions, and planning units. As explained in Chapter 4, the planning data scope can only be defined by subnetworks because the supply planning operators are network planning algorithms in nature. Figure 11.2 shows how the planning scope delineation can be used to select scenarios, versions, and planning units (subnetworks).

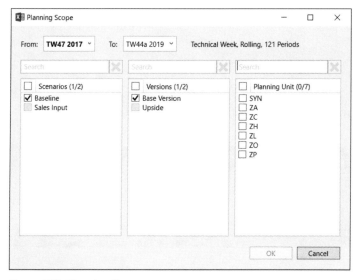

Figure 11.2 Planning Scope

4. In the section below the **Planning Scope** selection, **Time** is the first component of the Excel planning view you'll define. Planning views can use flexible time dimensions, making it possible to combine time granularities. This could be used, for example, to visualize four weeks in weekly buckets, but the remainder of the year in months. Leveraging the capabilities of totals in the planning view makes it possible, for example, to introduce a **Rest of Year** column. The result of this selection can be found in Figure 11.3, where the planning view visualizes the first four weeks,

followed by four months, and a column depicting the rest of the calendar year as a total. The results of this Excel planning view are shown in Figure 11.4.

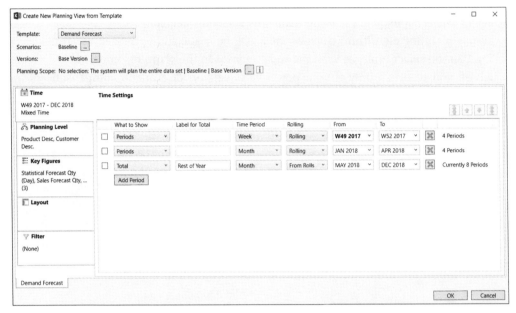

Figure 11.3 Telescopic Time Dimension in Excel Planning View

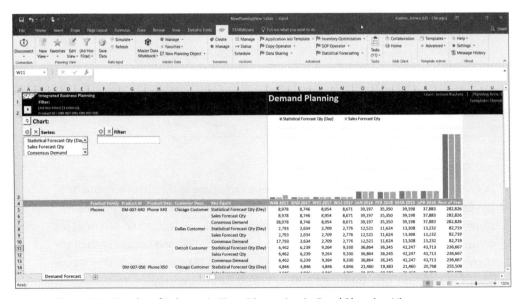

Figure 11.4 Results of Telescopic Time Dimension in Excel Planning View

5. Define the dimensions to visualize in terms of the planning level of the key figures. This can be done in the view planning level section, where you can select the
different attributes that make up the planning level. Figure 11.5 shows the dialog to
perform the selection. It's important to think through the order of the selected levels, as this drastically influences the usability of the planning views. It's advisable
to start from the highest level and become more granular so that the grouping of
the attributes in the planning levels makes sense. Depending on the implementation, you can opt to combine a description and identifier in one attribute, or to
split them as in the example shown for a product (ID and description).

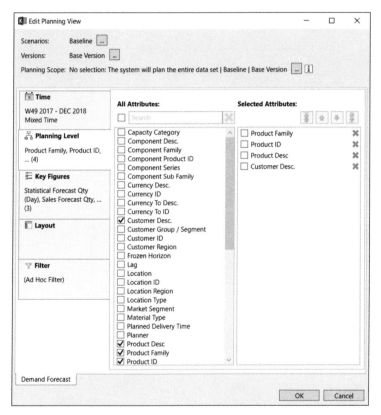

Figure 11.5 Planning Level

The example in Figure 11.5 shows a planning view starting at the product family,
then shows the product identifier followed by the individual product description
and the customer description. This planning view is very typical for detailed
demand planning on customer and product levels.

6. After selecting the planning level, select the key figures to appear in the planning view, as shown in Figure 11.6. This can be done in the **Key Figures** section when creating or editing a planning view. When adding key figures, it's important to consider the planning level selected in the prior step and how it relates to the base planning level of the key figure. If you selected planning levels that aren't part of the base planning level of the key figure, they will appear in the planning view with the descriptor **None**. The planning view will group the key figures per planning level before using the sequence specified in the create/edit planning view dialog. For example, a key figure like net demand, which is defined at the product location level, will have **None** in the **Customer** field if this is selected as part of the planning level in the planning view.

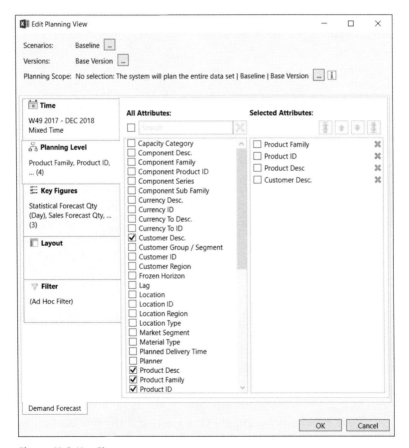

Figure 11.6 Key Figures

Remember that it's impossible to select a time granularity that's more granular than what the key figure is specified for. For example, if a key figure is defined in monthly buckets, it will be greyed out when selecting weekly buckets in the time dimension of the planning view.

> **Note**
>
> For more technical users, it's possible to see the technical names of the key figures by right-clicking the **All Key Figures** header of the dialog, which opens a dropdown in which you can see the description of the key figure, its technical name, or both.

7. Once all key figures have been selected, the **Layout** section lets you alter the way the key planning view formatting is performed. In standard planning views, the time dimension is maintained on the column axis, whereas the attributes of the planning level and the key figures are maintained as rows.

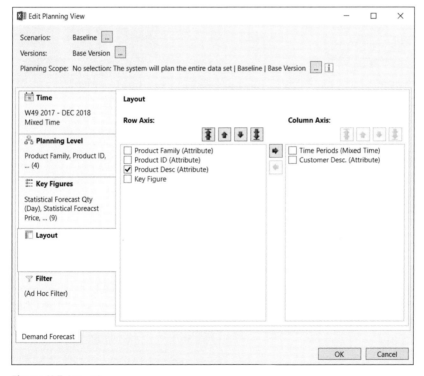

Figure 11.7 Layout

8. For particular use cases, you can opt to divert from this standard—for example, to show only one time bucket but the product as a column, as shown in Figure 11.7, which results in the planning view shown in Figure 11.8.

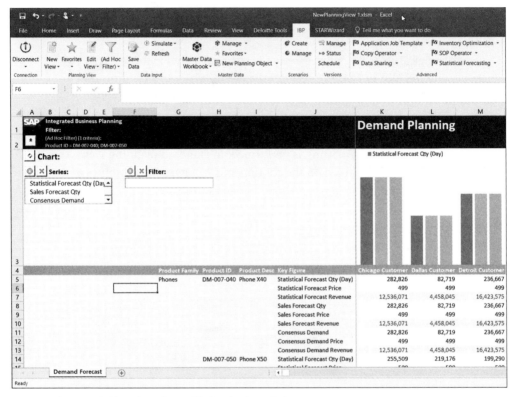

Figure 11.8 Planning View with Products as Columns

9. The last section in creating or editing a planning view allows you to specify a filter. Filtering in planning views is key to performance because it can reduce the number of records to be pulled from the database. Filters can be created ad hoc for the planning view or can be stored. Storing filters allows you to easily toggle between the various stored filters while working in the planning view by using the **Filter** dropdown in the **IBP** tab in Excel.

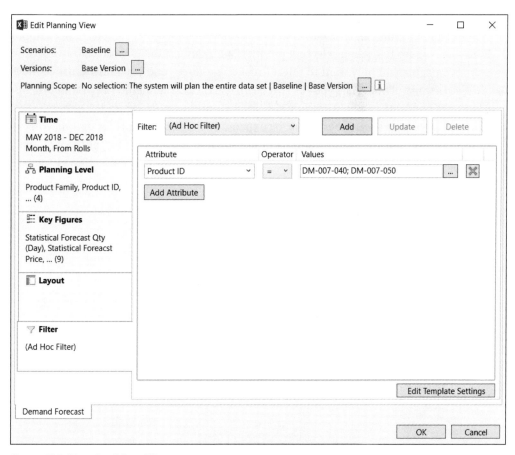

Figure 11.9 Planning View Filters

10. In Figure 11.9, a filter is shown that selects a subset of products. The filter currently isn't saved but can be by clicking the **Add** button at the top. Once a filter is stored, it can be assigned to other planning views easily with the provided name.

    Because planning view filters play a critical role in performance, system administrators can opt to enforce the usage of filters via a global parameter in the configuration. They can choose to require a filter and to display an error if no filter is available or a warning.

11. To bring more structure into the filtering capability, cascading filters can be applied. This can be done on the selection screen of a specific filter. For example, in Figure 11.9, when selecting products, you can use the ellipsis (...) button. Now, imagine you only want to select finished products, and you know finished products are of **Material Type FERT**: you can use the cascading filter to prefilter the list of available products to only the finished products. In Figure 11.10, the product selection is shown; at the top, by expanding the **Cascading Filter** option, you can filter down the list for **Material Type** equal to **FERT**. Don't forget to click **Apply** when a cascading filter is selected to filter the products for selection at the bottom.

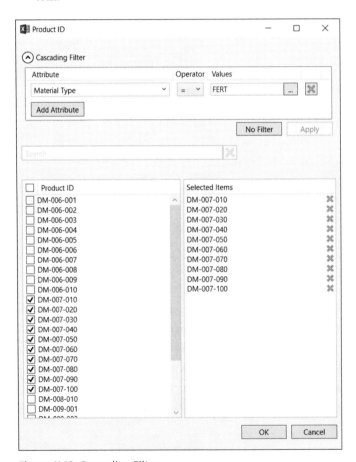

Figure 11.10 Cascading Filters

12. Finally, at the bottom of the planning view filtering dialog, as shown in Figure 11.9, there is an **Edit Template Setting** button. When you click this button, you as the template administrator can pass the filters provided in the template on to another user. Figure 11.11 shows the following options:

- **Don't Copy**
  The filter will not be passed on when a user builds a new planning view from this template.

- **Copy as a Suggestion**
  The filter will be passed on to a user building a planning view from this template, but the user can overwrite it.

- **Copy as Mandatory**
  The filter will be passed on and the user can not remove it.

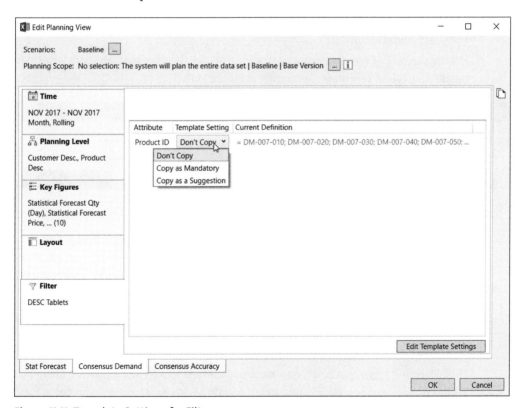

Figure 11.11 Template Settings for Filters

System administrators can make the use of filters in planning views mandatory in general by setting the global parameter FORCE_PLANNING_VIEW_FILTER to either **Mandatory** or **Warning** for the corresponding behavior.

11.1.2   Templates and Favorites

Once a planning view has been created, it can be stored. Some planning views are meant to be used widely in a planning organization and hence can be considered templates. In most organizations, power users are granted the role of template administrator, allowing them to create, update, delete, and organize templates. Regular end users tend to be at the receiving end of templates but will still appreciate the ability to make changes to the provided templates and store those changes. This can be achieved by using planning view favorites.

Template Administration

Having the role of template administrator provides the user with an extra section in the **IBP** tab, called **Templates**, as shown in Figure 11.12.

Figure 11.12 Template Administration

In template administration, you can add the current planning view as a template, update a template previously been created by the content in the current planning view, delete existing planning views, and organize the folder structure of the planning views.

Adding a planning view opens a dialog in which a name can be given and a folder can be selected for the planning view. The organization of planning views allows you to change the folder structure of the templates as shown in the upper section of Figure 11.13. Planning views can be given a name, and added to a folder. Updating templates looks very similar. To delete templates, a pop up allows you to select and delete templates which you no longer need. Organizing templates in a folder structure is often a good idea to make the templates more accessible by users.

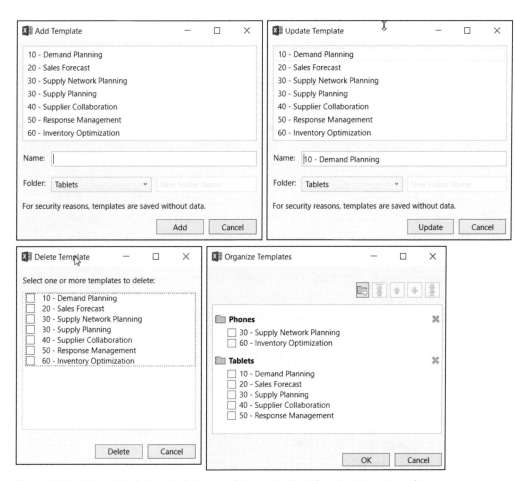

Figure 11.13 Adding, Updating, Deleting, and Organization Planning View Templates

Favorites

Users who aren't considered template administrators will open planning views either from the **New View** button in the **IBP** tab or via their favorites. When creating a new planning view from a blank Excel sheet, you can opt to create it from a template or not. We recommend creating new planning views with reference to templates because the templates include the formatting of the planning view. Creating a new planning view without reference to a template will result in a template without any formatting, which can be hard to interpret.

When creating a planning view from a template, most users want to leverage the user-defined characteristics of planning views by making edits to them. Because it would be inconvenient for users to have to make the same edits to planning views all the time, users can save the edits to the planning view in their favorites, which are user-specific but can be shared with other users.

After creation of the planning view, as described in the previous section, a user can add the planning view as a favorite via the **Add** option in the **Favorites** dropdown. The options to add, update, delete, and organize operate in the same way as the corresponding options for templates, as shown in Figure 11.13. The only extra option for favorites, because they're user-specific by default, is to share the template with a colleague using the **Share** option. Favorites can be shared with individual users or user groups.

With the sharing being initiated by the user who creates the planning view, it's important to consider the users you shared your favorite with when making updates. When updating a shared template, the system will show a warning if the template is shared to inform you of the repercussions of the change for the users who have access to the favorite. On the other hand, at the receiving end of shared favorites, users can opt out of sharing via the **Organize Template** option. Just move the shared favorite to the **Opt Out** folder and it won't appear in the dropdown list anymore. Getting it back is convenient as well: move it back up out of the **Opt Out** folder.

11.2   Formatting Planning Views

A good planning view will have to be formatted in a way that makes it easy to use. Moreover, planning views can become actual reports used in meetings or shared with stakeholders. Hence, it's imperative to make them look functional, easy-to-use, and professional. Because SAP IBP generates the table that makes up the main section of the planning view and the size of the table depends on the exact modalities of the planning view, which are controlled by a user, formatting of planning views requires a robust approach. This approach is covered by leveraging a formatting sheet to control the general layout options of the planning view.

In this section, we'll provide some basic layout tips prior to moving to more specific options available in planning views. We'll cover local calculations in the Excel planning views, called *local members* in SAP IBP. Finally, we'll close this section with an in-depth description of the EPM formatting sheet, which controls the layout of the SAP IBP Excel planning views.

11.2.1   Basic Layout Tips

When crafting the formatting of a new Excel planning view, there are a couple of tips that can fundamentally improve the layout of the workbook. First, the most important is to start from a good baseline. SAP Note 1790530 provides a link to a foundational set of planning views that form a good basis for building enterprise-specific templates.

If you do decide to start from a completely blank planning view, remember that the data table, which is the only thing the SAP IBP system populates when starting a new planning view, has the first value field on the cell selected. Figure 11.14 shows that when selecting cell D9 when creating a new planning view without reference to a template, this cell would become the first content field.

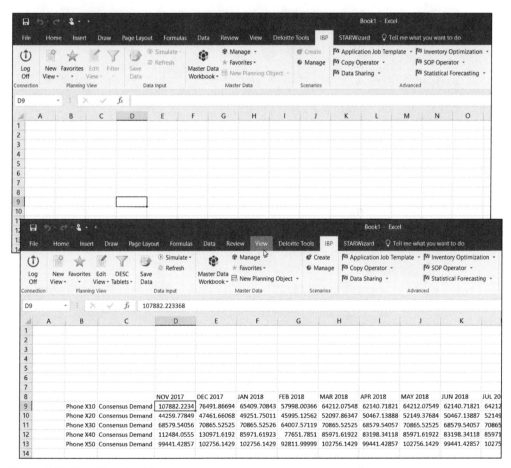

Figure 11.14 New Planning View

When creating a new planning view without reference to a template, it becomes clear that only the most basic information is automatically populated by SAP IBP. All the other information enters in after formatting the planning view. Most information for formatting the planning view can be found using Excel formulas, which are exposed by SAP Integrated Business Planning, add-in for Microsoft Excel. For example, the column headings can be found using the SOP_Heading Excel formula, followed by the number of the column, counting from the columns closest to the data fields.

Table 11.1 shows a sample of the available fields, but note that new fields are added in every release and are easy to retrieve in SAP IBP. Just go to a planning view, type a formula starting with "=SOP" or "=EPM", and a dropdown list of all available fields will be displayed.

Formula	Description	Example Value
SOP_Heading1	First column header measured from data fields	Key Figures
SOP_Heading2	Second column header measured from data fields	Product Description
SOP_Connection_Name	Connection name	SAP Active Planning Area
SOP_Planning_Area	Planning area description	D01ACTIVE
EPMUser()	User ID	Jeroen Kusters
SOP_Filter_Name	Name of filter applied	Ad Hoc Filter
SOP_Template_Name	Name of template if template is used	Demand Planning
SOP_Favorite_Name	Name of favorite if favorite is used	Demand Planning
SOP_Planning_Area_Scope	Planning scope as selected in the planning view	No Selection
SOP_Refresh_Timestamp	The timestamp for the last view refresh	2017-Sep-08 15:05:03

Table 11.1 Formulas in SAP Integrated Business Planning, Add-in for Microsoft Excel

The next step to make a good Excel planning view is to be smart about merging cells at the header level. This allows for decoupling the planning view data at the bottom, which auto-sizes with the data and columns selected in the planning view, from the header, which typically should remain stable over time.

11.2.2   Sheet Options and Local Members

To modify the content displayed in the data table, which is generated by SAP IBP, use the sheet options that can be selected from the **Edit View** dropdown in the **Planning View** group.

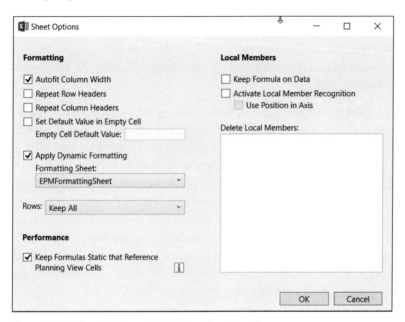

Figure 11.15 Sheet Options for Editing Planning Views

Basic formatting options can be selected at the top left, as shown in Figure 11.15:

- **Autofit Column Width** allows you to switch on/off the autofitting of column headers for controlling the size of, for example, attribute columns labeled with key figure names.

- **Repeat Row** or **Column Headers** is very useful if you want to use the standard Excel filtering capabilities. For example, it can ensure the product description is repeated if multiple key figures are generated.

- **Set Default Value in Empty Cell** for blank values can be useful for filtering or differentiating zero values from blank values.

- **Apply Dynamic Formatting** will be covered in Section 11.2.3.
- In the **Rows** section, you can select what should happen with zero and blank rows from the following options:
  - **Keep All**
  - **Hide Empty**
  - **Hide Empty and Zero Values**
  - **Remove Empty and Zero Values**
- Finally, the **Performance** setting lets you speed up the performance of the planning view. The only exception, and the reason you're given control over this field, is if there are formulas in the planning view that reference changeable cells (and aren't local members, as discussed ahead). If this parameter is set, the fields aren't recalculated automatically.

The right-hand side of the options window shows options for **Local Members**. The use of local members makes it possible to create standard Excel formulas in the planning view, which are just regular calculations. The data table rendered by SAP IBP can change all the time, but when adding a formula, the expectation is that the formula will remain stable under changing planning view conditions—for example, when adding or removing filters. Local members achieve this objective and need to be activated in the planning view by selecting the **Activate Local Member Recognition** setting in the sheet options. When this option is selected, you can insert a row in the data table section of the planning view and give it a row header in the key figure column and a formula in the first data field. Pressing Enter will make the local member recognition feature calculate the formula for all planning objects.

For the Excel planning view in Figure 11.16, imagine you want to calculate the difference between the statistical forecast and the sales forecast. You can do so as follows:

1. Activate local member recognition in the planning view options.
2. Insert a row under the sales forecast line of the first planning object (row 6 in this example).
3. Type a name in the key figure column (column K in this example).
4. Type a formula in the first data field (cell K9 in this case)—for example, *Statistical Forecast - Sales Forecast* (=K5-K6).
5. Press Enter.

The result is shown in Figure 11.17. Although you only typed the formula for the first product and for the first cell, the calculations have been made for all products and all columns. This planning view can now be saved as a template or favorite.

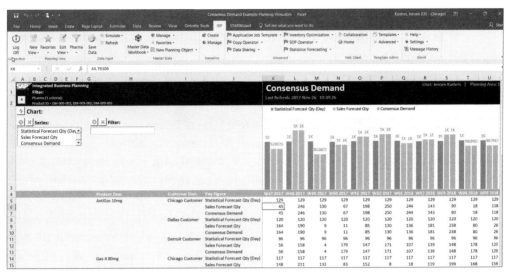

Figure 11.16 Planning View before Activating Local Members

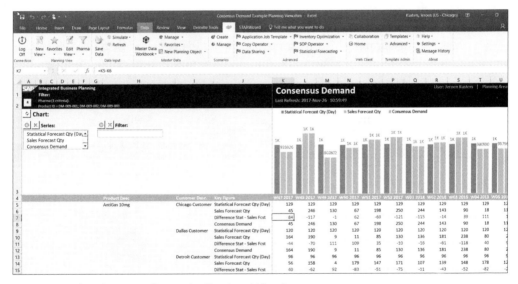

Figure 11.17 Planning Vew after Activating Local Members

Although local members provide a lot of opportunities to add custom calculations to the planning view, there are a couple of points worth noting:

- Local members aren't stored in the database and thus aren't available in dashboards or for outbound integration.

- Local members are very sensitive to structural changes to the planning views and hence should be removed before adding key figures or planning levels to ensure consistency.

11.2.3   EPM Formatting Sheet

Different fields in the planning view might have different requirements for visualizing the data content; for example, some fields might be percentages or currencies, whereas others are expected to be positive rounded numbers. In some cases, it might add value to use conditional formatting to highlight specific values, such as when a projected inventory becomes negative, representing a shortage.

The EPM formatting sheet allows for the general formatting of the planning view. It can be accessed by selecting **View Formats** from the **Edit View** dropdown in the **Planning View** group. Clicking this option opens a hidden Excel sheet, called EPMFormattingSheet by default. Looking back at the sheet options in Figure 11.15, it's possible to have multiple EPM formatting sheets, which can be assigned to the different main sheets in the workbook.

The EPM formatting sheet shown in Figure 11.18 allows for formatting the cells by specifying a hierarchy of formatting that applies to the fields. All the elements in the formatting sheet have a checkbox which lets you toggle them active/inactive.

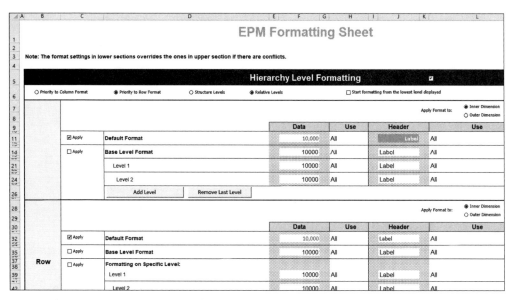

Figure 11.18 EPM Formatting Sheet

Every section of the EPM formatting sheet provides the layout for the data and the header. To influence the layout of the values, you can update the formatting of the cell representing the value (e.g., cell F11) with the formatting you want. The column header is maintained in the header column (in this case, column J). The fields next to the formatting fields, under the **Use** header, can be selected to mark which formatting elements should be carried over, as shown in Figure 11.19.

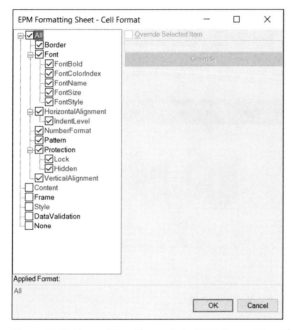

Figure 11.19 Formatting Elements in EPM Formatting Sheet

As an example, referring back to the local member in the previous session, it's possible to change the font color of the local member to become red when the value is negative. This corresponds to cases in which the sales forecast is higher than the statistical forecast and hence the sales planner might be overestimating future sales. To model this, navigate to the **Dimension Member/Property Formatting** section in the EPM formatting sheet and look for **Local Member Default Format** in the **Row** section. Make the conditional formatting—red for negative values—apply to all local members by following these steps;

1. Select **Apply** in front of **Local Member Default Format**.
2. Select the **Data** field with the value 10.000 in the **Local Member Default Format** header line.

3. Click **Conditional Formatting**, and apply a new conditional formatting rule to make the field red if the value is smaller than O.

4. Double-click the **Use** field next to the **10.000** field, and select **All**.

5. To not affect the column header, select **None** for the use of the header field.

6. Go back to the planning view, and click **Refresh**.

The results look like Figure 11.20.

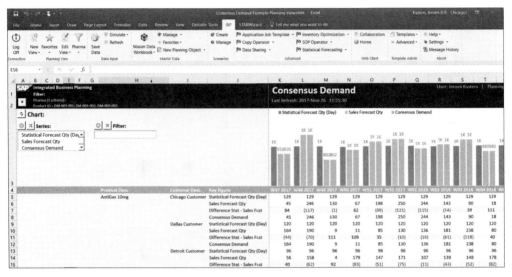

Figure 11.20 Conditional Formatting on Local Member

> **Note**
>
> The SAP Help website (*help.sap.com/IBP-REF*), as well SAP Note 1790530, provide much more information about using the EPM formatting sheet.

11.3   Using Charts

Charts are the most foundational capability planners want to use with Excel as a user interface for the SAP IBP system. It's possible to create Excel-based charts that leverage normal Excel capabilities. However, with the flexibility to create and change planning views, this section will cover a more sustainable way to create charts in SAP IBP planning views, ensuring they remain usable when the planning view changes.

SAP Note 1790530 covers SAP's predelivered planning views and introduces Visual Basic for Applications-based templates you can download when starting your SAP IBP implementation. The templates documented in *How to Use Template VBA* are the most recent version. In this section, we'll take these templates as a starting point and review the following benefits:

- A stable set of VBA-powered templates that are sustainable when users change their planning views
- Flexibility for users to maintain their charts as a self-service capability

How to Use Template VBA gives a complete walkthrough of how to use the planning view. Figure 11.21 gives an example of a planning view as delivered by SAP. At the top left, you can select a time series to represent. Click the **X** icon to remove the selected key figures. Select key figures in column J to add them with the **+** icon. The same process applies for filters, adding planning levels and removing them with the provided icons.

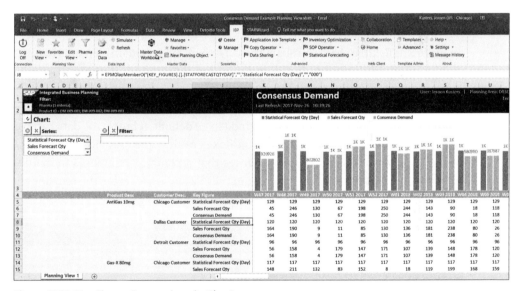

Figure 11.21 Key Figure Comparison in Charts

It's also possible to filter on a key figure while selecting different planning level elements to differentiate as time series. In Figure 11.22, you can see the statistical forecast differentiated by customer.

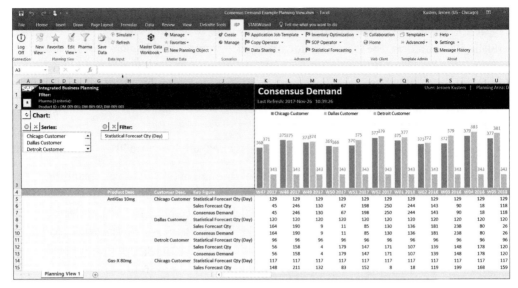

Figure 11.22 Customer Comparison in Chart

To make this flexible charting capability work, there are two main elements required:

1. Chart feeder hidden sheet

2. VBA code

The chart feeder is an Excel sheet that's hidden by default; it builds the data based on the selection performed in the selection boxes as described previously. The chart feeder is shown in Figure 11.23; you can see that it contains references to the filter information and the series information in cells B2 and B3, whereas the remainder of the table is the consolidated information from the planning view.

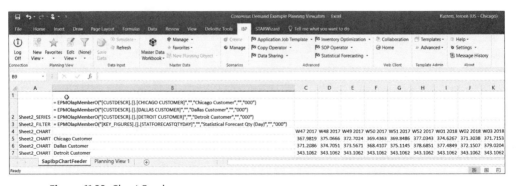

Figure 11.23 Chart Feeder

The VBA code ensures the chart feeder is rebuilt when changes to the selection criteria are made. The chart handler module in the VBA code is responsible for modeling the data in a way that's consumable by the chart in Excel. Documenting the details of the VBA code falls outside of the scope of this book, but more information can be found in the **How to Use Template VBA** section of SAP Note 1790530.

As a final comment, during implementation there is a choice of which template to use. The SAP Note comes with two sets of templates:

1. Templates with VBA code embedded
2. Templates relying on a VBA add-in for templates

In the first set of templates, the VBA code to control the chart is embedded in every workbook saved as a template. This makes it possible to deploy the templates to users without having to implement an additional add-in, allowing everyone with SAP Integrated Business Planning, add-in for Microsoft Excel to visualize data in the planning views with VBA-powered charts. However, this comes at a cost of updating the VBA code in every template if there are changes required, either to add functionality or to fix problems with the charts.

The alternative is to use templates that don't have all the code embedded but use an additional add-in instead. In this case, the main code to populate the chart feeder that controls the charts is available in a centralized add-in, allowing you to make changes centrally and deploy a new add-in when the VBA code needs updating. The downside is that a new add-in needs to be deployed. This is a choice that can be made during implementation; however, in most cases the embedded VBA code seems like the more pragmatic solution.

11.4   Master Data Worksheets

Although most of planning view usage in SAP IBP is typically centered on the planning functions described thus far in this chapter, SAP Integrated Business Planning, add-in for Microsoft Excel lets you maintain master data en masse in so-called master data workbooks. Over time, the concept of master data workbooks has expanded to also allow mass maintenance of planning objects. In this section, we'll give an overview of the creation and maintenance of master data workbooks and the functionality of planning object creation.

11.4.1   Master Data Workbooks

Master data workbooks let you visualize and maintain master data en masse in SAP IBP system using SAP Integrated Business Planning, add-in for Microsoft Excel. Although planning views are commonly used by all users, master data workbooks tend to be reserved for expert users who need to visualize all raw master data and possibly make changes. The approach of manually maintaining master data in the Excel add-in needs to be aligned with the integration strategy of the SAP IBP system, as discussed in Chapter 14.

Master data workbooks operate very similarly to planning worksheets and are generated via the **IBP** tab in the Excel ribbon, in the **Master Data** section, where the **Master Data Workbook** button provides a dropdown to create or change an existing master data workbook.

Creating a master data workbook uses a similar dialog compared to the planning view creation but comprises fewer steps. As shown in Figure 11.24, a master data workbook can have a filter maintained at the top and lets you select the master data type in the middle section. More than one sheet can be included by using the tabs at the bottom. If you want to edit the master data in the master data workbook, the **Edit** flag needs to be set.

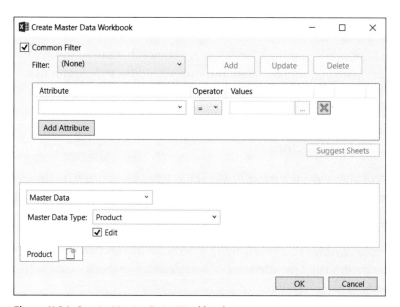

Figure 11.24 Create Master Data Workbook

After opening the master data workbook, it's possible to perform a mass change or create new master data records by editing or adding them in the workbook as shown in Figure 11.25. Master data workbooks can be stored as favorites just like planning views can, with the same ability to create, update, delete, share, and organize master data favorites.

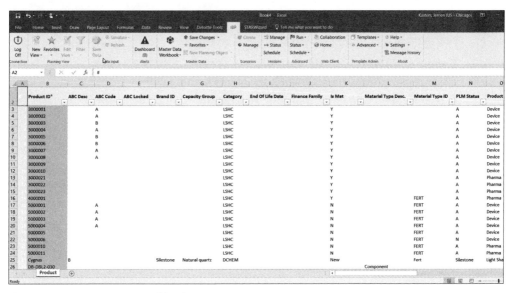

Figure 11.25 Master Data Workbook

11.4.2 Planning Object Creation

Planning objects are the planning level elements that contain data. For example, if a consensus demand key figure is maintained on the product-customer level, every combination of customer and product represents a planning object. This planning object either can exist—for example, because the customer has ordered this product in the past and hence has a sales history for it—or cannot exist, because no key figure has ever been created for this customer product. If a planning object exists, for any key figure at the same planning level (in this case, product-customer), you can maintain any other key figure at the same planning level in the planning view. However, if the combination has never been created, you need to create the object before you can maintain the key figure at that level.

In general, SAP IBP dynamically generates planning objects via its algorithms and integrations. For example, integration of the sales history on a product-customer level will create all the combinations of products and customers for which sales orders have occurred. Even if the sales history is available at a different planning level—for example, product-location-customer—the statistical forecast would generate a forecast on product-customer level, but the combinations would be created by the statistical forecasting algorithm. Only if no integration or algorithm will generate the planning object do you have to create it yourself. This is the case for new product introductions, for example, when you need to plan products that have never been sold before.

There are two ways you can create planning objects. First, they can be created in a traditional planning view, leveraging the **New Planning Object** button available in the **Master Data** section of the planning view, as shown in Figure 11.26.

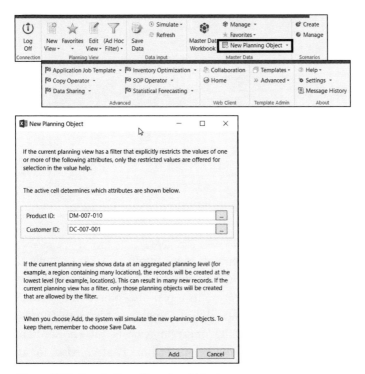

Figure 11.26 Create New Planning Object

It's best practice to create the objects at the lowest level, at the root of the planning view, to ensure strict control over which objects are created. Creating the planning levels on an aggregate level will generate all underlying planning combinations, which could result in creating more objects than you intended.

If your intention is to mass create planning combinations, a better approach is to leverage the planning object creations via the master data workbooks. In the same way, as shown in Section 11.4.1, a master data workbook can include sheets that control the planning object creation. This is done by selecting **Planning Object with Key Figure Data** from the unnamed dropdown in the **Product** area (shown in Figure 11.24, in which it has **Master Data** selected), then selecting the planning level at which the key figure is stored. In this case, looking at the consensus demand, which is stored at the product-customer level, you can generate the planning objects together with the demand—for example, for a new product introduction.

Generating the master data workbook as shown in Figure 11.27 gives a workbook as shown in Figure 11.28, in which combinations can be added. Given how the workbook is structured, this can only be done at the base planning level, which was suggested as a best practice for manual creation in the planning view as well.

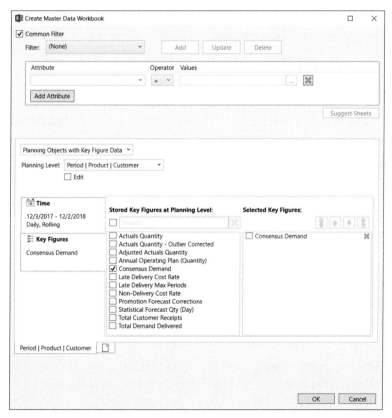

Figure 11.27 Define Planning Object Creation/Change Master Data Workbook

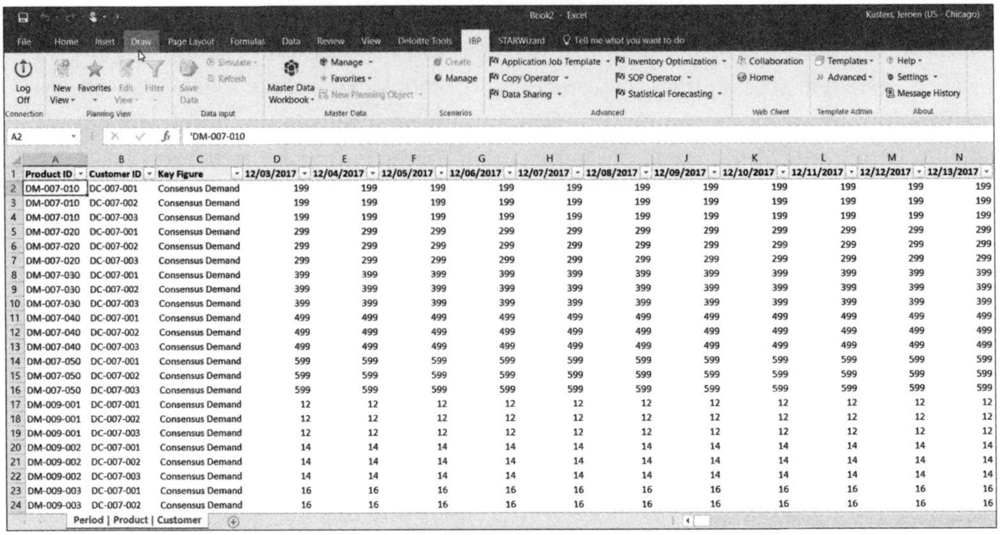

Product ID	Customer ID	Key Figure	12/03/2017	12/04/2017	12/05/2017	12/06/2017	12/07/2017	12/08/2017	12/09/2017	12/10/2017	12/11/2017	12/12/2017	12/13/2017
DM-007-010	DC-007-001	Consensus Demand	199	199	199	199	199	199	199	199	199	199	199
DM-007-010	DC-007-002	Consensus Demand	199	199	199	199	199	199	199	199	199	199	199
DM-007-010	DC-007-003	Consensus Demand	199	199	199	199	199	199	199	199	199	199	199
DM-007-020	DC-007-001	Consensus Demand	299	299	299	299	299	299	299	299	299	299	299
DM-007-020	DC-007-002	Consensus Demand	299	299	299	299	299	299	299	299	299	299	299
DM-007-020	DC-007-003	Consensus Demand	299	299	299	299	299	299	299	299	299	299	299
DM-007-030	DC-007-001	Consensus Demand	399	399	399	399	399	399	399	399	399	399	399
DM-007-030	DC-007-002	Consensus Demand	399	399	399	399	399	399	399	399	399	399	399
DM-007-030	DC-007-003	Consensus Demand	399	399	399	399	399	399	399	399	399	399	399
DM-007-040	DC-007-001	Consensus Demand	499	499	499	499	499	499	499	499	499	499	499
DM-007-040	DC-007-002	Consensus Demand	499	499	499	499	499	499	499	499	499	499	499
DM-007-040	DC-007-003	Consensus Demand	499	499	499	499	499	499	499	499	499	499	499
DM-007-050	DC-007-001	Consensus Demand	599	599	599	599	599	599	599	599	599	599	599
DM-007-050	DC-007-002	Consensus Demand	599	599	599	599	599	599	599	599	599	599	599
DM-007-050	DC-007-003	Consensus Demand	599	599	599	599	599	599	599	599	599	599	599
DM-009-001	DC-007-001	Consensus Demand	12	12	12	12	12	12	12	12	12	12	12
DM-009-001	DC-007-002	Consensus Demand	12	12	12	12	12	12	12	12	12	12	12
DM-009-001	DC-007-003	Consensus Demand	12	12	12	12	12	12	12	12	12	12	12
DM-009-002	DC-007-001	Consensus Demand	14	14	14	14	14	14	14	14	14	14	14
DM-009-002	DC-007-002	Consensus Demand	14	14	14	14	14	14	14	14	14	14	14
DM-009-002	DC-007-003	Consensus Demand	14	14	14	14	14	14	14	14	14	14	14
DM-009-003	DC-007-001	Consensus Demand	16	16	16	16	16	16	16	16	16	16	16
DM-009-003	DC-007-002	Consensus Demand	16	16	16	16	16	16	16	16	16	16	16

Figure 11.28 Planning Object Creation/Change via Master Data Workbook

11.5 Using Microsoft Visual Basic for Applications

Section 11.4 on using charts in SAP IBP Excel planning views gives a first glimpse of the possibilities Microsoft Excel delivers to control data visualization in planning views. Although the possibilities of using VBA to extend SAP Integrated Business Planning, add-in for Microsoft Excel are almost endless, in this section we'll introduce just two practical use cases.

11.5.1 VBA for Formulas in Local Members

In Section 11.2.2, we introduced the concept of local members, planning view elements that can use a formula to calculate key figures based on other elements available in the planning view. Although this is a very efficient way to add custom calculations without burdening the planning area by adding more calculated key figures, it comes with some restrictions.

For example, imagine trying to build local members that cross period boundaries, such as a newly calculated projected inventory key figure. Because the first period typically needs to be a bit different (e.g., use the initial inventory instead of the last period's projected inventory), and the end of the time horizon doesn't have a next period, it's a good idea to use a custom formula to correct for these quirks. This custom formula can be created in VBA and stored in the planning view (provided you create the planning view as macro-enabled).

11.5.2   VBA Hooks

The other opportunity to influence the behavior of SAP IBP with VBA is by enabling VBA hooks. VBA hooks let you implement code on specific events. As of version 1802, there are four planning view hooks available and two master data planning view hooks, as follows:

- **Planning view hooks**
  - Before saving data, which is called before SAP Integrated Business Planning, add-in for Microsoft Excel sends data from Excel to the backend SAP IBP system. This hook can be used for implementing extra validations or corrections to the data being sent to the backend IBP database
  - After using the **Refresh** button.
  - Before simulation.
  - Before creating a simulation.
- **Master data workbook hooks**
  - Before clicking **Update**, which is used before the changes during the mass maintenance of master data are sent to the backend.
  - After clicking **Refresh**, which is called when the mass master data view is created or refreshed.

The VBA hooks can be used by expert users to implement additional capabilities and have to be activated by the system administrator via a global parameter. The global parameters ACTIVATE_VBA_HOOKS for planning view hooks and ACTIVATE_MD_VBA_HOOK for master data workbook hooks can take the value Mandatory or Optional. If the parameter is mandatory and no VBA hook is found, the SAP IBP code will stop and the action won't be performed. The optional setting allows the code to finish without considering a VBA hook in case none is implemented in the planning view.

11.6   Summary

In this chapter, we covered the main functionality available in the Excel planning views, which are the main user interface for the SAP IBP system. Starting with a detailed overview of building and changing existing planning views allowed us to go deeper into more advanced capabilities to take maximum advantage of this flexible environment. We covered the formatting of the planning view and how the EPM formatting sheet can provide consistency and stability for advanced formatting. Then, we discussed using charts and how they can be controlled by leveraging the SAP-provided, VBA-enabled templates. We explained the master data templates, which allow the creation and maintenance of planning data, and the planning object creation that can prove very valuable in, for example,e new product introductions.

We closed the chapter by reviewing the availability of Visual Basic for Applications, both inside the planning view and as a medium to interact with the data when it's shared with the backend SAP IBP database. Although building planning views is often more an art than a science, these building blocks allow you to go out and build the planning views that are perfect for your business scenarios and user populations.

Chapter 12

Key Performance Indicators and Performance Monitoring

Analytics is an essential part of an effective S&OP process. This chapter discusses how big and small sets of data are used to monitor performance at various stages in the S&OP process.

Supply chain management has become a complex function due to the sheer complexity of dependencies that exist between various teams, departments, and even different companies across international boundaries. To work in these ever-changing market conditions and to improve the supply chain process, supply chain professionals need sufficient information and visibility not only within the organization but also across partner companies. Defining a proper set of metrics, managing them, and driving continuous improvement to meet customer requirements and organizational goals are the critical issues of managing a supply chain successfully.

Currently, data is used reactively by evaluating the performance of decisions made in the past. Companies must leverage the data available from various sources in the organization to build metrics that provide visibility and helps determine the feasibility of pursuing future plans. Assessing the performance of the past and gaining visibility into the future are the key fundamental takeaways that an organization gains from robust performance metrics. SAP IBP offers the capability to collect data from various data sources via SAP Cloud Platform Integration and provides a flexible platform to build key performance indicator reports.

This chapters focuses on why an organization needs performance measurements, standard metrics that are available to evaluate the performance of the supply chain organization. It also discusses methodologies used to monitor your performance and ensure continuous improvement. Chapter 13 focuses on SAP IBP tool's analytics capability and how it solves the need to build analytics charts and dashboards.

In this chapter, we'll delve into the details of performance metrics represented by KPIs for the S&OP process by getting into the specifics of every review cycle. For every organization aligned to S&OP cycles, a KPI can be selected. We'll also discuss S&OP process monitoring and continuous improvement through usage of performance metrics.

12.1   Key Performance Indicators in SAP IBP

We've discussed the importance of measuring the performance of an organization from different perspectives to get a holistic view of where the organization is heading. As part of this process, it's very important to define KPIs that are aligned with an organization's goal.

A KPI is a measurable value that defines how the supply chain function is performing achieving business objectives. The success of a function in the supply chain is often defined by how close the performance is to the target goal or simply if the organization is approaching the desired standards. Defining standard KPIs helps benchmark an organization's performance against other peers operating in the same industry.

To make KPIs clearer and better able to meet their purposes, they should have the following traits:

- **Specific**
  A KPI should be clear and specific, focusing on the problem area that it needs to measure. If the KPI isn't defined specifically, then the organization will measure without understanding how it helps in continuous improvement. For example, imagine a company finds over time that it's holding huge inventory across the supply chain. The dollar values locked up in the inventory are huge. If the organization wants to reduce its inventory holdings, it must measure specific KPIs like production reliability, distribution reliability, lost sales due to delays in shipments, and so on. The KPIs may measure different values, but they all measure supply and demand variability that causes excess inventory.

- **Measurable**
  Can we improve something that we can't measure? It's important to define measurable KPIs so that we can track the current status and progress made towards the benchmark.

- **Achievable**
  Goals must be defined in a way that is achievable in the given period of time. An achievable goal motivates a team to progress. Eventually, this helps identify overlooked opportunities for improvement.

In the supply chain scenario, the target for forecast accuracy can be set as a KPI, but the management must set achievable targets so that the team can march toward an achievable goal rather than be demotivated by the goal by itself.

- **Relevant**
  A KPI goal should be relevant for the current time period, and it should drive the entire team forward. The supply chain team must understand that the goal is relevant and, with the right support, achievable.

- **Time-bound**
  Every goal is time bound, with a target date to achieve it. Usually, organizations set KPI goals quarterly so that they can be evaluated periodically and the next target can be set. Small time-bound targets motivate the team to move toward the final goal.

SAP IBP provides rich analytics features to build different analytics charts and group them into a dashboard. Dashboards have various charts and information elements consolidated concisely. In the following subsections, we'll look at various KPIs you can use in different S&OP processes.

SAP IBP dashboards and analytics get real-time data from the connected system. Beyond measuring past performance, KPIs also can be used as a platform to initiate discussions with partners and understand how we can collaborate well on future transactions. The dashboards can be shared through portals, and partners need not have access to the system.

Once KPIs are identified and measured, it's important to act on the results to improve future performance. This can be achieved when a well-defined goal is set, its performance measured on KPIs, root-cause identified, and performance monitored.

Some of the following important KPIs can be used in the demand planning, sales, and production and inventory areas of the supply chain. These KPIs are measured and reviewed periodically for improvement:

- S&OP lead time
- Case fill rates
- Inventory days of supply (DOS)
- Demand plan accuracy and bias
- Delivered cost per case
- Schedule acceptance
- Promotion performance
- Product availability
- Responsiveness to demand
- Customer service
- Responsiveness to channel
- Deployment adherence

In the following sections, we've categorized some of these KPIs under each S&OP process that may be more relevant to review. The objective is to organize a list of

12

commonly used KPIs in the S&OP process. You should analyze the applicability of these KPIs for your purposes before applying them.

Figure 12.1 shows an example of dashboards that can be built in SAP IBP with demand review KPIs.

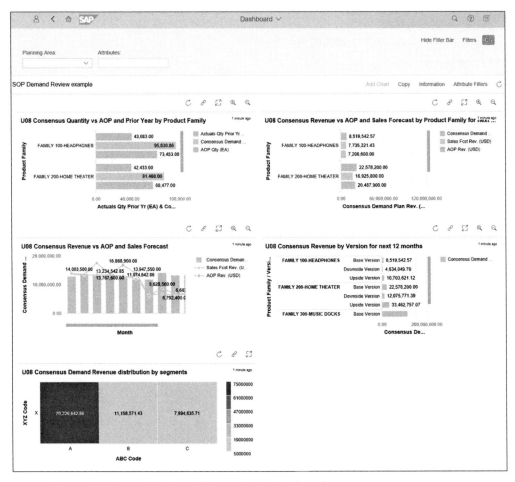

Figure 12.1 Demand Review KPI Example in Dashboard

12.1.1   Demand Review KPIs

The demand review process is the first step of the S&OP, and it focuses on reviewing forecast demand, sales input from various regions, and marketing intelligence. Demand review process discussions usually focus on how well the organization forecasted in the past and whether it needs to improve the process to make the consensus demand as close to actual sales as possible.

The following are some of the KPIs that can be helpful during the demand review process:

- **Forecast accuracy**
  Forecast accuracy is the measure of accuracy with which demand is predicted by the statistical tool. This enables an organization to provide a reliable signal for operations planning and the S&OP process. This is calculated by comparing the actual value with the forecasted value via the following formula:

  $$Statistical\ Forecast\ Accuracy = \frac{\left(Sum\ of\ Actual\ sales - Sum\ of\ Statistical\ Forecast\right)}{Sum\ of\ Actual\ sales}$$

- **Forecast bias**
  Forecast bias is a measure of the tendency for a forecast to be consistently higher or lower than actual results. This KPI helps the organization to better plan the operations and to improve revenue and decrease cost. It uses the following formula:

  $$Forecast\ Bias(\%) = \frac{Cumulative\ sum\ of\left(Actual\ order\ quantity - Forecast\right)}{Sum\ of\ Actual\ order\ quantity}$$

  Forecast bias is usually calculated individually for each period, with a positive or negative bias depending on the sales of the period. However, the cumulative sum of forecast bias over a period of time (typically a quarter or year) gives an accurate picture of the bias.

  Organizations must decide at what level they need to measure the forecast bias. For example, for some industries, it makes sense to measure forecast bias at an SKU level; for some, it could be at a category or family level. The level at which this KPI is to be measured must be determined before deciding on the data collection strategy. In general, forecast numbers are more accurate when aggregated at the product family level.

- **Unit forecast accuracy as a percentage of units shipped**
  The unit forecast accuracy is a percentage calculated by dividing the number of units forecasted by the number of units shipped out to the customer:

  $$Unit\ Forecast\ Accuracy = \left(\frac{Number\ of\ forecasted\ unit}{Number\ of\ units\ shipped}\right)\%$$

- **The functional accuracy of demand input**

  During the demand review process, different organizational functions like marketing, sales, demand planning, and finance provide their input to shape the unconstrained forecast to be as accurate as possible.

  The accuracy of demand input from these functions must be measured separately to understand the impact they're making on forecast accuracy. The level of forecast accuracy calculation may be different for these functions depending on the granularity they operate upon.

  The marketing team is usually measured on forecast accuracy at the product category or subchannel level and on how the input provided by the team shaped the consensus forecast accuracy numbers.

  The sales team's demand input accuracy is measured at a product category/subchannel level and on how the input provided by the team contributed to the overall consensus forecast accuracy on that level.

  The demand planning team usually provides the initial statistical forecast for other teams to work on and makes a final adjustment to the demand. The demand planning team's accuracy is measured by statistical forecast accuracy, adjusted statistical forecast accuracy, and how it contributes to the consensus forecast accuracy.

  The finance team's forecast accuracy is measured by its ability to identify and close financial gaps that may arrive due to the gap between the forecast and actuals.

- **Demand variability**

  Demand variability measures variability of demand in a specific period of time. Demand variation happens throughout the year. However, there could be some periods that show a pattern of variability—seasonality, promotion, and so on. Capturing significant demand variability that occurs helps demand planners and the marketing team make adjustments to the forecast numbers when this event occurs again.

  For example, an automotive antifreeze manufacturer performs a statistical forecast for the next two to three years. The demand planner knows from the previously measured metrics of demand variability that the demand for the products shoots up in the first week of November and stays stable until April in some regions of the United States. Therefore, these adjustments are made to the statistical forecast before its released for other functions to add their intelligence.

- **Forecast stability**

  Forecast stability is the measure of how stable the forecast numbers are when measured from one period to another. A stable forecast is required to plan medium and long-term operations and asset availability. Long-term forecasts are generally stable, and they tend to fluctuate in the near short term because different short-term fluctuations in the market and economic conditions contribute to the numbers.

- **Product profitability**
  Measures the profit (in dollars) of each product. This helps planners cumulate profit numbers at a product family or category level so that the discussions can be focused on variations shown for high profitability groups of items.

- **Percent revenue from new product platform/product line**
  Measures the percentage of revenue contributed by a new product line against the total sales of the organization.

12.1.2 Supply Review KPIs

The S&OP supply review process focuses on the unconstrained forecast provided and whether the manufacturing plants and suppliers have enough capacity to meet the demand. If there's a capacity shortfall, you must determine the options available to meet the demand and identify the need to modify forecast numbers, such as constrain the forecast for the available capacity.

Figure 12.2 and Figure 12.3 show an example supply review dashboard with supply review-related KPIs.

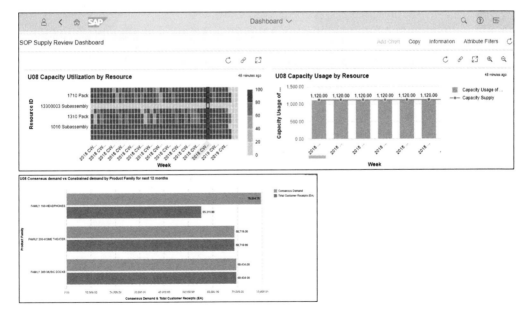

Figure 12.2 Supply Review KPI Examples in Dashboard: Part I

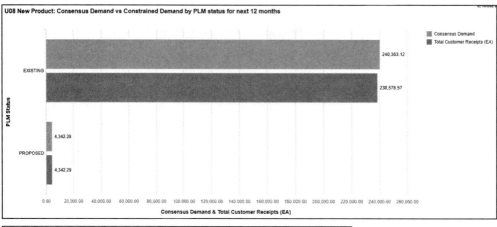

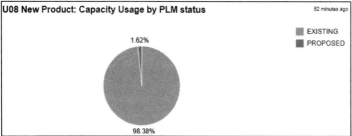

Figure 12.3 Supply Review KPI Examples in Dashboard: Part II

Some of the KPIs that may be helpful in the supply review process are as follows:

- **Cost of goods sold as a percent of revenue**
  Cost of goods sold is the measure of total direct and indirect costs incurred in producing goods like the cost of purchasing raw materials, cost of production, labor, and other overhead.

  Cost of goods sold as a percent of revenue is the measure of the percentage of the total cost of goods sold against the total revenue:

$$Cost\ of\ Goods\ sold\ \%\ of\ Revenue = \left(\frac{Direct\ Material\ cost + Labor + Overhead}{Revenue} \right)\%$$

- **Fill rate percentage**
  This is a measure of customer service based on a number of units delivered on or before a customer-requested delivery date. This helps to improve customer service levels to customers and drive revenue. The formula is as follows:

$$Customer\ Fill\ Rate = \frac{\#\ units\ delivered\ on\ or\ before\ customer\ Requested\ Delivery\ date}{Total\ \#\ of\ units\ orders\ by\ customer}$$

- **Perfect order percentage**

  This is a measure of service based on a number of orders delivered in full on or before a customer-requested delivery date:

  $$Perfect\ order\ \% = \left(\frac{\#\ units\ delivered\ on\ or\ before\ customer\ Requested\ Delivery\ date\ as\ a\ complete\ order}{Total\ \#\ of\ units\ orders\ by\ customer} \right)\%$$

- **Finished goods inventory turns**

  This is the measure of how many times the inventory cycles or turns over in a year. Inventory turns can be calculated by value or unit, but make sure it's consistent:

  $$Finished\ Goods\ Inventory\ Turns = \frac{Annual\ cost\ of\ Goods\ Sold}{Average\ Inventory\ value}$$

- **Average inventory level**

  This is the measure of average finished goods inventory stored across the supply chain in a dollar value. This helps an organization visualize the working capital locked in the network. It uses the following formula:

  $$Average\ Inventory\ level = Actual\ month\ end\ inventory\ in\ units \times Cost\ per\ unit$$

- **Raw material inventory**

  Raw material inventory is the metric that provides visibility into raw materials available in the manufacturing facility and in transit. In general, inventory managers maintain inventory at A-, B-, and C-class items.

- **Finished goods days of supply**

  This is the measure of the finished goods inventory level at each manufacturing facility and distribution center compared to the demand. This measure helps organizations visualize working capital impact and assess how equipped they are for serving customers.

  $$Finished\ Goods\ Days\ of\ Supply = \left(\frac{Month\ ending\ inventory\ level}{Sum\ of\ 3\ months\ customer\ shipments} \right) \times 90$$

- **Inventory carrying cost**

  This is the measure of the cost incurred in storing inventory over a period of time. The cost incurred by carrying inventory can be associated with inventory storage space, labor, freight, insurance, and cost of capital.

12

- **Obsolete inventory percentage**

  This is the percentage of the cost of obsolete inventory as compared to the total inventory. Obsolete inventory can be expired inventory on hand or inventory that can't be sold to customers.

- **Transportation costs**

  This is the measure of the total cost incurred for transportation over a period of time; this includes the cost of freight, labor, supplies, and other expenses involved in moving goods from one place to another.

- **Planning SG&A costs**

  Sales, general, and administrative costs include expenses related to marketing, promotion, and distribution of goods and services. SG&A costs are usually expressed as a percentage of cost incurred compared to the total cost of goods sold.

- **Capacity utilization percentage**

  Capacity utilization can be calculated for manufacturing or warehousing capacity. *Manufacturing capacity utilization* is the measure of comparison between actual production and the maximum available manufacturing capacity:

  $$Manufacturing\ capacity\ utilization = \left(\frac{Actual\ Production\ volume}{Total\ Available\ Production\ Capacity} \right)\%$$

  Warehousing capacity utilization is the measure of space utilized by inventory at a given location. This measure helps an organization determine space needs across the network and reduce warehousing costs:

  $$Warehousing\ capacity\ utilization = \left(\frac{Average\ Inventory\ (Pallets)}{Capacity\ (Pallet\ space) \times Stacking\ factor} \right)\%$$

- **Production adherence**

  This is the measure of how well a company stuck to its production plan. The production adherence KPI helps you visualize how reliable manufacturing assets are in meeting the planned production output:

  $$Production\ Adherance\ \% = \left(\frac{Planned\ Production - Actual\ Production\ output}{Planned\ Production} \right)\%$$

- **Operating equipment efficiency (OEE)**

  Overall equipment efficiency is a cumulative effect of metrics used to measure the utilization and efficiency of a manufacturing operation or piece of equipment. A piece of equipment's effectiveness can be calculated by focusing on different areas in which failure can happen, like equipment failure, setup and adjustment, idling, scrap, and rework.

- **First-pass quality yield**
This is also known as throughput yield. It's defined as a number of units coming out of a manufacturing process divided by the number of units provided as an input into the process over a period of time.

12.1.3 Operating Review KPIs

In the operating review of the S&OP process, leaders from all functions are present. Exceptions are discussed and resolved. This process is also a platform to discuss opportunities that all functions cohesively visualize and devise a strategy for.

The following are some of the KPIs that may be of interest in the operating review process:

- **Cost/benefit of outsourcing function**
The operating review of the S&OP process reviews the consensus demand, whether the company has the capacity to meet the demand, and whether it's economical to produce in house rather than outsource. A KPI consolidating various costs involved in producing in house versus outsourcing can be a great tool for cost/benefit analysis of outsourcing.

- **Manufacturing cycle time**
Manufacturing lead time measures the time taken to produce a finished product from the time the order is released to the production floor.

- **Cash to cash cycle time**
The cash conversion cycle measures the time taken between cash outlay and cash recovery. Cash outlay typically happens when the company spends to acquire raw materials and pay suppliers. Cash recovery happens after the customer pays after receiving the goods and services:

  Cash to Cash cycle time = Days sales outstanding + Inventory Days' of supply – Days payable outstanding

- **Cumulative supply chain lead time**
This is the total time it takes for supply chain activities like demand planning, S&OP, and supply planning to be complete and the orders released for execution. This is one of the key differentiators for companies in the consumer products segment that innovates and releases new products in the market frequently.

- **Manufacturing nonconformance rate**
  This is the measure of how many times the manufacturing process has not been in conformance with requirements. The output may be rejected or reworked. It's important to document all instances/rates at which the manufacturing process has been nonconforming to guidelines.

- **Transportation cost as percent of sales**
  This is the measure of proportional to transportation costs compared to the total sales. Transportation costs include all costs incurred in moving raw materials to the manufacturing site, finished goods transfer to the warehouse, and finally to the end customer:

$$Transportation\ cost\ as\ \%\ of\ Sales = \left(\frac{Total\ Transportation\ cost}{Total\ Sales} \right)\%$$

- **Percent of fleet utilization**
  This is a measure of the total trucks in the fleet that were effectively put to use during the evaluation period. If the fleet is underutilized, that's an indicator to evaluate whether you can cut down the fleet strength. If the fleet is fully utilized, then the company has to look into other options available to meet future needs.

- **Primary carrier utilization percentage**
  Some companies use multiple modes of transportation/multiple carriers to move their products: trucks, intermodal, ships, air, and so on. One of the carrier modes is usually defined as the primary carrier that meets the requirements on time at a lesser cost. Other modes are also available to meet ad hoc demand. This KPI measures the utilization of the primary carrier for utilization.

- **On-time delivery percentage**
  This is the measure of process and supply chain efficiency which measures the number of finished goods and services delivered to end customers on time and in full.

- **Ship to deliver cycle time**
  This is the measure of the time it takes for the finished goods to leave the company and to reach the end customer. This is an important KPI for companies that do business globally and ship through the ocean. The transit time of the finished goods is measured in dollars that the company has to consider for working capital calculation.

- **Returned goods inventory**
  This is the measure of returned goods inventory available across the supply chain.

12.1.4 Executive Review KPIs

In the executive review process, senior leadership is provided with the outcome of the S&OP process and approvals are sought for exceptions. This is also a platform for the leadership to get visibility into the past performance and the strategic direction the company needs to take going forward.

The following are some of the KPIs that may be of interest for the executive review process of the S&OP process:

- **Return on supply chain fixed asset**
  Measure of the return an organization receives on its invested capital in supply chain fixed assets. This includes the fixed assets used to plan, source, make, deliver, and return:

$$Return\,on\,Supply\,Chain\,Fixed\,Asset = \left(\frac{Supply\,chain\,Revenue - COGS - Supply\,chain\,Management\,cost}{Supply\,Chain\,Fixed\,assets} \right)$$

- **Return on asset**
  This is one of the KPIs that shareholders are directly interested in. Return on asset is a financial ratio that shows the percentage of profit of the organization versus the value of the total fixed assets it owns:

$$Return\,on\,Asset = \left(\frac{Net\,Income}{Total\,assets} \right)$$

- **Return on working capital**
  This is the measure of the magnitude of investment relative to a company's working capital position versus the revenue generated from a supply chain. Components include accounts receivable, accounts payable, inventory, supply chain revenue, cost of goods sold, and supply chain management costs:

$$Return\,on\,Working\,Capital = \left(\frac{Supply\,chain\,Revenue - COGS - Supply\,chain\,Management\,cost}{Working\,capital} \right)$$

- **Scrap and rework percentage**
  This is the measure of scrap or rework of the manufacturing process. This KPI gives visibility into the reliability of the manufacturing process. During the executive process, this helps when making a strategic decision on investments in the manufacturing process.

- **Total logistics cost as percent of sales**
  This is the measure of total logistics cost compared to the total sales.

- **Miles per unit of product or total transportation emissions**
  This is the measure of the carbon footprint products are leaving while being transported across the network. Consumers these days have become environmentally conscious, and it's important to measure these parameters to stay within a set limit.

- **Service level**
  This is a cumulative measure of how well the company able to meet customer requirements on time and in full. Various KPIs that contribute to calculating the service levels include on time in full (OTIF), stockouts, fill rate, perfect order, and so on.

- **Redistribution and expedite costs**
  Organizations have preferred modes of transport, like truck or ship. In some situations, expedited shipments must be made to meet the customer requirements through other expensive and expedited mode like air/third-party shipping. This KPI measures the costs incurred for transportation by choosing the expedited mode of transport.

In this section, we defined various KPIs that could be useful for the S&OP process. It's also important to provide tools to supply chain professionals to visualize these KPIs in a more constructive way that triggers actions to be taken. SAP IBP provides various analytics tools to visualize these KPIs. In Chapter 13, we'll look into the details of analytics features in SAP IBP.

12.2   Monitoring and Continuous Improvement

Supply chain KPIs are analogous to an aircraft dashboard. An aircraft's cockpit has hundreds of indicators that are measured in real time. Can the measured data itself drive the aircraft and take us to the target destination? Definitely not. The pilot looks at these indicators and steers the aircraft in the right direction to its destination. A dashboard is a tool that helps a pilot make decisions. Similarly, big data analytics and KPI dashboards provide the past performance of the organization, early warnings about some problems and opportunities that lie ahead. Supply chain professionals must use these KPIs to avoid problems and tap opportunities.

In this section, we'll look at the managerial approach of monitoring supply chain performance and taking an organization toward a continuous improvement path. Defining the right KPI metrics and defining benchmarks are most essential aspects of continuous improvement.

12.2.1   Balanced Scorecard

Before looking into the balanced scorecard approach, let's look into the case of a smartphone manufacturer, XYZ Corporation. XYZ Corporation was the market leader in the smartphone market in the early 2000s, but it couldn't retain the market leader position for long. Did it do anything wrong while in the leading position? Absolutely not. The company did well based on all metrics focused on the internal functioning of the organization. However, the organization failed to innovate and lost visibility into future market needs. New smartphone technology changes disrupted the market, and XYZ Corporation was out of market. This case helps highlight the importance of measuring performance in a holistic manner, looking into past financial performance and an ability to innovate and stay relevant with the changing market needs.

The balanced scorecard methodology includes financial measures of performance and outcomes of actions already taken. It complements the financial performance with operational measures of customer satisfaction, internal processes, innovations, and improvement activities.

A balanced scorecard provides holistic supply chain professionals a chance to consider all the important operational measures together. This helps in visualizing whether the performance improvement shown in one area of operation is achieved at the expense of others. A balanced score card can be analyzed through different dimensions, known as perspectives. These dimensions or perspectives are as follows:

- **Customer perspective**
  Companies must evaluate what their customers value a lot. Performance indicators must be designed from a customer service perspective, mostly focusing on quality and service.

- **Internal business perspective**
  To meet customer needs, organizations must be efficient in their internal operations. The internal measures of the balanced scorecard should focus on a major business process like cycle time or productivity.

- **Innovation perspective**
  Markets are becoming global, and customer needs are changing. While focusing on the customer's perspective and measuring internal business, it's important to innovate and evolve products and service offerings. We've seen in the telecom industry that market leaders doing everything well internally to meet customer demand failed because they didn't forcast the future market.

- **Financial perspective**
  If the organization has done well on the customer and internal perspectives,

improved financial performance is the outcome. The financial goals of the supply chain organization should be aligned with the profitability, growth, and shareholder value.

12.2.2   Root-Cause Analysis

In the S&OP process, KPIs provide the metrics of a supply chain function behavior at the organizational or product category level. Later, these metrics are drilled down in different granularities to see all possible reasons for the behavior. Identifying the root cause of a problem involves listing all possible reasons and mapping the occurrences.

For example, let's consider a typical problem that a supply chain faces: long manufacturing lead times. The first step toward facing this problem is to understand the current manufacturing lead time and benchmark it toward industry leaders. Later, you can drill down into all lead times involved in the manufacturing process, like raw material transportation lead time, manufacturing setup time, manufacturing time, time spent on rework, time taken from the shop floor to a truck for outbound delivery, and so on. You need to get data for all these lead times and then can nail down the root cause of the problem.

Different tools are available for root-cause analysis, like fishbone diagrams, decision trees, and so on. In this section, we'll walk through an example of a problem and see how a decision tree helps nail down the root cause.

ABC Corporation identifies that the on-time delivery of orders metric isn't performing well—and is performing below the industry benchmark. Figure 12.4 illustrates a decision tree prepared to identify the root cause. The first level of the decision tree identifies various modes of transport and the percentage of late orders that falls into this category. The next level will identify the lead time of the order placed. One of the observations from the decision tree indicates that truck deliveries with an order placed with a lead time of fewer than two days fail to meet the delivery date. One reason for this could be receiving orders on Friday to deliver on Monday.

The next level of investigation goes in the direction of loading the materials in the carrier. How often were materials loaded onto the carrier on time? Nearly 17 percent of the time, materials were not loaded on time. This opens the investigation of what didn't go well in loading: issues with material handling, personnel availability, and so on. The problem statement started with on-time delivery, which lead into different areas of the supply chain and helped unearth different problem areas.

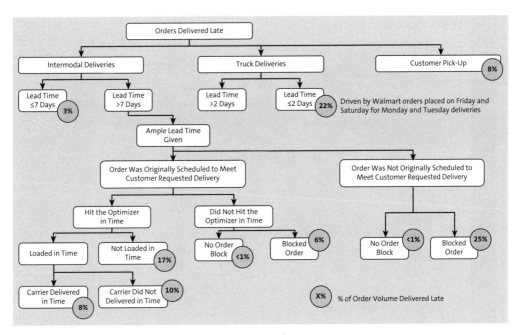

Figure 12.4 Root-Cause Analysis Decision Tree Example

12.2.3   Define, Measure, Analyze, Improve, and Control

Define, measure, analyze, improve, and control (DMAIC) is a management tool that's data-driven and is used to improve, optimize, and stabilize business processes. DMAIC is the best tool to define a problem, measure performance, analyze the root cause, and steer the process towards continuous improvement. As shown in Figure 12.5, DMAIC is a cyclical process, and it keeps improving the process and defines benchmarks of performance.

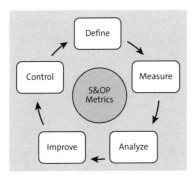

Figure 12.5 DMAIC Process for Continuous Improvement

There are various stages in the DMAIC process:

- **Define**

  This is the first step of the process, in which the problem statement is defined. When defining a problem, you first should validate via past performance if it's a real problem and the impact it makes on the customer. How does the customer value this problem? What is the impact it makes and its severity? Identifying this information helps in defining the magnitude of the problem and allocating resources to fix it. The next step in this stage is defining the goal statement that's time-bound—for example, bringing down the cost of production by 5 percent but cutting waste within the next 12 months.

- **Measure**

  Data is measured throughout the process and all the stages. However, in this stage, you map the current process and collect data on the current process performance. This helps determine the baseline against which improvement will be compared in future. In this stage, you should also focus on identifying the possible sources of data and ensure the reliability of the data.

- **Analyze**

  In this phase, the data collected is analyzed to identify the root cause of the problem. The collected data is displayed in an easily digestible visual format using charts and graphs. This helps to visualize the data trend and the possible root cause of the problem. After data is collected, it's also important to visually inspect the data before analyzing it further. The analysis is done with various tools such as fishbone diagrams or decision trees to derive the root cause. Analysis results must be recorded and discussed internally to determine if the root cause is valid. Data from different sources can be collected to validate the root cause.

- **Improve**

  Once the root cause is identified and the teams are convinced about the root cause, the next step is to brainstorm all possible solutions that can improve the performance and fix the identified problems. From the brainstormed solutions, you select a practical solution that can be implemented in the given time period. As you implement the solution to improve the process, you must measure the results periodically to assess if the solution is fixing the problem.

- **Control**

  This is the final stage of the process, in which you monitor and control the improvement solution implemented and make it sustainable for the future. All the improvement solutions implemented are documented for future reference and the lessons learned are implemented in other areas of the organization. During this stage, you also devise a mechanism to sustain the improvements that were implemented.

12.3   Summary

Big data analytics and KPIs provide pointers to assess how the supply chain organization is performing and the direction it needs to be taken. By implementing a structured S&OP process and a continuous improvement process, the supply chain process can be improved, thereby increasing revenue and shareholder value.

12

Chapter 13

Dashboard and Analytics

SAP IBP's analytics and dashboard capabilities have revolutionized the usage of KPIs and application reports in S&OP processes. This chapter explains how to set up, use, and manage advanced analytics and dashboards to control the input and output of the S&OP process.

SAP IBP's analytics and dashboard capabilities have revolutionized the usage of KPIs and application reports in S&OP processes. This chapter explains how to set up, use, and manage advanced analytics and dashboards to control the input and output of the S&OP process.

In the previous chapter, you learned about various key performance indicators and the methodology to measure the supply chain's performance and monitor the KPIs. In this chapter, the focus will be on the rich analytics capabilities that are available in SAP IBP, which help supply chain managers gain visibility into the performance of the supply chain.

Supply chain managers know they need real-time analytics to help them have real-time visibility and gain insights into the supply chain. *Real-time analytics* refers to getting the information from the source as it's happening now. This real-time information is needed for supply chain leaders to make decisions that matter today. Decisions made based on real-time data drive the strategy of the business. Gone are the days when managers wait for a day or week for the transaction data to flow to the analytics system and to develop charts and then make a decision based on the same. SAP IBP can pull real-time data from multiple source systems and provide analytics insights for users to take action.

SAP IBP helps unleash the power of real-time analytics, which enables businesses to make data-driven decisions. Without a data-driven approach, decisions are based only on conjectures from observation and gut feelings. This approach is prone to a lot of mistakes and it can cost a company a huge fortune, depending on at what level this decision has been applied. By looking into real-time data analytics, leaders can make effective decisions at the strategic, tactical, and operational levels, which leads to a positive outcome for businesses. Better decisions lead to serving customers effectively and making the process efficient.

SAP IBP's analytics function provides a lean approach to analytics chart building. This means users can define their own charts with key figures in the areas that matter to them. For example, a demand planner of a retail chain can build her own analytics chart that shows the consensus demand for Brand A that she manages, region-wise, for the next two quarters. This chart helps her make decisions about spreading out the demand across the region or see alerts if any action is to be taken. Analytics charts help visually highlight areas where actions need to be taken.

Just like analytics charts, dashboards can be configured in the system by the user. A dashboard is a collection of advanced analytics charts that are logically grouped together on a single screen to gain visibility into the supply chain from various KPI dimensions. For example, a supply planner can develop a dashboard that shows all supply-related KPIs, resource utilization across geographic areas, and inventory across distribution centers. This dashboard can provide insights into the supply chain network and identify actions to be taken where necessary.

13.1   Advanced Analytics

SAP IBP contains huge dataset that's either integrated from connected systems or derived from planning and processes. In the Analytics app in SAP IBP, there are various forms and charts to use to show data. However, in the S&OP process, we often struggle to identify which is the best chart to visually make an impact on leadership or to drive a suitable decision.

Before getting into the technical aspects of building and managing analytics charts, it's important to understand some principles and theory behind data visualization. SAP IBP users and configuration consultants sometimes wear the analytics hat while building charts. Laws of grouping or Gestalt laws of grouping help us understand how humans perceive patterns and objects. The principles are organized under the following categories:

- *Proximity:* Objects, even when they are of different shapes that are close together, are perceived as a group.
- *Similarity:* Objects that share similar attributes like shape or color are perceived as a group.

- *Continuity and connectedness:* This refers to the natural tendency of the mind to recognize patterns that are familiar and fill in any information that may be missing. Objects that tend to have a continuity or border are perceived as a group.
- *Closure:* An open structure can be easily perceived as closed and complete. This is applied in charts with multiple objects; the mind can perceive broken objects and can form boundaries itself and perceive them as different groups.

Understanding these principles and applying them helps in building charts that clearly represent large quantities of data coherently and help a user to decode the relationships in the data by reducing the distortion of data. Data in the chart is analyzed through different chart formats based on the data properties and expectations of the information from the charts. Different types of analytics charts commonly used for supply chain analytics are discussed next.

13.1.1 Types of Analytics and Charts

To visualize data, SAP IBP has provided various types of charts, like comparison, trend, distribution, and geographic. Depending on the usage of the data and the insights to derive, we can use the most appropriate chart.

Comparison

Hillary is the demand planning manager of the personal electronics division of her company. She manages headphones, home theatre, and music docks under her portfolio. Every month before preparing for the demand review process, she looks into the demand forecasting performance of the past and compares what the Consensus demand error looks like month to month. This helps her strategize the demand forecasting process in the future and trends to watch out for. In such scenarios, a comparison chart can be used effectively to gain insights.

For comparison charts, SAP IBP has provided various types of charts, like **Bar**, **Column**, **Dual X-Axis Bar**, **Dual Y-Axis Column**, **Heat Map**, and **Table** (see Figure 13.1).

Figure 13.1 Comparison Charts

Figure 13.2 shows an example of a bar comparison chart. Some of the best practices for using comparison charts include using consistent colors through the charts to highlight meaningful changes over a period of time. It's advisable to use a horizontal axis for better visibility. In heatmaps, it's best to use a single color with different shades that help to visually differentiate between different levels of data.

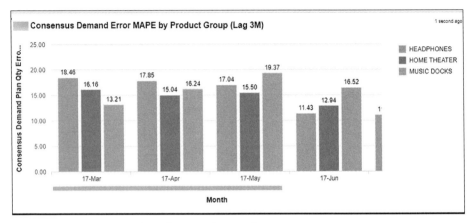

Figure 13.2 Comparison Chart Illustrated Example

Trend

John is a sales manager for the West region. His team generates forecast numbers based on the marketing input and field intelligence. John is interested in visualizing the sales forecast trend for the whole year and how it looks against the actual quantity delivered at the same time the previous year. Trend graphs can be leveraged to provide visibility into time-based data trend.

For trend charts, SAP IBP has provided various chart types, like **Line**, **Dual Y-Axis Line**, **Combination**, and **Dual Y-Axis Column** (see Figure 13.3).

Figure 13.3 Trend Charts

Some of the best practices for using trend graphs are to use solid lines so that the trend is visually easier to understand and to restrict the number of lines to be as minimal as possible to avoid possible clutter. It's also advisable to define the range of the graph so that the trend line lies within the range of the graph and within two-thirds of the chart area. Figure 13.4 shows an example of a trend graph tracking the sales forecast and actual quantity.

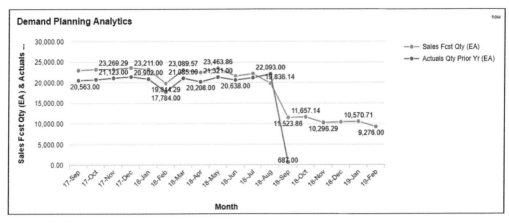

Figure 13.4 Illustrated Example of Trend Graph

Distribution

Greg is a supply planner for Brand A globally and he's interested in visualizing how much of resource is used for manufacturing Brand A across various manufacturing facilities. Distribution graphs help him visualize the capacity distribution of Brand A across various manufacturing facilities. This helps clarify which regions cater to the supply needs of the brand globally.

SAP IBP provides various charts in the distribution category, like **Pie**, **Donut**, **Stacked Column**, **Stacked Bar**, **Dual Stacked Column**, **Dual Stacked Bar**, **100% Stacked Bar**, **100% Stacked Column**, **100% Dual Stacked Bar**, **100% Dual Stacked Column**, and **Scatterplot** (see Figure 13.5).

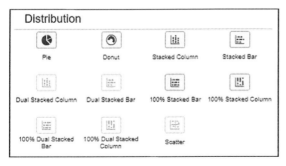

Figure 13.5 Distribution Charts

415

Some of the best practices for using distribution charts are to keep the number of categories as minimal possible so that the slices can be visually differentiated and, for building scatter plot comparisons, important to include more data so that meaningful inferences can be made. An example of a distribution chart is shown in Figure 13.6.

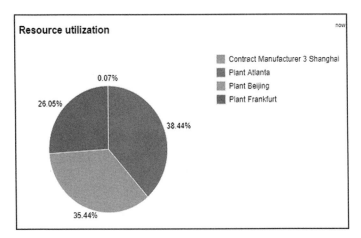

Figure 13.6 Illustrated Example of Distribution Chart

Geographic

Amit is the brand manager of a specific brand of handset in the EMEA region. He's interested in visualizing the geographic distribution of demand across various countries in EMEA region. This type of graph helps him make decisions about resource allocation for each country, depending on how deep the market is. Geographic charts help visualize the distribution of demand across geographic regions and represents the weight or volume of business coming out of each of these countries.

SAP IBP provides various charts in the geographic category like **Choropleth**, **Geo Pie**, and **Geo Bubble** (see Figure 13.7).

Figure 13.7 Geographic Charts

Some of the best practices for effectively using geographic charts are to define the country and geo attributes in the master data type and define the region and category as minimally as possible so that they're visually distinguishable. Figure 13.8 shows an example of a geographic chart.

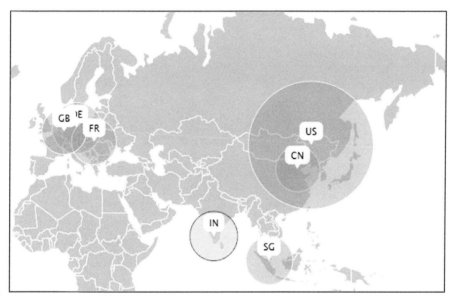

Figure 13.8 Illustrated Example of Geographic Chart

13.1.2   Creating Advanced Analytics Charts

In this section, we'll walk through the process of creating analytics charts in SAP IBP. The Analytics app can be accessed from the SAP Fiori launchpad, under the **General Planner** group (see Figure 13.9). In the Analytics app, all the available analytics graphs are listed. To create a new chart, follow these steps:

1. Click the **New Chart** button. This opens a pop-up window in which you can select the type of charts like **Chart** or **Supply Network** (see Figure 13.10).

Figure 13.9 Advanced Analytics App

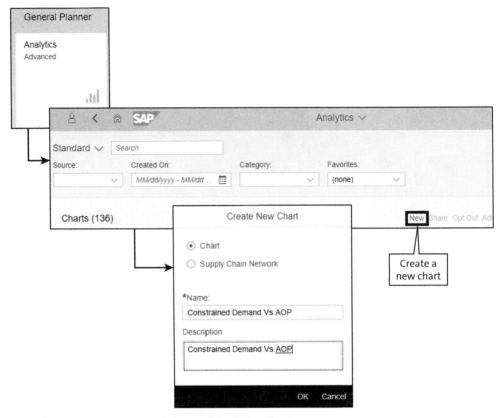

Figure 13.10 Create New Advanced Analytics Chart

2. On the next page, specify various basic parameters for the chart. As illustrated in Figure 13.11, following are the **Basic Settings** to maintain:

   – **Planning Area**
   Specify the planning area from which the data is to be pulled for building the graph. In general, the default planning area appears here, but you can change it as needed.

   – **Key Figures**
   Specify the key figures for which the graph is required to be built. In this example, we're building a chart to compare the trend of constrained demand revenue, sales demand revenue, and AOP revenue. All key figures in the selected planning area are available to choose from.

Figure 13.11 Basic Settings for Chart

- **Filter for Key Figure Values**
  You can specify filters while creating the chart by specifying a range of values to be fetched. This is particularly useful in cases in which the plant supervisor wants to build a resource utilization chart for highlighting underutilized assets.

- **Group By**
  Helps in grouping the data in the X or Y axis. This is particularly helpful to reduce the clutter of the graph by grouping the graph elements.

- **Currency/Unit of Measure To ID**
  Helps in specifying the unit of measure of conversion for quantity and currency conversion. This gives all the elements in the graph the same base unit of measure.

– **Type of Chart**
  You need to choose the type of chart to be configured. The desired chart must be chosen based on your requirements. In the current version of SAP IBP, there are 24 different types of charts available, grouped under four categories: **Comparison**, **Trend**, **Distribution**, and **Geographic**.

3. After specifying the basic parameters, maintain parameters like **Axis** and **Value Display** under **Chart Options** (as illustrated in Figure 13.12).

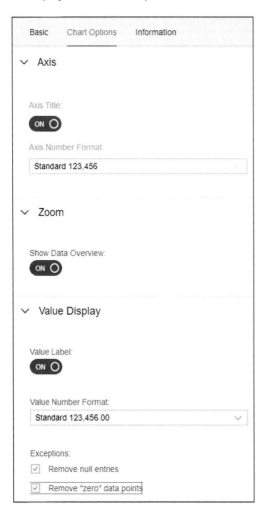

Figure 13.12 Advanced Analytics: Chart Options

The following options can enhance the look and readability of your graph:

– **Axis Title**
This switches on or off the display of the axis titles.

– **Axis Number Format**
There are different standard number formats available to choose from to display the axis number values.

– **Show Data Overview**
We can switch this on or off to show or hide the data overview.

– **Color**
There are two color options available to choose from: **Automatic** or **Custom Colors**. In the automatic mode, the system chooses the colors that best illustrate the graphical content. The system provides multiple color palette options to choose from, such as **Qualitative**, **Sequential**, **Reverse Qualitative**, and **Reverse Sequential**.

– **Value Label**
Values displayed on the label of the graph can be switched on or off from this option.

– **Value Label Type**
With this option, you can choose if the label values are to be displayed in a value or percentage. By default, the value is selected, but it can be changed. Typically, you use percentage displays for showing production capacity utilization, warehouse capacity utilization, market share by brand, and so on.

– **Value Number Format**
There are different standard value number formats available to choose from to display the label values.

– **Exceptions**
This option helps in removing null entries and zeros from the graphical display. It's generally a best practice to remove null values from the display and show only the period that has values. This reduces the clutter in the graph and helps in building trends with available values.

4. In the **Information** area, provide general information about the chart and configure the sharing options available (see Figure 13.13).

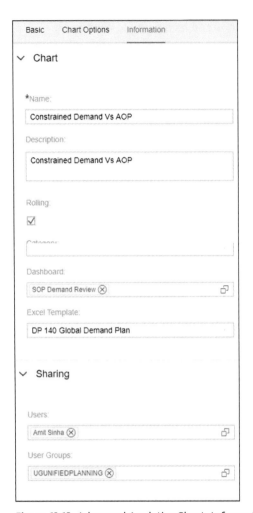

Figure 13.13 Advanced Analytics Chart: Information

The general information to provide is as follows:

- **Name and Description**
  The name and description of the analytics chart can be changed here.

- **Rolling**
  Checking this option makes sure that the selected period of the chart is a rolling period. For example, say that you're interested in visualizing the supply parameters for the next three quarters. When the chart is created, you need to select the

next three-quarter period, and selecting the **Rolling** option ensures this display period is calculated dynamically when the chart is refreshed.

- **Category**
  This a free text field that helps to categorize the chart.

- **Dashboard**
  A dashboard can be built by consolidating multiple analytics charts into a single view. Here, you can specify the dashboard in which this analytics chart is to be included.

- **Excel Template**
  While creating the Excel planning view, you can plug in the chart that helps planners to visualize the change. For example, an Excel planning view in which the sales team updates the demand numbers can show the brand-level demand distribution of the region. This helps the sales team to immediately visualize the impact of the numbers at a brand level across the region.

- **Sharing**
  You can share charts either with specific users or with a user group. To share an analytics chart with a user group, the group must have been created already. For more details, see Chapter 7.

13.1.3   Managing Advanced Analytics Charts

Now that the chart is created and shared with various user groups, we'll look at how different users can manage the chart. For example, say that you create a chart to show inventory availability across the supply chain. However, a brand manager wants to look at the details of a specific brand that she manages. This section covers some of the options available to manage analytics charts.

Once the chart is selected from the list of available charts, the top portion of the chart will include fields to help manage the selection of time period, attributes, and versions/scenarios, as shown in Figure 13.14.

Figure 13.14 Managing Period and Attribute Selection

Attribute, time period, and simulation properties of the chart are managed in the following fields:

- **Versions/Scenarios**
  You can choose the version and scenario of interest to you from this option. All versions and scenarios that are available in the planning area are available to select.

- **Period Type**
  You can choose the period type required here. The available period types to choose are based on period types that are configured in the planning area.

- **From/To**
  Here, you can choose the selection and display periods.

- **Attributes**
  Attribute-based selections can be made here. All master data types and the corresponding attributes are listed here to be chosen. For example, if you want to look into the resource utilization of specific resources, proceed as follows (see Figure 13.15):

  - Select the **Resource** for the master data type under **Attributes**. Multiple master data types can be selected by selecting them one by one. In this case, you can choose **Product** as well if you want to visualize resource utilization by specific brand.

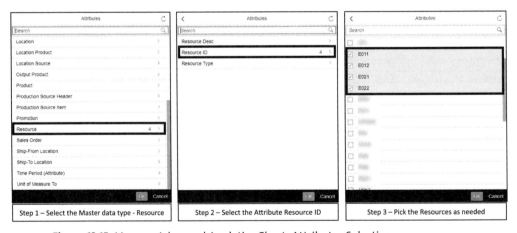

Figure 13.15 Manage Advanced Analytics Chart: Attributes Selection

– Next, select the attribute for generating the chart for specific selection. For example, a chart can be generated for particular product group. This is done by selecting the attribute **Product Group** and then providing the value of the **Product Group**, for example **GROUP1** and **GROUP2**. In this way, the chart is generated only for the items in product group 1 and product group 2.

After the chart is displayed for the period and attribute selections are made, there are some tools available in the chart that enhance the visual representation of the chart, as follows (see Figure 13.16):

- **Drill down**

  Drill down is an important aspect of the advanced analytics chart. Drill down helps in visualizing the chart at an aggregated level, and drilling down the values to the level below that helps in visualizing and interpreting the data details better. Drill down helps in deep analysis of charts and enhances the ability to nail down the root cause of the issue.

  This process is called the "focus and drill down" approach to analysis. The chart by default is loaded at a higher level and you can pick a specific period to drill down into to better understand an issue or detail.

Figure 13.16 Chart Options

Example

Let's examine a case study. Greg is the supply planner for a company that produces granola bars. There are multiple resources available to produce these bars, and some resources are shared by multiple brands depending on the allergen content. As illustrated in Figure 13.17, the resource utilization chart shows the list of resources and the share of each brand. Greg picks line E011; he wants to know which products of that brand take up 33.02 percent of the resource. He selects the brand and resource and clicks the **Drill Down** button. A drilldown chart now opens, which shows the list of products that constitute 33 percent of the load. Further analysis of the drill down value for the capacity percentage value is shown in Figure 13.18.

This type of drilldown analysis helps Greg make decisions about moving products from one resource to another and sharing the load as needed while taking allergen/resource restrictions into consideration.

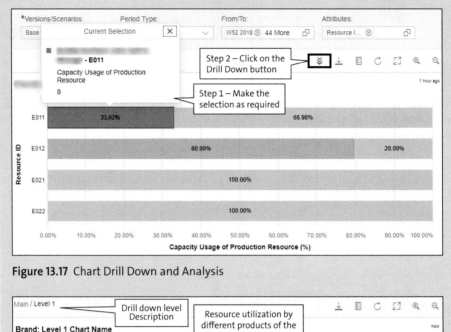

Figure 13.17 Chart Drill Down and Analysis

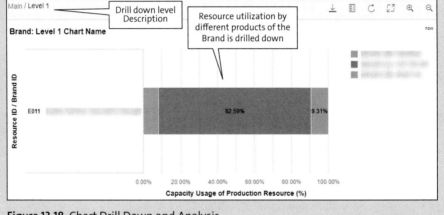

Figure 13.18 Chart Drill Down and Analysis

- **Download**

  You can download the details of the chart. The chart contents can be downloaded at each drilldown level.

- **Legend**

  The chart legend can be hidden or shown by clicking this button.

- **Refresh**
This is an interesting aspect of the advanced analytics chart. The **Refresh** button pulls data in real time from the backend SAP HANA database and displays it in the chart.

- **Full Screen**
The chart can be seen full screen or within the app window.

- **Zoom In/Out**
These buttons let you zoom in or out to better see the chart details.

There are a few chart options available at the bottom of the chart that can also be leveraged to share, copy, and edit the analytics chart, as follows (see Figure 13.19):

- **Edit**
This option opens the chart in edit mode so that you can make changes to it. Note that only the owner of the chart (the user who created the chart) can edit it.

- **Copy**
This option lets you make a copy of an existing chart and create a new one.

- **Hide Details**
This option hides the details of the chart to provide more space for the chart to be displayed.

- **Share options**
The chart can be shared for collaboration with other users. Following are the options available to share the chart.

    - **Send E-Mail**

    - **Share on SAP Jam**

    - **Save as Tile**

In Chapter 7, we discussed sharing analytics charts in SAP Jam in detail.

Figure 13.19 Chart Options: Share and Copy

13.2 Advanced Dashboards

SAP IBP provides greater flexibility to define, create, and manage dashboards without the need to do any configuration. Once all prerequisite elements like planning areas, transaction data, and analytics charts are configured and available, all pieces can be put together to create a dashboard. The dashboard can be managed from the Advanced Dashboards app available under the **General Planner** group in the SAP Fiori launchpad.

Before getting into the technical aspects of managing dashboard in SAP IBP, let's go over some general principles/best practices to follow to build a good dashboard. The following are some design principles you can consider as guidelines to build a good dashboard:

- It's important to understand the *target audience* for a dashboard and what details that audience will be interested in. You also need to be cognizant of the actions expected to be taken based on the insights from the dashboard.

- An understanding of the *detail level* that will be of interest to the audience will help. Always start from charts at a higher level and show charts with more details as users drill down.

- It's a good practice to use a *consistent color palette* for all the charts in a dashboard to avoid distortion.

- Be consistent with *axes and periodicities of time*. A dashboard created for S&OP review can have a monthly periodicity, for example, because the target audience will be interested in the quarter by quarter value.

- If two charts show the same details but for two different product groups, they should be placed *close to each other* to enable easy comparison.

- Finally, based on the charts to be incorporated in the dashboard, *visualize the layout* of the dashboard before building it in the system.

13.2.1 Creating Advanced Dashboards

Dashboards in SAP IBP can be created and managed from the Dashboards: Advanced app available in the **General Planner** group of the SAP Fiori launchpad (see Figure 13.20). Opening the Dashboards app shows the list of dashboards already created. From here, click the **New** button to open a pop-up window in which you can provide details of the dashboard, like **Name**, **Description**, **Category**, and whether you want it to be a **Favorite**. Once you're finished, click **Save** (see Figure 13.21).

Figure 13.20 Advanced Dashboards App

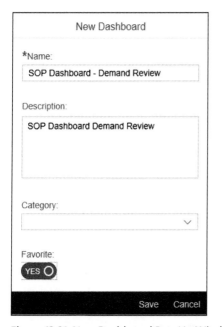

Figure 13.21 New Dashboard Pop-Up Window

On the next screen, you can add multiple charts to the dashboard by clicking the **Add Chart** button. From the pop-up window that opens (see Figure 13.22), you can select charts to add. As mentioned earlier, you can add an analytics chart to a dashboard directly from the Analytics app as well.

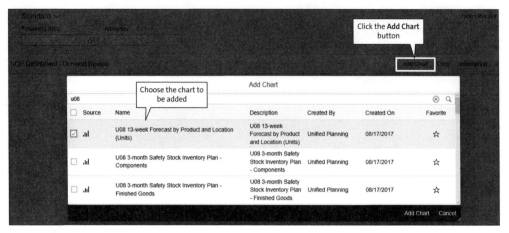

Figure 13.22 Adding Charts to Dashboard

13.2.2   Using Advanced Dashboards

Each dashboard serves a specific purpose and targets a specific audience. Therefore, you create a different dashboard for each process. For example, the demand review process targets demand planners, who will be interested in visualizing brands and region-level demand and comparing the forecast accuracy of one period with another. Dashboards can be marked as favorites to be listed at the top of the list for easy access.

In the following sections, some sample dashboards are shown for each S&OP process step. These dashboards can be used as a guide to developing dashboards for each process, but you'll need to analyze your specific business requirements to design your own dashboards.

Demand Review

Figure 13.23 and Figure 13.24 illustrate a sample dashboard created for the demand review process. The following are the analytics charts included in the dashboard:

- **Consensus Quantity vs AOP and Prior Year by Product Family**
- **Consensus Quantity vs AOP and Sales Forecast by Product Family for Next 12 Months**
- **Consensus Revenue vs AOP and Sales Forecast**
- **Consensus Revenue by Version for Next 12 Months**

- Consensus Demand Revenue distribution by segments
- 13-Week Forecast by Product and Location (Units)
- Demand Forecast by Location for Next 13 Weeks (Units)

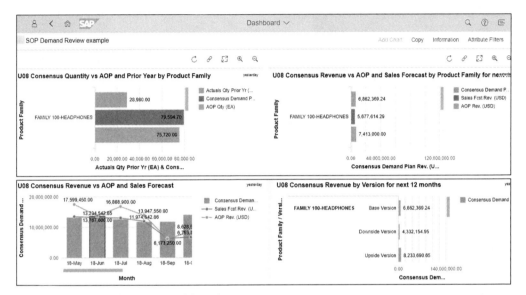

Figure 13.23 Demand Review Dashboard: Part I

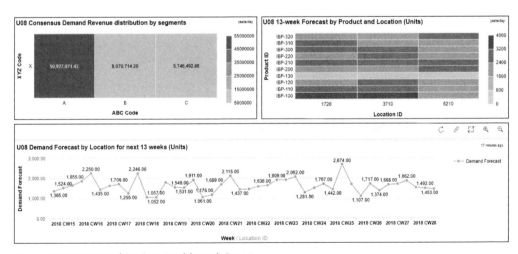

Figure 13.24 Demand Review Dashboard: Part II

Supply Review

Figure 13.25 and Figure 13.26 illustrate a sample dashboard created for the supply review process. The following are the analytics charts included in the dashboard:

- Capacity Utilization by Resource
- Capacity Usage by Resource
- Consensus Demand vs Constrained Demand by Product Family for Next 12 Months
- New Product: Consensus Demand vs Constrained Demand by PLM Status for Next 12 Months
- New Product: Capacity Usage by PLM Status
- Supply Network Visualization

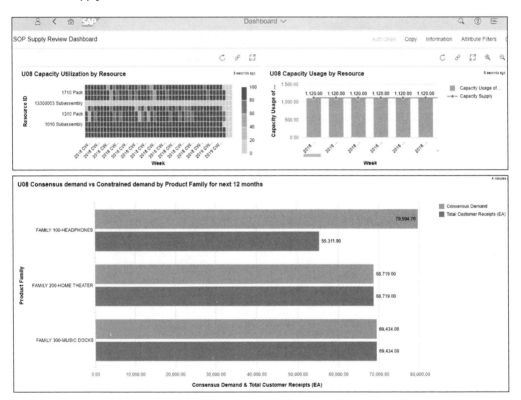

Figure 13.25 Supply Review Dashboard: Part I

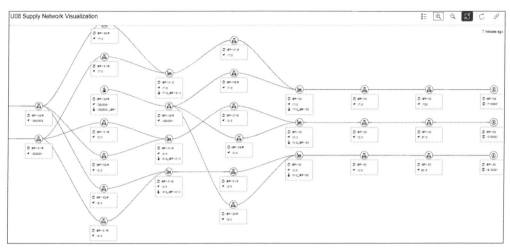

Figure 13.26 Supply Review Dashboard: Part II

Operating Review

Figure 13.27 shows a sample dashboard created for the operating review process. The following are the analytics charts included in the dashboard:

- Quarterly Demand Revenue vs AOP and Actuals
- Constrained Revenue vs AOP and Sales Forecast
- Gross Profit by Version

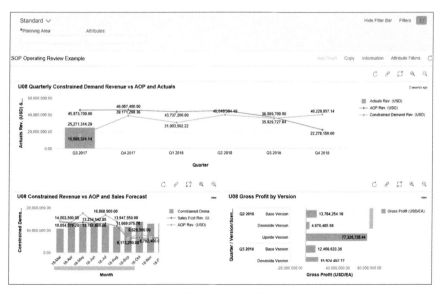

Figure 13.27 Operating Review Dashboard Example

Executive Review

Figure 13.28, Figure 13.29, and Figure 13.30 show a sample dashboard created for the executive review process. Note here that all charts are in the periodicity of months or quarters. This periodicity is decided based on the target audience of the executive review process. The following are the analytics charts included in the dashboard:

- Quarterly Constrained Demand Revenue vs AOP and Actuals
- Constrained Revenue vs AOP and Sales Forecast
- Gross Profit of a Product Group
- New Product: Consensus Demand vs Constrained Demand by PLM Status for Next 12 Months
- Gross Profit by Product and Customer Group
- Gross Profit by PLM status and Product
- Consensus Demand vs Constrained Demand by Product Family
- Capacity Utilization by Resource
- Constrained Revenue by Version
- Constrained Demand Revenue vs Consensus Demand Revenue by Segment
- Gross profit by Version
- Capacity by PLM Status

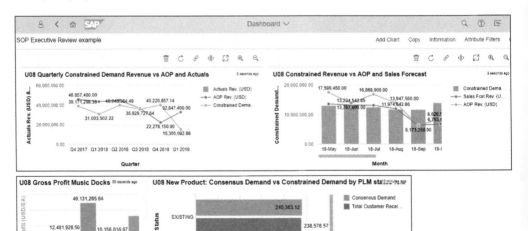

Figure 13.28 Executive Review Dashboard: Part I

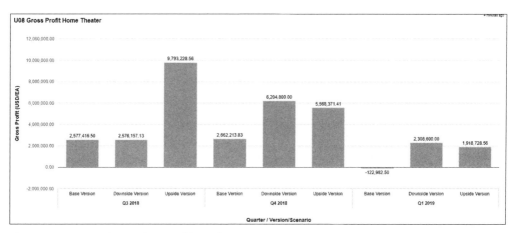

Figure 13.29 Executive Review Dashboard: Part II

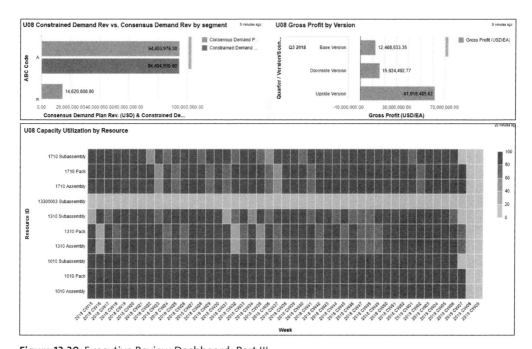

Figure 13.30 Executive Review Dashboard: Part III

13.2.3   Managing Advanced Dashboards

After the dashboards are created, you can manage them from the Dashboard app. Some options include refreshing data, resizing charts, and sharing them for collaboration.

The following are some of the significant options available in the app to manage dashboards:

- **Refresh**
  You can refresh data loaded to all the charts with one click to get real-time data. In addition, each chart can be refreshed individually.

- **Resize Chart**
  You can resize each chart individually by determining its size and location. **Columns** and **Rows** have four size options (from **1** to **4**) to choose from (see Figure 13.31).

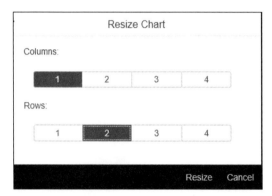

Figure 13.31 Resize Chart

- **Share**
  A dashboard can be shared with specific users or with an SAP Jam group for collaboration. **Send E-Mail** or **Share on SAP Jam** are the options available for collaboration.

13.3   Summary

SAP IBP offers a flexible tool to build real-time analytics charts and dashboards. Real-time analytics, following chart design principles, help business leaders to determine the right decisions to make and actions to take. SAP IBP helps consolidate real-time data and visualization details. Business leaders must gain insight to decide the right course of action that aligns with the strategy of their businesses.

Chapter 14

Integrating SAP IBP for Sales and Operations

SAP Integrated Business Planning provides integration mechanisms to import master and transactional data from external data sources and export the output back to the downstream systems. In this chapter, we'll discuss these integration options for SAP IBP.

In Chapter 2, we covered the planning model and its entities in SAP IBP. Before a user can perform any planning-relevant tasks, one of the prerequisites is to load data into the planning model to enable subsequent planning processes. SAP IBP is a decision-support system, so the decisions made need to be sent back to downstream systems for further processing.

In this chapter, we'll cover the integration mechanisms available for inbound and outbound data from SAP Integrated Business Planning for sales and operations, which is primarily used for the tactical planning process. The data elements include the master data and transactional data, which are interfaced from source systems such as SAP ERP, SAP S/4HANA, or other external systems. We'll also touch on the integration technologies available depending on the use cases you plan to implement in SAP IBP.

14.1 Data Integration Scenarios

In this section, we'll go over the different integration mechanisms available in SAP Integrated Business Planning. Before we delve deeper, let's review the planning processes supported in SAP IBP:

- Mid- to long-term tactical planning
- Short-term operational planning

The objects typically used to model mid- to long-term tactical planning processes (which includes S&OP) in SAP IBP are called *configurable data objects*. These objects provide flexibility to model customer-specific business processes. Simple master data types, compound master data types, reference types, virtual master data types, and key figures are used to model such configurable data objects.

The objects used to model operational planning processes in SAP IBP are of the *order* type. This is because operational planning processes require close integration with execution systems such as SAP ERP or SAP S/4HANA. To enable tight integration with execution systems, SAP IBP offers a static order data model. The static order data model objects are modeled as external master data types in planning model configuration. In addition, the static data model objects have limited flexibility compared to configurable data objects.

Depending on the integration scenario or planning process, data can be transferred using generic tools or dedicated integration technologies such as SAP Cloud Platform Integration for data services and SAP HANA smart data integration (SDI; see Table 14.1).

Processes	Tactical Planning	Operational Planning
Characteristics	Time-series based planning: configurable data objects, high flexibility, periodic data transfers	Order-based planning: static data model, limited flexibility, order elements, periodic data transfers
Integration mechanism	SAP Cloud Platform Integration for data services or manual data integration from Web UI	SAP Cloud Platform Smart Data Integration (OpenAPI)
Source and target data sources	SAP ERP, SAP APO, SAP BPC, SAP CRM, SAP S/4HANA and any external source	SAP ERP, SAP S/4HANA and any other source

Table 14.1 Overview of Main Integration Scenarios

14.2   Integration for Tactical Planning

Figure 14.1 illustrates the typical inbound and outbound data feeds for enabling the S&OP process from various source systems, such as SAP ERP, SAP Advanced Planning and Optimization (SAP APO), SAP Customer Relationship Management (SAP CRM), SAP Business Warehouse (SAP BW), financial planning applications, and so on.

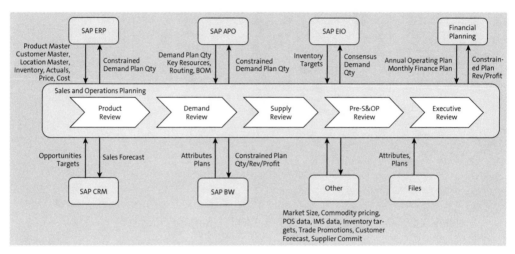

Figure 14.1 Typical Data Feeds for S&OP Process

SAP IBP provides different integration options to enable bidirectional data transfer. Figure 14.2 illustrates the integration options available for tactical planning processes for importing data to and exporting data from SAP IBP. The options for importing and exporting data are as follows:

- **Integration using SAP Cloud Platform Integration for data services**
  SAP Cloud Platform Integration for data services is used for bidirectional data transfers—that is, for importing and exporting master data and transaction data to or from SAP IBP.

- **Manual data integration using the web interface**
  Using the web interface provided via SAP Fiori applications, you can manually upload master data and transactional data into SAP IBP.

- **Export of key figure data using OData services**
  This option is used to export only the time-series data from SAP IBP.

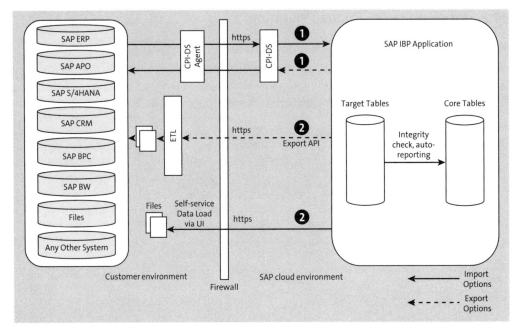

Figure 14.2 Data Integration Options for Tactical Planning Processes

In the following subsections, we'll go over each integration option in more detail.

14.2.1   SAP Cloud Platform Integration for Data Services

SAP Cloud Platform Integration for data services is a cloud-based data-integration tool for batch/scheduled data integration between on-premise applications and cloud applications. SAP Cloud Platform Integration for data services is included as part of the SAP IBP subscription at no additional cost to customers.

The following are some the key capabilities of SAP Cloud Platform Integration for data services:

- Provides secure direct access to multiple SAP ERP sources to extract, transform, and load data to targeted cloud applications
- Reads and writes from/to heterogeneous sources—databases (SAP HANA, DB2, Oracle, SQL Server) and files (XML or delimited)

- Provides a role-based web UI for designing, executing, and monitoring extract, transform, load (ETL) jobs
- Gives end-to-end visibility into data loads into SAP Integrated Business Planning and configurable email notifications for alerts on integration flow operations
- Offers a built-in scheduler or can invoke integration flow from third-party applications through a web services call

Figure 14.3 shows the SAP Cloud Platform Integration for data services architecture for SAP IBP. On the left-hand side, you can see the various on-premise source systems, such as SAP ERP, SAP APO, databases, and files.

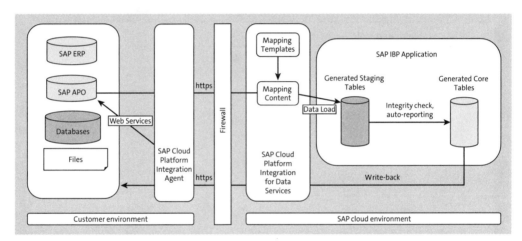

Figure 14.3 SAP Cloud Platform Integration for Data Services Architecture for SAP IBP

There is a lightweight installation of the SAP Cloud Platform Integration for data services agent inside the customer's firewall. The agent securely transfers data from on-premise systems to the cloud by communicating with SAP apps through RFC or with other databases or files. The data is sent to the cloud via HTTPS and is streamed from source to target and never persisted. The communication is always from the agent to the cloud, with no need for VPN, reverse proxy, or other firewall exceptions. The data services agent uses *long polling*: it places a request with the server and waits for a response when a task is ready to execute.

On the right-hand side, in the cloud, is the wizard-driven UI that lets you browse metadata to define integration flows. SAP Cloud Platform Integration for data services has access to the SAP IBP staging tables with read and/or write access. For importing data into SAP IBP, the data is put into the staging tables with write access. Then the postprocessing in SAP IBP is triggered to perform integrity checks and move the data to core tables.

SAP Cloud Platform Integration for data services has a web-based, wizard-driven UI (see Figure 14.4) to browse metadata directly and design integration flows. You can manage integration flows from anywhere via a secure browser. Integration flows persist in the SAP Cloud Platform Integration for data services repository, enabling reuse.

Figure 14.4 Designer's Data Flow Editor for Mappings

SAP Cloud Platform Integration for data services also provides a dashboard to monitor the status of the SAP Cloud Platform Integration for data services tasks (see Figure 14.5).

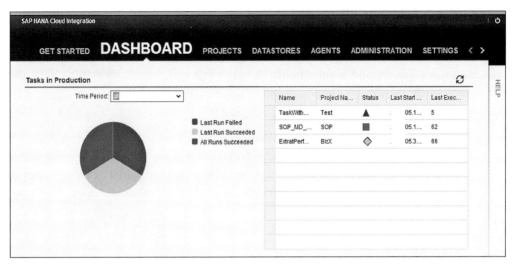

Figure 14.5 Dashboard for Monitoring Tasks

SAP Cloud Platform Integration for data services lets you connect directly to SAP ERP, SAP S/4HANA, and SAP APO to extract and pipe from the on-premise source systems to SAP IBP–generated target tables securely via HTTPS, without data persisting in files anywhere.

SAP Cloud Platform Integration for data services can also directly read from SAP IBP's calculation scenario object and write back to flat files on-premise securely via HTTPS or write directly back to SAP ERP or SAP APO via web service calls.

The following are the high-level steps you need to follow to set up the integration for SAP Cloud Platform Integration for data services:

1. Install and configure the SAP Cloud Platform for data services agent on your on-premise system.

2. Configure the connection to the SAP Integrated Business Planning system.

3. Define data stores.

4. Import tables and extractors.

5. Create a project.

6. Create a task using a predefined template.

7. Execute the task.

8. Promote the task to production.

9. Schedule the task.

There are predefined templates available, which are dataflows with mappings from SAP ERP or SAP APO to a data model in SAP IBP. These templates can be used as is or can be used as a starting point for further customization. The templates are designed to meet the specific requirements of SAP Integrated Business Planning data and reduce the time needed to get up and running with the application.

There are three types of templates available:

1. General-purpose templates contain information to process the data after it's loaded. The SOP_APO_Task and SOP_ECC_Task general-purpose templates contain global variables, preload scripts, and post-load scripts. After using either of these templates to create a task, you can add data store information and build your own data flows.

2. Master data templates

3. Key figure templates

Table 14.2 lists the predefined templates for moving master data and key figures from SAP ERP and SAP S/4HANA to SAP IBP. The details of each template can be found in the SAP Cloud Platform Integration guide on SAP IBP's main help page.

Object	SAP Cloud Platform Integration for Data Services Template	Data Flow	Sources
Master Data			
Product	SOP_MD_ ProductMaster	DF_SOP_ ProductMaster	Extractor OMATERIAL_ ATTR, table MAKT
Location	SOP_MD_ LocationMaster	DF_SOP_ LocationMaster	Extractor OPLANT_ATTR_ SOP, table T001W
Location product	SOP_MD_ LocationProd	DF_SOP_ LocationProduct	Tables MARA, MARC, MBEW
Customer	SOP_MD_ CustomerMaster	DF_SOP_ CustomerMaster	Extractor OCUSTOMER_ ATTR, tables KNVP, KNVH
Sales order	IBP_MD_SalesOrder_ InitialLoad	DF_IBP_SalesOrder_ InitialLoad	Extractor 2LIS_11_ VASCL
	IBP_MD_SalesOrder_ DeltaLoad	DF_IBP_SalesOrder_ DeltaLoad	Extractor 2LIS_11_ VASCL

Table 14.2 Predefined Templates for SAP ERP and SAP S/4HANA

Object	SAP Cloud Platform Integration for Data Services Template	Data Flow	Sources
Delivery	`IBP_MD_Deliveries_ InitialLoad`	`DF_IBP_Deliveries_ InitialLoad`	Extractor 2LIS_12_ VCITM
	`IBP_MD_Deliveries_ DeltaLoad`	`DF_IBP_Deliveries_ DeltaLoad`	Extractor 2LIS_12_ VCITM
Key Figures			
Actuals/ shipment history	`SOP_KF_Actuals`	`DF_SOP_Actuals`	Extractor 2LIS_12_ VCITM, tables VBRK, VBRP
Inventory	`SOP_KF_Inventory`	`DF_SOP_Inventory`	Tables MARA, MARC, MARD
Open orders	`SOP_KF_OpenOrders`	`DF_SOP_OpenOrders`	Extractors 2LIS_11_ VAHDR, 2LIS_11_VAITM, 2LIS_11_VASTI
Sales forecast price	`SOP_KF_ SalesForecastPrice`	`DF_SOP_ SalesForecastPrice`	Extractor 2LIS_13_ VDITM
None	`SOP_ECC_Task`	Task without data flow containing global variables and settings fitting to SAP ERP integration	

Table 14.2 Predefined Templates for SAP ERP and SAP S/4HANA (Cont.)

Table 14.3 lists the predefined templates for moving master data and key figures from SAP APO and SAP S/4HANA on-premise to SAP IBP. It also lists the template to send the key figure data from SAP IBP to SAP APO as planned independent requirements.

Object	Template	Data Flow	Sources or Targets
Master Data			
Resource	`SOP_MD_Resource`	`DF_SOP_Resource`	Table /SAPAPO/ RES_HEAD

Table 14.3 Predefined Templates for SAP APO

Object	Template	Data Flow	Sources or Targets
Planning area	IBP_MD_PlanningArea	DF_IBP_ProductMaster	Extractor 9ADP_CUSTOM_PRODUCT*, tables /BIO/9ATMATNR, /SAPAPO/MATKEY, T006A
		DF_IBP_LocationMaster	Extractor 9ADP_CUSTOM_LOCATION*, table /BIO/9ATLOCNO
		DF_IBP_UnitsOfMeasure	Extractor 9ADP_CUSTOM_PRODUCT*, tables /SAPAPO/MATKEY, /SAPAPO/MARM, T006A
		DF_IBP_UnitsOfMeasure_Conversion	Extractor 9ADP_CUSTOM_PRODUCT*, tables /SAPAPO/MATKEY, /SAPAPO/MARM
Key Figures			
Capacity limits	SOP_KF_CapacityLimit	DF_SOP_Capacity	Extractor 9ACAPACITY, table /SAPAPO/RES_HEAD
Capacity consumptions	SOP_KF_Consumption	DF_SOP_Consumption	Function modules BAPI_LOCSRVAPS_GET_LIST2, BAPI_PDSSRVAPS_GETLIST
Demand plan	IBP_KF_DemandPlanning	IBP_KF_DemandPlanning	Extractor 9ADP_CUSTOM_TOTAL_DEMAND_PLAN*
None	SOP_APO_Task	Task without data flow containing global variables and settings fitting to SAP APO integration	
Key Figures from SAP IBP to SAP APO			
Planned independent requirements	IBP_KF_PlannedIndependentRequirements	DF_IBP_SensedDemand	Target is customer-generated web service for BAPI_PIRSRVAPS_SAVEMULTI

Table 14.3 Predefined Templates for SAP APO (Cont.)

14.2.2 Manual Data Integration Using Web Interface

SAP IBP provides an SAP Fiori app called Data Integration Jobs for importing data manually through a file-based format. It only supports importing data into generated tables or configurable data objects for master data, time profiles, key figures, and snapshots. This self-service SAP Fiori app doesn't support downloading or exporting any data from SAP IBP system. It also doesn't support external master data that's part of the static order data model.

It's important to note that uploading data using this app is only recommended during early stages of the implementation or on an exception basis by super users in the productive system. For the typical end user, there are other ways to accomplish business tasks.

Figure 14.6 illustrates the manual data integration scenario. The data files are uploaded using the Data Integration Jobs app. The data is uploaded into the staging tables and then processed further with integrity checks into the core tables.

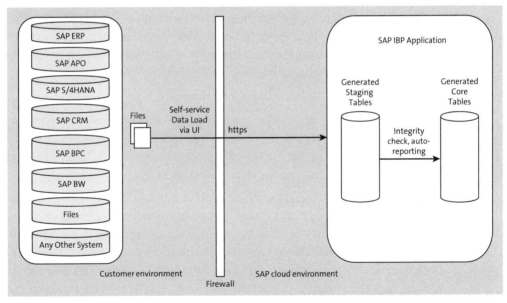

Figure 14.6 Manual Data Integration Using Web Interface

The Data Integration Jobs app (see Figure 14.7) is part of the **Administrator** SAP Fiori launchpad group and is available to the users with the correct permissions.

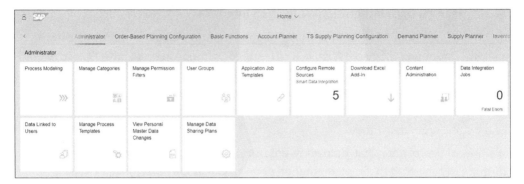

Figure 14.7 Data Integration Jobs SAP Fiori App

The key capabilities using this application are as follows:

- Download templates for time periods, master data, key figures, and snapshots
- Import time periods, master data, key figures, and snapshots

In the rest of this section, we'll cover the internal integration within SAP IBP for the configurable object data type in more detail. This is applicable to all integration mechanisms for tactical planning processes, such as SAP Cloud Platform Integration for data services, manual integration, or exporting via a web service.

There are two phases of the data integration process:

1. For manual file upload, the system reads and loads the contents of the file into a staging table, which is an intermediate storage space. If the data can't be parsed, the system will reject the file. For SAP Cloud Integration Platform for data services, the data is directly loaded into the respective staging tables.

2. From the intermediate staging table, the data is moved to the application tables. Records may be rejected in this phase. The possible reasons for rejection can include corresponding master data not existing, records failing referential integrity checks, and so on. When this occurs, the rejection appears as a rejection code. The system retains data load reports for seven days by default. The data load reports and the import status of the data integration jobs can be seen on the main data integration **Job Details** screen. The import status is represented by a colored icon (see Figure 14.8).

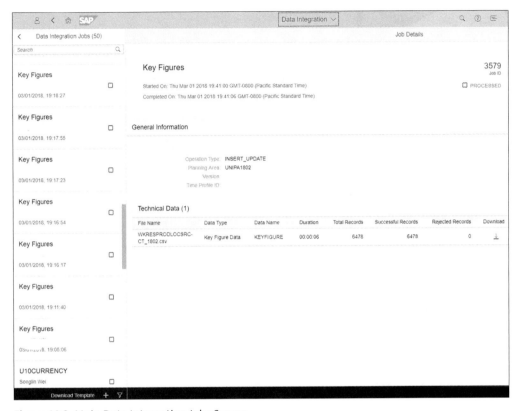

Figure 14.8 Main Data Integration Jobs Screen

The data for configured data objects is imported in the following sequence:

1. Time periods
2. Master data related to master data objects
3. Key figures
4. Snapshots

For manual file-based integration, you can download the templates for each of the objects as a starting point from the data integration **Job Details** main screen.

Time Periods

Typically, time period data is imported manually via files from the Data Integration Jobs app because it's loaded infrequently. Prefilled template options can be used, or if you want to extend the existing time horizon, you can download the existing time period data and upload it again.

There are two **Operation Type** options: **Replace** and **Delete**. **Replace** replaces the existing time period data with the new time period data from the files. **Delete** deletes the time period data specified in the data file (see Figure 14.9).

Figure 14.9 Data Integration for Time Periods

Master Data

Master data can be loaded either via SAP Cloud Platform Integration for data services or from the Data Integration Jobs app. Simple and compound master data types are the only configurable master data objects in which data can be loaded.

The following operation types are available for master data:

- **Insert or Update**
  With this operation type, the system updates existing master data and inserts new records into SAP IBP.

- **Delete**
  Using this operation type, you can specify which master data rows are deleted from the master data object. The delete operation cascade-deletes the dependent master data objects and/or key figure data for related planning areas.

The related master data objects are compound master data objects that refer to the deleted master data object. For these compound master data objects, the system deletes all the rows that have the originally deleted rows as a part of their key.

For example, say you have a product simple master data type with PRDID as its key and a location-product compound master data type with PRDID and LOCID as key attributes. Now, if a product is deleted from the simple master data type, then it will also delete all corresponding rows from location-product for the deleted product.

The key figure values are deleted from the planning areas if they're related to the deleted master data object in the following two cases:

– The master data type key attributes are the same as or are a subset of the key figure base planning level root attributes. For example, for a master data object product with a key attribute PRDID and a key figure with PRDID and LOCID as root attributes of its base planning level, values of the key figure are deleted for all values of PRDID that are deleted. This is independent of the LOCID values of the key figure planning combinations.

– Nonkey attributes of the master data object are the same as or are a subset of the key figure base planning level root attributes, and no other master data object rows remain that have the same nonkey attributes. For example, for a simple master data object product with a nonkey attribute PRODBRAND (product brand) and a key figure with root attributes of its base planning level being PRODBRAND and LOCREGION (location region), values of this key figure are deleted when there are no more products for the corresponding product family. This is independent of the LOCREGION values.

- **Replace**
  With this operation type, any master data in the new data load that doesn't already exist in the SAP IBP system is inserted. Any master data in the new load that already exists in the SAP IBP system is updated. Master data that already exists in the system but isn't included in the new load is deleted. The results of such an operation is that any associated master data, related planning combinations, and transaction or key figure data is also cascade-deleted.

  This operation type must be used with extreme caution as you risk deleting data unintentionally.

  Figure 14.10 illustrates the replace operation for master data.

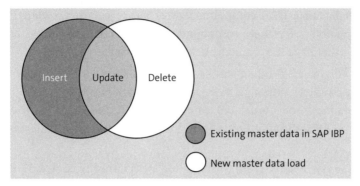

Figure 14.10 Replace Operation Type for Master Data

Key Figures

Key figure data can be loaded either via SAP Cloud Platform Integration for data services or from the Data Integration Jobs app. Key figure data can only be imported into stored key figures. You can't load data into key figures based on static order model data using SAP Cloud Platform Integration for data services or the Data Integration Jobs app.

The following operation types are available for master data:

- **Insert or Update**
  With this operation type, the system updates existing key figure data and inserts new records into SAP IBP.

- **Delete**
  Using this operation type lets you clear all the key figure values for the records or values specified in the data load. When you load data into the system, you can explicitly specify the stored key figures that you want to delete. This operation type doesn't delete the time series records; it only nullifies the values.

- **Replace**
  With this operation type, the key figure data for combinations present in the new data load (via SAP Cloud Platform Integration for data services or a file) that doesn't already exist in the system is inserted. The key figure data for combinations that overlap with existing data in the system is updated. Any existing key figure data in the system that isn't included in the new data load is cleared (i.e., the key figure and any related transaction data is updated with NULL).

This operation type is used in scenarios in which you want to delete (nullify) all existing data for a specific key figure and replace it with new data.

Figure 14.11 illustrates the replace operation.

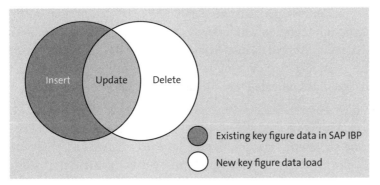

Figure 14.11 Replace Operation Type for Key Figure Data

Snapshots

Using this option, snapshot data can be imported only in change history-enabled key figures configured as snapshots of the change history type. Such snapshots are used by the Demand Sensing application.

14.2.3   Export of Key Figure Data Using OData Services

SAP IBP provides an OData service to extract key figure data. This service isn't recommended for mass extraction of key figures. For extracting mass volumes of key figure data, we recommend that you use SAP Cloud Platform Integration for data services, as discussed in the previous sections.

The use cases for this service include extracting the key figure data to be integrated with external on-premise systems or external reporting tools. To extract the data, you need to provide the level of the attributes, key figures, and the selection filters for the data you want to extract. The OData service returns the requested data in JSON format. The data can be returned for any planning area, version, or scenario.

To access the SAP IBP system from outside the cloud securely and extract data using this OData service, certain steps must be completed, such as creating an inbound communication user and a communication arrangement using a communication scenario (SAP_COM_0143). In addition, you also need to create an external data access user group and assign business users to it.

14.3   Integration for Operational Planning

As we noted earlier, the object type used to model operational planning processes in SAP IBP is the *order* type. This is because operational planning processes require close integration with execution systems such as SAP ERP, SAP S/4HANA, or non-SAP ERP systems. To enable tight integration with execution systems, SAP IBP offers a static order data model. The static order data model objects are modeled as external master data types in planning model configuration in SAP IBP. In addition, the static data model has limited flexibility compared to configurable data objects.

Order-based planning requires master data, transactional data, and configuration data to work. This data is not created directly in SAP IBP. A connection is established between SAP IBP and an external system, and then the necessary data is integrated from that system. Once the data is available in SAP IBP, you can use it as the basis for your planning. There is periodic data transfer from any system to SAP IBP. Also, there is periodic data transfer of planning results from SAP IBP to other SAP/non-SAP systems.

Figure 14.12 illustrates the architecture for the order-based planning process using SAP HANA smart data integration and Open API.

For order-based planning, you always need to use Open API using SAP HANA smart data integration. This is mandatory for SAP IBP for response and supply.

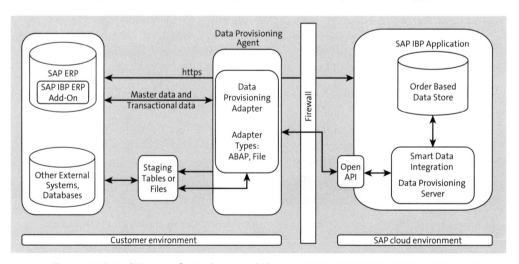

Figure 14.12 Architecture for Order-Based Planning Using SAP HANA SDI and Open API

There are two types of adapters available depending on whether you can use out-of-the-box integration between SAP IBP and SAP ERP or SAP S/4HANA.

If you can use the out-of-the box integration, then SAP IBP provides a supply chain integration SAP ERP add-on. The data provisioning adapter type in this case is ABAP. The data provisioning adapter establishes the connection with the SAP IBP system. The out-of-the-box integration option using the SAP ERP add-on is depicted in the top portion of Figure 14.12. On the left side, you see the on-premise source system, which in this scenario will be either SAP ERP or SAP S/4HANA. The supply chain integration SAP IBP add-on collects the required master and transactional data from SAP ERP or SAP S/4HANA and transforms data into the format required for SAP IBP. The master and transactional data is then sent to SAP IBP via inbound integration as a basis for planning purposes. After the planning is done in SAP IBP, the results can be sent back to the target system (either SAP ERP or SAP S/4HANA).

The other option available for integration is using the data provisioning adapter of the *file* type. This option is depicted in the bottom portion of Figure 14.12.

The relevant master data, transactional data, and configuration data is taken from the source system and written into individual tables, which are then stored in the staging area, which can be a file share.

The first step for using the file-based adapter is that data is extracted and transformed from your source system into the staging area. Once the adapter is up and running, all the data (i.e., all the master data, transactional data, and configuration data) is transferred from the inbound staging area to the SAP IBP system using SDI.

For outbound integration, you extract the order-based planning data from your SAP IBP system into the outbound staging area. Once the outbound adapter is up and running, all the data (order details and order confirmation details) is transferred from the outbound staging area to your target system using SDI.

Table 14.4 lists the master data, transactional data, and stock supported for inbound and outbound integration.

Object Type	From SAP ERP to SAP IBP	From SAP IBP to SAP ERP
Master data	Material	
	Location (DC, plant, vendor, customer)	
	Location material	

Table 14.4 Inbound and Outbound Integration data

Object Type	From SAP ERP to SAP IBP	From SAP IBP to SAP ERP
	Transportation lane	
	Resource	
	Production data structure	
Transactional data	Sales order	Planned order
	Inbound delivery	Purchase requisition
	Outbound delivery	Stock transfer requisition
	Purchase requisition	Sales order confirmation
	Purchase order	
	Stock transfer requisition	
	Stock transfer order	
	Planned order	
	Production order	
	Acknowledgement	
Stock	Unrestricted-use stock	
	Unrestricted-use vendor consignment stock	
	Quality inspection stock	
	Vendor consignment stock in quality inspection	
	Blocked stock	
	Blocked vendor consignment stock	

Table 14.4 Inbound and Outbound Integration data (Cont.)

14.4   Other Integrations

SAP IBP integrates with external systems to consolidate data for S&OP. This includes financial integration with SAP BPC, opportunities integration with SAP BPC, promotions integration with SAP Trade Promotion Management, and integration with SAP ERP or SAP S/4HANA.

14.4.1   Financial Integration with SAP BPC

SAP IBP can be integrated with financial plans from external systems like SAP Business Planning and Consolidation. The integration layer is SAP Cloud Platform Integration for data services for integration between SAP BPC on-premise and SAP IBP deployed in the cloud. From SAP BPC, usually the annual operating plans (AOPs) and budget plans are provided as input for SAP IBP, along with any other cost-related data.

In SAP IBP, this financial information is used for calculating margin and revenue calculations. In SAP IBP, the AOP input is the taken as a target to meet the tactical and operational plans, the constrained demand revenues are compared against the targets, and the plan is adjusted to meet the target. Figure 14.13 shows the integration between SAP BPC and SAP IBP with inputs and outputs. SAP provides the integration content or guidelines via SAP Note 2428919.

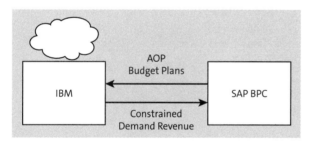

Figure 14.13 SAP IBP to SAP BPC Integrtation

14.4.2   Opportunities Integration with SAP Hybris Cloud for Customer

Opportunities that are planned in SAP Hybris Cloud for Customer can be integrated with SAP Integrated Business Planning, where they are included in the sales forecasting and consensus demand planning processes. The integration layer is SAP Cloud Platform Integration for data services to copy between the two cloud-based solutions (see Figure 14.14). SAP also provides out-of-the-box integration guidelines for transferring sales opportunities that are at a certain process stage and have a certain probability value to SAP IBP. Once this information is transferred to SAP IBP, it can be part of the sales forecasting process and consequently part of consensus demand planning.

Figure 14.14 SAP IBP to SAP Hybris Cloud for Customer Integration

14.5   Summary

In this chapter, we covered the integration mechanisms available for inbound and outbound data from SAP Integrated Business Planning for sales and operations. The data elements included the master data and transactional data interfaced from source systems such as SAP ERP, SAP S/4HANA, and other external systems. In addition, we also touched other integration technologies available depending on the use cases you plan to implement in SAP IBP specifically for operational planning processes.

Chapter 15
Roles and Security

In this chapter, we'll discuss the robust user management and security model in SAP IBP, which provides the right level of data and functional access for user, thus enabling multiple cross-functional teams across different regions and business units to work with the system securely.

SAP IBP provides robust identity and access management to control access to application functions and data, along with secure access to SAP IBP's cloud environment. The authorization concept in SAP IBP is much simpler to configure from the web UI without the overhead of logging into multiple systems and complex security profiles.

You will typically access SAP IBP in the cloud; via SAP Integrated Business Planning, add-in for Microsoft Excel deployed on your local system; or from the browser window to access the web UI. You can access SAP IBP from anywhere, whether from within a corporate firewall or outside the network via the Internet. No matter what the access method, is, SAP IBP provides a secure connection via single sign-on and SAML2-based authentication.

In the following sections, we'll cover security management to access SAP IBP through single sign-on and other secure access methods in detail, user management and business roles to manage user access to different application functions and planning area content, and permission filters to manage the visibility and editability of data. Finally, we'll cover the infrastructure management of SAP IBP.

15.1 Security Management

SAP IBP uses SAP Cloud Platform Identity Authentication for identity and access management, which provides safe and secure access to SAP IBP. There are two ways in which customers can access SAP IBP:

1. **Through SAP Cloud Platform Identity Authentication**
   Figure 15.1 shows the system landscape of a user's authentication for SAP IBP. This

is the default authentication provided by SAP when a new customer tenant is provisioned. The administrator user is provided access to SAP IBP and its associated SAP Cloud Platform Identity Authentication. The administrator creates business users in SAP IBP, then loads and stores these users into SAP Cloud Platform Identity Authentication, which is the identity provider in this setup to authenticate a user via his ID or email as configured by the administrator.

When the end user logs into SAP IBP through a browser for the web UI or through the Excel add-in using single sign-on and SAML2-based authentication, SAP IBP redirects the request to SAP Cloud Platform Identity Authentication to check if the user is allowed to login. If authentication is successful, then the user roles and data access profiles of the user are checked in SAP IBP and the user is allowed to access different applications and data as defined by the roles and permission filters set for the user.

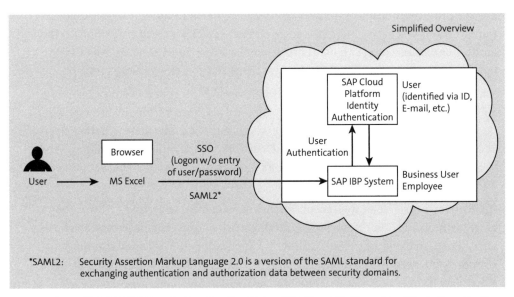

Figure 15.1 SAP IBP User Authentication Using SAP Cloud Platform Identity Authentication

2. **Through your organization's cloud identity**
   In this case, your organization's identity provider (IdP) will be used with SAP Cloud Platform Identity Authentication in a proxy model for user authentication. Figure 15.2 shows the system landscape in which users are centrally stored and managed in your identity provider, like Microsoft ADFS. In this setup, when the user logs into SAP IBP from her browser or the Excel add-in with single sign-on, SAP IBP redirects the request to SAP Cloud Platform Identity Authentication, which runs in a

proxy mode, routing the user authentication request to the customer's identity provider. If authentication is successful, the user is allowed access to SAP IBP application UIs and data based on her roles and permission filters setup.

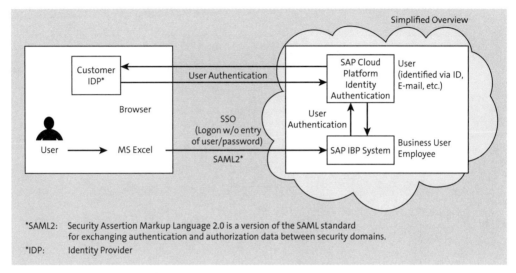

Figure 15.2 SAP IBP User Authentication Using Customer IDP

SAP IBP uses SAP S/4HANA user management and its underlying artifacts, such as Transaction SU01 for user management and Transaction PFCG for role maintenance, which have been proven to be standard for access control. To ease setup, SAP IBP provides user-friendly SAP Fiori UIs for creating and managing users, roles, and permissions. The core areas of user management and access control in SAP IBP involve the following: users, business roles, catalogs, and permission filters.

Figure 15.3 shows the permission model in SAP IBP to control access to application functions and data. This will be discussed in detail in later sections of this chapter. The permissions model starts with the creation of an employee containing the user's details and then moves to creating a business user through which the user can login to the system. Users are assigned business roles that contain business catalogs to grant access to the SAP Fiori apps in SAP IBP, along with restrictions to control areas like planning areas, master data types, key figures, versions, data lifecycles, and so on.

Finally, permissions filters can be defined and assigned to business users or roles to grant permissions for which master data attribute values and key figures the user has visibility into and editability access for. For example, sales planner A may be given access to view and edit data only for country X.

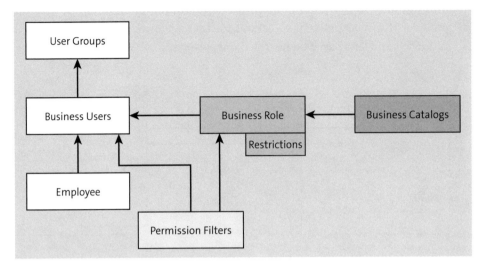

Figure 15.3 Permissions Model in SAP IBP

15.2   User Management

User management in SAP IBP covers all the administrative functions to create and maintain users to access SAP IBP. These users are created using the Maintain Employees and Maintain Business Users SAP Fiori apps and then uploaded to the SAP Cloud Platform Identity Authentication service for secure authentication, single sign-on, and user management in SAP Cloud Platform. The following subsections cover details of how to perform user management in SAP IBP by creating employees and business users, maintaining users in the SAP Cloud Platform Identity Authentication service, and finally how to manage user groups in SAP IBP.

15.2.1   Creating Users

As part of the onboarding process for SAP IBP, the IT administrator contact identified by your organization gets an email with access information that includes the following:

- The URL for the SAP IBP application, along with administrator login credentials
- The URL for the SAP Cloud Identity Administrative Console, along with login credentials

As mentioned before, there are two methods of user authentication in SAP IBP: through SAP Cloud Platform Identity Authentication or through a customer's IDP. When logged in as the administrator via the non-SAML-based URL provided for initial login, navigate to the **Identity and Access Management** group in the SAP Fiori launchpad to access SAP Fiori apps for maintaining users and roles in SAP IBP, as shown in Figure 15.4. These apps include Maintain Business Users, Maintain Business Roles, Business Role Templates, and others.

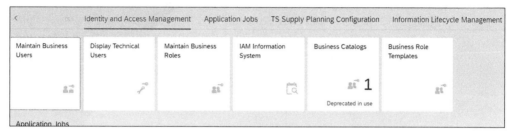

Figure 15.4 Identity and Access Mangement in SAP Fiori Launchpad for SAP IBP

The process of creating users in an SAP Cloud Platform Identity Authentication–based setup is as follows:

1. **Create employees**
   From the Maintain Employees SAP Fiori app, you first create employee records for all the users that will be accessing the SAP IBP system. These records contain unique employee IDs and other personal information, like first name, last name, email, phone, and address. For example, employee John Smith with ID DM56908 can be created as shown in Figure 15.5.

Figure 15.5 Maintain Employees SAP Fiori App

You can also use the **Upload** function available in the Maintain Employees app to upload a list of employees from a CSV file.

2. **Create and maintain business users**

   For the employees created in previous step, you next create business users in SAP IBP. Business user are users who can login to SAP IBP with the required functional and data-related authorizations to securely access the application. In the Maintain Business Users SAP Fiori app, you'll see a list of business users already created in the system. To create a new user, click the **New** button in the app and select the employee for whom a user needs to be created. For example, for the demand planner, a business user is created as shown in Figure 15.6. Here, account validity (**Valid From** and **Valid To**) can be maintained for the user under **User Data**, as well as some **Regional Settings**, along with the assignment of business roles.

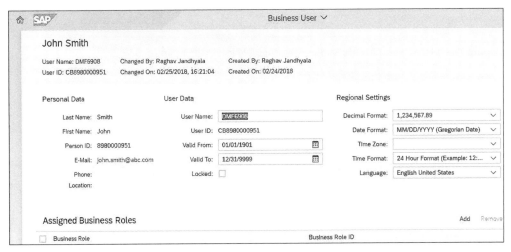

Figure 15.6 Maintain Business Users SAP Fiori App

> **Note**
>
> For the **User Name** field, you should enter the employee ID of the employee for whom the business user is being created.

3. **Download the business users**

   For SAP Cloud Platform Identity Authentication-based user authentication, click the **Download** button in the Maintain Business Users app as shown in Figure 15.7.

This downloads all the business users into a CSV file, which will be uploaded next to SAP Cloud Platform Identity Authentication.

Figure 15.7 Download Business Users

4. **Upload users into SAP Cloud Platform Identity Authentication**
   Login to the SAP Cloud Platform Identity Authentication administrative console in with the administrative credentials that were provided during customer on-boarding. Under **Custom Applications**, select your application URL and click **Upload Users** to upload the CSV files as shown in Figure 15.8. After upload, an email will be sent to the users for activation and access to the application. From the URL link, the user can also change the password to login to SAP IBP.

Figure 15.8 Upload Users to SAP Cloud Platform Identity Authentication

If you're using a corporate IdP, then the process is similar, except that SAP Cloud Identity Authentication needs to be configured as a proxy. The steps are as follows:

1. Login to the SAP Cloud Identity Authentication administrative console with the administrative credentials.

2. In the Corporate Provider Identity app, configure **Trusted Identity Providers** for the **Corporate Identity Provider**.

3. In the Application SAP Fiori app, select your SAP IBP URL and click **Identity Provider** to choose the configured **Corporate IDP**.

4. With this setup, the corporate IDP acts as a proxy for SAP Cloud Identity Authentication, and users are copied to the corporate IDP automatically.

15.2.2   User Groups

Users who perform similar business functions can be grouped in SAP IBP into user groups. For example, the NA Demand Planners user group might contain a list of users who are demand planners for North America. Users can be assigned to one or more user groups. Figure 15.9 shows the User Group SAP Fiori app in SAP IBP for an example user group: DEMAND_REVIEW, containing users who are responsible for demand planning in SAP IBP. Many functional areas in SAP IBP use user groups to collaborate or share information with all users in the group.

Figure 15.9 Maintain User Groups in SAP IBP

Some examples of the functionalities that can be assigned to user groups are as follows:

- Permission filters can be assigned to all users in the user group. For example, the NA Demand Planners user group can be assigned permissions to edit only NA planning data.

- User groups can be assigned to process steps that indicate which users can be assigned planning tasks and participate in the process progress.

- Analytics Charts and Dashboards can be shared with user groups.
- User-defined scenarios created in excel add-in can be shared with user groups

User groups can be maintained in the User Group SAP Fiori app under the **Administrative** group in the SAP Fiori launchpad for SAP IBP. To create a new user group, click **Add** and enter the **Name** and **Description** of the new user group. Then choose users that can be assigned to this user group.

15.3 Business Roles Management

Business roles are assigned to users to control which SAP Fiori applications, business functions, and planning data they're allowed to access. In addition, permission filters can be assigned directly to business roles to control the planning data that a user is allowed to view and modify.

For example, for newly created demand planner John Smith, you might grant access to general planner SAP Fiori apps like Analytics, Dashboards, Application Jobs, and so on, along with demand planner-specific apps like Manage Statistical Forecast. You can assign only demand-specific key figures in the planning model to this user so that he can focus on his area of responsibility.

There are five main aspects of creating a business role:

1. **Create a business role from a template or new**
   In the Maintain Business Roles SAP Fiori app, you can see a list of existing roles. You can choose to create a new business role from system-delivered templates or create one from scratch. To create a new role from a template, click the **Create from Template** button in the Maintain Business Roles SAP Fiori app and choose one of the predelivered templates. To create a business role from scratch, click **New** and provide the required information, like **Role ID**, **Name**, and **Description**.

   For example, you can create a new role for demand planners as shown in Figure 15.10 as follows:

   - Select **Create from Template** ❶ in the Maintain Business Roles SAP Fiori app.
   - Select the **Demand Planner (IBP)** template ❷ from the predelivered templates ❸.
   - In **Assigned Business Catalogs** ❹, choose all the predelivered catalogs or add/remove existing business role catalogs.

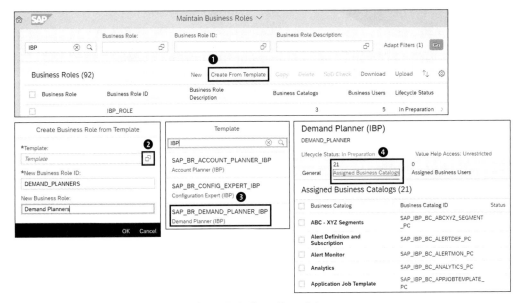

Figure 15.10 Create New Business Role from Template

2. **Assign business catalogs**

   Business catalogs provide access to SAP Fiori apps. When you choose a new role from template, a list of business catalogs associated with that role are added to the new role. You also can add or remove catalogs for the business role. For example, the Basic Planning Tasks business catalog provides access to the following:

   - SAP Integrated Business Planning, add-in for Microsoft Excel
   - Application Jobs app
   - Application Job Templates app
   - Change History app

   A list of available business catalogs, along with the details of the group to which they belong, SAP Fiori apps to which they provide access, and their restrictions, is available in the application help for SAP IBP under **Identity and Access Management • App Descriptions • Maintain Business Roles • Assign Business Catalogs**.

3. **Maintain restrictions**

   Restrictions can be maintained for a business role to limit the data and functions of SAP IBP that can be accessed by users with that business role. Read and write access restrictions can be defined for the authorization objects that control access to SAP IBP functions. Examples of restrictions include planning areas and key figures that the user can view and edit, master data types the user can be allowed to access, data lifecycle management, and so on.

Restrictions are defined for a business role under the **Maintain Restrictions** area. Possible restrictions include read access types of **Unrestricted** (default) and **Restricted** and write access types of **Unrestricted**, **Restricted**, and **No Access** (default). Restrictions can be defined when the **Restrictions** access type is selected. The values for the restriction also can be defined.

For example, the **General** restriction area includes the following restriction fields:

- **Administration Functions**
- **Reason Code ID**
- **Permission Filter ID**
- **Response Management Scenario Scope**
- **Application Logs**

The **Key Figures** restriction area includes the following fields:

- **Planning Area**
- **Key Figures**

Suppose you want to limit users' access to planning area RJSAPIBP1. In the Maintain Business Users SAP Fiori app, select **Maintain Restrictions** and choose **Restricted** for the write access type. Then select **Planning Area** under **General** and choose the planning areas that the user has access to. To further restrict access to key figures, you can choose the **Key Figures** restriction area and select specific key figures, such as **Demand Plan Qty.** and **Consensus Demand Qty.** In general, for an S&OP planning process, you'll need the following business roles:

- Sales planners
- Marketing planners
- Demand planners
- Supply planners
- Supply chain analyst
- Expert user/administrator
- Integration expert

4. **Activate the business role**

   Once the business role is created, click the **Generate** button to activate it. Once the role is active, it can be assigned to users.

15

5. **Assign business role to users**

   Business roles can be assigned to users in two ways:

   - In the Maintain Business Roles SAP Fiori app, choose the role, then navigate to the **Assigned Business Users** tab. Here, you can select the business users previously created and assign them to the role.

   - In the Maintain Business Users SAP Fiori app, choose the user and navigate to the **Assign Business Role** section. Here, you can add or remove the predefined business roles to or from the user.

15.4   Permission Filters

Permission filters define the scope of data visibility and editability for users. This is a very powerful functionality in SAP IBP, providing secure access to data across all functional areas where the data is read or modified by planners using the Excel add-in, analytics, or planning operators.

Permission filters are assigned to user groups or business roles. The definition of permission filters has two aspects: read criteria and write criteria.

In this section, we'll cover the read and write criteria functionality in the permission filters in detail, with examples of how to setup permission filters. We'll then cover how permission filters can be used in process management to grant permissions to edit key figure values only when the process step dates are reached and the process is in progress.

15.4.1   Read Criteria

The read criteria of permissions filters determine what planning data is visible to the user by defining attribute conditions. For example, the North America demand planners are granted access to **Product Category = PC** and **Region = North America**. These planners have access to subsets of data that they can read/write, but they can't see other data, related to, say, **Region = Europe**.

Multiple attribute conditions can be defined in a permission filter. For example, permission filter **VF1** for read access can be defined for **Product Category** and **Region** attributes as follows: **Product Category = PC, Product Category = Printers, Region = North America, Region = Central America**. When such a condition is entered, the same attributes are combined with OR conditions and different attributes combined with AND conditions—for example, **(Product Category = PC OR Printers) AND (Region = North**

America OR Central America). Figure 15.11 shows an example of a permission filter created with read access set to filter condition **Product Family = FAMILY 100-HEAD-PHONES**. This permission filter, when assigned to a user in SAP IBP, will grant access only to products belonging to the **FAMILY 100-HEADPHONES** product family.

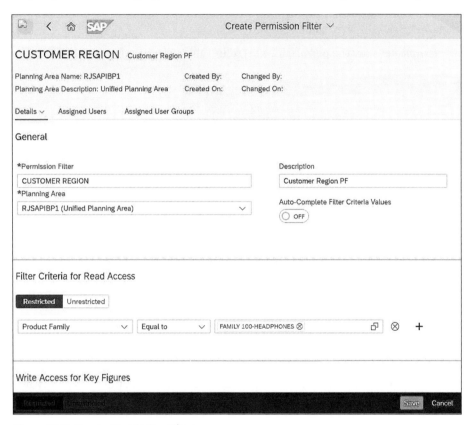

Figure 15.11 Create Permission Filter

For master data, the permission filters are applied to all the master data records for the master data type in which the corresponding attribute value exists. Therefore, when the demand planner user logs in to Excel or analytics or any other area in SAP IBP in which attributes are displayed, she will be able to see only a subset of data. For example, in Excel, when the demand planner filters for product category, she can see only PCs and printers; when she filters for products, she can see only the products that belong to those categories. In addition, the attribute values will be applied for all displayed key figures, limiting the access to master data and key figures that the user is allowed to view or modify.

More than one permission filter can be defined and applied to a user. In this case, it should be noted that the permission filters are combined as a union of individual permission filter data sets, granting larger data set access. For example, if a user is provided two read permission filters—**PF1**: **Product Category = PC** and **PF2**: **Region = North America**—then this user can see all data and is not just restricted to PCs and North America. This is explained below:

For example, let's say the permissions listed in Table 15.1 are assigned to the user.

Permission Filter	Product Category	Region
PF1	PC	All
PF2	All	North America

Table 15.1 Example Permission Filter Setup

When the first permission filter is applied, the user can see all regions; when the second permission filter is applied, the user can see all product categories, thereby granting access to a larger data set. Therefore, it's important to review the filter settings and assign the right levels of permission filters to users so that they can access only the data they're limited to.

15.4.2   Write Criteria

Permission filters support write criteria for being able to edit only a certain set of master data attribute values and key figures. For example, sales managers should only be able to work on their region-specific sales numbers but need visibility into the sales figures from other regions for planning, as shown in Table 15.2.

User	Access	Region A	Region B
Sales manager 1	Write access	X	
Sales manager 1	Read access	X	X
Sales manager 2	Write access		X
Sales manager 2	Read access	X	X

Table 15.2 Access Control Granting Read Access for All Regions but Write Access Only to Specific Regions

In Excel planning views, when the sales managers are working on their data, they should only be able to modify data for the regions for which they're assigned write access.

Write criteria in permission filters optionally can be defined to further restrict the data that the user can edit. If the write criteria are not defined, then the permissions defined in the read criteria give access to both read and write key figures.

When you choose the **No Access** setting for the filter criteria for write access, then the user can only view data and not edit any key figures. Note that key figures that are editable first need to be assigned to the role with restrictions for read/write.

Let's illustrate this with an example: Key figure **Sales Forecast Qty** in planning area **SAPIBP1** is configured as an editable key figure. A business role called **Sales Planners** is defined. In this role, the restrictions are defined such that the key figure and planning area are unrestricted for write access. This business role is then assigned to the two sales managers.

Now, say you define a permission filter, **Sales Region**, with read access restricted for the **Region = Region A AND Region B** attribute. Then, you assign this sales region permission filter to the two sales managers. This provides full read and write access to regions A and B to sales managers.

You now want to further restrict what regions each of the sales planners are allowed to edit. For this, add to the permission filters a write access restriction as follows, thereby creating two separate permission filters:

Permission filter **Sales Region-A** has read access for region A and region B, along with write access for region A. Similarly, permission filter **Sales Region-B** has read access for region A and region B, along with write access for region B. The **Sales Region-A** permission filter is assigned to sales manager 1 and **Sales Region-B** is assigned to sales manager 2.

Now, when sales manager 1 logs into Excel, he can view the sales forecast quantity for both region A and region B, but can only edit the same for region A. Moreover, when this user views data across regions—say, editing by **Product Category = PC**—Excel displays data that sums across all regions. If the user tries to make a change at this aggregated level, the system will perform an editability check and return an error to the user indicating that the permission filters assigned to him do not allow him to edit data because he has no write access to region B.

When the user adds filter criteria in Excel for region A, the editability check will be successful and he can enter data at the aggregated level.

The permission filters write access also lets you define what key figures can be edited. For example, if the role provides write access to KF1 and KF2 and the permission filter is defined with write access for **Key Figure = KF1**, then this user can only edit key figure KF1, not KF2.

15.4.3   Permission Filters in Process Stage

Permission filters can be assigned as part of a process management template in the step definition. This controls which key figures should be allowed to be edited by which users during a process stage; for example, you can lock sales key figures from editing after the sales planning step is completed. Multiple permission filters can be assigned to one or more process step participants or groups in the Manage Process Templates SAP Fiori app, as shown in Figure 15.12.

Figure 15.12 Permission Filters Assignment to Process Management

15.5   Infrastructure Management

SAP IBP is deployed on SAP Cloud Platform, providing quick access to application functionality, fast implementation time, and capability to support changing business needs and growth. There are minimal IT efforts involved for customers because both hardware and software operations and maintenance are included in the cloud subscription provided by SAP.

SAP data centers run in secured and safe environments, thereby providing the following:

- Certified operations
- Advanced network security
- Reliable data backup
- Built-in compliance, integrity, and confidentiality

The implementation of technical and organizational security and data protection measures is regularly audited and verified by
achieving different certifications and attestations. Figure 15.13 lists the SAP Cloud Platform certifications and attestations.

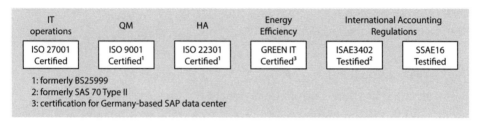

Figure 15.13 SAP Cloud Platform Certifications and Attestations

SAP Cloud Platform security provides the following:

- **Secure operations/internal control framework**
  - Asset management
  - Change management
  - Incident management
  - Antivirus and malware management
  - Backup/restore management
  - Identity and access management
  - Advanced IT security architecture, providing isolated, separated landscapes per customer and security-hardened systems
- **Threat and vulnerability management**
  - Security patch management
  - Penetration testing
  - Vulnerability scanning
  - 24-7 security monitoring center

- **Physical security**
  - Video and sensor surveillance
  - Access logging
  - Security guards
  - Fire detection and extinguishing system
  - Uninterruptible power supply
  - Biometric access control in certain locations
- **Network security**
  - Network admission control
  - Intrusion prevention systems
  - Network filtering
  - Two-factor authentication
  - Proxies
  - Internet content filtering
  - Customer data flow control with regional data storage (e.g., EU-, US-Cloud)

SAP IBP customers have worldwide coverage with SAP data centers running SAP IBP across multiple geographic regions. These include Pennsylvania, United States; Germany; Moscow, Russia; Shanghai, China; and Sydney, Australia.

15.6   Summary

In this chapter, we covered various aspects of roles and security for accessing SAP IBP deployed on SAP Cloud Platform. We looked at identity and access management for single sign-on for SAP IBP, user management to create and maintain users, and business roles to grant access to application UIs. We also covered general restrictions on application functions and planning models, permission filters to control data visibility and editability, and finally concluded with an overview of infrastructure management, looking at the network and infrastructure security and secure monitoring and operations.

Chapter 16
SAP IBP Case Studies

This chapter will make the contents of this book come to life via two case studies. Our objective is to describe market trends driving the process focus of the implementation, the capabilities delivered, and the benefits realized.

The case studies in this chapter are based on SAP IBP implementations from real companies. For each case study, we'll provide some background on the company prior to the implementation, as well as discuss the challenges the company was facing. We'll look at the process scope of the companies' SAP IBP projects, providing you with a peek inside the actual methods and development of their landscape. Finally, we'll look at the capabilities that each company gained, as well as the concrete benefits the solution provided them with.

Our first case study comes from the high-tech industry and walks through a fairly standard implementation. In our second case study, we'll introduce an innovative SAP IBP project for a life sciences and health care client, demonstrating the flexibility of SAP IBP and the opportunity for value-adding solution extensions.

16.1   High-Tech OEM

Our case study comprises the implementation roadmap of a high-tech original equipment manufacturer (OEM), delivering high-end servers to corporate customers. We'll start by describing the market trends that drove this company to pursue an SAP Integrated Business Planning roadmap and the company's key challenges. We'll show how those challenges drove the process scope to deliver a strong planning capability and what benefits resulted from the implementation.

16.1.1   Market Drivers

Before going through the process with this company, let's first look at the company's background and then introduce the key challenges that were being addressed by the implementation of an S&OP process leveraging the SAP IBP solution.

Company Background

Driving success in an international, high-tech OEM, configuring five servers every minute, delivering seven terabytes of memory to clients every minute, and shipping up to 12 network drives every minute is an involved endeavor. At any given moment, this organization operates with over 200 suppliers and has over 10,000 active SKUs, delivering products to over 100,000 customers scattered across the globe. Most of those products are manufactured by original device manufacturers (ODMs) that work for various OEMs at any given moment in time. The company had a limited in-house manufacturing capability, which was focused on highly complex configurations requiring extensive testing.

The intricacies in the supply network are abundant, with different manufacturing paradigms from traditional make-to-stock processes for most off-the-shelf network devices and directly sold components, to purely engineering-to-order products for high-end clients, and anything in between. The majority of the complexity is formed by configure-to-order offerings in which clients can compose their own servers by selecting all the critical elements. Some of those elements tie directly to the requested components (e.g., which exact memory the client prefers in their server), whereas others have more delicate relationships to ensure the right heat sync in the end-state device.

Over the years, this company has grown to become one of the bigger high-tech OEMs in the market, resulting in the accumulation of complexity. As the market has become increasingly complicated, this complexity has infiltrated the company's processes in the same way. This resulted in processes that carried a lot of legacy complexity with them, building a strong basis for trying a supply chain planning transformation.

Challenges

At the start of the engagement, the organization was running a *manually-managed supply chain planning process*, in which its servers and components were planned manually throughout complex supply chain networks, resulting in limited visibility over the various layers of in-house manufacturing, contract manufacturers, and multitiered suppliers. The process of assembling new servers could follow one of many supply network models, and the complexity of the server would often drive the path toward outsourced manufacturing via ODMs or in-house manufacturing.

The collaboration process with suppliers and ODMs was based on an outdated, peer-to-peer technology, impossible to keep aligned with the changing business reality. Although collaboration was critical in the process, given the shortage of specific key commodities (e.g., processors, memory, solid-state drives), it was a very expensive and time-consuming process to bring new suppliers on board, limiting the agility of the supply chain drastically. It was hard to make the technology evolve with changes in the industry's business processes, such as evolving towards attribute-based collaboration. For example, in the memory business, collaboration is moving towards density (1,000 terabytes in memory) rather than product-based collaboration (32,000 memory modules of 32 gigabytes each).

The signals shared with the suppliers exhibited high variability week to week, resulting in a lack of trust in the data, which in turn resulted in unreliable supplier commitments. This lack of trust due to the bad signal reduced the effectivity of the objective of supplier collaboration—that is, increasing the bullwhip effect.

16.1.2   Process Scope

To deliver an integrated business planning capability, supported by the SAP IBP technology platform, this organization elected to follow a release-based approach. The initial focus was on the automation of the supply planning processes, combined with automated supplier collaboration capabilities leveraging the Ariba Network. In the next phase, demand planning was addressed, followed by the driving a true S&OP process. The last phase focused on improving shortage management by enabling the response management capabilities in the SAP solution. Throughout all the phases, visibility and management-by-exception capabilities were key, which were delivered as part of SAP Supply Chain Control Tower.

Phase 1: Supply Planning and Collaboration

The focus of the supply planning scope was to drive *automated supply network propagation*, in which the demand was propagated through the various network models using the unconstrained supply heuristic as described in Chapter 4, providing end-to-end visibility into the steps of propagation from consensus demand out of demand planning up to the unconstrained requirements plan for the supplier. Due to the global nature of operations, there was a strong focus on modeling inter-regional demand flows to establish a truly global demand picture in which intercompany flows would be reflected as dependent demand streams. The plan was operationalized via a connection to traditional SAP ERP-based material requirements planning to generate purchase requisitions.

There was a lot of focus on *demand supply matching*, providing interactive planning views for users to perform supply demand matching on the component level, analyzing shortages and adjusting plans. This was required both on the commodity level for components from the supplier and on the assembly levels to provide a clear signal to ODMs.

To bring all the information together, *data visualization and executive reporting* was required. Dashboards were used to provide real-time insights into all the planning information, from demand plans to unconstrained requirement plans, supplier commitments, and projected inventory. A report on excess inventory was delivered as an input to the excess and obsolescence processes. To deliver actionable management-by-exception capabilities to planners, custom alerts were used for comparison between the current version of the plan and the previous one, as well as to identify shortages and supplier commitment discrepancies.

Supplier collaboration was automated via the SAP IBP and SAP Ariba connection, allowing suppliers to log into the SAP Ariba portal directly for retrieving critical information such as unconstrained requirement plans and for providing commitments and inventory levels. The project delivered easy supplier onboarding without IT work, as opposed to the former, heavily customized supplier network collaboration environment.

Phase 2: Demand Planning

The first focus of the demand planning process was establishing a renewed *segmentation approach*. The flexible SAP IBP data model allowed the company to build faster and better aggregation and disaggregation capabilities across product hierarchy levels, such as product family, product line, category, and the like. An automated ABC classification based on revenue contributions was combined with an XYZ classification based on variability, allowing users to focus manual efforts where they were needed most. The planning was expanded from regional (three main regions globally) to individual planning for Tier 1 customers where relevant, combined with a lower level of granularity in the planning, which aligned more with the regional rollup structure put in place.

Based on the segmented demand, an *advanced statistical forecasting* process was put in place. An automated outlier detection and correction based on user defined control limits also was put in place in preparation for robust statistical forecasting. Planning views showing a comparison of multiple statistical models at different hierarchy levels was made available, in which super users could fine-tune statistical methods interactively. There was support for automated models that can select optimal model parameters to detect trends/seasonality, replacing home-grown statistical forecasting tools; the new models leveraged advanced R-algorithms.

Building a tight integration with supply planning allowed the company to start running the demand planning process *location agnostic*. This allows demand planners to do what they do best—forecast what direction the market is going to take—rather than combining this effort with a supply dimension by introducing the location as part of the demand planning process.

Given the strong presence of configure-to-order materials in the company's product offerings, the requirement to build a *variant configuration-based planning solution* was critical. A server could have one of many memory options, processors, or drives, which could be hard to predict up front. This was addressed by building a specific attachment rate–based forecasting process, in which the critical commodities such as processors, memory, and disk drives were forecasted based on the servers they would be connected to. The flexible data model and key figure configuration allowed the company to build an integrated capability in which users could maintain key information about the relationship of the components to the servers, server families, or product lines, and the system would suggest the connection rate by looking at past attachment. This automated a lot of the demand planning process, allowing users to shift attention from baseline plan generation to reviewing the critical items, thus maximizing their value impact.

Building the demand planning process in a second phase, with supply planning already there, opened the door to leveraging SAP IBP as the baseline platform for running the company's S&OP process. Strengthening the baseline planning capabilities with a strong set of key performance indicators and metrics completed the circle to establish a true supply chain control tower.

Phase 3: Response Management

Although a lot of companies that set out on a complex planning transformation journey suffer shortages, the best way to make shortages manageable is by improving the planning process itself. This is what this organization did in the first two phases, focusing on demand and supply planning. After stabilization of demand and supply planning, improving the shortage management capabilities via response management is the final piece of the puzzle.

Providing response management delivers a near-term shortage management capability on a lower level of granularity, providing visibility into orders. The shortage management capability will deliver order-level pegging, allowing employees to follow up on the gating factors of all the sales orders while providing visibility for every sales order in terms of which supply elements fulfill the order.

16.1.3 Capabilities

We've covered the main process scope, which delivered a solid technology foundation. Now, let's zoom into the planning capability this enabled, before examining the benefits in the last section.

From a demand planning perspective, a solid improvement in planning accuracy was achieved via more advanced segmentation and statistical forecasting capabilities, which all leveraged the same data model. Removing the shadow IT that was used for statistical forecasting before, which had proven to be adopted very sparsely, ensured a strong adoption of new processes across locations.

In the supply planning space, establishing a supply network planning process powered by SAP IBP for supply, which automates the unconstrained demand propagation through all the complex supply networks, resulted in a transparent and stable unconstrained requirement plan for suppliers. Leveraging the scenario planning capability allowed the organization to model different responses to disruptions, increasing the response accuracy.

The supply plan was shared with suppliers in an automated way via the SAP Ariba Supply Chain Collaboration, which is natively connected to SAP IBP via data sharing agreements. After maintaining the Ariba Network ID in SAP IBP, the plan can be shared immediately from the Excel planning views, and suppliers can commit immediately in their Ariba Network web portals to provide instantaneous commitment sharing.

In the next step, the planners can use the supply commitments to perform effective supply demand matching, building a procurement plan for the near term, as well as production plans to be shared with both in-house manufacturing and outsourced manufacturing locations.

Finally, the program closed the loop with the response management capability, allowing detailed order-level pegging visibility into sales orders and how they related to the corresponding supply elements.

All the main planning capabilities were integrated into the S&OP process, which brought detailed demand and supply planning information to a higher level, allowing executives to immediately assess the risk and opportunities in the supply chain. Leveraging SAP Supply Chain Control Tower, visibility was ensured throughout the supply chain, with solid management by exception using the user-defined alerting mechanisms.

16.1.4 Benefits

All those capabilities together delivered on the benefit promise this organization had set out to fulfill. The biggest benefit realized was an increase in planning agility. Bringing all information together in one platform, with end-to-end visibility, allowed the company to assess the impact of demand and supply disruptions and provide corrective action in a matter of hours. The scenario planning capability in turn ensured a strong improvement in planning quality, as it was possible to assess different versions of responses to supply disruptions and select the most optimal one.

On the supplier collaboration side, it was possible to share new versions of the plan immediately and ensure high quality of the shared plan. Quality was ensured via the direct connectivity of SAP IBP with SAP Ariba, which contrasted sharply with the legacy process, in which the plan went through various transformations after leaving the legacy planning system prior to arriving at the supplier, which meant a lot of time spent on reconciling potential differences. The ability to share the plan from Excel allowed planners to interact more intensely with suppliers and partners, taking away the one-day latency that had existed before.

In supplier onboarding, there was a solid cost reduction and increase in agility because suppliers could be onboarded in the Ariba Network. Once onboarded in the Ariba Network, the planner himself could maintain the Ariba Network ID in SAP IBP, allowing him to immediately share data with the supplier.

Building the demand planning capability in SAP IBP not only delivered a strong increase in demand planning accuracy but also allowed the company to bring the complete S&OP process together in the SAP IBP solution. This allowed for a much more accurate and agile S&OP cycle in which executives could immediately use SAP IBP to visualize data, assess the impact of disruptions, and make quality decisions.

16.2 Life Sciences and Health Care

This case study will go into the details of the journey of a life sciences and health care company, executed in 2016, which pioneered shelf-life visibility capabilities that have since been embedded in the standard SAP solution. We'll follow a similar structure to the previous case study, starting with the drivers for change, followed by the process scope, in which we will zoom into the specific requirements, and closing with the delivered capabilities and derived benefits.

16.2.1 Market Drivers

In the following subsections, we'll first look at the company's background before diving into the challenges it was facing.

Company Background

This project involved the implementation of SAP IBP for sales and operations for the American division of a major medical devices manufacturer. The company produces a variety of devices, from inexpensive consumables to very specialized devices used in advanced medical procedures. The products were sold via various sales channels, both direct to hospitals and via distributors, and with various modalities of inventory management. A lot of inventory was tied up in sales reps' vehicles, and as common practice a broad spectrum of possible products was delivered to physicians because it was hard to assess the exact needs prior to medical procedures. In those cases, physicians could select what they needed and return the other products.

Challenges

The described inventory models resulted in very limited visibility in this organization's planning environment. This environment was characterized as a combination of local Excel sheets and financial planning solutions. This unreliable information was compounded by the complexity of a limited shelf-life, often a factor in the life sciences and health care industry. There was no single source of truth nor of planning information (demand signals) or available supply (inventories were split among sales reps, clients, and various distribution centers, all with their own remaining shelf-lives).

The production and procurement plans were established in a completely manual way after long negotiations with all organizational entities, which operated based on their own plans. This was a very time-consuming process, with more negotiation than value-adding discussion to deliver the organizational goals of keeping the inventory under control while delivering extraordinary customer service.

16.2.2   Process Scope

The primary vision was to implement SAP IBP for sales and operations to deliver end-to-end visibility and one common version of the truth in inventory and demand.

Supply Chain Visibility

The standard capabilities of SAP in 2016 were uniquely suitable to address this company's concerns because it provided a very user-friendly way for planners to leverage the user experience they had learned to master over time: Microsoft Excel. Yet moving to SAP IBP took away the nuisance of having disconnected spreadsheets and as many plans as there were planning employees. All the data was available in one common environment, allowing the organization to leverage the SAP IBP dashboards and Excel sheets in its S&OP cycle, thus strengthening the business process by providing the foundational information.

Shelf-Life Visibility

At the time of implementation, the standard SAP capability wasn't sufficient to address data visualization of shelf-life implications on system performance. The main requirement in this space was to provide shelf-life visibility and ensure that products running out of shelf-life underwent the following actions:

- Identified via management by exception, to help sales ensure they were pushed in the channel
- Withdrawn from planning to ensure expired products wouldn't be considered available inventory

To address this requirement, the solution integrator Deloitte worked closely with the SAP development group to establish a solution in this space. This solution is now part of the predelivered SAP planning areas and documented as part of the standard environment. In this case study, however, we'll talk about the process of how SAP IBP can support custom, new requirements as part of a solution implementation, providing customer-specific solutions to particular business problems.

To deliver the solution to address these requirements, first the master data structure had to be established. Shelf-life applies of course to a batch of products, which wasn't

16

available as standard in the SAP IBP sample planning areas. Hence a new master data type called *batch* was set up. The batch information reflects the product and location and creates a new batch ID. The batch comes with a batch inventory, as well as a last ship date, as shown in Figure 16.1.

	A	B	C	D	E	F	G
1	Batch Lot Code	Location ID	Product ID	Batch Inventory	Batch Last Ship Date	Batch Sequence	
2	TESTBATCH3	1102	10000001	1000	2016-12-15	2	
3	TESTBATCH2	1102	10000001	1800	2016-09-15	1	
4							

Figure 16.1 Batch Master Data

To make use of the batch in the planning level, the batch needs to be considered part of the planning level. This means a new planning level, period-product-location-batch, becomes the baseline for the batch inventory. The shelf life itself can be set up as an attribute as key figure for the initial period only, allowing the initial inventory to become available on the batch level.

In the next step, logic needed to be established to derive the actual shelf-life visibility. This was performed by assuming a first-in, first-out setup from a planning perspective, assuming the oldest batch would be shipped out first. In other words, we start consuming the stock from the oldest batch first; if it runs out, we move to the next batch and then to the next to calculate the **Projected Batch Inventory**.

The projected batch life takes the initial batch inventory and subtracts the dependent demand to reflect the remaining inventory in the corresponding batch over time. As you may be aware, this is not a standard capability in key figure modeling in SAP IBP because the calculation involves considering the previous bucket. We can define the calculation as follows:

Projected Batch Inventory = Previous Projected Batch Inventory – Dependent Demand

Yet standard key figure configuration doesn't let you calculate based on previous buckets. Moreover, the calculation complexity is slightly higher because batches that have expired can't be used, and the sequence of the batch needs to be adhered to. A hint of the sequence adherence can be seen in Figure 16.1, where the batch sequence is depicted, allowing easy visibility for which batch to consider first. Because these requirements go beyond the capability of standard SAP, L-Code was leveraged to meet this requirement. L-Code provides a way to implement custom calculations in SAP IBP. L-Code is implemented by SAP and can be delivered as part of the cloud agreement by opening a support ticket.

This setup allows us to calculate the remaining batch life, which is only the first step. To meet our two requirements, normal key figure modeling can be applied to finalize the setup. First, based on the batch last ship date, the inventory left in the period that corresponds to the last ship date essentially should be scrapped. Identifying this quantity allows us to raise an alert, which can be used to inform sales people to take action and push the remaining stock into the channel.

Once the batch stock due to expire is identified, action should be taken to ensure the supply planning algorithms consider this. In this project, the S&OP heuristic was applied; to withdraw the expired inventory, the inventory correction key figure was used. By copying the inventory due to expire into the inventory correction as a negative correction, the heuristic could understand that the inventory was no longer available and plan accordingly.

Automation of Production and Procurement Plans

Once the main problem of ensuring the right information was available for planning was considered, this project leveraged the S&OP heuristic to drive calculation of the production and procurement plans. Those plans, while unconstrained in nature, were adjusted by supply planners and buyers to correctly reflect capacity limitations or supplier restrictions.

Conclusion

Although this approach of leveraging L-Code should be considered a last resort, it demonstrates one of the ways to extend the SAP IBP solution to cater to specific problem statements that seem hard to address even after reading this book.

Moreover, though this was a real problem statement for a project that occurred in 2016, the solution was released as part of the standard solution in version 1708. This illustrates that SAP actively seeks improvements from clients and adopts best practices into the next releases of the standard solution, ensuring future state maintenance and extension of the product's capabilities.

16.2.3   Capabilities

By combining the standard behavior from SAP IBP, the main reason for this organization to embark on its integrated business planning journey, with the flexibility of specifying custom specifications delivered in the context of the cloud offering from SAP, the following key capabilities were delivered:

16

- Leveraging SAP IBP to enable an S&OP process and a planning cadence to enable different business functions, including marketing, finance, and supply chain, and thus reach a realistic consensus sales forecast instead of operating in silos
- Providing visibility into inventory due to run out of shelf-life and proactively informing sales to ensure reductions in scrapping and driving active push to market for products running short on shelf-life
- Building automated supply planning capability that considers shelf-life restrictions and plans exactly the required quantities

16.2.4   Benefits

The biggest benefit identified was the central focus on one operating plan. In an organization in which competing plans had been the topic of highly debated daily meetings, everyone having visibility into the different organizational silos and being able to learn from each other and have one final source of the truth saved a tremendous amount of time. Combined with full automation of the production and procurement plan generation, this allowed planners to dedicate their time to value-adding planning activities rather than remain in regular firefighting mode.

16.3   Summary

In this chapter, we covered real-life use cases of how SAP IBP has been implemented for two organizations: one high-tech OEM and a life sciences and health care company. The objective was to show the typical challenges which led to the selection of SAP IBP as a planning solution, the processes which were enabled by the solution, the capabilities this brought to those organizations, and the benefits that resulted from the implementation. We hope this allows you to form a better understanding of how a real-life implementation could look for your organization, what you can expect from the improvement, and how your company will benefit from it.

The Authors

Raghav Jandhyala is a senior director of product management at SAP for SAP Integrated Business Planning. He is responsible for sales and operations planning, unified planning processes, and best practices in SAP IBP. Raghav has more than 16 years of experience in different fields, including supply chain management, retail, and banking, along with strong technical background in development and adoption of business applications. Previously in his career, Raghav worked as a business consultant, development architect, customer success and solutions manager, and product manager. Raghav has worked with SAP IBP from its inception and is responsible for developing the roadmap for SAP IBP for sales and operations. Currently, he works with multiple SAP IBP customers on new innovations, business transformations initiatives, and as a trusted advisor for their global rollouts.

Jeroen Kusters is a senior manager for Deloitte Consulting LLP with more than 10 years of supply chain planning experience. Jeroen started his career implementing SAP APO environments, with a focus on demand planning and service parts planning. Since 2013, his focus has been on SAP Integrated Business Planning; he works closely with SAP to drive new functionality enabling best-practice supply chain planning business processes.

Pramod Mane is a senior director of product management at SAP for SAP Integrated Business Planning. He has more than 17 years of supply chain planning experience. At SAP he is responsible for the roadmap and direction for supply chain planning applications covering sales and operations planning (S&OP) and business network collaboration. Pramod was part of the initial product development team for SAP Sales and Operations Planning on SAP HANA.

Pramod works closely with customers and partners to drive innovation and has acted as a trusted advisor to many customers during their supply chain transformation journey. Pramod started his career at JDA Software where he was part of the supply chain product development team; he later implemented these solutions as part of a professional services group. Pramod holds a BS in mechanical engineering from the University of Pune (India), a MS in industrial engineering from SUNY Buffalo, and an MBA from the University of Maryland, College Park.

Amit Sinha is a leader in SAP supply chain practices at Deloitte Consulting LLP. He has more than 14 years of experience in supply chain planning and business transformation projects. He has worked extensively with different industry sectors across the globe in the areas of sales and operations planning, demand planning, supply planning, inventory optimization, and supply chain analytics. He is an expert in SAP IBP and other SAP supply chain applications. Amit has also authored a text book on supply chain management, published numerous articles in international journals, and has been a speaker at supply chain conferences.

Index

D

- Configure and use the S&OP, demand, response and supply, and inventory planning applications

- Measure your progress with the SAP Supply Chain Control Tower

- Deploy SAP IBP and set it up in your landscape

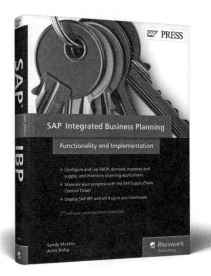

Sandy Markin, Amit Sinha

SAP Integrated Business Planning

Functionality and Implementation

What does it mean to move your supply chain to the cloud? With this guide to SAP Integrated Business Planning, get the complete S&OP, demand, response and supply, and inventory planning picture—and then learn to monitor and control these processes. You'll understand how to set up and use your SAP IBP system, from planning models to user roles. Using industry case studies, see what it takes to ensure a successful adoption of SAP IBP.

504 pages, 2nd edition, avail. 06/2018
E-Book: $69.99 | **Print:** $79.95 | **Bundle:** $89.99

www.sap-press.com/4615

- Learn what SAP S/4HANA offers for supply chain management: manufacturing, warehousing, procurement, and beyond

- Explore embedded analytics and key SAP Fiori applications for supply chain processes

- Preview your migration to SAP S/4HANA

Deb Bhattacharjee, Eric Monti, Stephen Perel, Guillermo B. Vazquez

Logistics with SAP S/4HANA

An Introduction

Welcome to logistics in a digital world. From procurement to production and everything in between, see how SAP S/4HANA transforms your SAP Logistics landscape. Examine each supply chain line of business in SAP S/4HANA: sales order management, manufacturing, inventory management, plant maintenance, and more. Discover key innovations such as MRP Live and embedded SAP EWM. Explore the future of logistics with SAP!

500 pages, pub. 10/2017
E-Book: $59.99 | **Print:** $69.95 | **Bundle:** $79.99

www.sap-press.com/4485

- Model and optimize your demand and supply planning processes with SAP APO-DP and SAP APO-SNP

- Manage different products and supply chain planning scenarios

- Enhance SAP APO functionality using SAP HANA

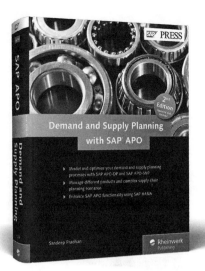

Sandeep Pradhan

Demand and Supply Planning with SAP APO

Keep up with consumer demand using this guide to SAP APO! Learn how to use DP and SNP to forecast demand and capture demand patterns to perform tactical supply planning. Blending big-picture descriptions with step-by-step instructions, this book offers information on everything from implementing SAP APO to using it for interactive, characteristic-based, and collaborative planning.

831 pages, 2nd edition, pub. 04/2016
E-Book: $69.99 | **Print:** $79.95 | **Bundle:** $89.99

www.sap-press.com/4011

Rheinwerk
Publishing

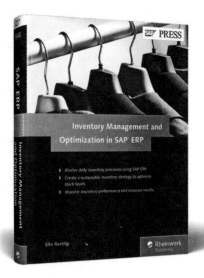

- Master daily inventory processes using SAP ERP

- Create a sustainable inventory strategy to optimize stock levels

- Monitor inventory performance and measure results

Elke Roettig

Inventory Management and Optimization in SAP ERP

Avoid having too little or too much stock on hand with this guide to inventory management and optimization with SAP ERP! Start by managing the stock you have through replenishment, goods issue, goods receipt, and internal transfers. Then plan for and optimize your future by avoiding bottlenecks, setting lead times, using simulations, and more. Finally, evaluate your operations using standard reports, the MRP Monitor, and KPIs. Keep your stock levels just right!

523 pages, pub. 02/2016
E-Book: $69.99 | **Print:** $79.95 | **Bundle:** $89.99

www.sap-press.com/3977

Interested in reading more?

Please visit our website for all new book
and e-book releases from SAP PRESS.

www.sap-press.com